KILL ME
Kiss Me

Volume 5
by Lee Young You

HAMBURG // LONDON //

Kill Me Kiss Me Vol. 5
Created by Lee Young You

Translation - Jihae Hong
English Adaptation - Paul Morrissey
Copy Editor - Suzanne Waldman
Retouch and Lettering - Eric Pineda
Production Artist - Vicente Rivera, Jr
Cover Design - Anna Kernbaum

Editor - Bryce P. Coleman
Digital Imaging Manager - Chris Buford
Pre-Press Manager - Antonio DePietro
Production Managers - Jennifer Miller and Mutsumi Miyazaki
Art Director - Matt Alford
Managing Editor - Jill Freshney
VP of Production - Ron Klamert
Editor-in-Chief - Mike Kiley
President and C.O.O. - John Parker
Publisher and C.E.O. - Stuart Levy

A  Manga

TOKYOPOP Inc.
5900 Wilshire Blvd. Suite 2000
Los Angeles, CA 90036

E-mail: info@TOKYOPOP.com
Come visit us online at www.TOKYOPOP.com

ISBN: 1-59532-420-8

First TOKYOPOP printing: February 2005
10 9 8 7 6 5 4 3 2 1
Printed in the USA

KILL ME Kiss Me

Story So Far...

When pretty-boy Jung-Woo's cousin, Tae, convinces him to switch identities with her, he figures his life can't get any more bizarre. But then this crazy girl, Que-Min, starts fixating on him, and local bad-ass Ghoon-Hahm suddenly decides to make Jung-Woo his new favorite punching bag. After Jung-Woo gets deathly ill, things go from weird to weirder when the violent Ghoon-Hahm is the one who nurses him back to health! Turns out that Ghoon-Hahm has had a crush on Que-Min for years, and he's determined to place himself firmly between Jung-Woo and his dream girl. Que-Min may have something to say about that, though, especially now that she's finally getting some attention from Jung-Woo. At last, this volatile lover's triangle reaches its melodramatic conclusion!

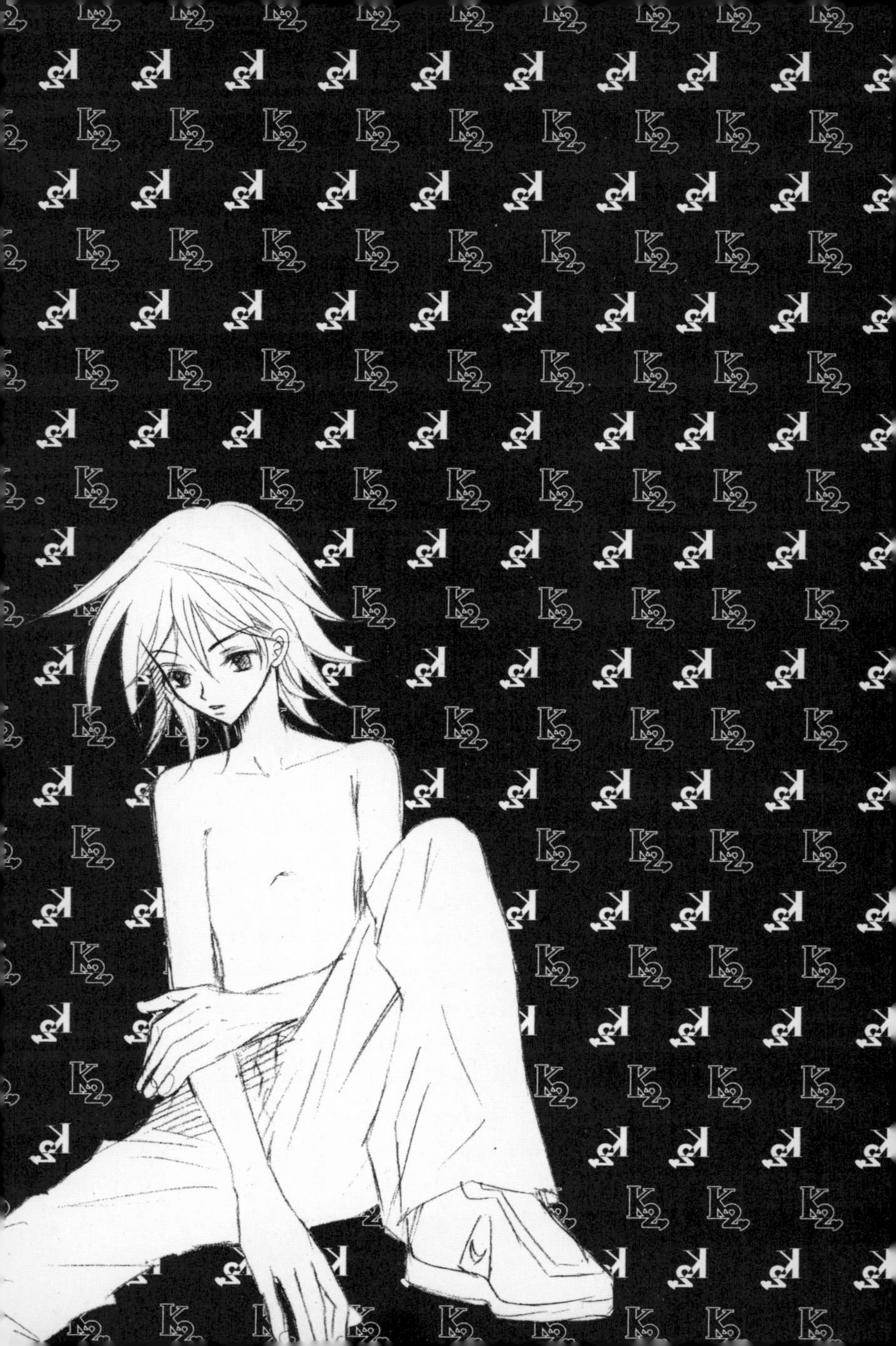

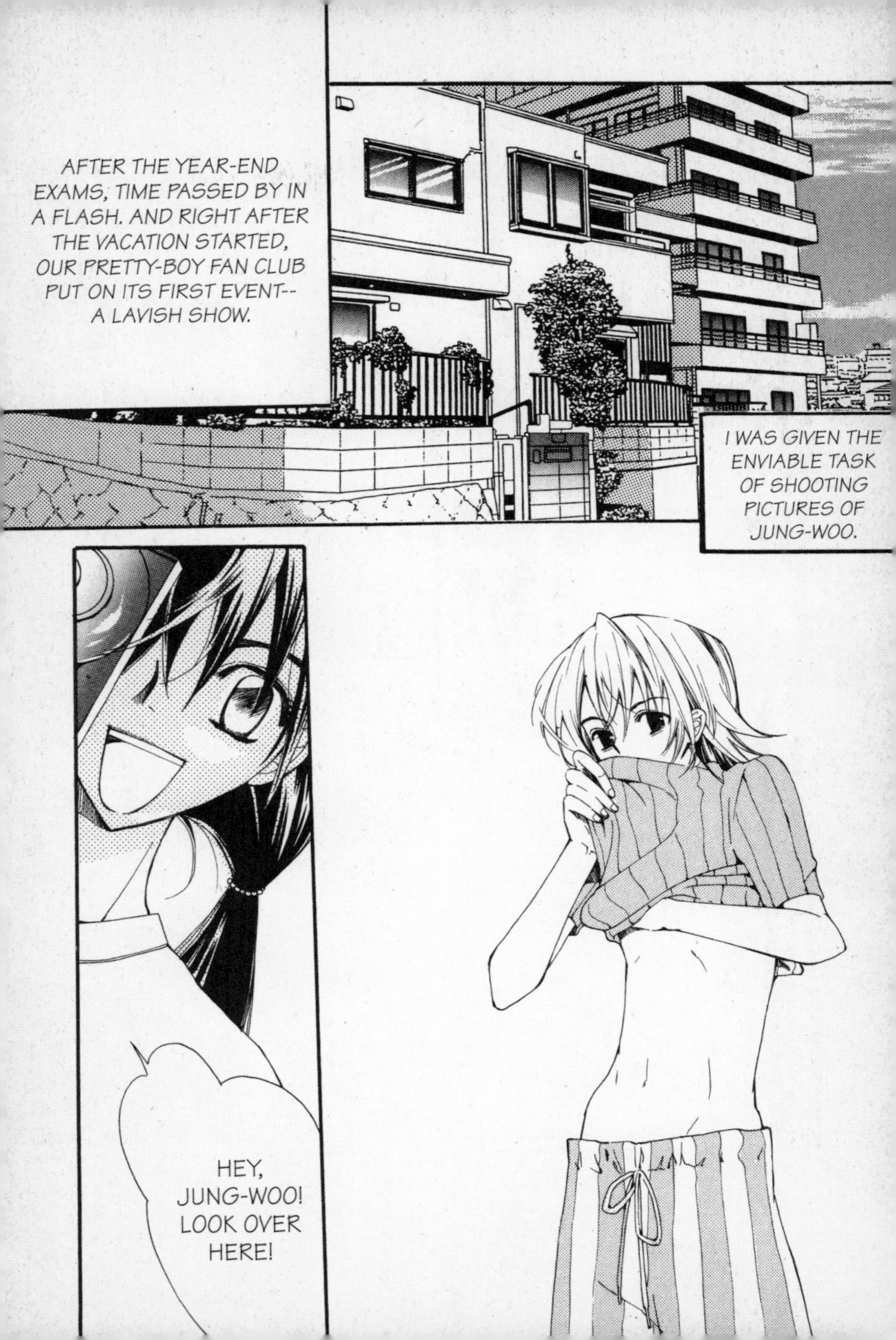
AFTER THE YEAR-END EXAMS, TIME PASSED BY IN A FLASH. AND RIGHT AFTER THE VACATION STARTED, OUR PRETTY-BOY FAN CLUB PUT ON ITS FIRST EVENT-- A LAVISH SHOW.
I WAS GIVEN THE ENVIABLE TASK OF SHOOTING PICTURES OF JUNG-WOO.
HEY, JUNG-WOO! LOOK OVER HERE!

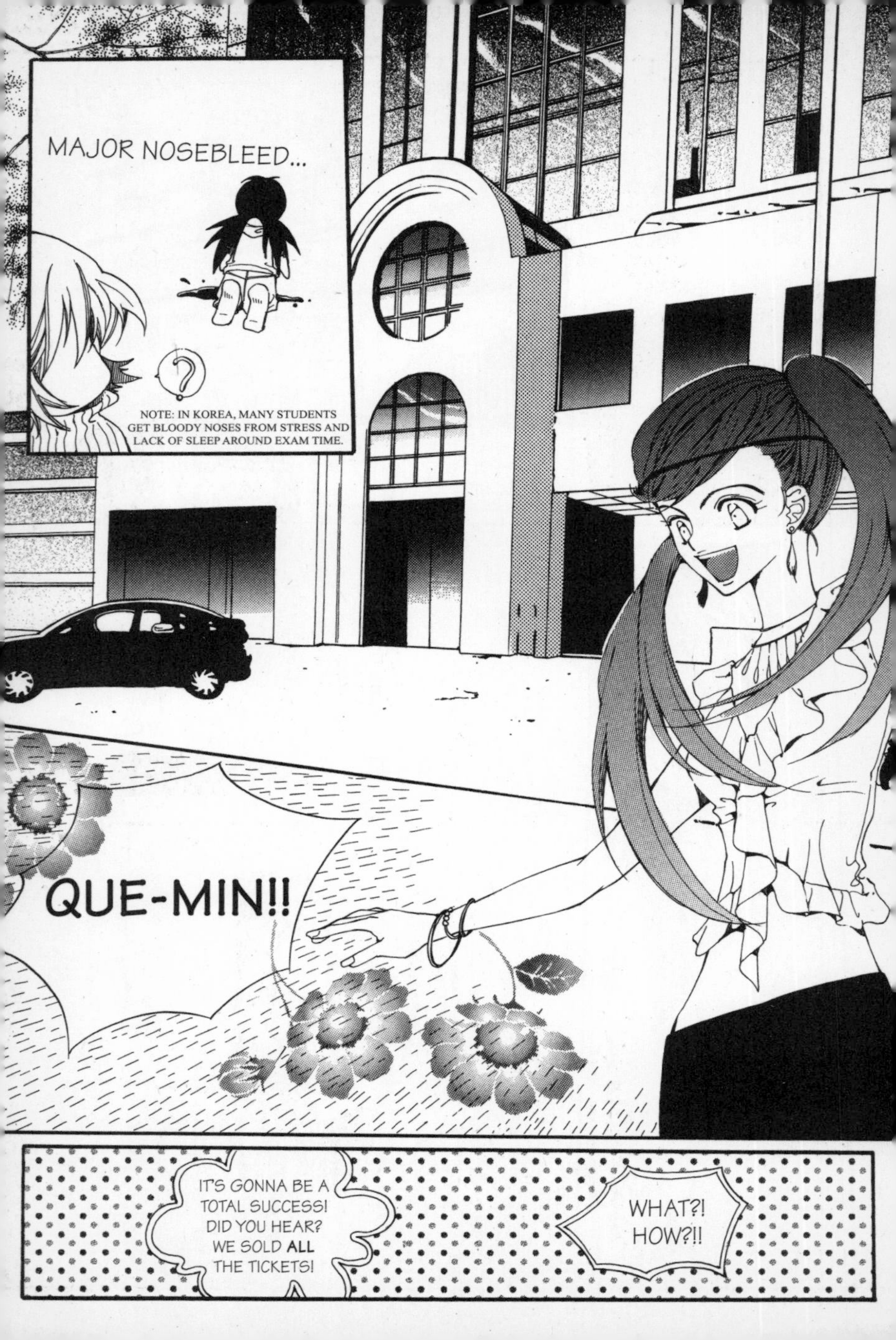
MAJOR NOSEBLEED...
?
NOTE: IN KOREA, MANY STUDENTS GET BLOODY NOSES FROM STRESS AND LACK OF SLEEP AROUND EXAM TIME.
QUE-MIN!!
IT'S GONNA BE A TOTAL SUCCESS! DID YOU HEAR? WE SOLD ALL THE TICKETS!
WHAT?! HOW?!!

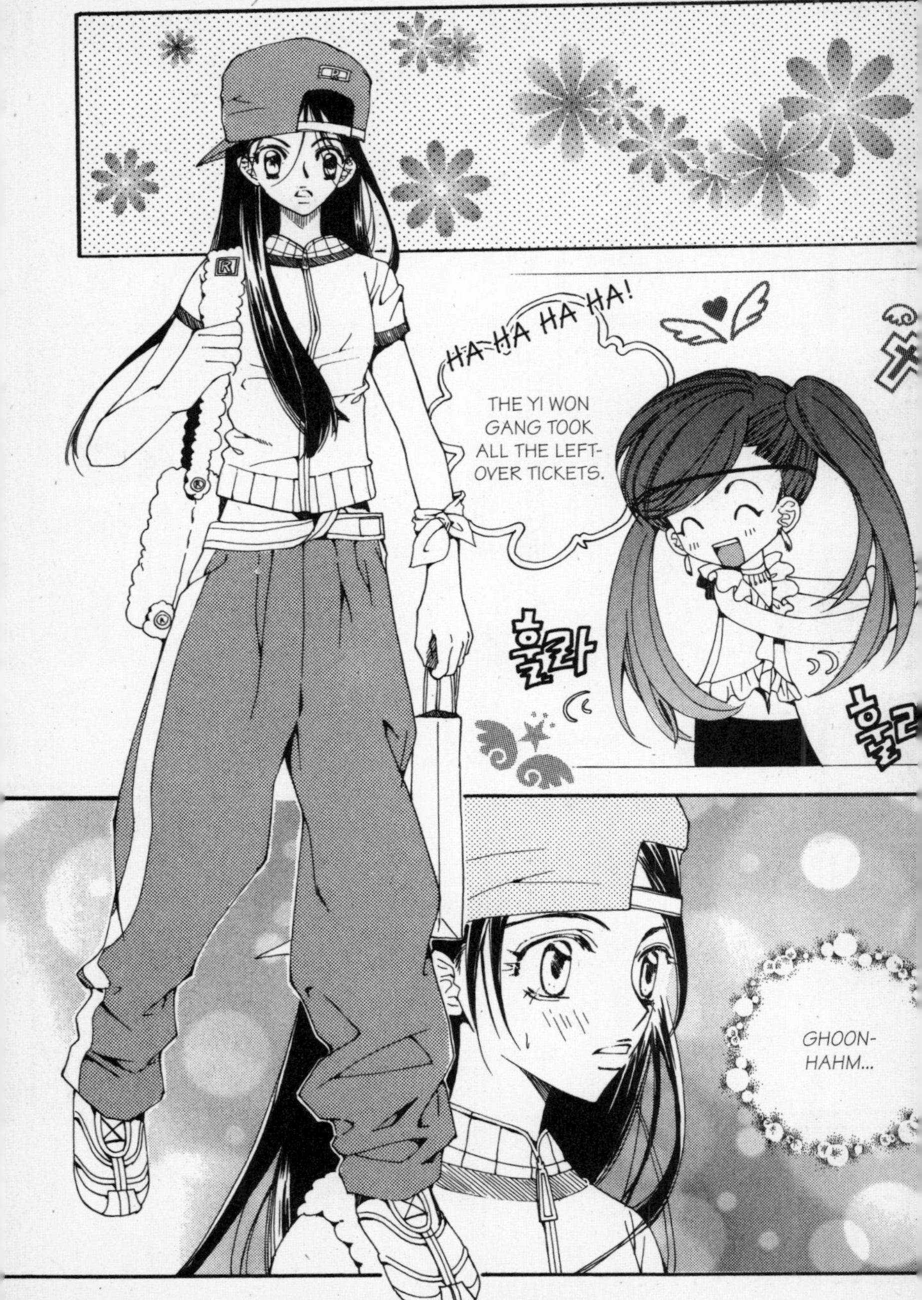
HA HA HA HA!
THE YI WON GANG TOOK ALL THE LEFT-OVER TICKETS.
GHOON-HAHM...

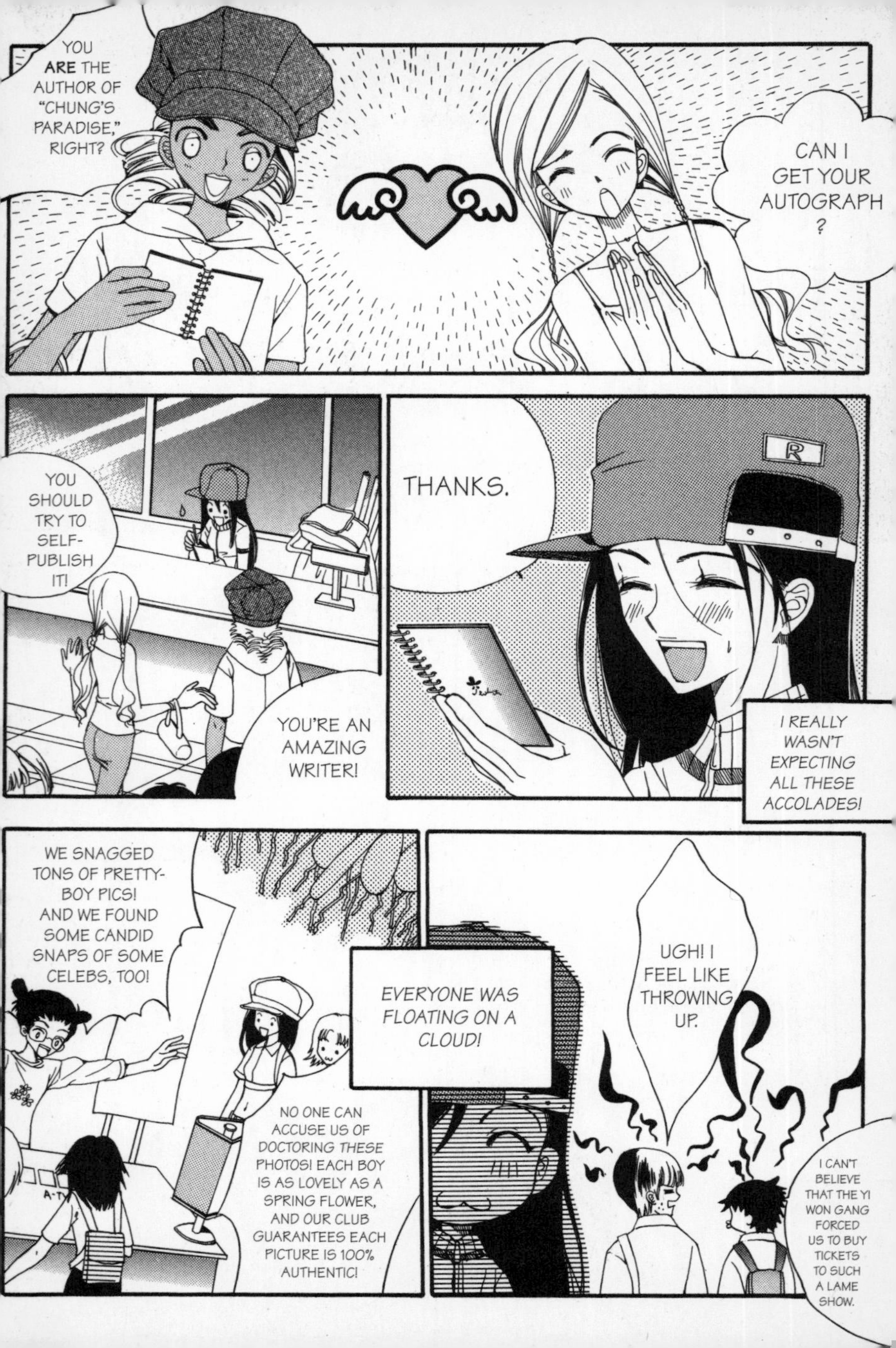
YOU **ARE** THE AUTHOR OF "CHUNG'S PARADISE," RIGHT?
CAN I GET YOUR AUTOGRAPH?
YOU SHOULD TRY TO SELF-PUBLISH IT!
YOU'RE AN AMAZING WRITER!
THANKS.
I REALLY WASN'T EXPECTING ALL THESE ACCOLADES!
WE SNAGGED TONS OF PRETTY-BOY PICS! AND WE FOUND SOME CANDID SNAPS OF SOME CELEBS, TOO!
NO ONE CAN ACCUSE US OF DOCTORING *THESE* PHOTOS! EACH BOY IS AS LOVELY AS A SPRING FLOWER, AND OUR CLUB GUARANTEES EACH PICTURE IS 100% AUTHENTIC!
EVERYONE WAS FLOATING ON A CLOUD!
UGH! I FEEL LIKE THROWING UP.
I CAN'T BELIEVE THAT THE YI WON GANG FORCED US TO BUY TICKETS TO SUCH A LAME SHOW.

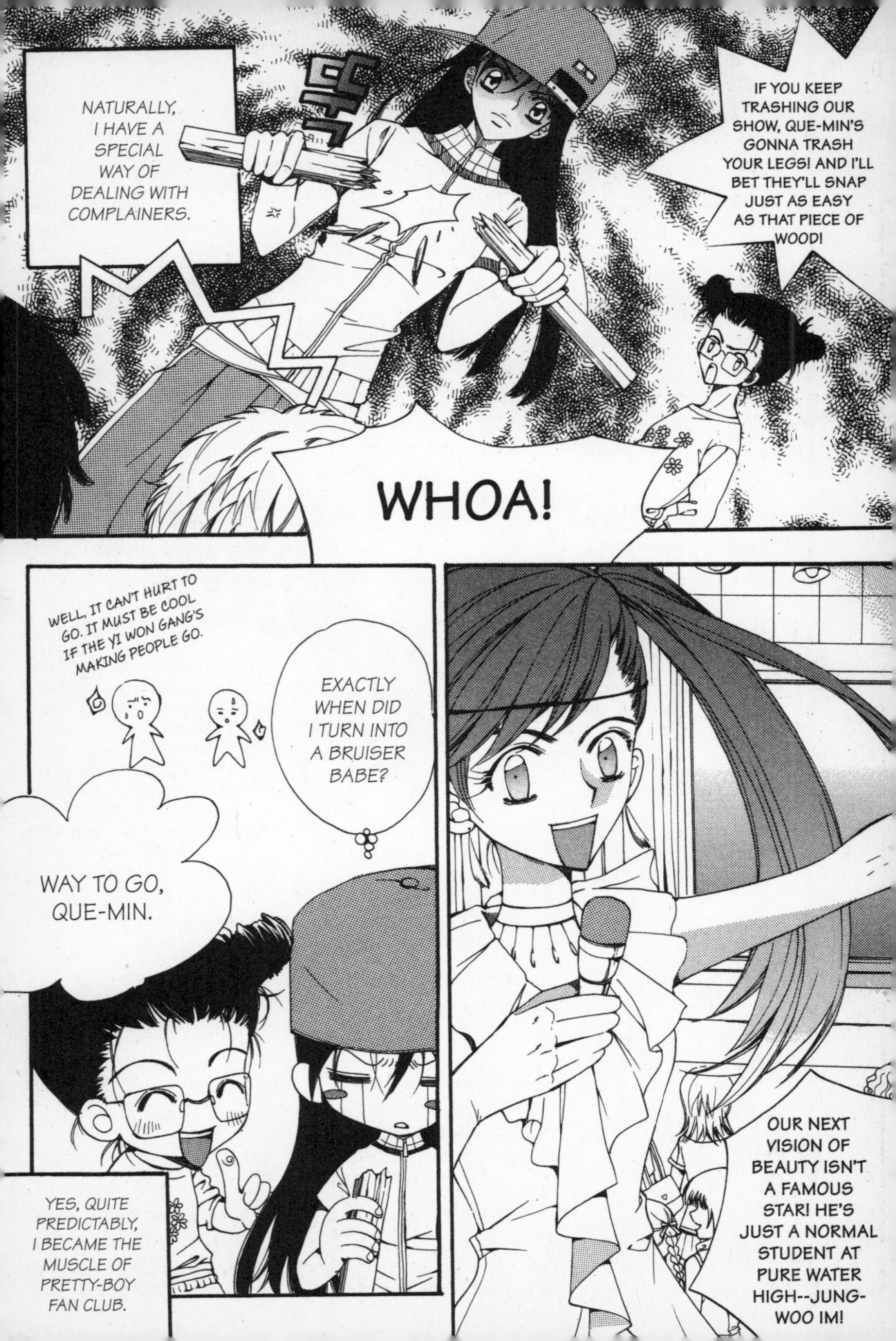
NATURALLY, I HAVE A SPECIAL WAY OF DEALING WITH COMPLAINERS.
IF YOU KEEP TRASHING OUR SHOW, QUE-MIN'S GONNA TRASH YOUR LEGS! AND I'LL BET THEY'LL SNAP JUST AS EASY AS THAT PIECE OF WOOD!
WHOA!
WELL, IT CAN'T HURT TO GO. IT MUST BE COOL IF THE YI WON GANG'S MAKING PEOPLE GO.
EXACTLY WHEN DID I TURN INTO A BRUISER BABE?
WAY TO GO, QUE-MIN.
YES, QUITE PREDICTABLY, I BECAME THE MUSCLE OF PRETTY-BOY FAN CLUB.
OUR NEXT VISION OF BEAUTY ISN'T A FAMOUS STAR! HE'S JUST A NORMAL STUDENT AT PURE WATER HIGH--JUNG-WOO IM!

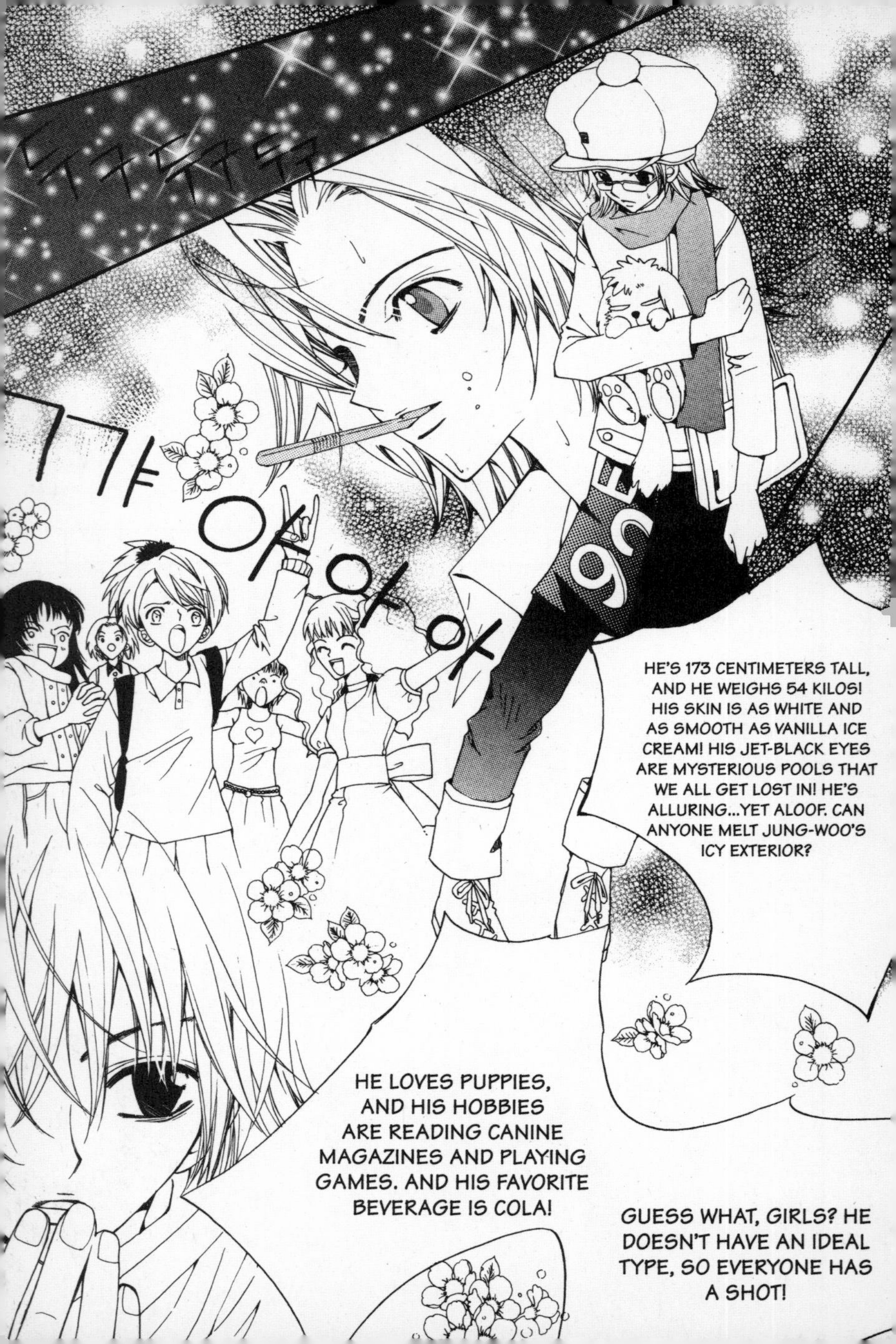
꺄아아아
HE'S 173 CENTIMETERS TALL, AND HE WEIGHS 54 KILOS! HIS SKIN IS AS WHITE AND AS SMOOTH AS VANILLA ICE CREAM! HIS JET-BLACK EYES ARE MYSTERIOUS POOLS THAT WE ALL GET LOST IN! HE'S ALLURING...YET ALOOF. CAN ANYONE MELT JUNG-WOO'S ICY EXTERIOR?
HE LOVES PUPPIES, AND HIS HOBBIES ARE READING CANINE MAGAZINES AND PLAYING GAMES. AND HIS FAVORITE BEVERAGE IS COLA!
GUESS WHAT, GIRLS? HE DOESN'T HAVE AN IDEAL TYPE, SO EVERYONE HAS A SHOT!

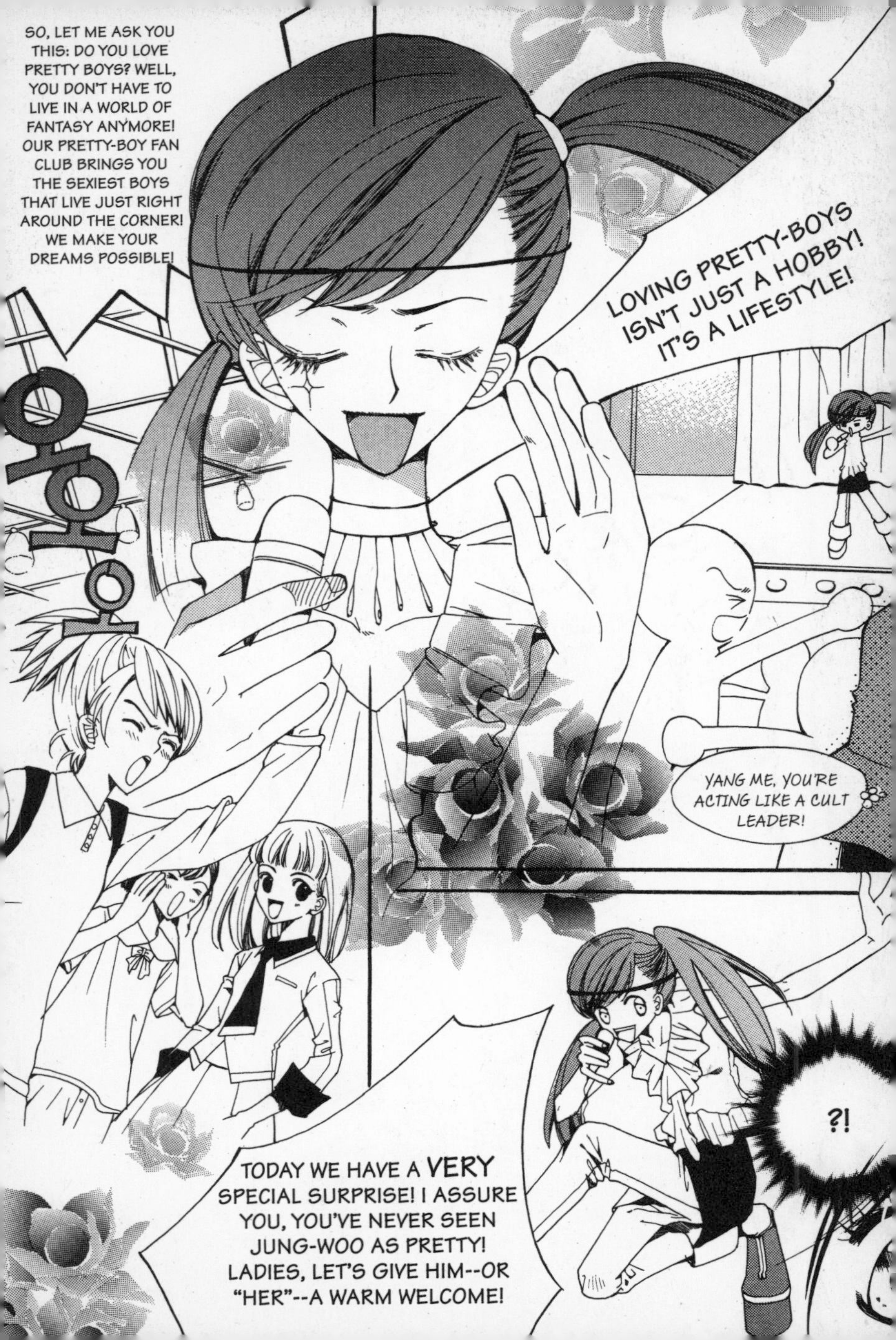
SO, LET ME ASK YOU THIS: DO YOU LOVE PRETTY BOYS? WELL, YOU DON'T HAVE TO LIVE IN A WORLD OF FANTASY ANYMORE! OUR PRETTY-BOY FAN CLUB BRINGS YOU THE SEXIEST BOYS THAT LIVE JUST RIGHT AROUND THE CORNER! WE MAKE YOUR DREAMS POSSIBLE!
LOVING PRETTY-BOYS ISN'T JUST A HOBBY! IT'S A LIFESTYLE!
YANG ME, YOU'RE ACTING LIKE A CULT LEADER!
TODAY WE HAVE A VERY SPECIAL SURPRISE! I ASSURE YOU, YOU'VE NEVER SEEN JUNG-WOO AS PRETTY! LADIES, LET'S GIVE HIM--OR "HER"--A WARM WELCOME!
?!

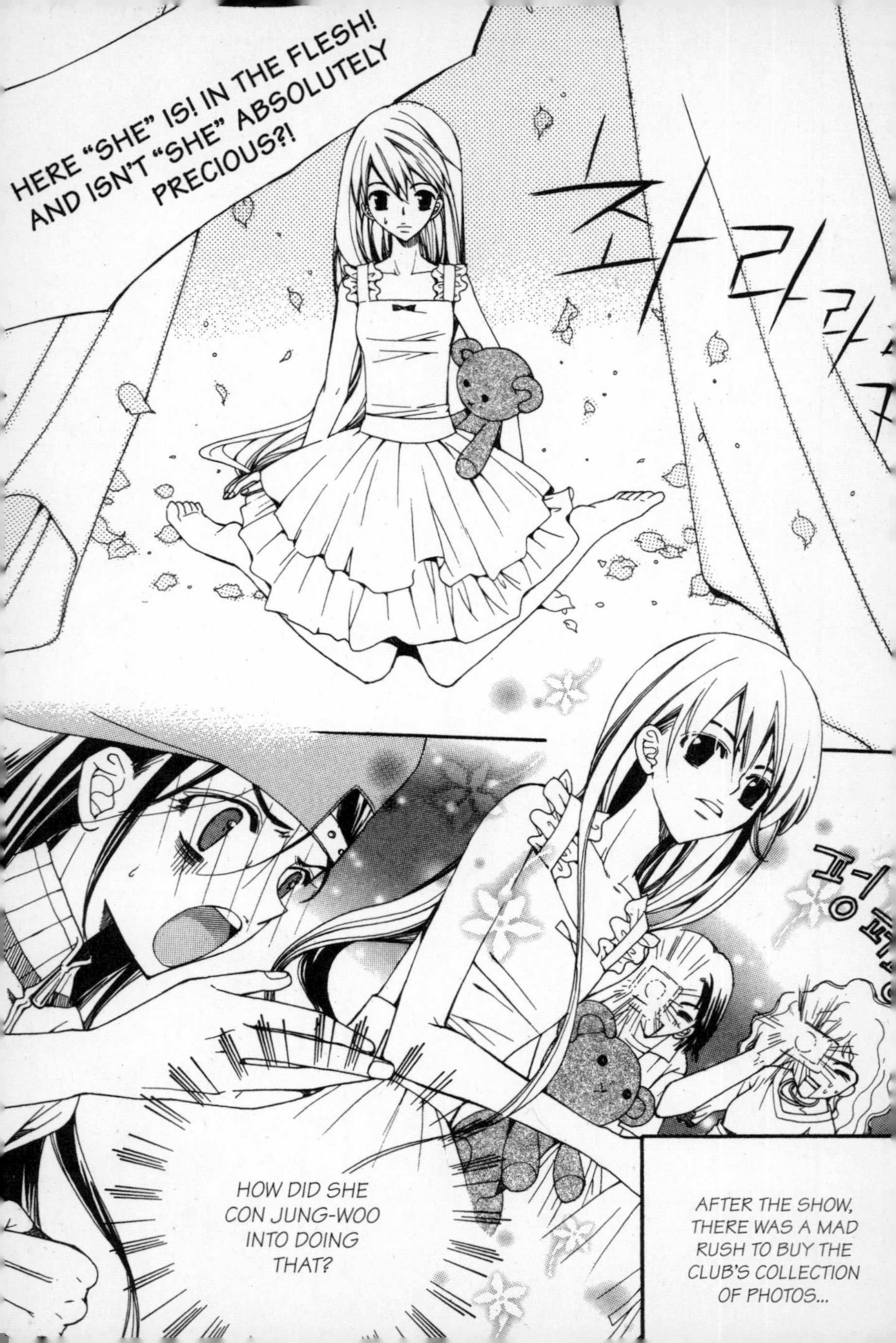
HERE "SHE" IS! IN THE FLESH! AND ISN'T "SHE" ABSOLUTELY PRECIOUS?!
HOW DID SHE CON JUNG-WOO INTO DOING THAT?
AFTER THE SHOW, THERE WAS A MAD RUSH TO BUY THE CLUB'S COLLECTION OF PHOTOS...

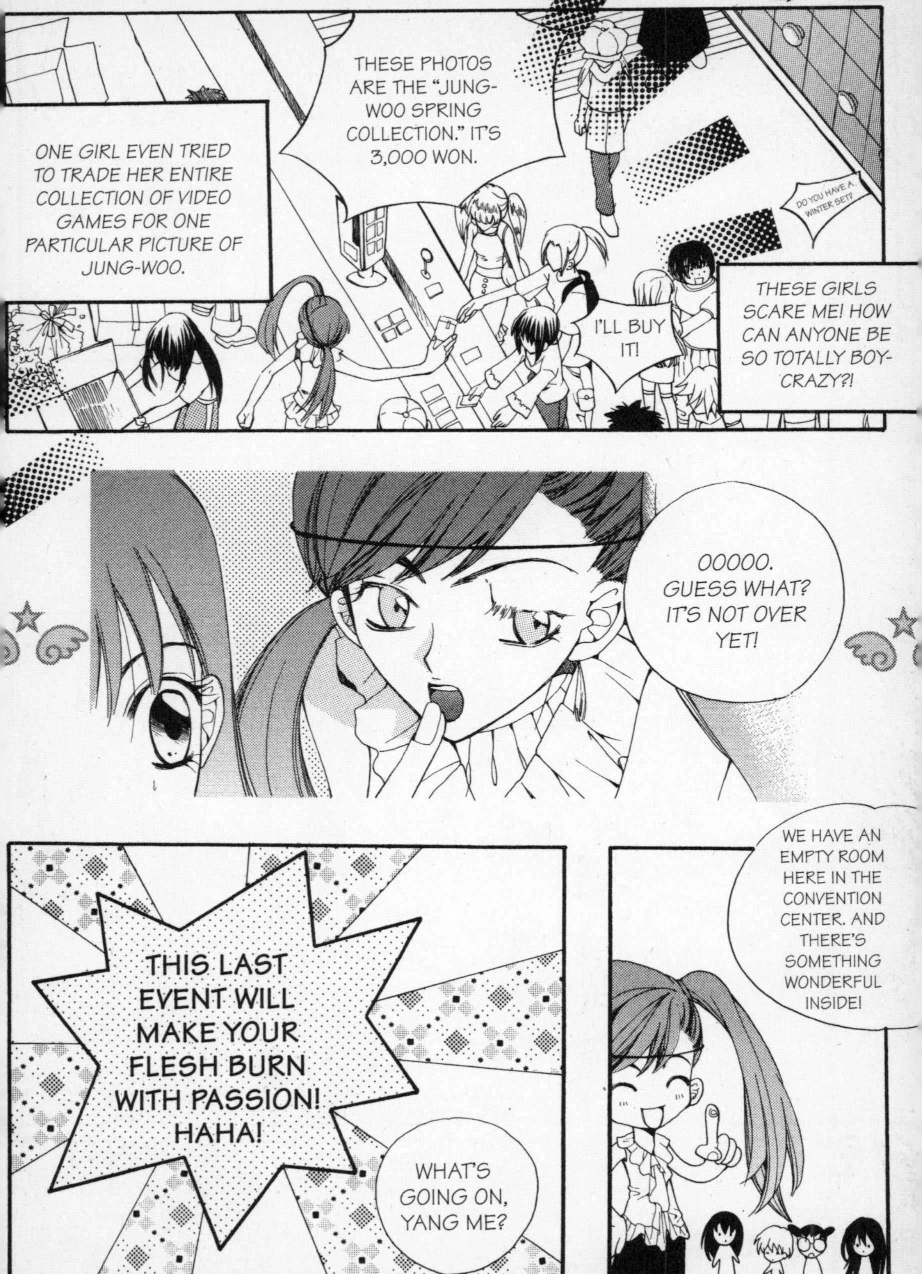
ONE GIRL EVEN TRIED TO TRADE HER ENTIRE COLLECTION OF VIDEO GAMES FOR ONE PARTICULAR PICTURE OF JUNG-WOO.
THESE PHOTOS ARE THE "JUNG-WOO SPRING COLLECTION." IT'S 3,000 WON.
DO YOU HAVE A WINTER SET?
I'LL BUY IT!
THESE GIRLS SCARE ME! HOW CAN ANYONE BE SO TOTALLY BOY-CRAZY?!
OOOOO. GUESS WHAT? IT'S NOT OVER YET!
THIS LAST EVENT WILL MAKE YOUR FLESH BURN WITH PASSION! HAHA!
WHAT'S GOING ON, YANG ME?
WE HAVE AN EMPTY ROOM HERE IN THE CONVENTION CENTER. AND THERE'S SOMETHING WONDERFUL INSIDE!

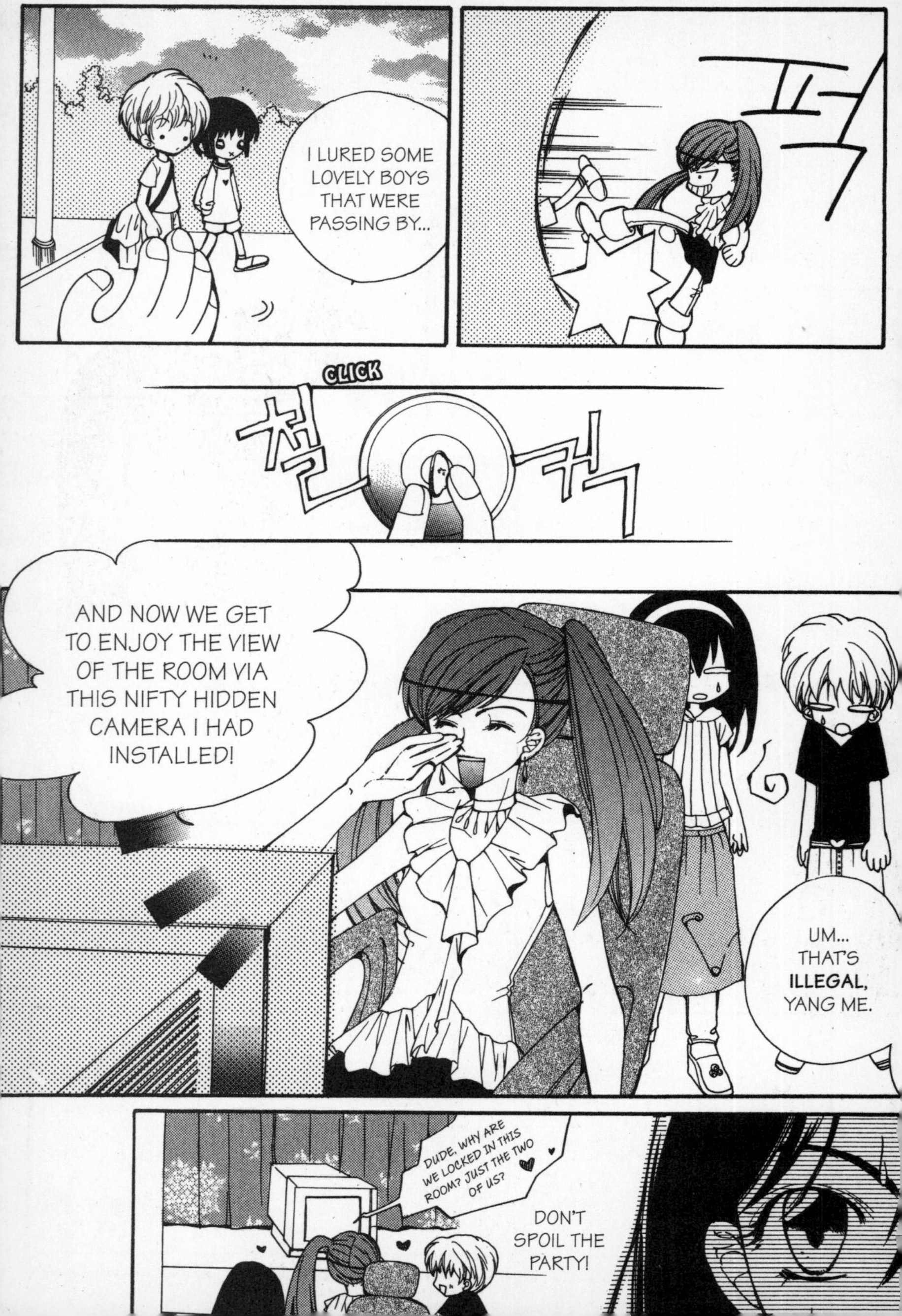
I LURED SOME LOVELY BOYS THAT WERE PASSING BY...
CLICK
철컥
AND NOW WE GET TO ENJOY THE VIEW OF THE ROOM VIA THIS NIFTY HIDDEN CAMERA I HAD INSTALLED!
UM... THAT'S **ILLEGAL,** YANG ME.
DUDE, WHY ARE WE LOCKED IN THIS ROOM? JUST THE TWO OF US?
DON'T SPOIL THE PARTY!

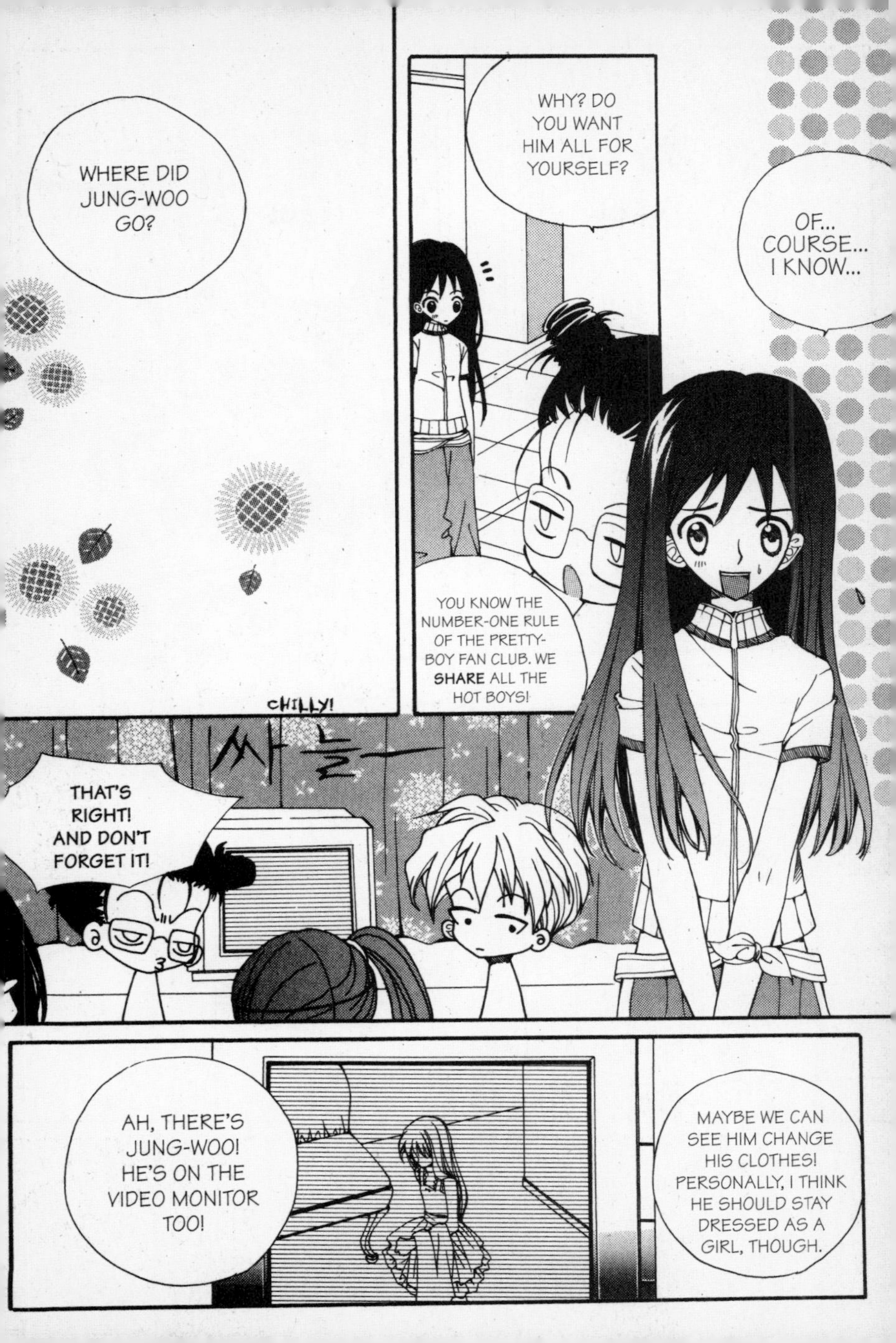
WHERE DID JUNG-WOO GO?
WHY? DO YOU WANT HIM ALL FOR YOURSELF?
YOU KNOW THE NUMBER-ONE RULE OF THE PRETTY-BOY FAN CLUB. WE **SHARE** ALL THE HOT BOYS!
OF... COURSE... I KNOW...
CHILLY!
싸늘—
THAT'S RIGHT! AND DON'T FORGET IT!
AH, THERE'S JUNG-WOO! HE'S ON THE VIDEO MONITOR TOO!
MAYBE WE CAN SEE HIM CHANGE HIS CLOTHES! PERSONALLY, I THINK HE SHOULD STAY DRESSED AS A GIRL, THOUGH.

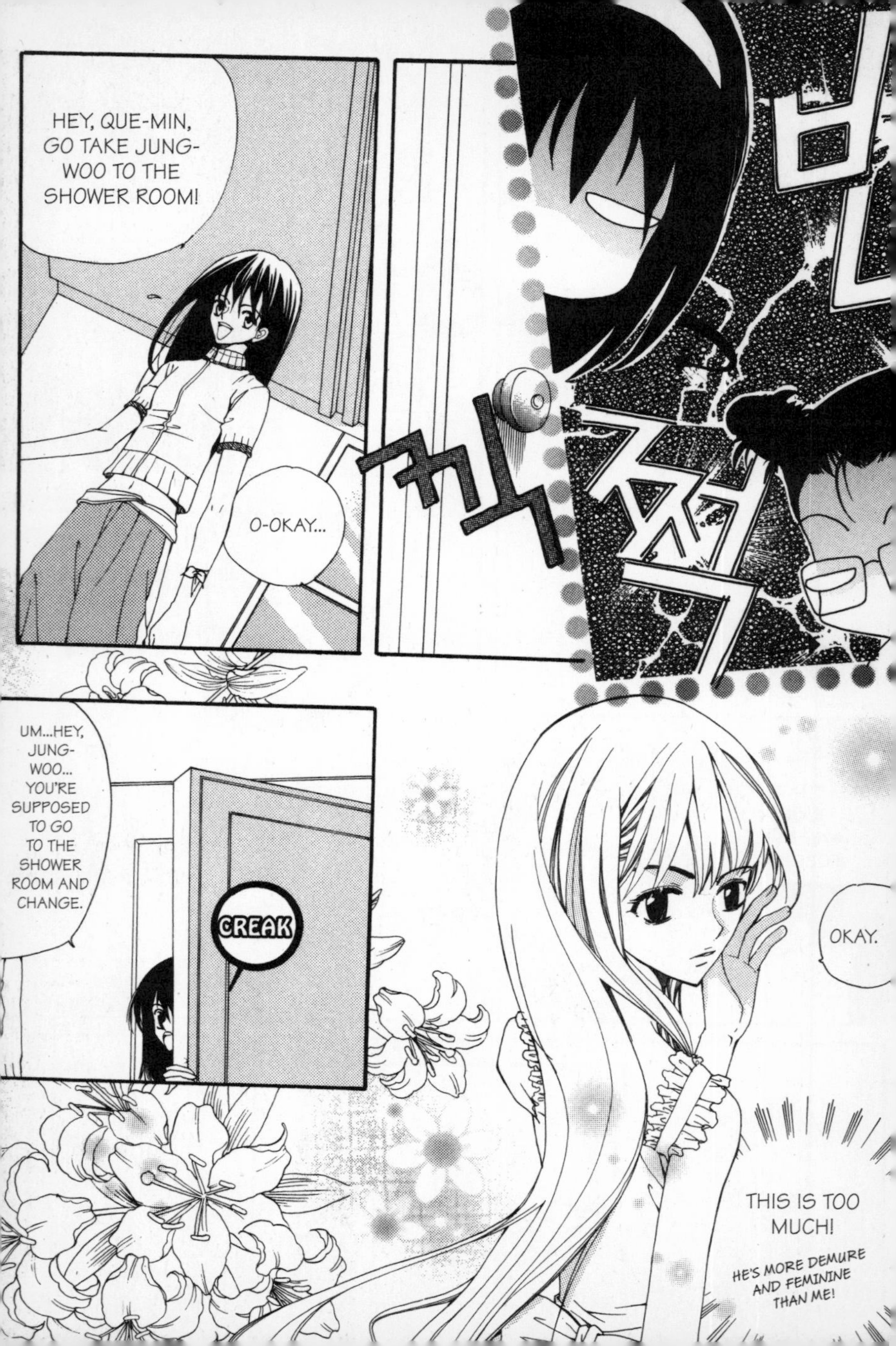
HEY, QUE-MIN, GO TAKE JUNG-WOO TO THE SHOWER ROOM!
O-OKAY...
UM...HEY, JUNG-WOO... YOU'RE SUPPOSED TO GO TO THE SHOWER ROOM AND CHANGE.
CREAK
OKAY.
THIS IS TOO MUCH!
HE'S MORE DEMURE AND FEMININE THAN ME!

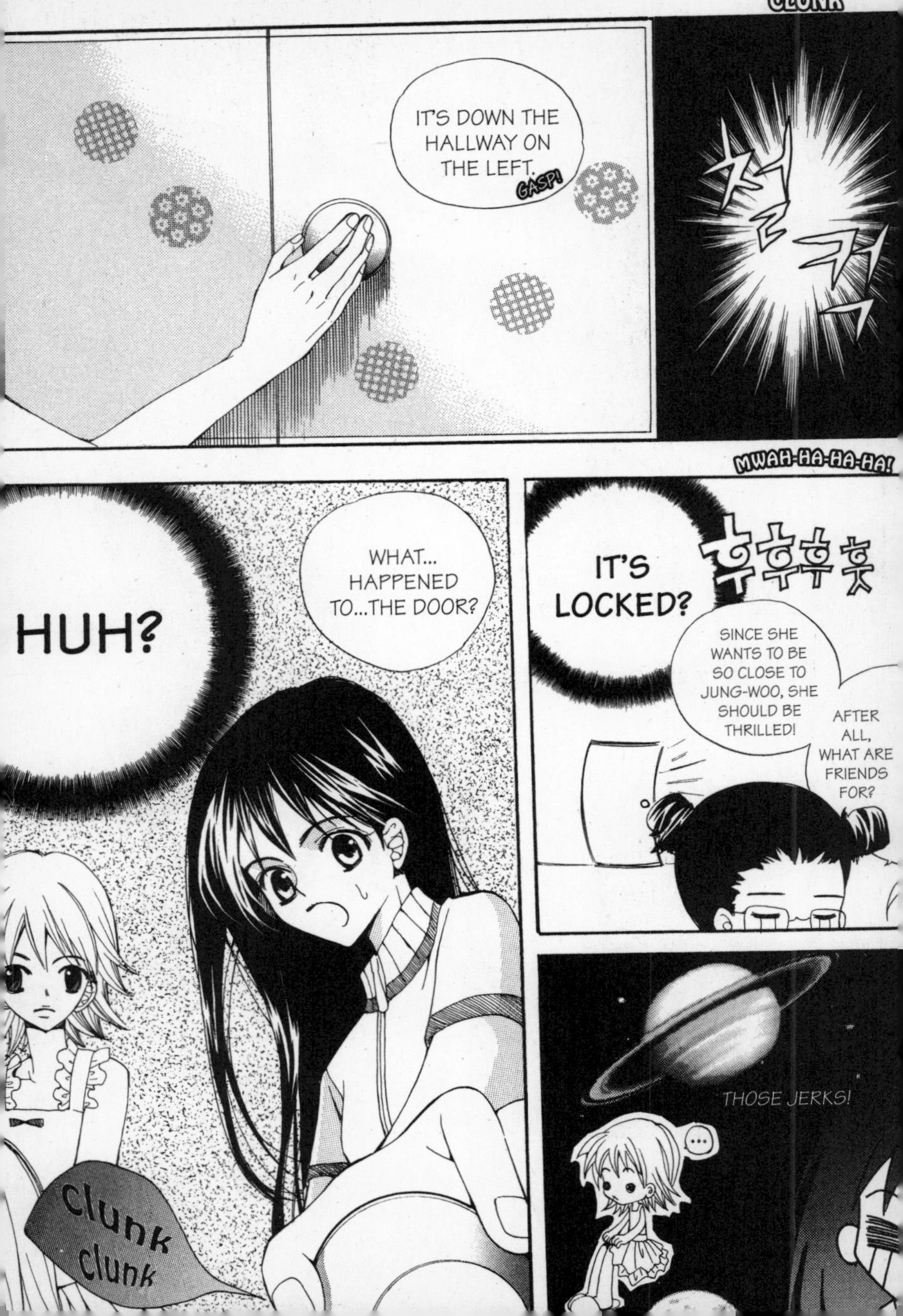
IT'S DOWN THE HALLWAY ON THE LEFT.
GASP!
CLUNK
HUH?
WHAT... HAPPENED TO...THE DOOR?
Clunk clunk
MWAH-HA-HA-HA!
IT'S LOCKED?
후후후훗
SINCE SHE WANTS TO BE SO CLOSE TO JUNG-WOO, SHE SHOULD BE THRILLED!
AFTER ALL, WHAT ARE FRIENDS FOR?
THOSE JERKS!
...

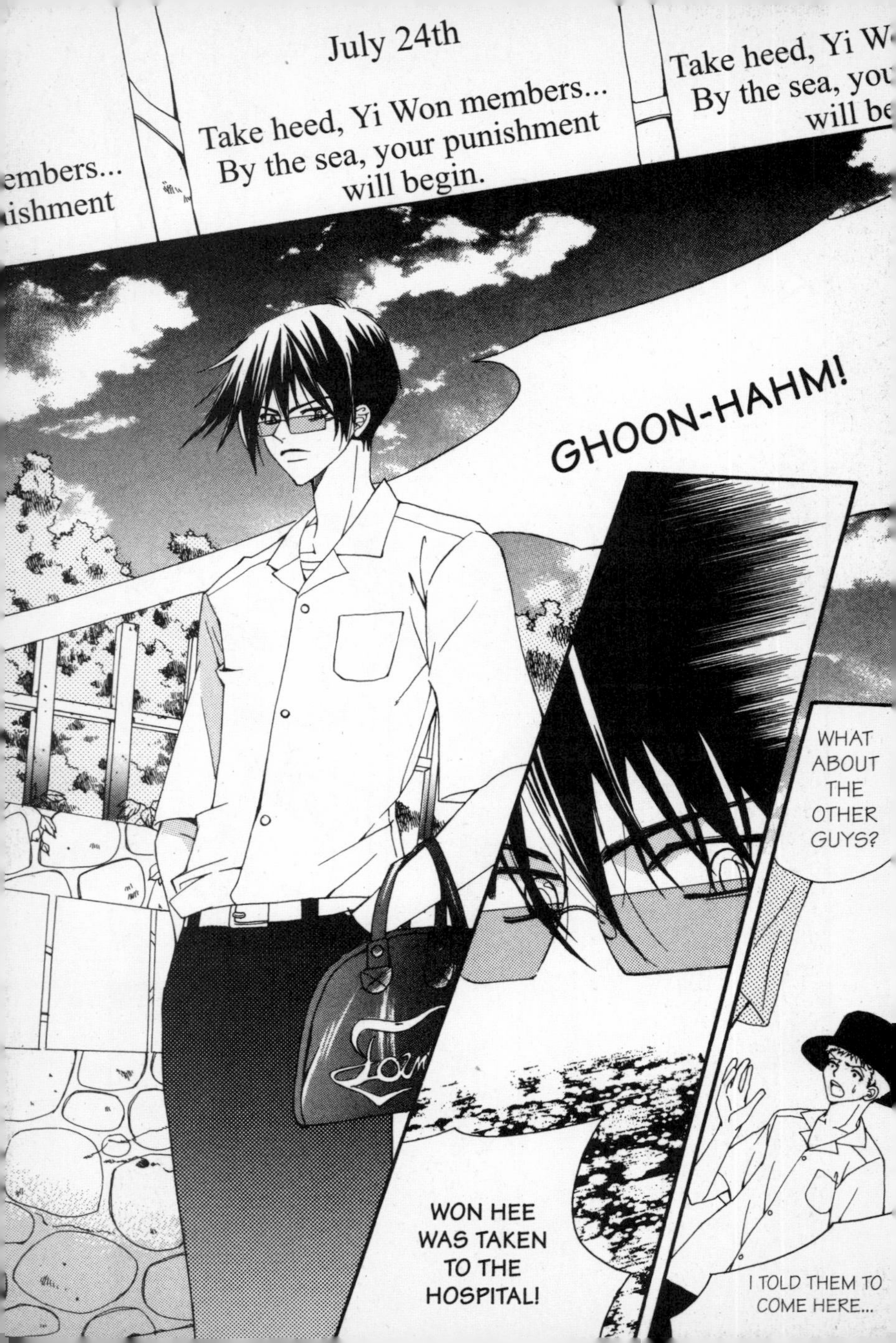
July 24th
Take heed, Yi Won members... By the sea, your punishment will begin.
GHOON-HAHM!
WON HEE WAS TAKEN TO THE HOSPITAL!
WHAT ABOUT THE OTHER GUYS?
I TOLD THEM TO COME HERE...

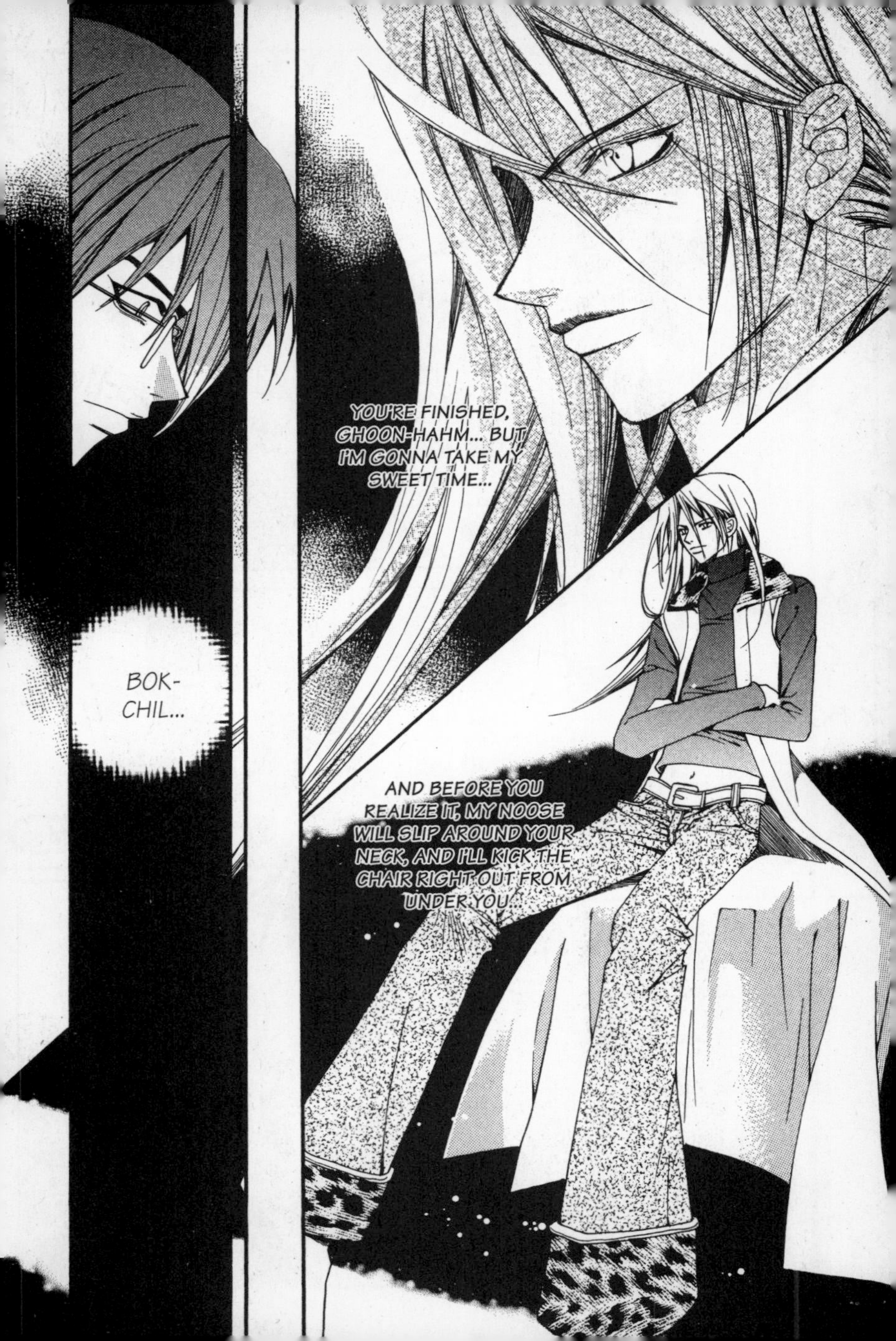
BOK-CHIL...
YOU'RE FINISHED, GHOON-HAHM... BUT I'M GONNA TAKE MY SWEET TIME...
AND BEFORE YOU REALIZE IT, MY NOOSE WILL SLIP AROUND YOUR NECK, AND I'LL KICK THE CHAIR RIGHT OUT FROM UNDER YOU...

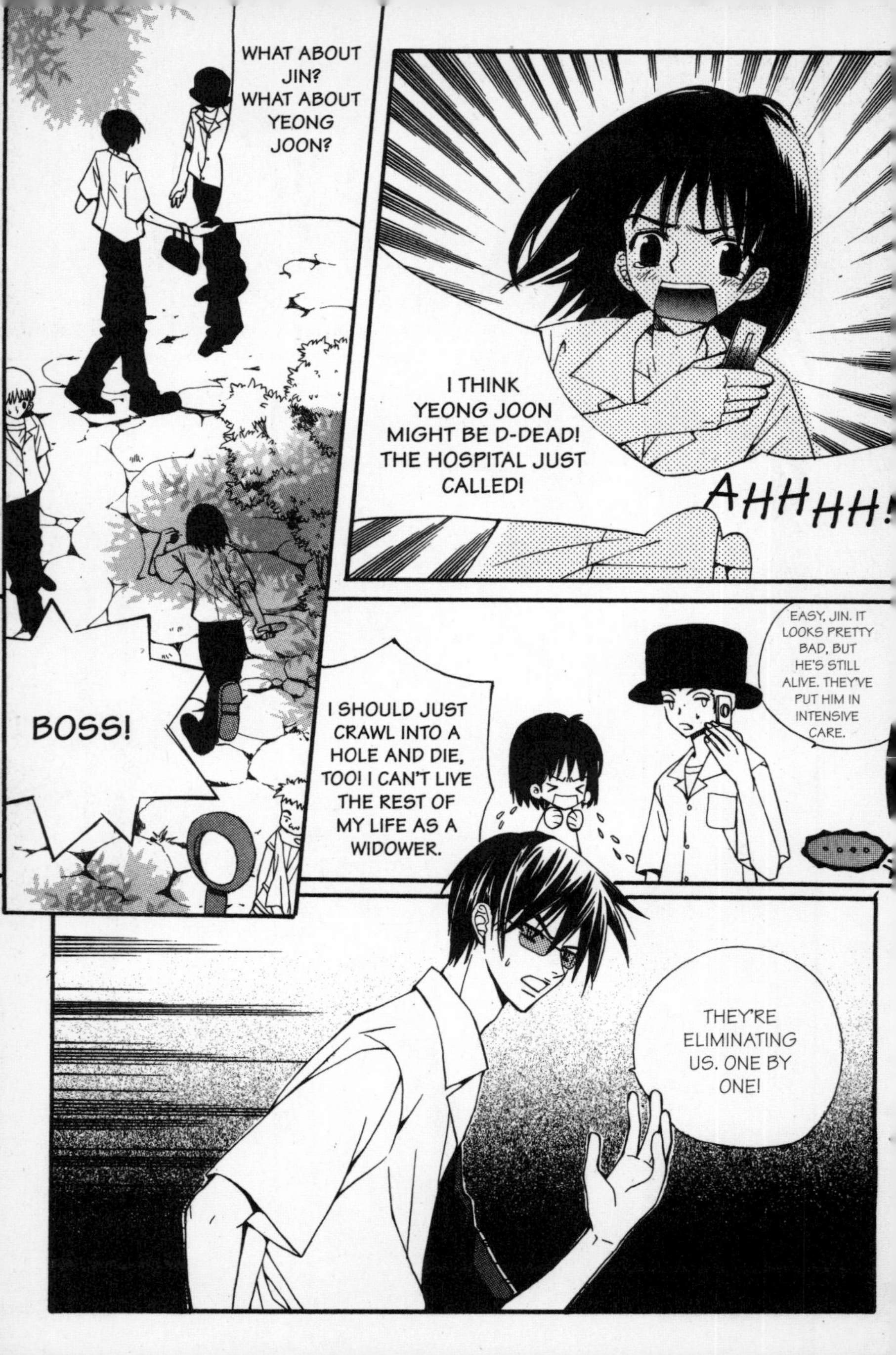
WHAT ABOUT JIN? WHAT ABOUT YEONG JOON?
BOSS!
I THINK YEONG JOON MIGHT BE D-DEAD! THE HOSPITAL JUST CALLED!
AHHHHH!
I SHOULD JUST CRAWL INTO A HOLE AND DIE, TOO! I CAN'T LIVE THE REST OF MY LIFE AS A WIDOWER.
EASY, JIN. IT LOOKS PRETTY BAD, BUT HE'S STILL ALIVE. THEY'VE PUT HIM IN INTENSIVE CARE.
....
THEY'RE ELIMINATING US. ONE BY ONE!

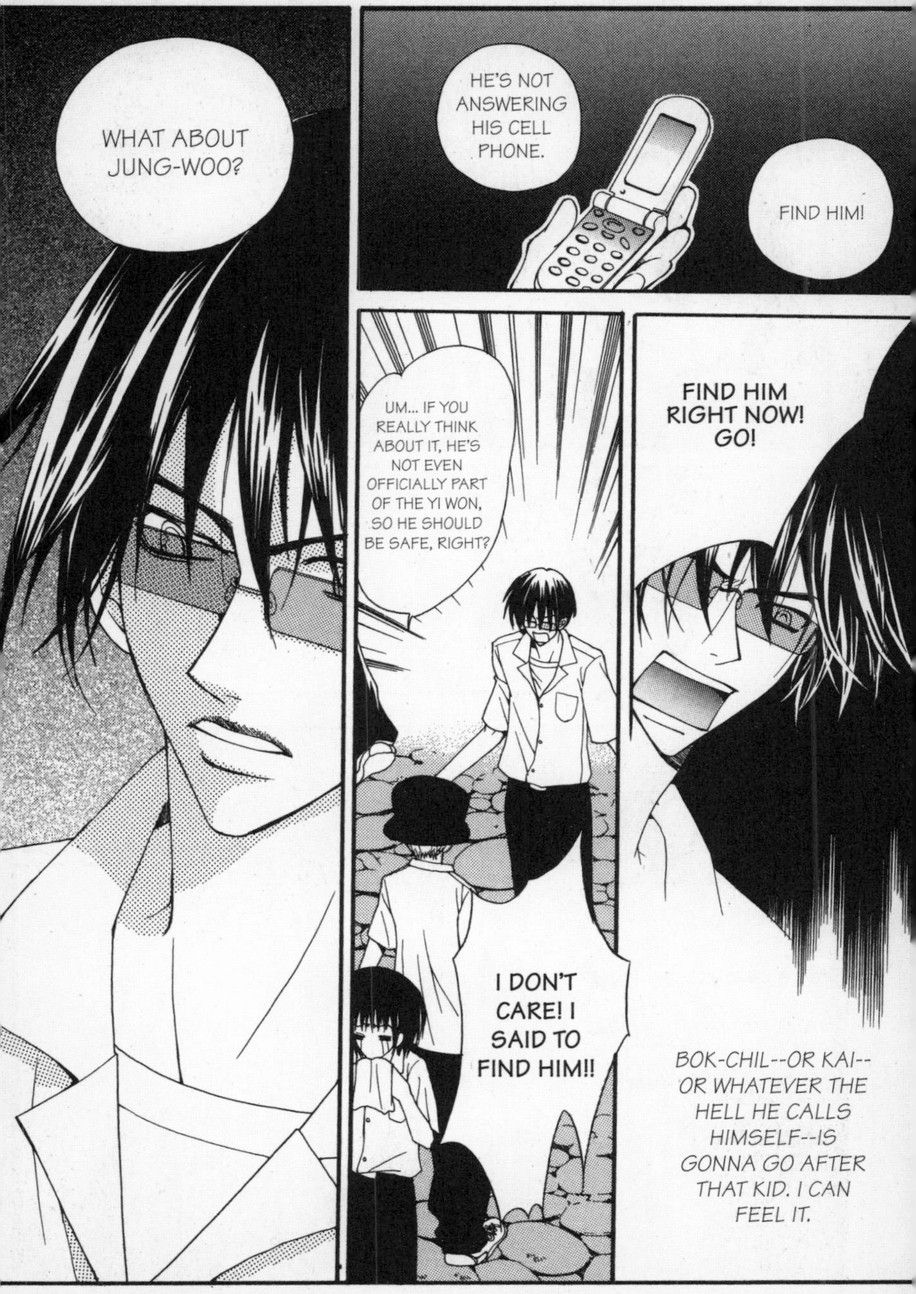
WHAT ABOUT JUNG-WOO?
HE'S NOT ANSWERING HIS CELL PHONE.
FIND HIM!
UM... IF YOU REALLY THINK ABOUT IT, HE'S NOT EVEN OFFICIALLY PART OF THE YI WON, SO HE SHOULD BE SAFE, RIGHT?
I DON'T CARE! I SAID TO FIND HIM!!
FIND HIM RIGHT NOW! GO!
BOK-CHIL--OR KAI--OR WHATEVER THE HELL HE CALLS HIMSELF--IS GONNA GO AFTER THAT KID. I CAN FEEL IT.

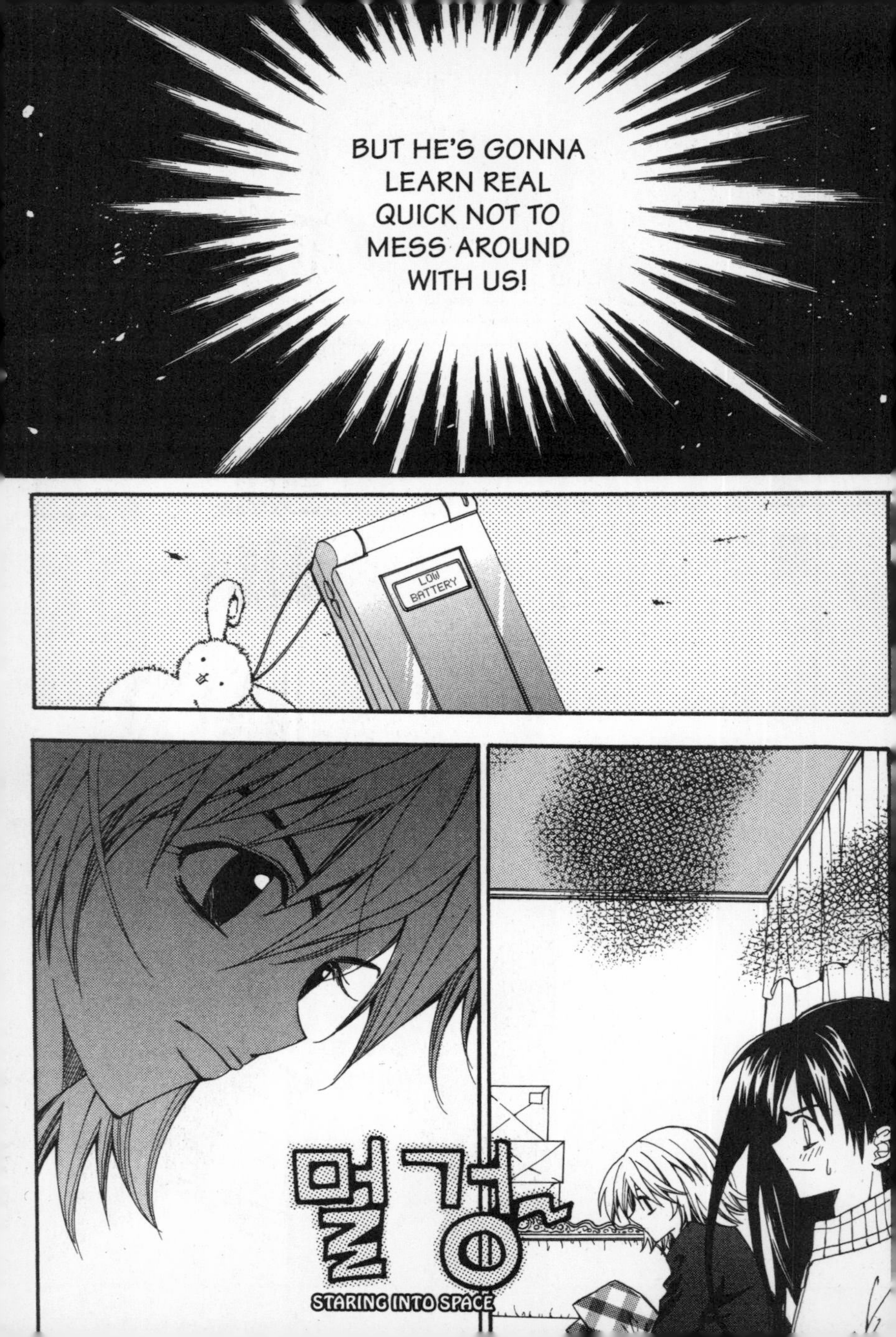
BUT HE'S GONNA LEARN REAL QUICK NOT TO MESS AROUND WITH US!
LOW BATTERY
STARING INTO SPACE

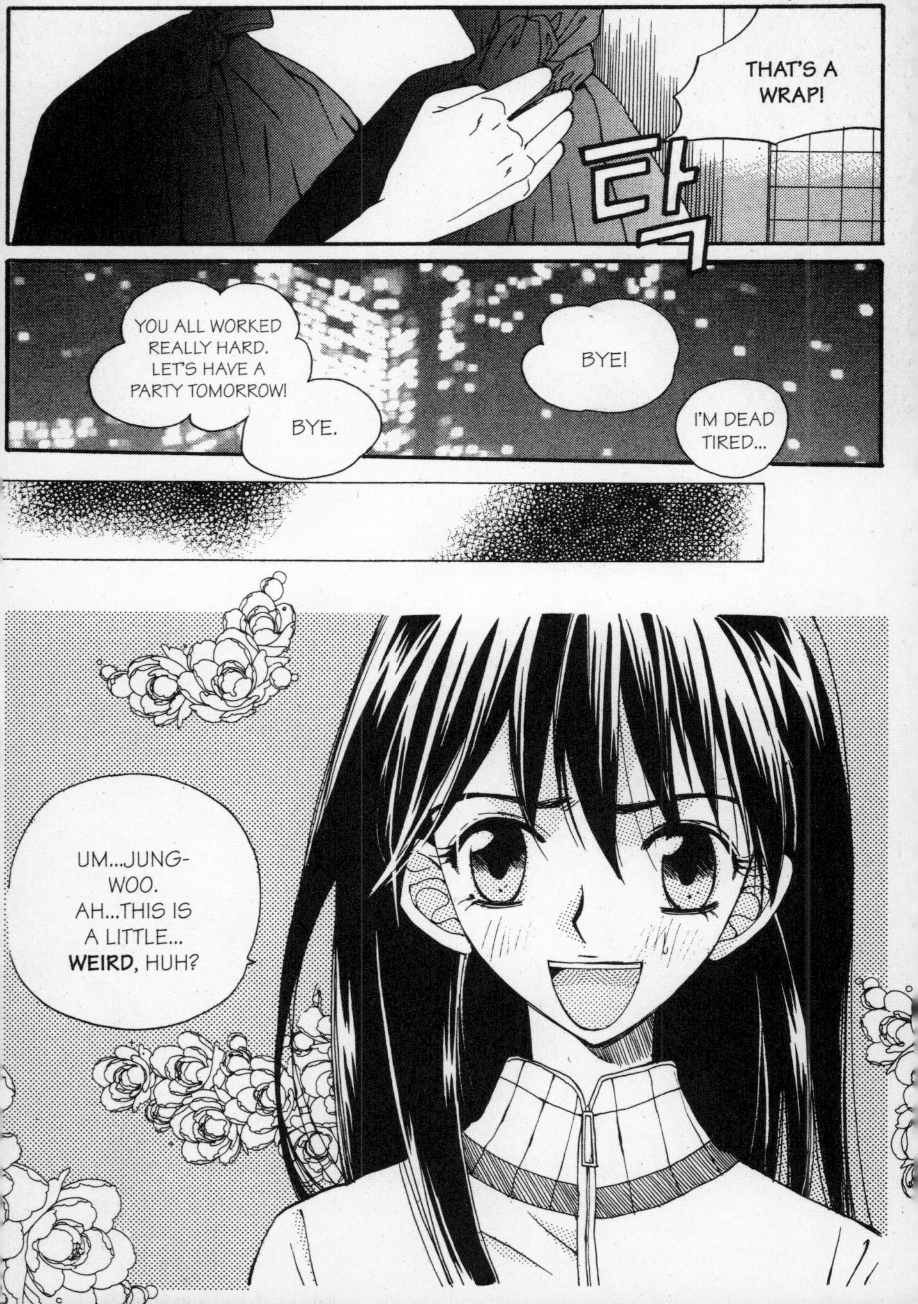
THAT'S A WRAP!
탁
YOU ALL WORKED REALLY HARD. LET'S HAVE A PARTY TOMORROW!
BYE.
BYE!
I'M DEAD TIRED...
UM...JUNG-WOO. AH...THIS IS A LITTLE... **WEIRD**, HUH?

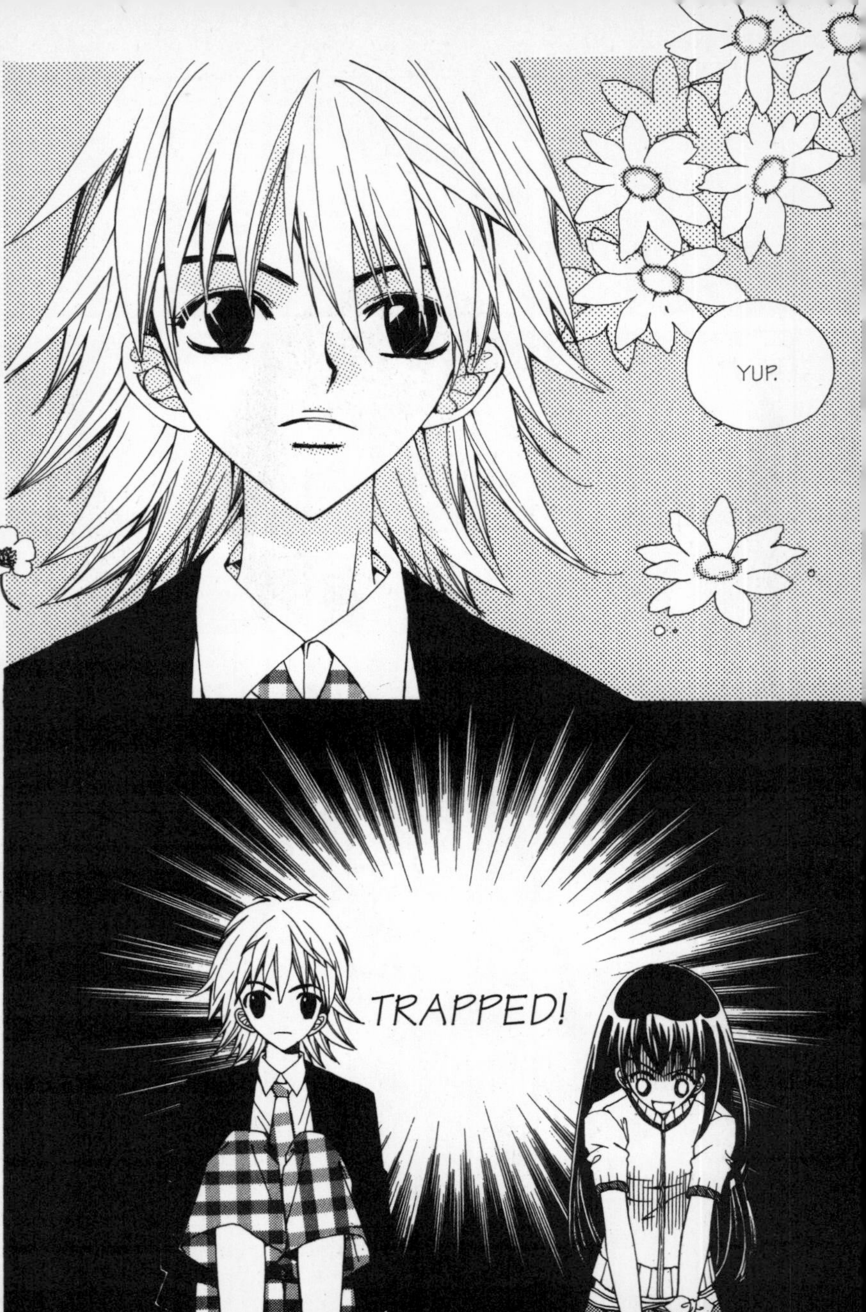
YUP.
TRAPPED!

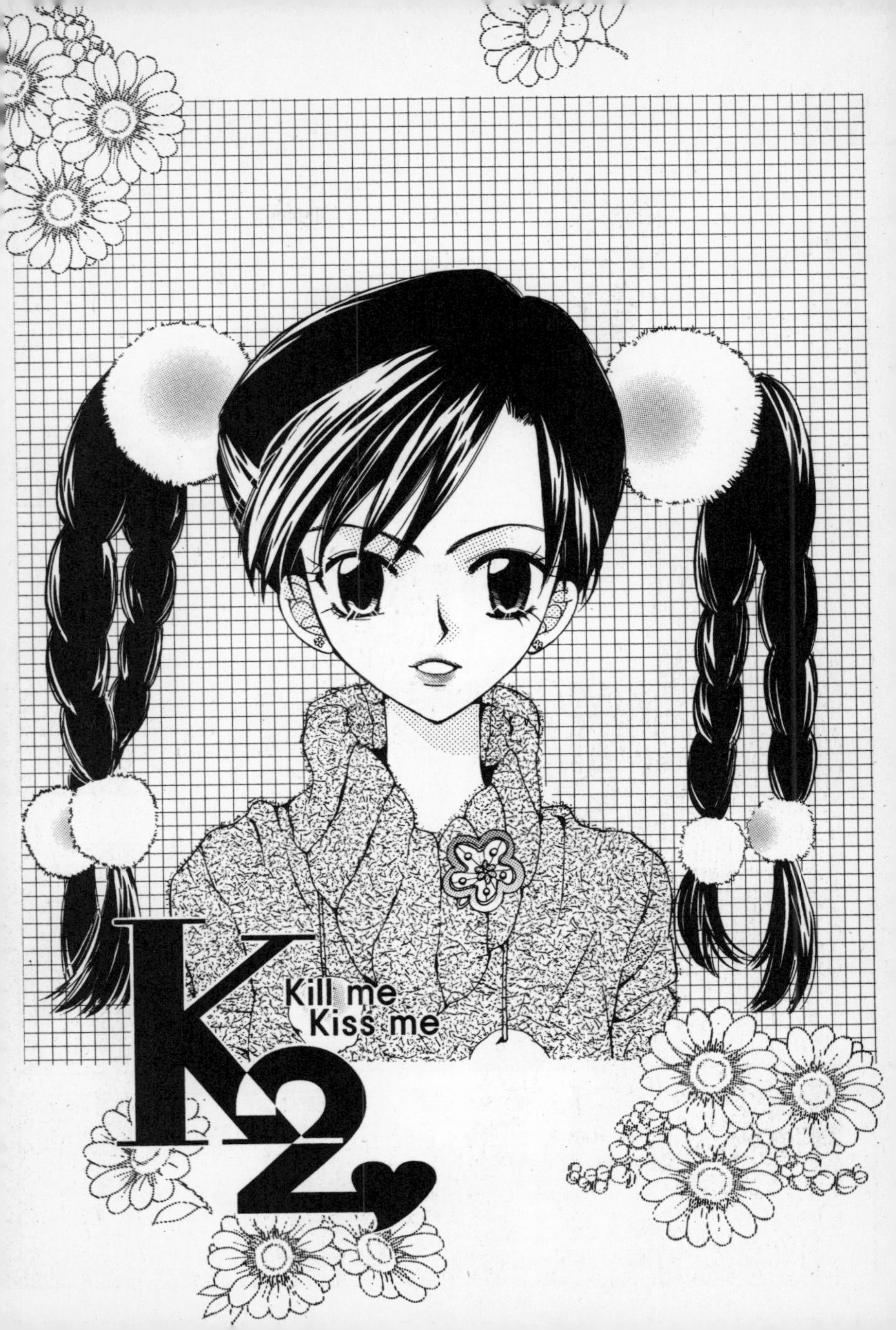
K2
Kill me
Kiss me

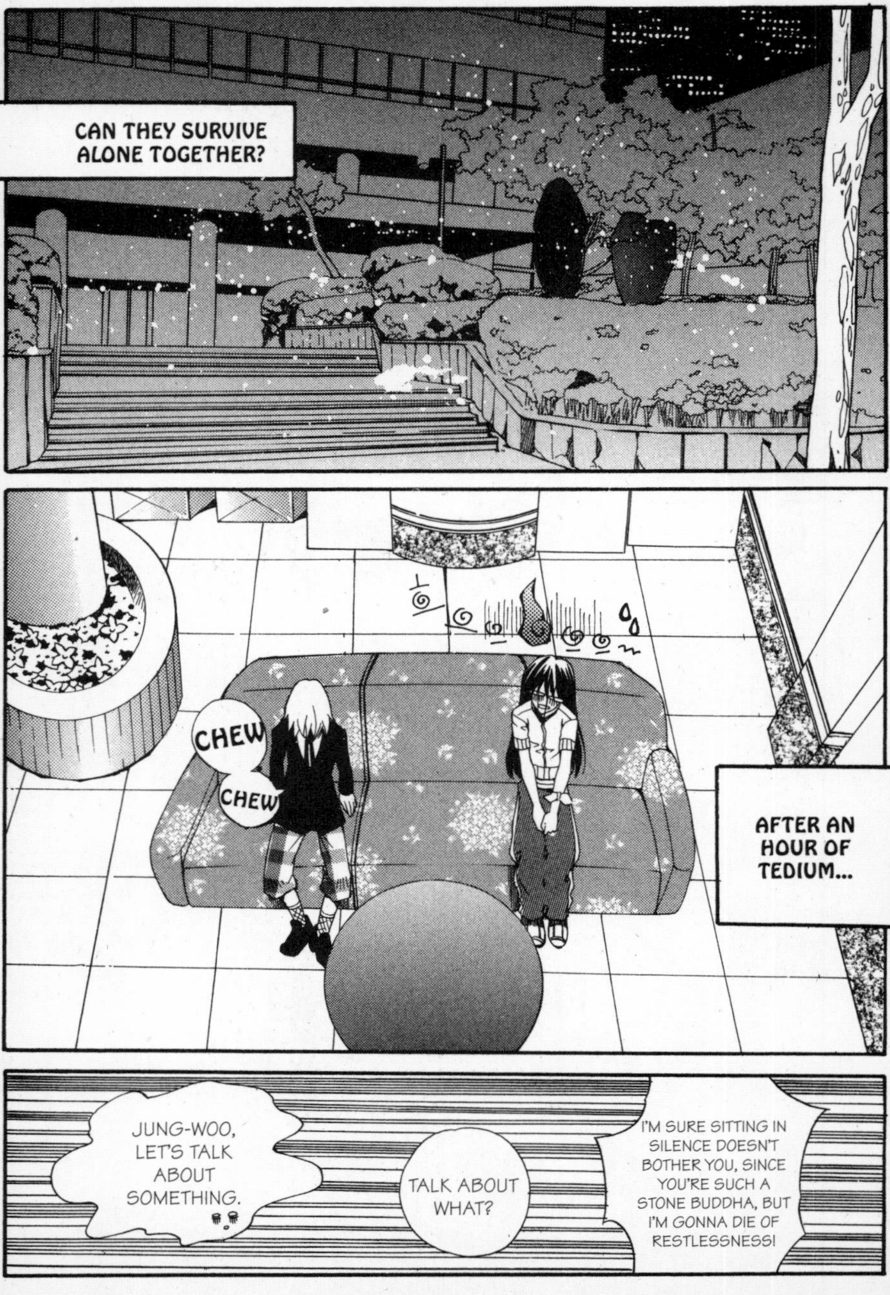
CAN THEY SURVIVE ALONE TOGETHER?
CHEW
CHEW
AFTER AN HOUR OF TEDIUM...
JUNG-WOO, LET'S TALK ABOUT SOMETHING.
TALK ABOUT WHAT?
I'M SURE SITTING IN SILENCE DOESN'T BOTHER YOU, SINCE YOU'RE SUCH A STONE BUDDHA, BUT I'M GONNA DIE OF RESTLESSNESS!

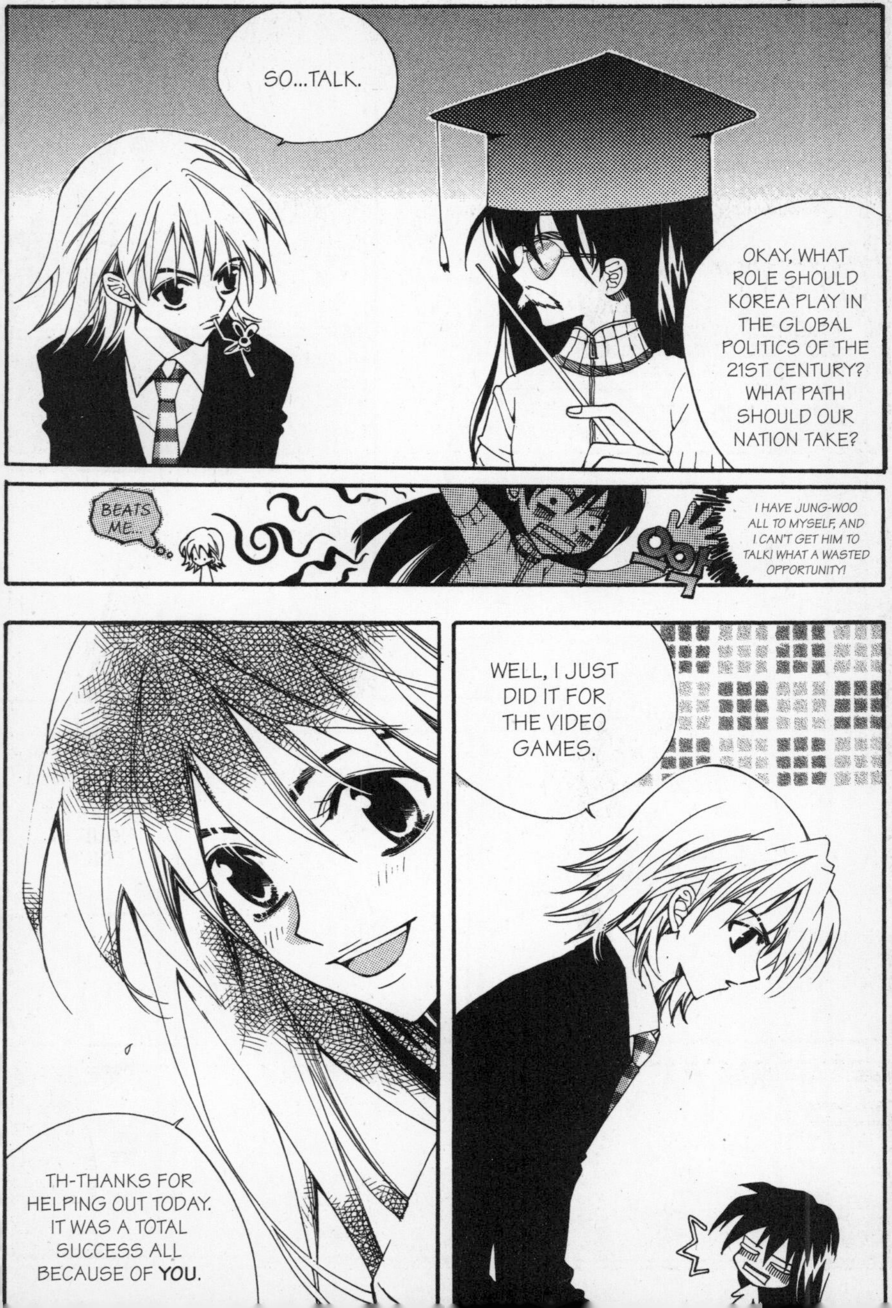
SO...TALK.
OKAY, WHAT ROLE SHOULD KOREA PLAY IN THE GLOBAL POLITICS OF THE 21ST CENTURY? WHAT PATH SHOULD OUR NATION TAKE?
BEATS ME..
I HAVE JUNG-WOO ALL TO MYSELF, AND I CAN'T GET HIM TO TALK! WHAT A WASTED OPPORTUNITY!
TH-THANKS FOR HELPING OUT TODAY. IT WAS A TOTAL SUCCESS ALL BECAUSE OF YOU.
WELL, I JUST DID IT FOR THE VIDEO GAMES.

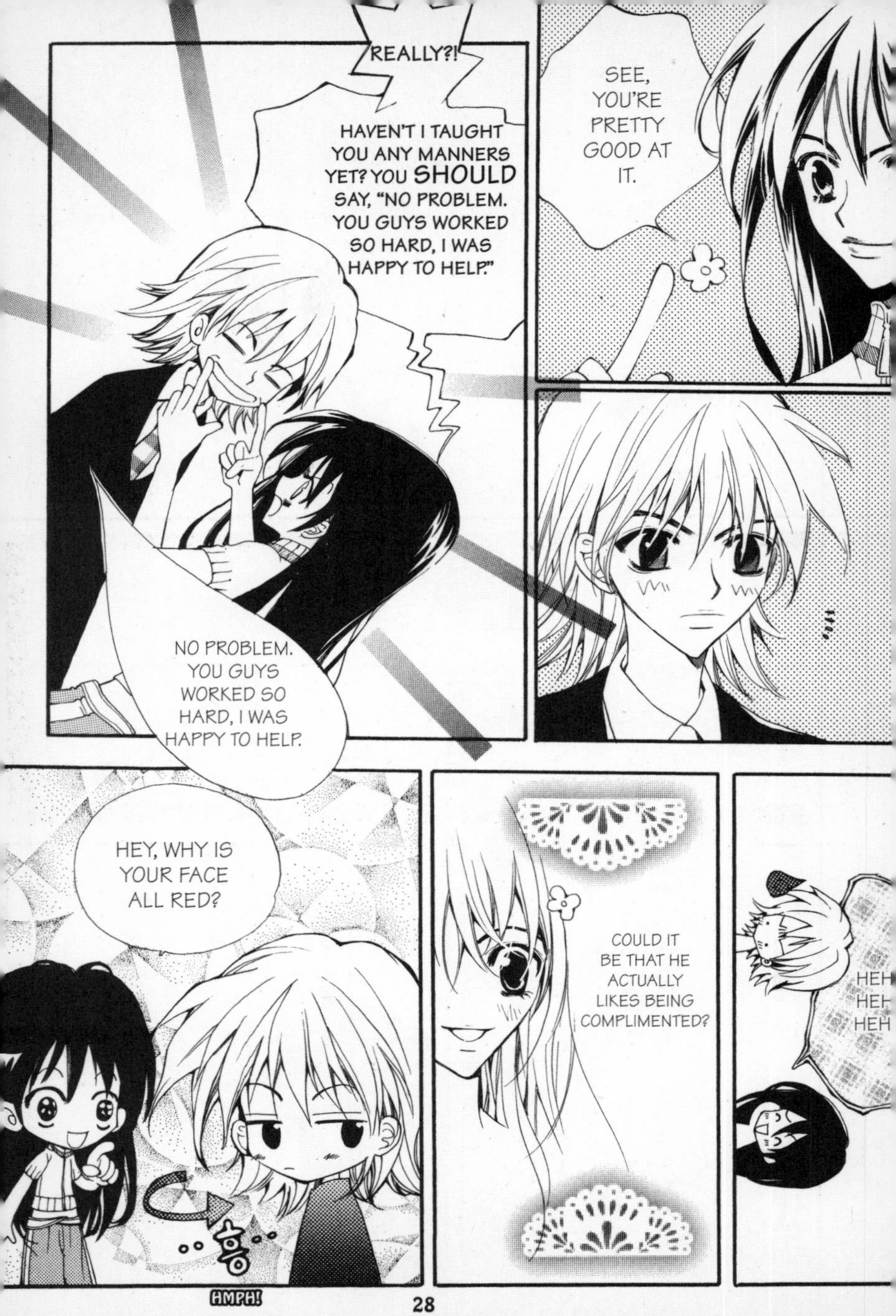
REALLY?!
HAVEN'T I TAUGHT YOU ANY MANNERS YET? YOU SHOULD SAY, "NO PROBLEM. YOU GUYS WORKED SO HARD, I WAS HAPPY TO HELP."
NO PROBLEM. YOU GUYS WORKED SO HARD, I WAS HAPPY TO HELP.
SEE, YOU'RE PRETTY GOOD AT IT.
HEY, WHY IS YOUR FACE ALL RED?
흥
AMPH!
COULD IT BE THAT HE ACTUALLY LIKES BEING COMPLIMENTED?
HEH HEH HEH

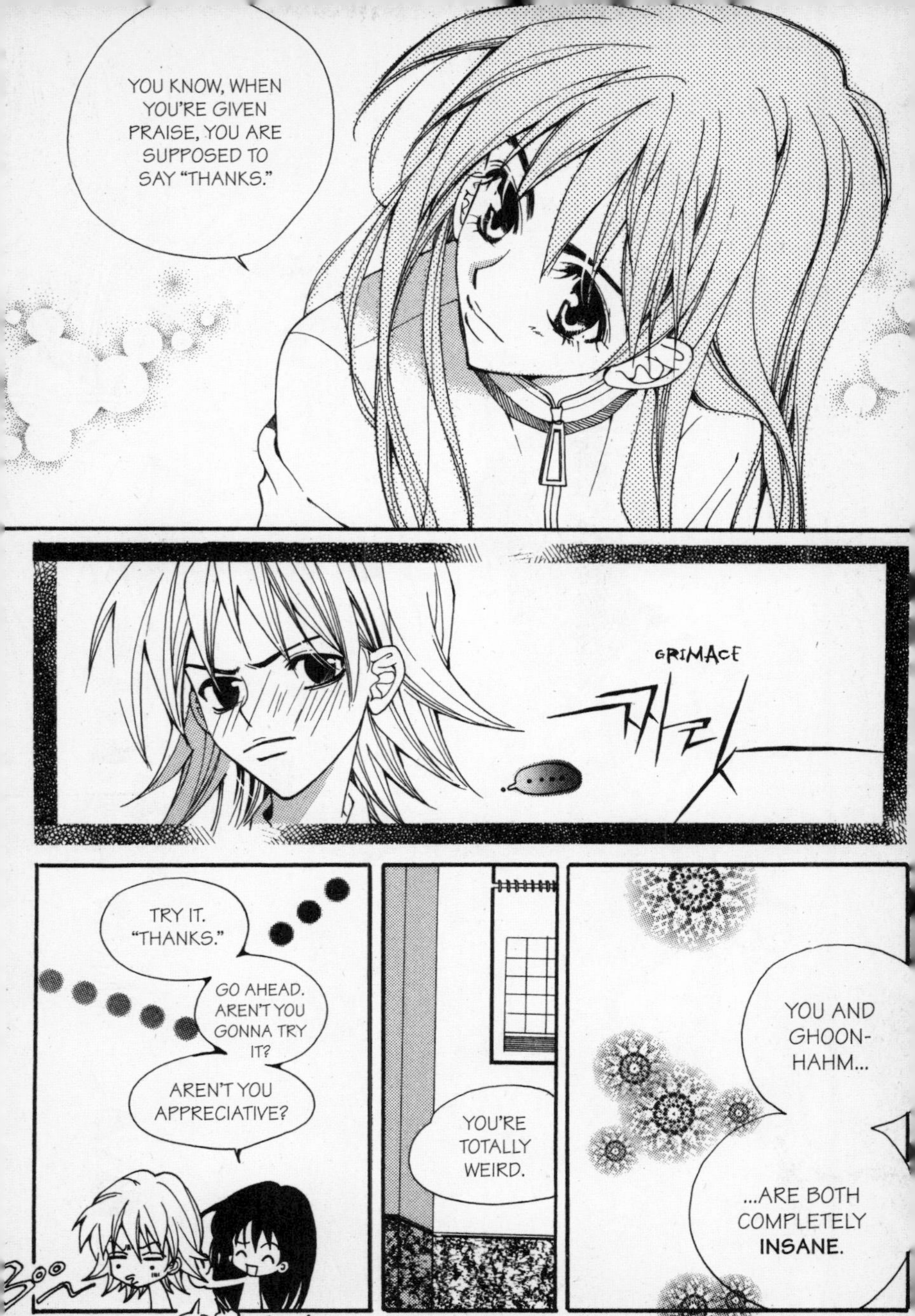
YOU KNOW, WHEN YOU'RE GIVEN PRAISE, YOU ARE SUPPOSED TO SAY "THANKS."
GRIMACE
....
TRY IT. "THANKS."
GO AHEAD. AREN'T YOU GONNA TRY IT?
AREN'T YOU APPRECIATIVE?
탁탁
YOU'RE TOTALLY WEIRD.
YOU AND GHOON-HAHM...
...ARE BOTH COMPLETELY **INSANE.**

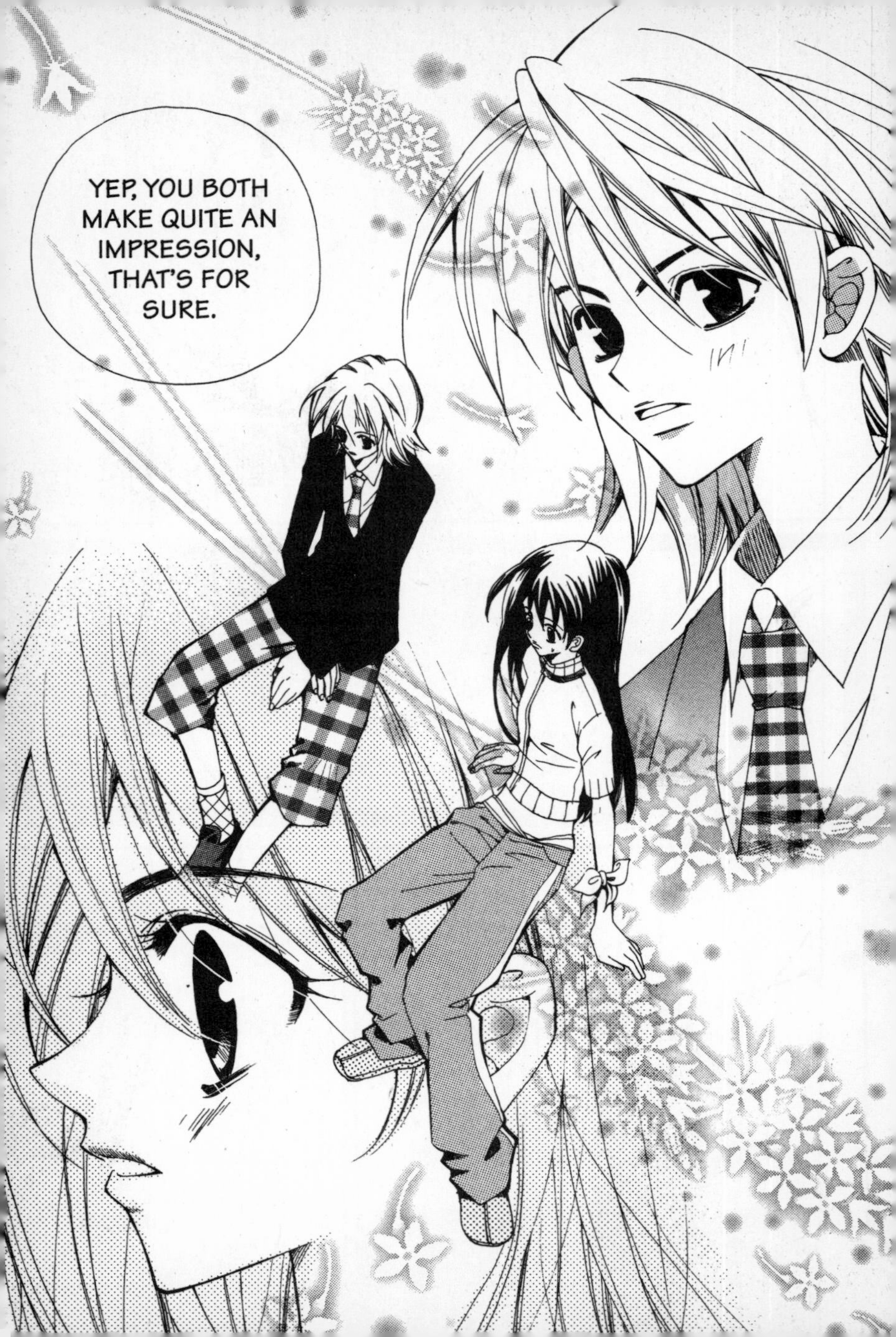
YEP, YOU BOTH MAKE QUITE AN IMPRESSION, THAT'S FOR SURE.

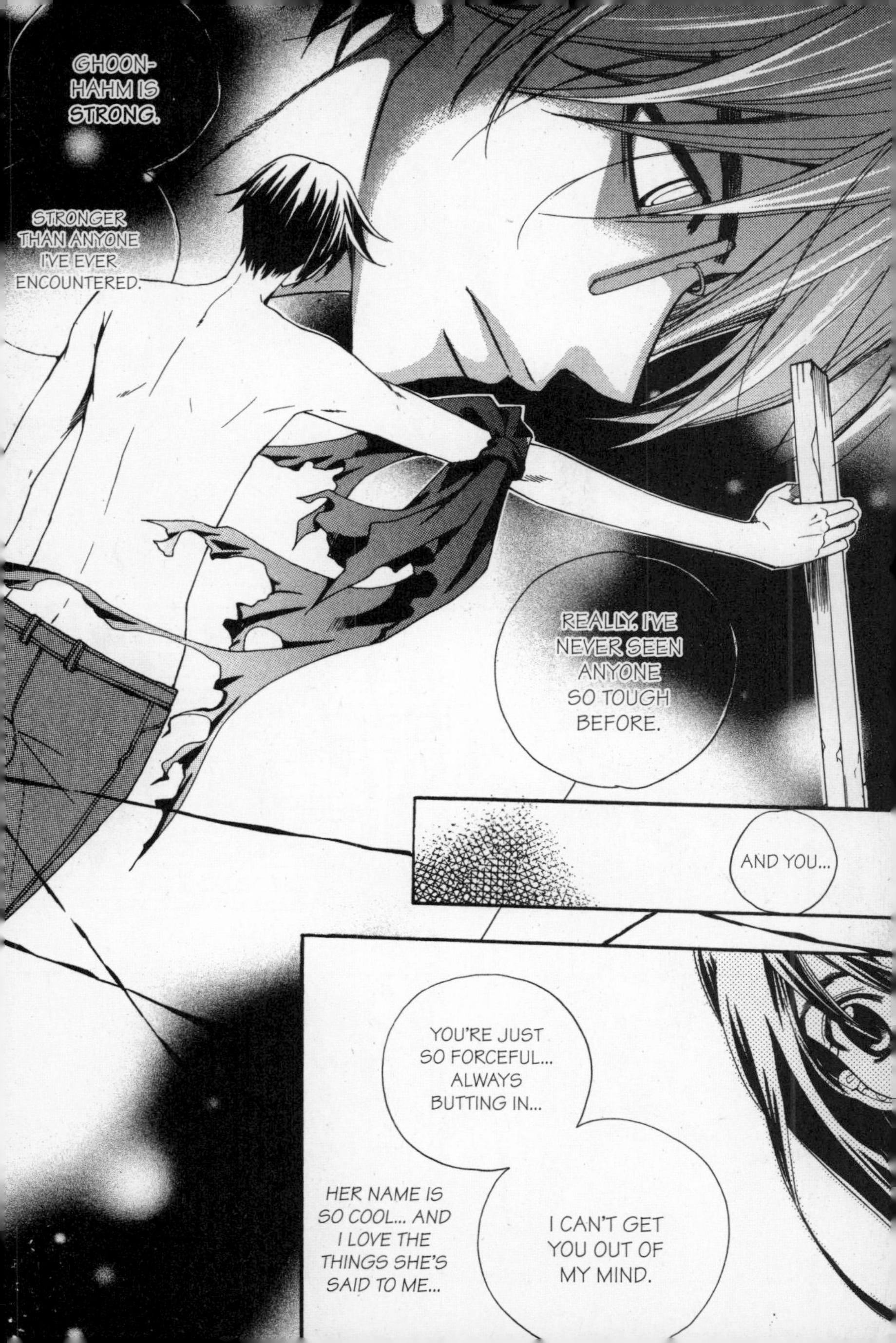
GHOON-HAHM IS STRONG.
STRONGER THAN ANYONE I'VE EVER ENCOUNTERED.
REALLY. I'VE NEVER SEEN ANYONE SO TOUGH BEFORE.
AND YOU...
YOU'RE JUST SO FORCEFUL... ALWAYS BUTTING IN...
HER NAME IS SO COOL... AND I LOVE THE THINGS SHE'S SAID TO ME...
I CAN'T GET YOU OUT OF MY MIND.

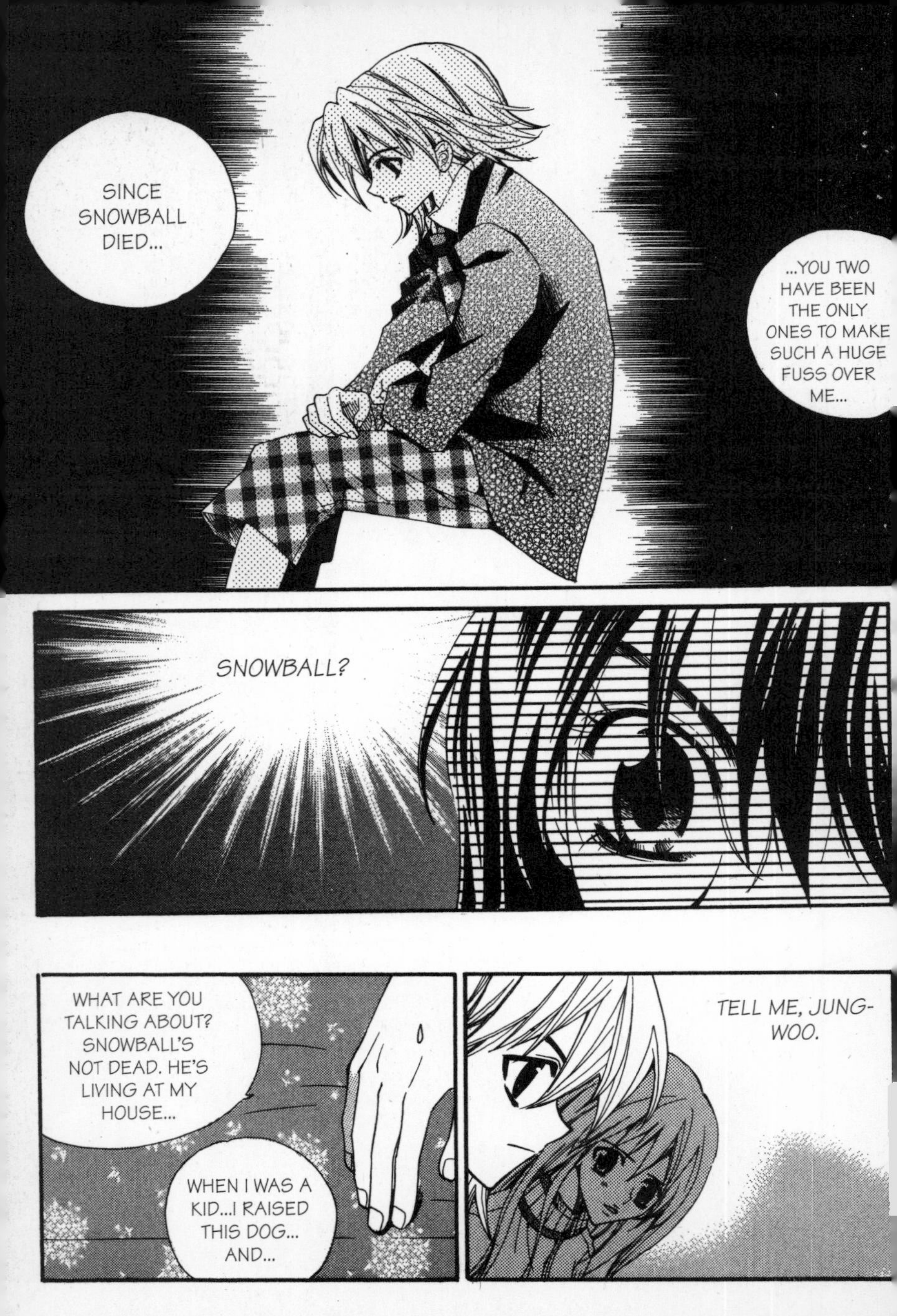
SINCE SNOWBALL DIED...
...YOU TWO HAVE BEEN THE ONLY ONES TO MAKE SUCH A HUGE FUSS OVER ME...
SNOWBALL?
WHAT ARE YOU TALKING ABOUT? SNOWBALL'S NOT DEAD. HE'S LIVING AT MY HOUSE...
WHEN I WAS A KID...I RAISED THIS DOG... AND...
TELL ME, JUNG-WOO.

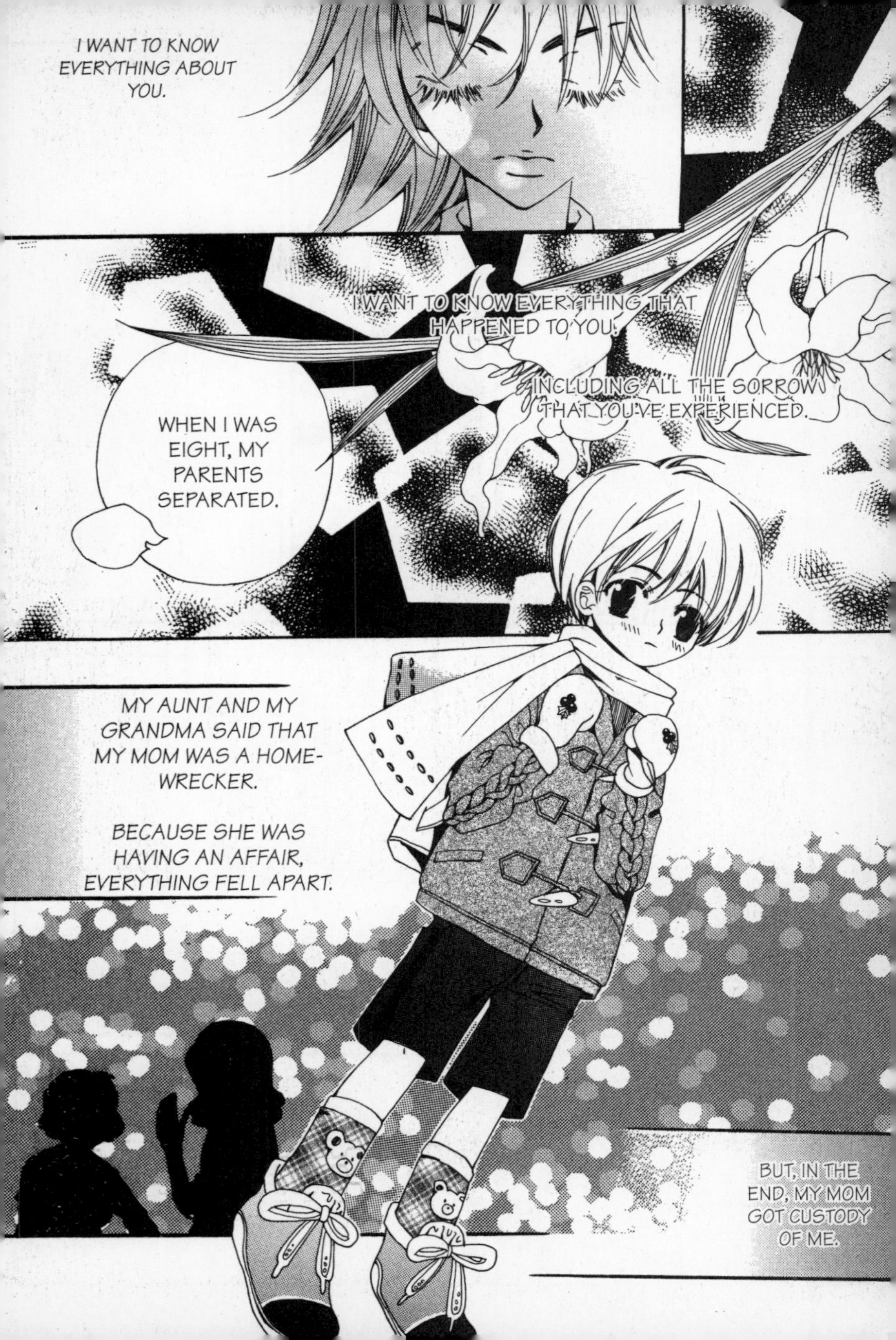
I WANT TO KNOW EVERYTHING ABOUT YOU.
I WANT TO KNOW EVERYTHING THAT HAPPENED TO YOU!
INCLUDING ALL THE SORROW THAT YOU'VE EXPERIENCED.
WHEN I WAS EIGHT, MY PARENTS SEPARATED.
MY AUNT AND MY GRANDMA SAID THAT MY MOM WAS A HOME-WRECKER.
BECAUSE SHE WAS HAVING AN AFFAIR, EVERYTHING FELL APART.
BUT, IN THE END, MY MOM GOT CUSTODY OF ME.

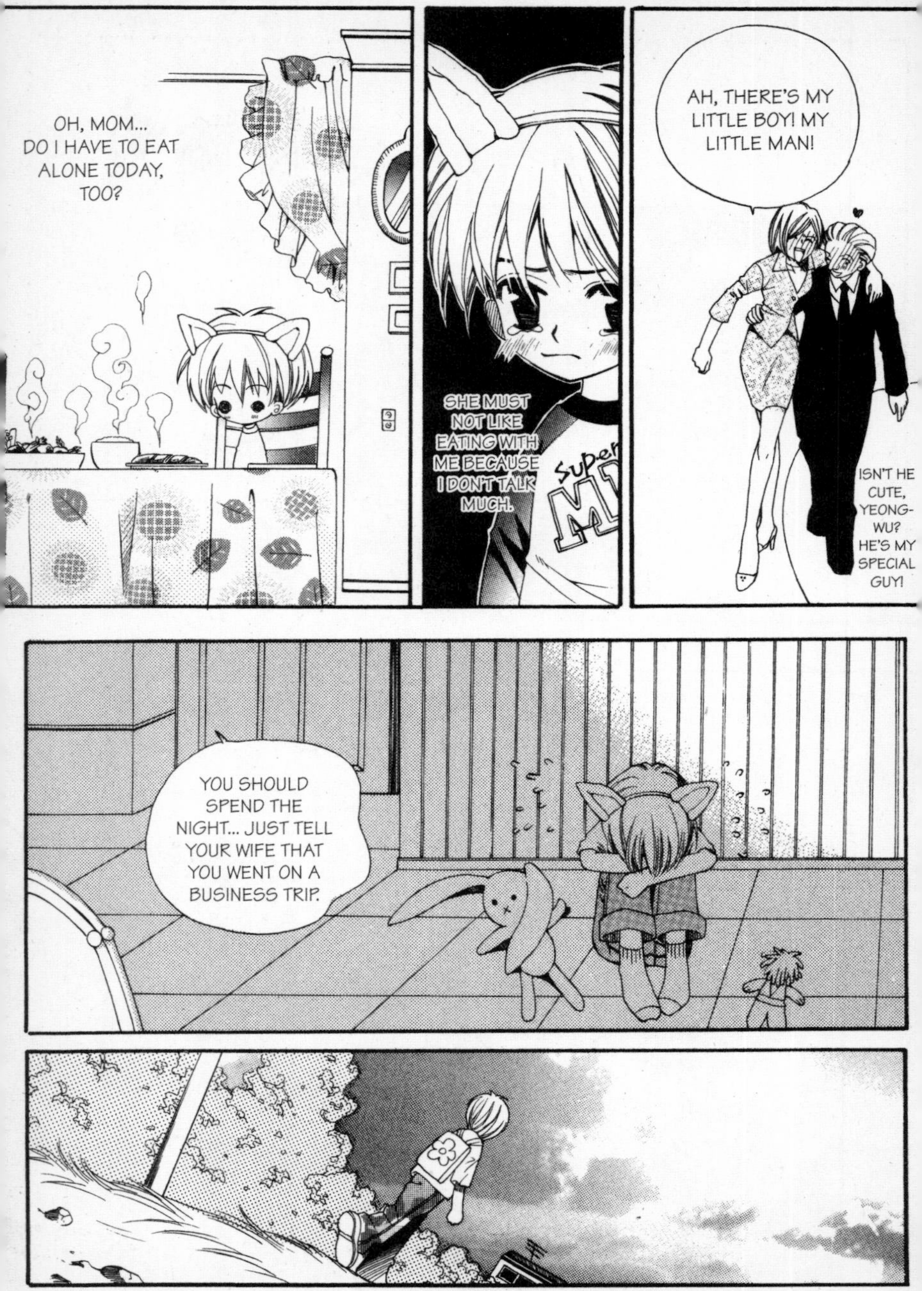
OH, MOM... DO I HAVE TO EAT ALONE TODAY, TOO?
SHE MUST NOT LIKE EATING WITH ME BECAUSE I DON'T TALK MUCH.
Super
AH, THERE'S MY LITTLE BOY! MY LITTLE MAN!
ISN'T HE CUTE, YEONG-WU? HE'S MY SPECIAL GUY!
YOU SHOULD SPEND THE NIGHT... JUST TELL YOUR WIFE THAT YOU WENT ON A BUSINESS TRIP.

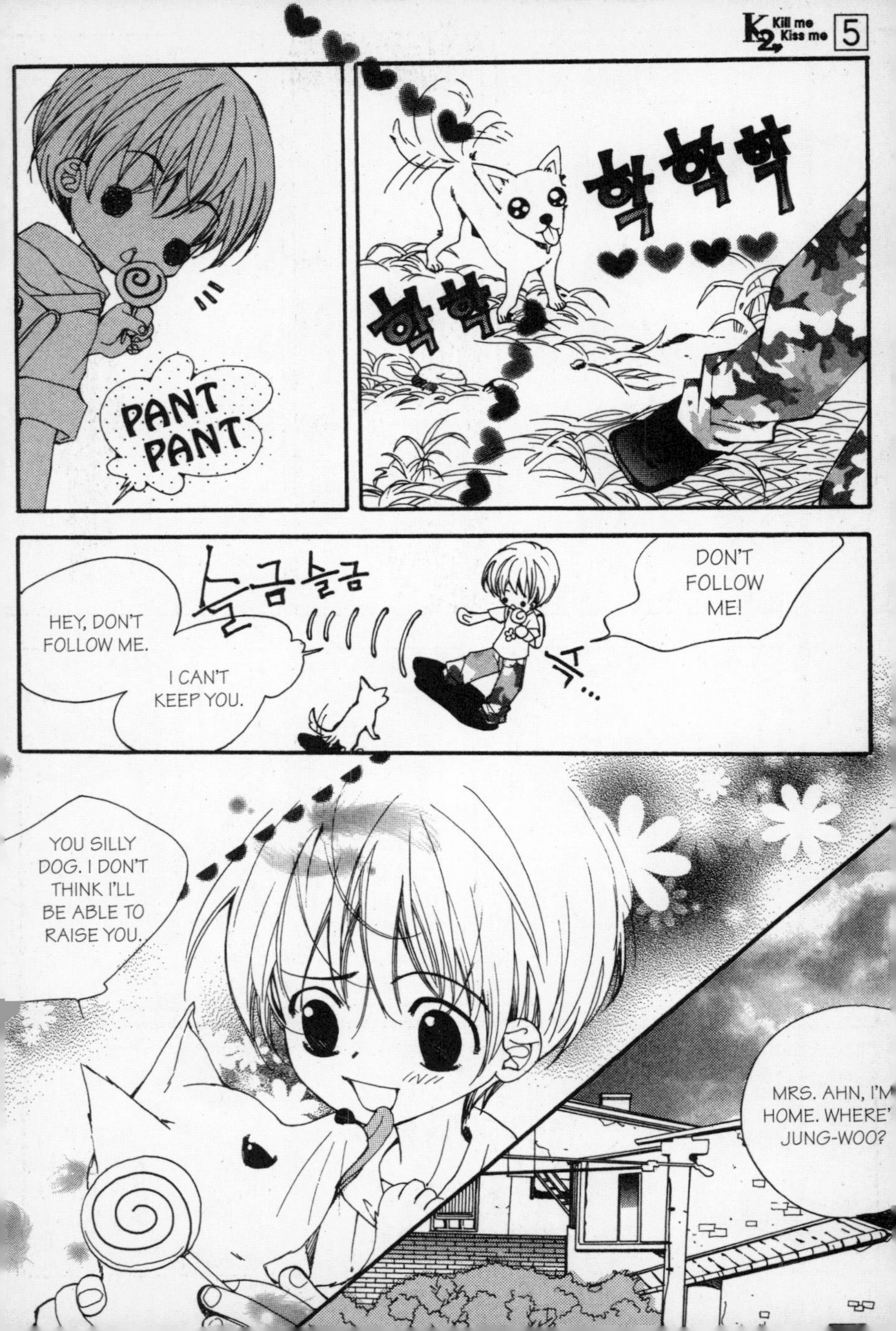
PANT PANT
헉헉헉
헉헉
HEY, DON'T FOLLOW ME.
I CAN'T KEEP YOU.
슬금슬금
슥...
DON'T FOLLOW ME!
YOU SILLY DOG. I DON'T THINK I'LL BE ABLE TO RAISE YOU.
MRS. AHN, I'M HOME. WHERE' JUNG-WOO?

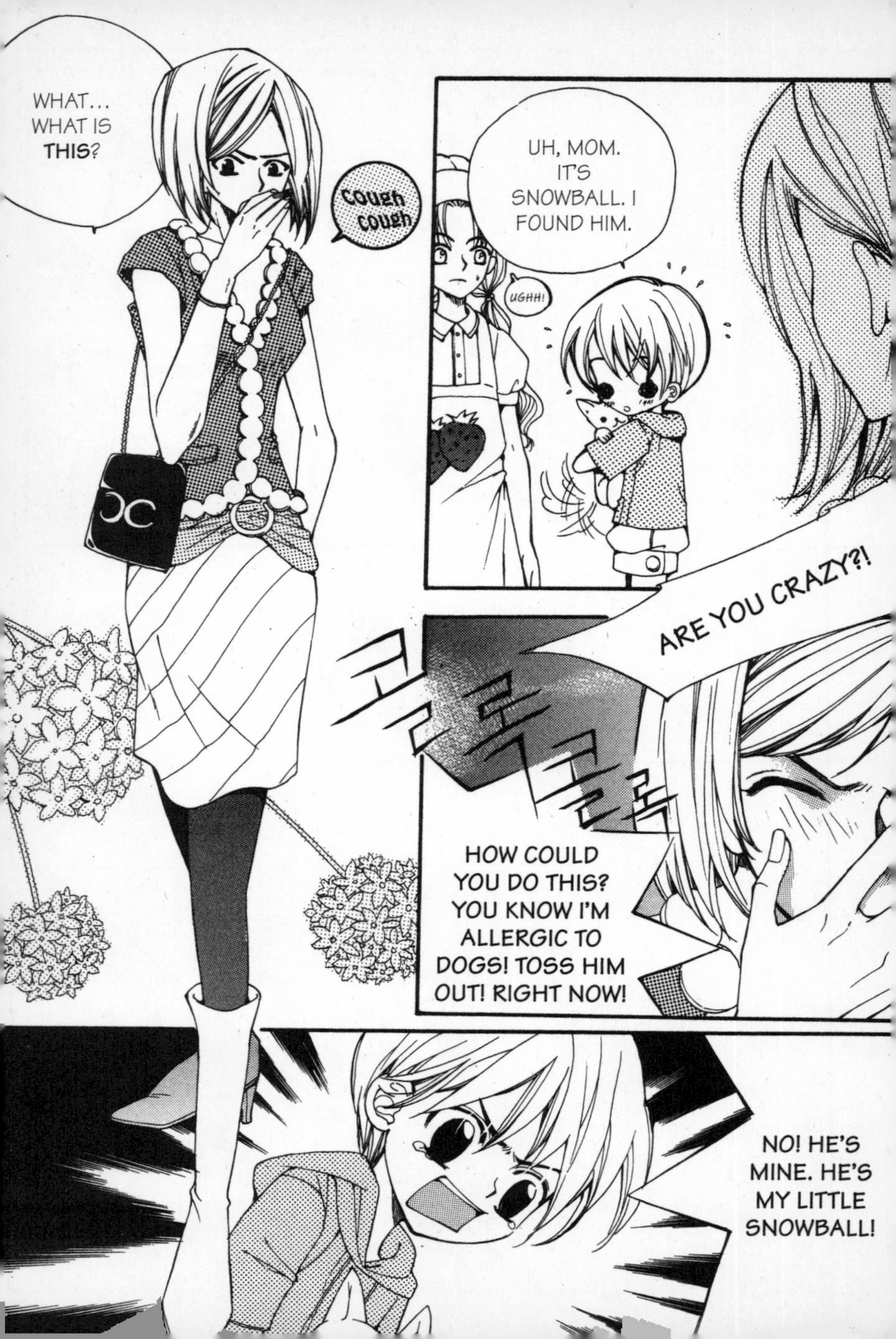
WHAT… WHAT IS THIS?
Cough cough
UH, MOM. IT'S SNOWBALL. I FOUND HIM.
UGHH!
ARE YOU CRAZY?!
콜록콜록
HOW COULD YOU DO THIS? YOU KNOW I'M ALLERGIC TO DOGS! TOSS HIM OUT! RIGHT NOW!
NO! HE'S MINE. HE'S MY LITTLE SNOWBALL!

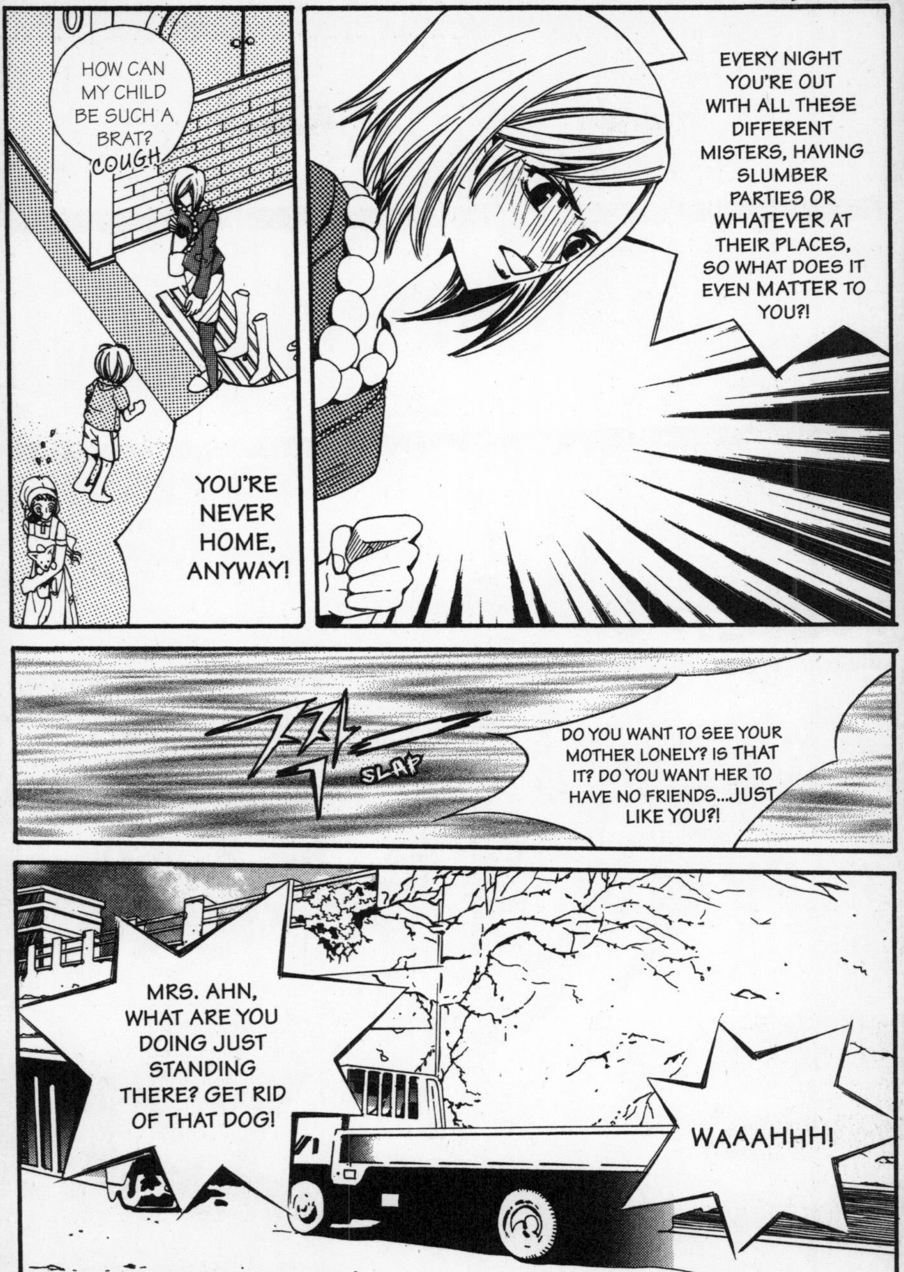
HOW CAN MY CHILD BE SUCH A BRAT?
COUGH
YOU'RE NEVER HOME, ANYWAY!
EVERY NIGHT YOU'RE OUT WITH ALL THESE DIFFERENT MISTERS, HAVING SLUMBER PARTIES OR WHATEVER AT THEIR PLACES, SO WHAT DOES IT EVEN MATTER TO YOU?!
SLAP
DO YOU WANT TO SEE YOUR MOTHER LONELY? IS THAT IT? DO YOU WANT HER TO HAVE NO FRIENDS...JUST LIKE YOU?!
MRS. AHN, WHAT ARE YOU DOING JUST STANDING THERE? GET RID OF THAT DOG!
WAAAHHH!

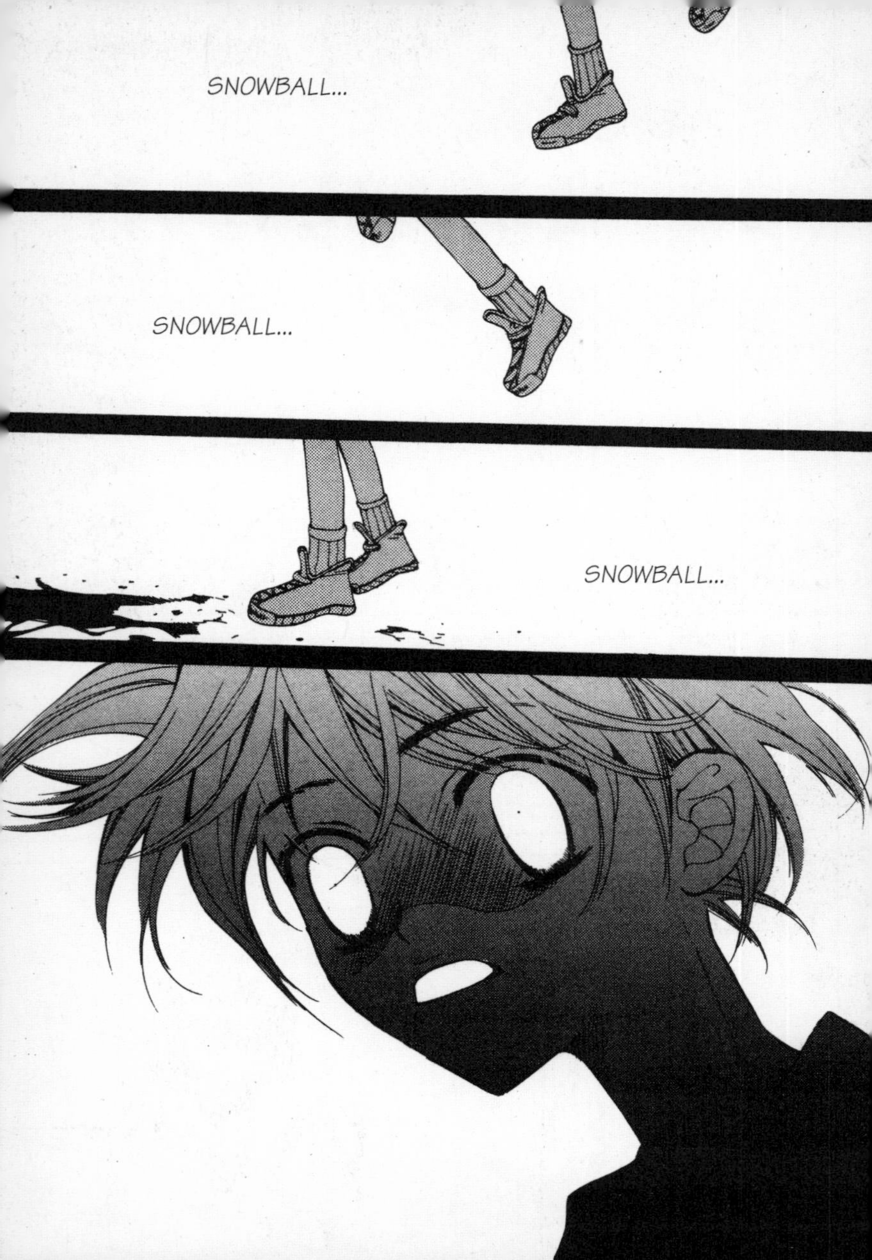
SNOWBALL...
SNOWBALL...
SNOWBALL...

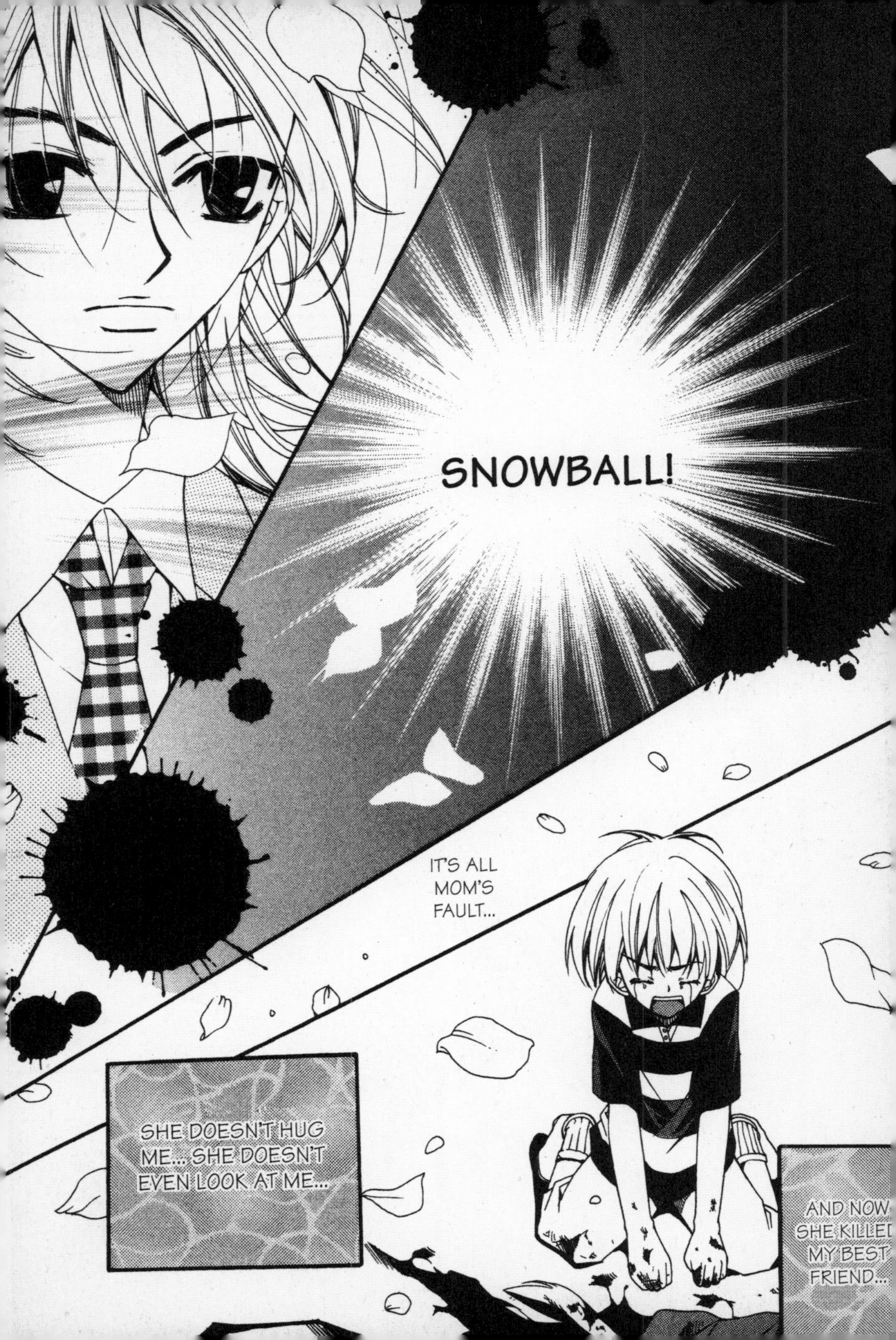
SNOWBALL!
IT'S ALL MOM'S FAULT...
SHE DOESN'T HUG ME... SHE DOESN'T EVEN LOOK AT ME...
AND NOW SHE KILLED MY BEST FRIEND...

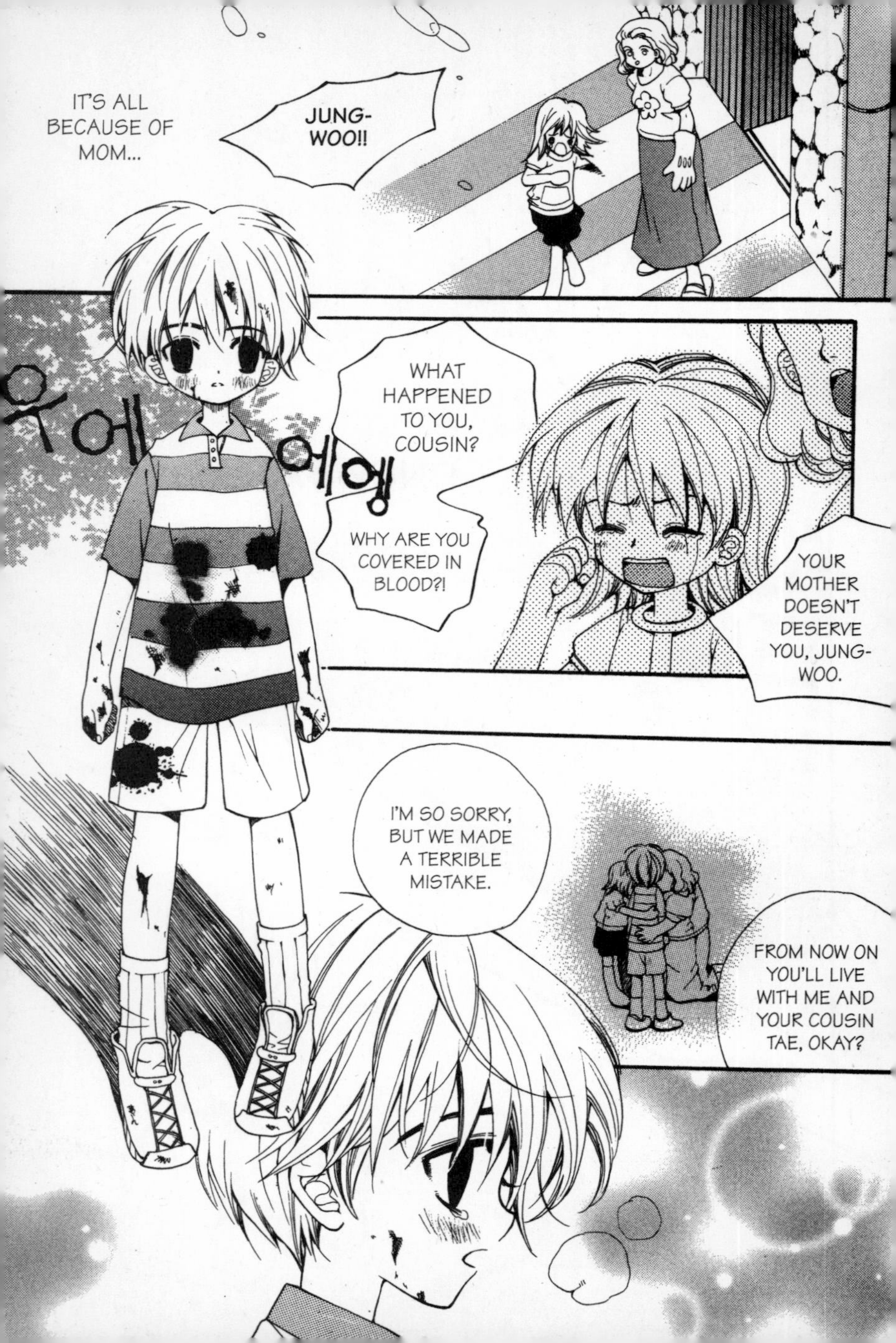
IT'S ALL BECAUSE OF MOM...
JUNG-WOO!!
우에
에엥
WHAT HAPPENED TO YOU, COUSIN?
WHY ARE YOU COVERED IN BLOOD?!
YOUR MOTHER DOESN'T DESERVE YOU, JUNG-WOO.
I'M SO SORRY, BUT WE MADE A TERRIBLE MISTAKE.
FROM NOW ON YOU'LL LIVE WITH ME AND YOUR COUSIN TAE, OKAY?

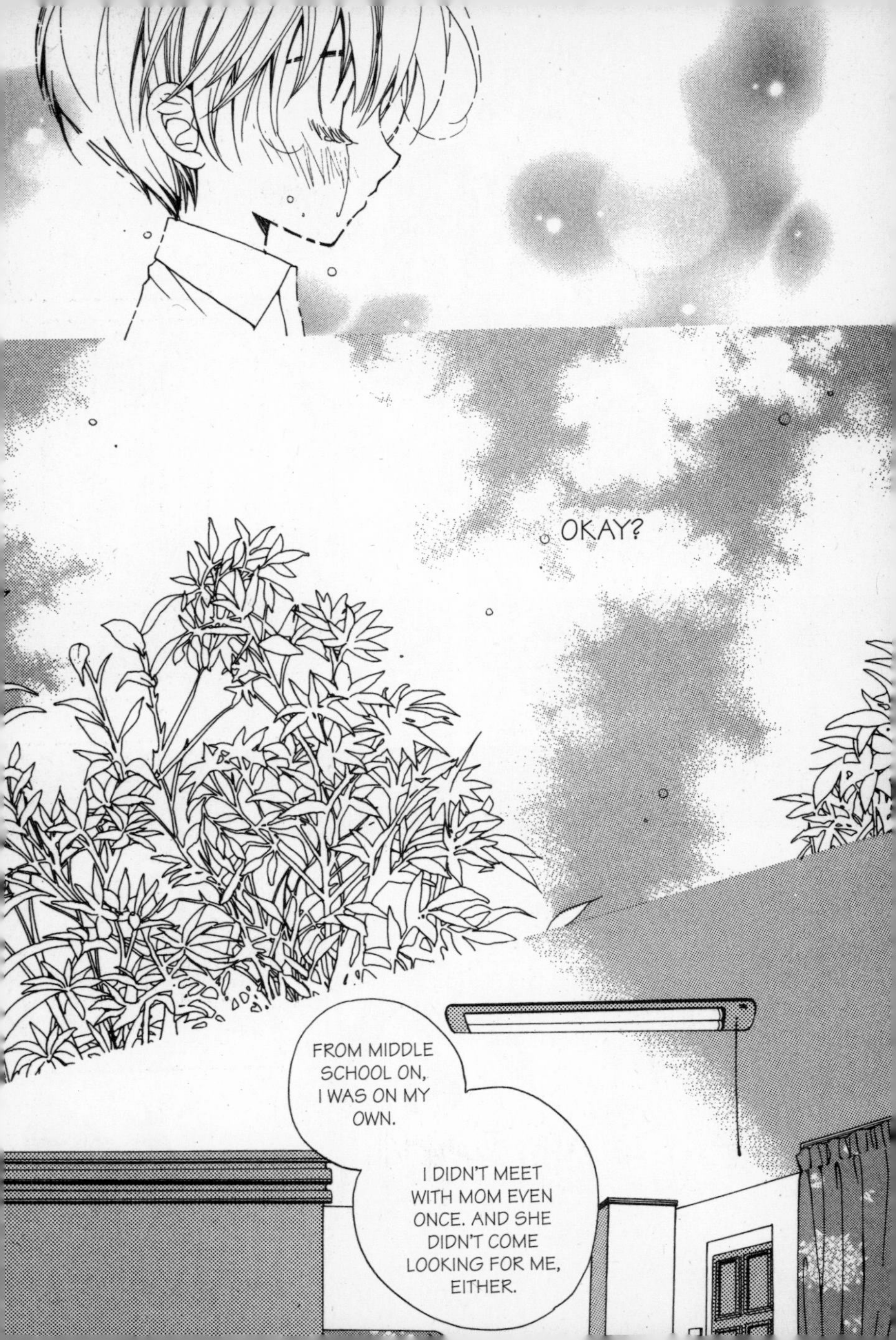
OKAY?
FROM MIDDLE SCHOOL ON, I WAS ON MY OWN.
I DIDN'T MEET WITH MOM EVEN ONCE. AND SHE DIDN'T COME LOOKING FOR ME, EITHER.

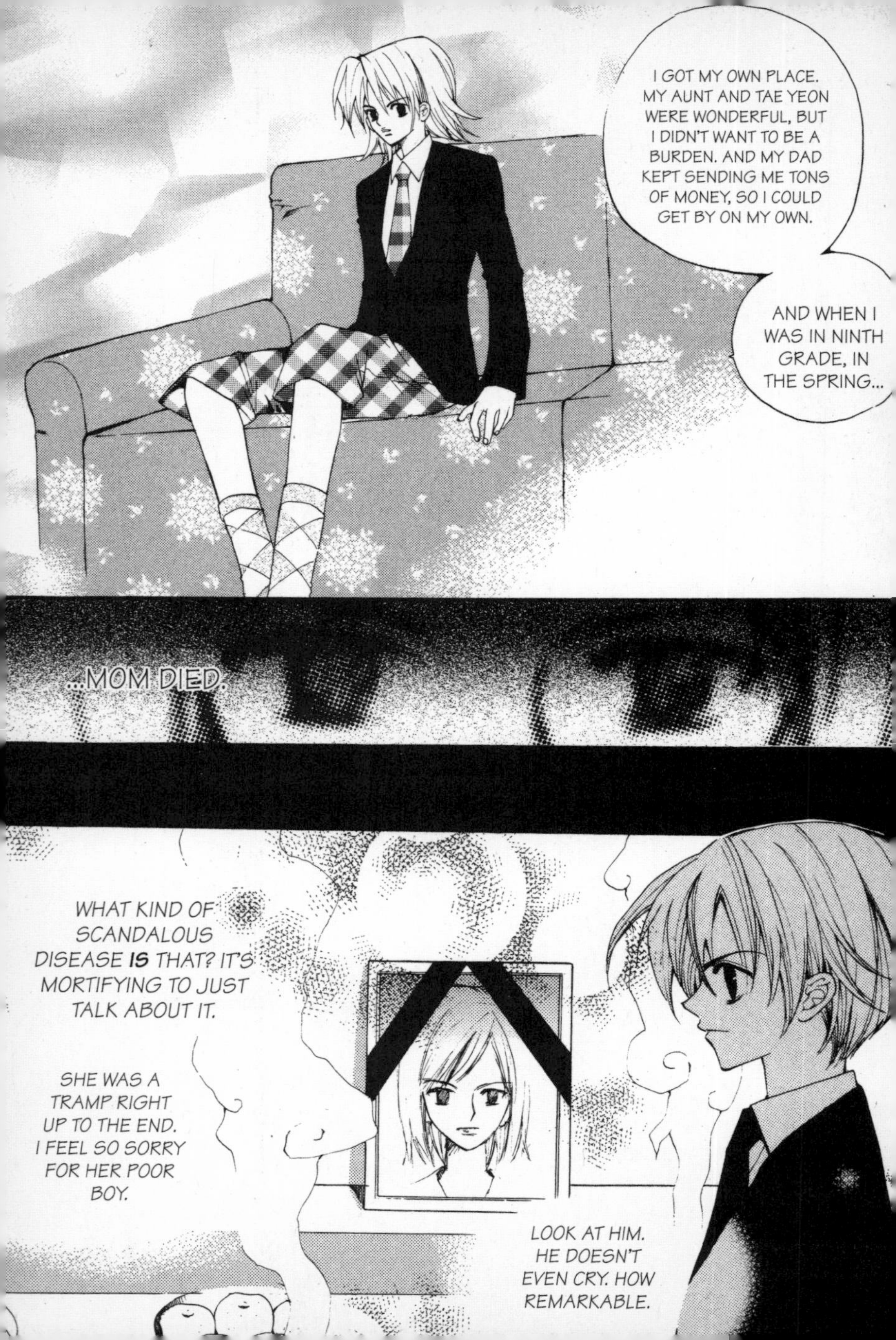
I GOT MY OWN PLACE. MY AUNT AND TAE YEON WERE WONDERFUL, BUT I DIDN'T WANT TO BE A BURDEN. AND MY DAD KEPT SENDING ME TONS OF MONEY, SO I COULD GET BY ON MY OWN.
AND WHEN I WAS IN NINTH GRADE, IN THE SPRING...
...MOM DIED.
WHAT KIND OF SCANDALOUS DISEASE **IS** THAT? IT'S MORTIFYING TO JUST TALK ABOUT IT.
SHE WAS A TRAMP RIGHT UP TO THE END. I FEEL SO SORRY FOR HER POOR BOY.
LOOK AT HIM. HE DOESN'T EVEN CRY. HOW REMARKABLE.

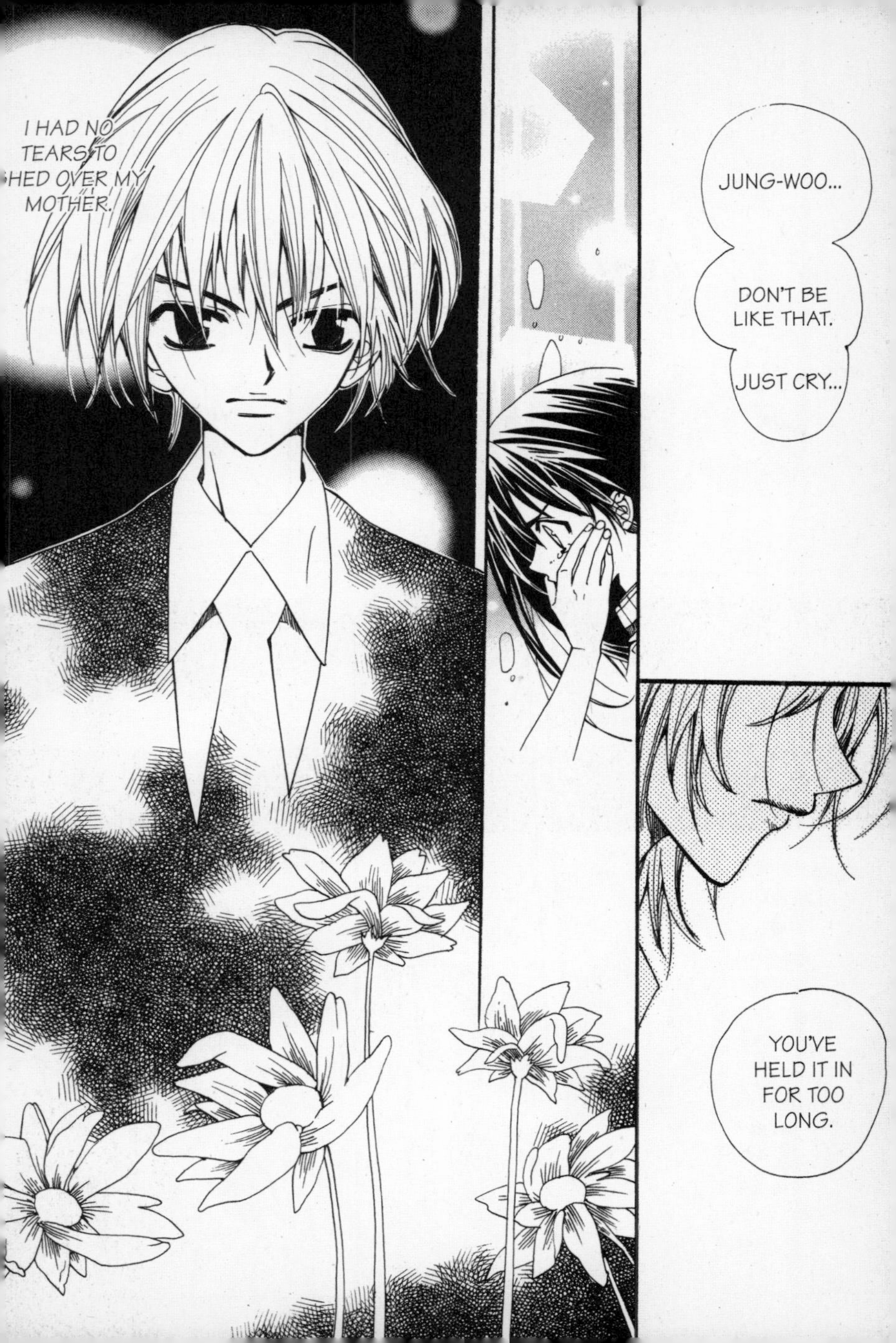
I HAD NO TEARS TO SHED OVER MY MOTHER.
JUNG-WOO...
DON'T BE LIKE THAT.
JUST CRY...
YOU'VE HELD IT IN FOR TOO LONG.

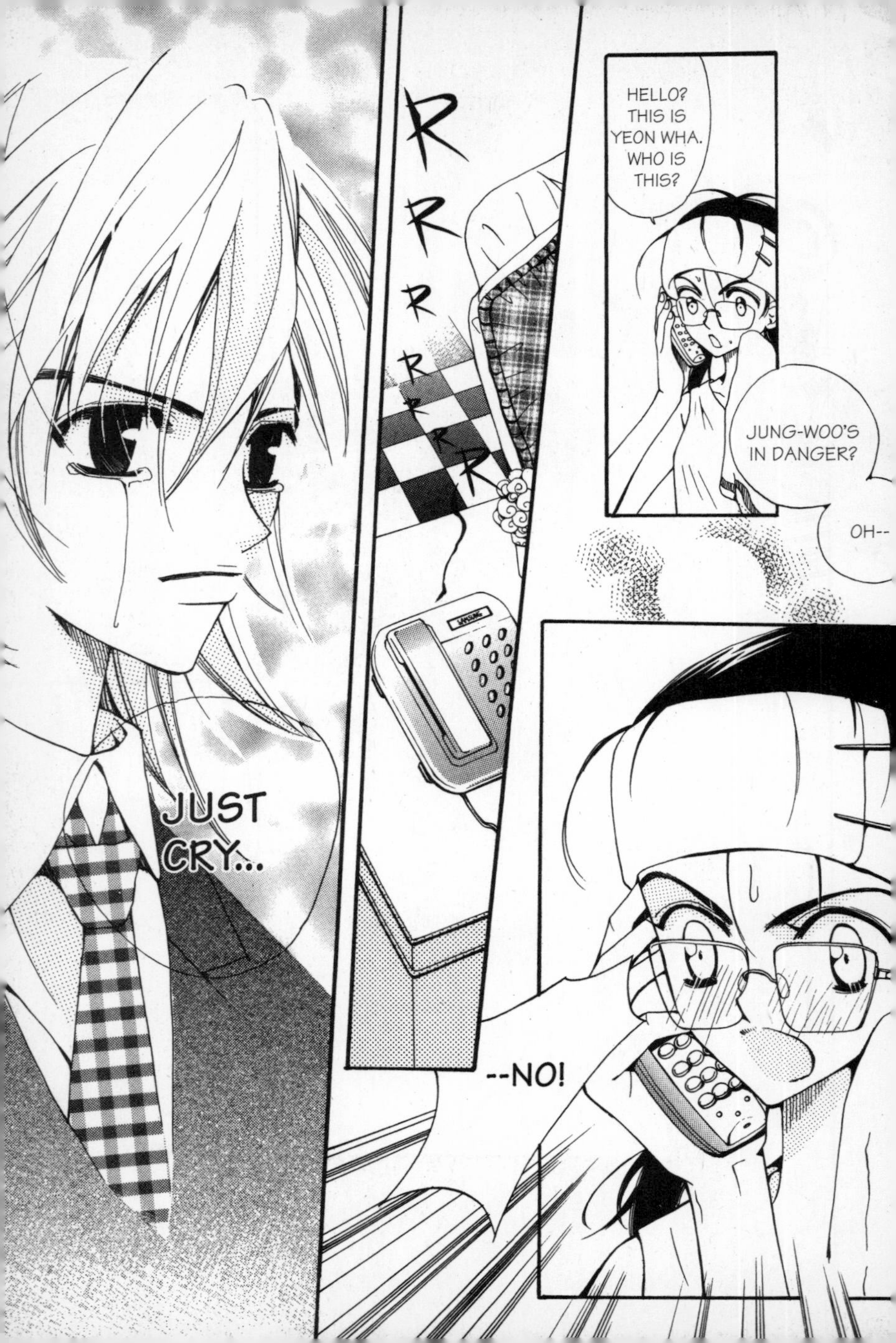
JUST CRY...
RRRRRRR
HELLO? THIS IS YEON WHA. WHO IS THIS?
JUNG-WOO'S IN DANGER?
OH--
--NO!

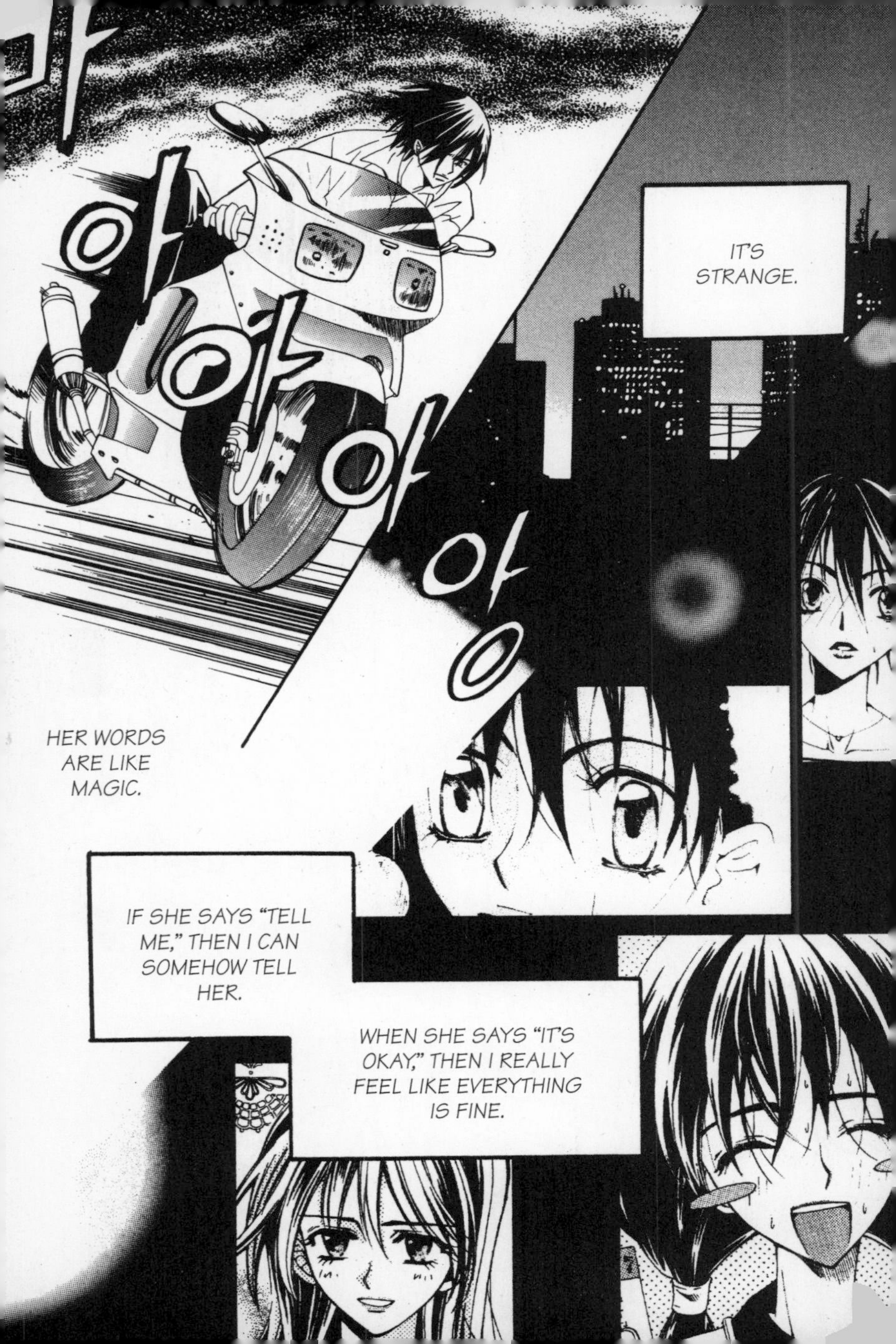
IT'S STRANGE.
HER WORDS ARE LIKE MAGIC.
IF SHE SAYS "TELL ME," THEN I CAN SOMEHOW TELL HER.
WHEN SHE SAYS "IT'S OKAY," THEN I REALLY FEEL LIKE EVERYTHING IS FINE.

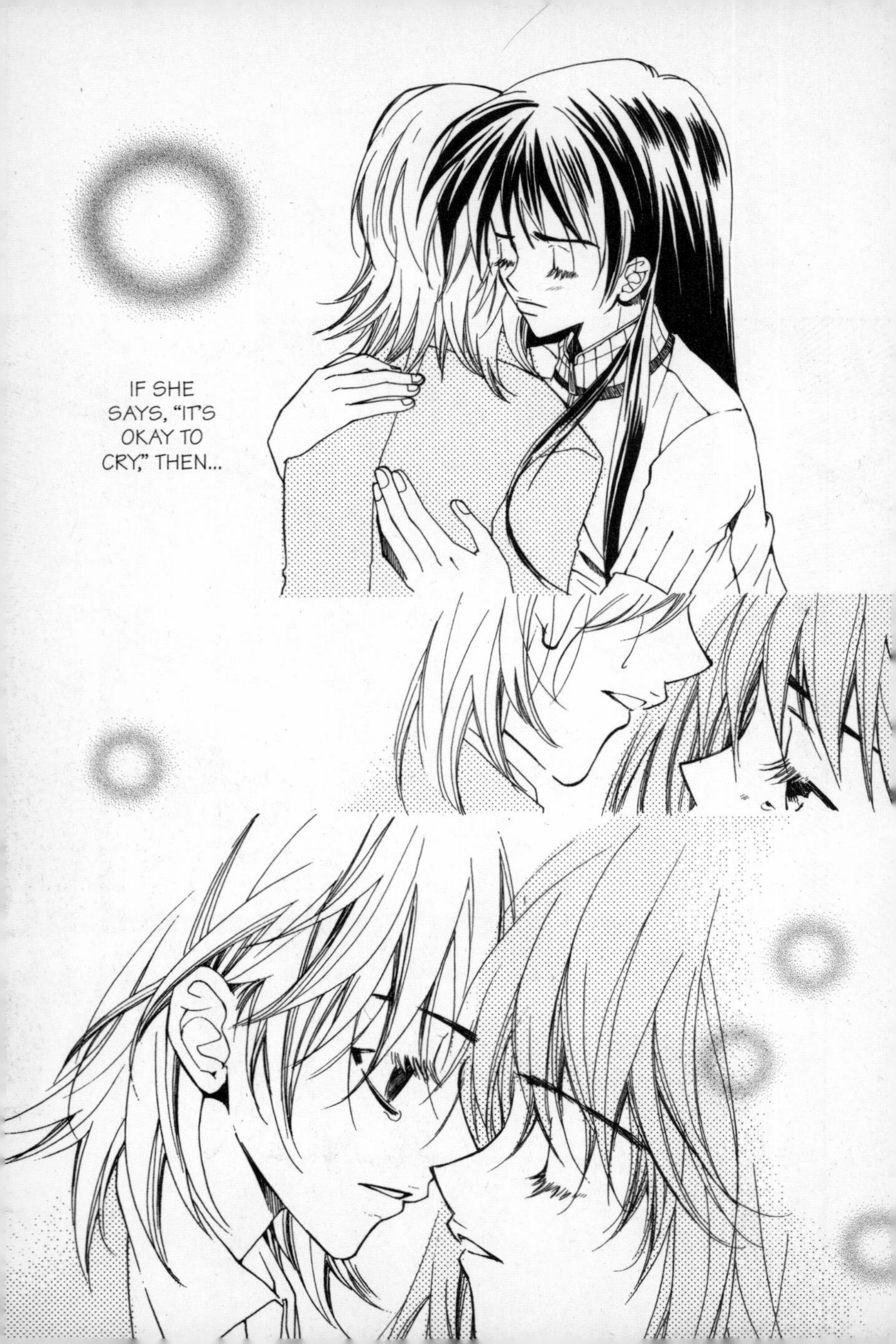
IF SHE SAYS, "IT'S OKAY TO CRY," THEN...

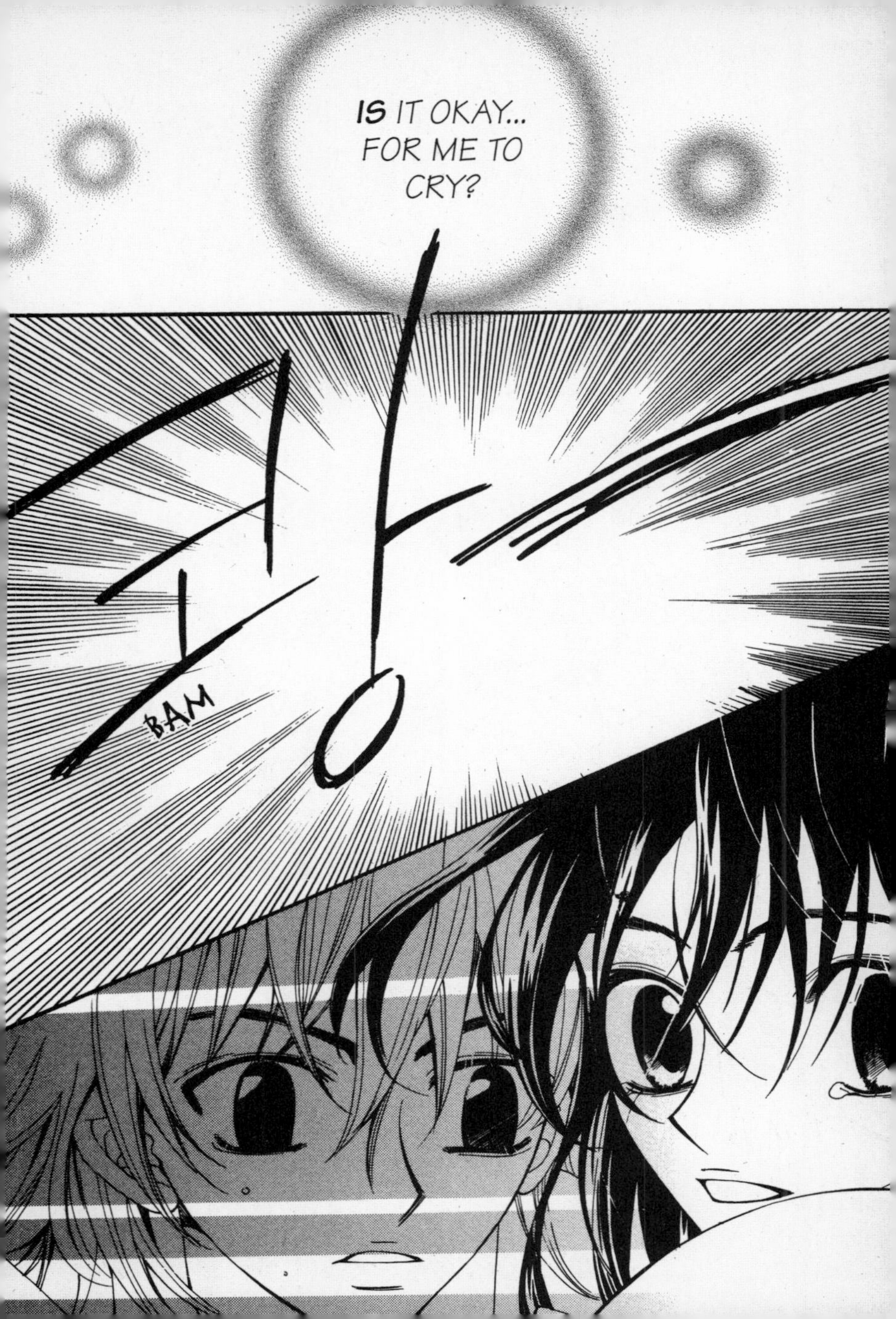
IS IT OKAY... FOR ME TO CRY?
BAM

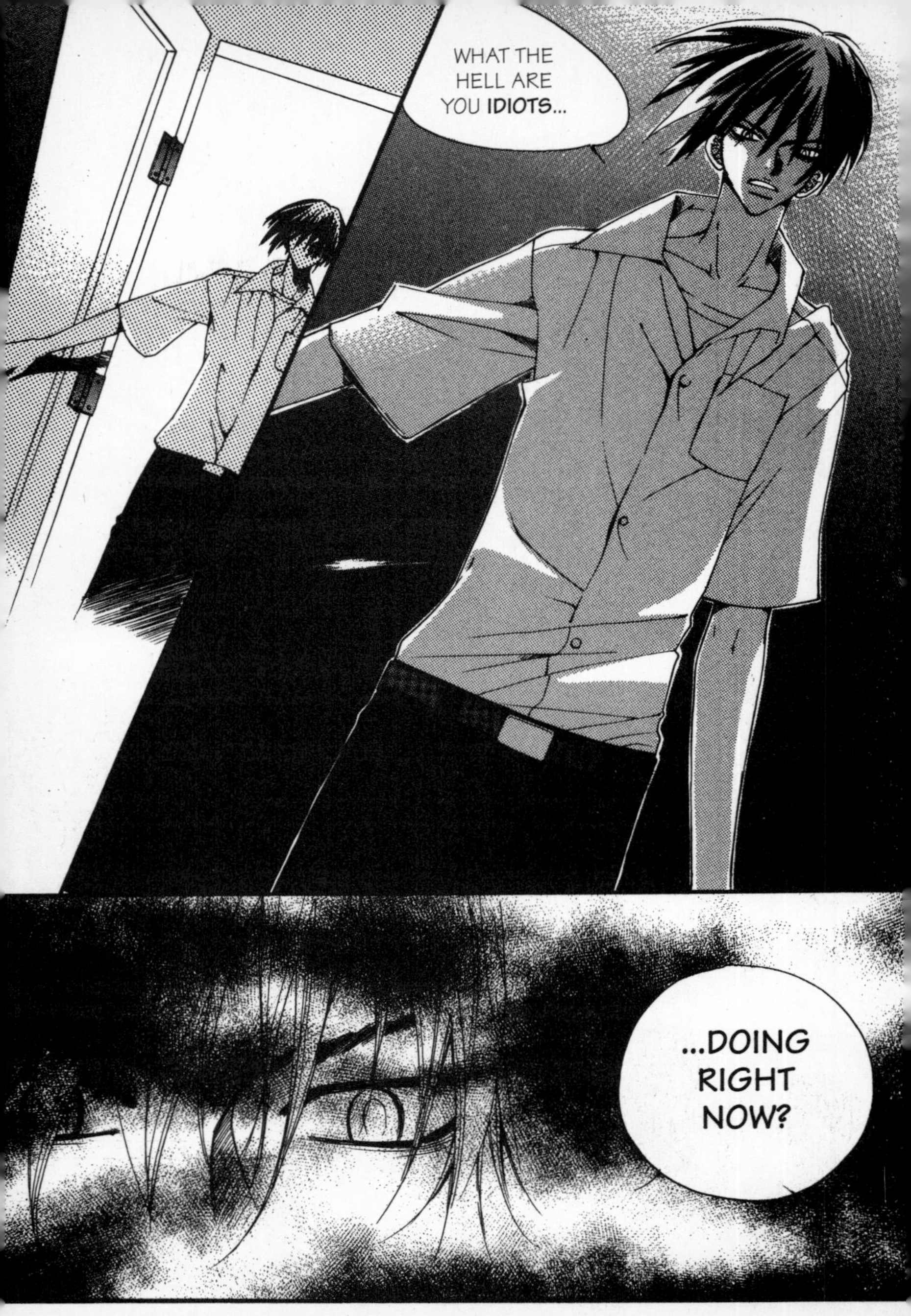
WHAT THE HELL ARE YOU **IDIOTS**...
...DOING RIGHT NOW?

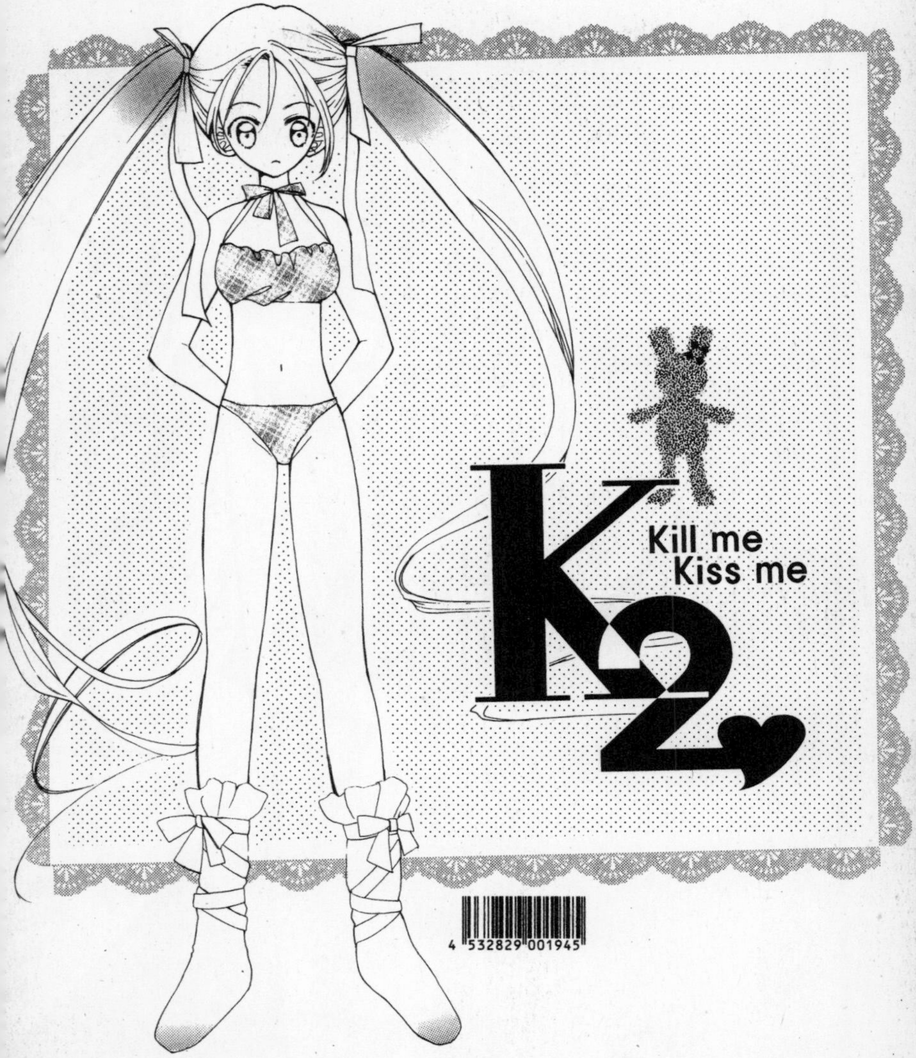
K2
Kill me
Kiss me

4 532829 001945

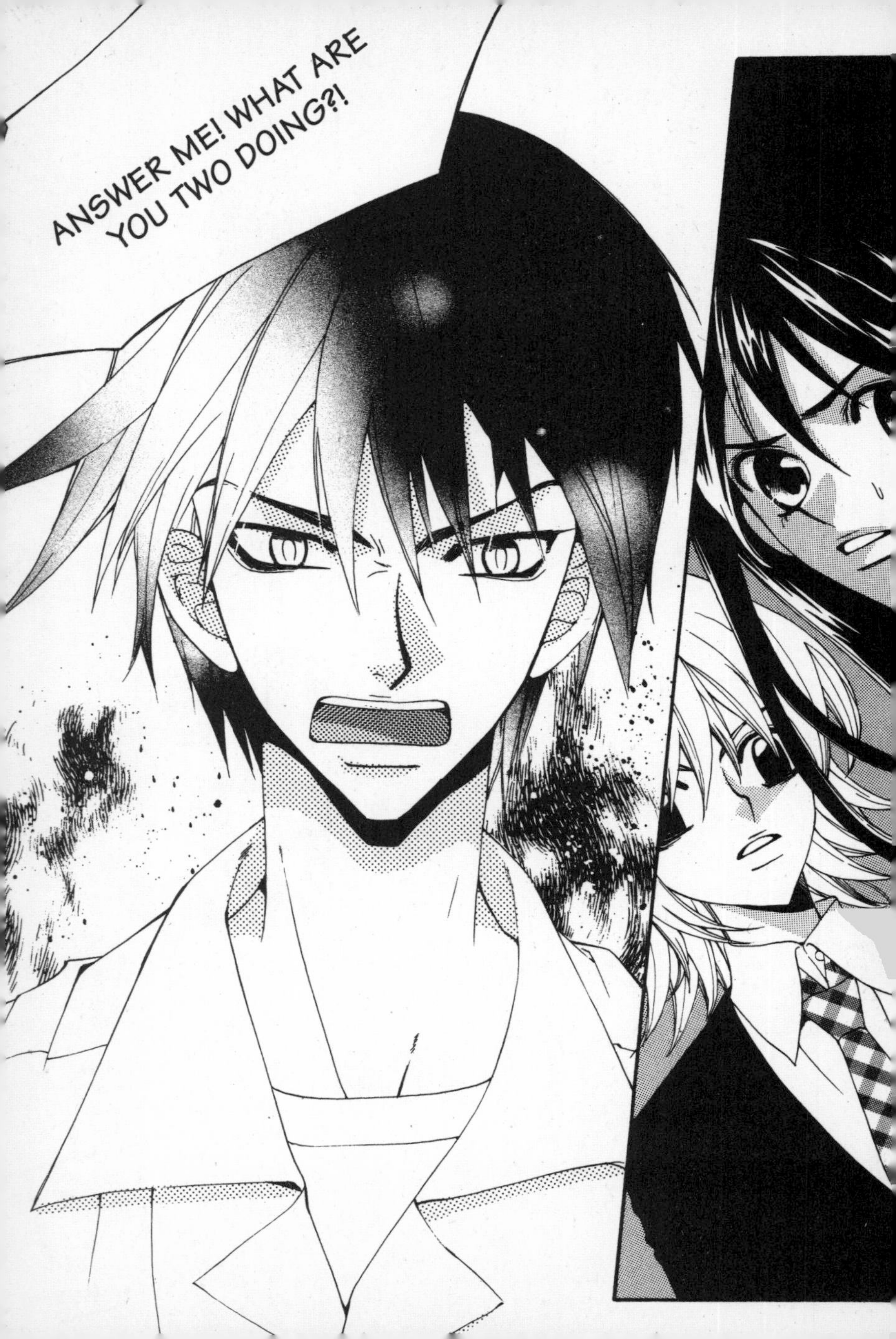
ANSWER ME! WHAT ARE YOU TWO DOING?!

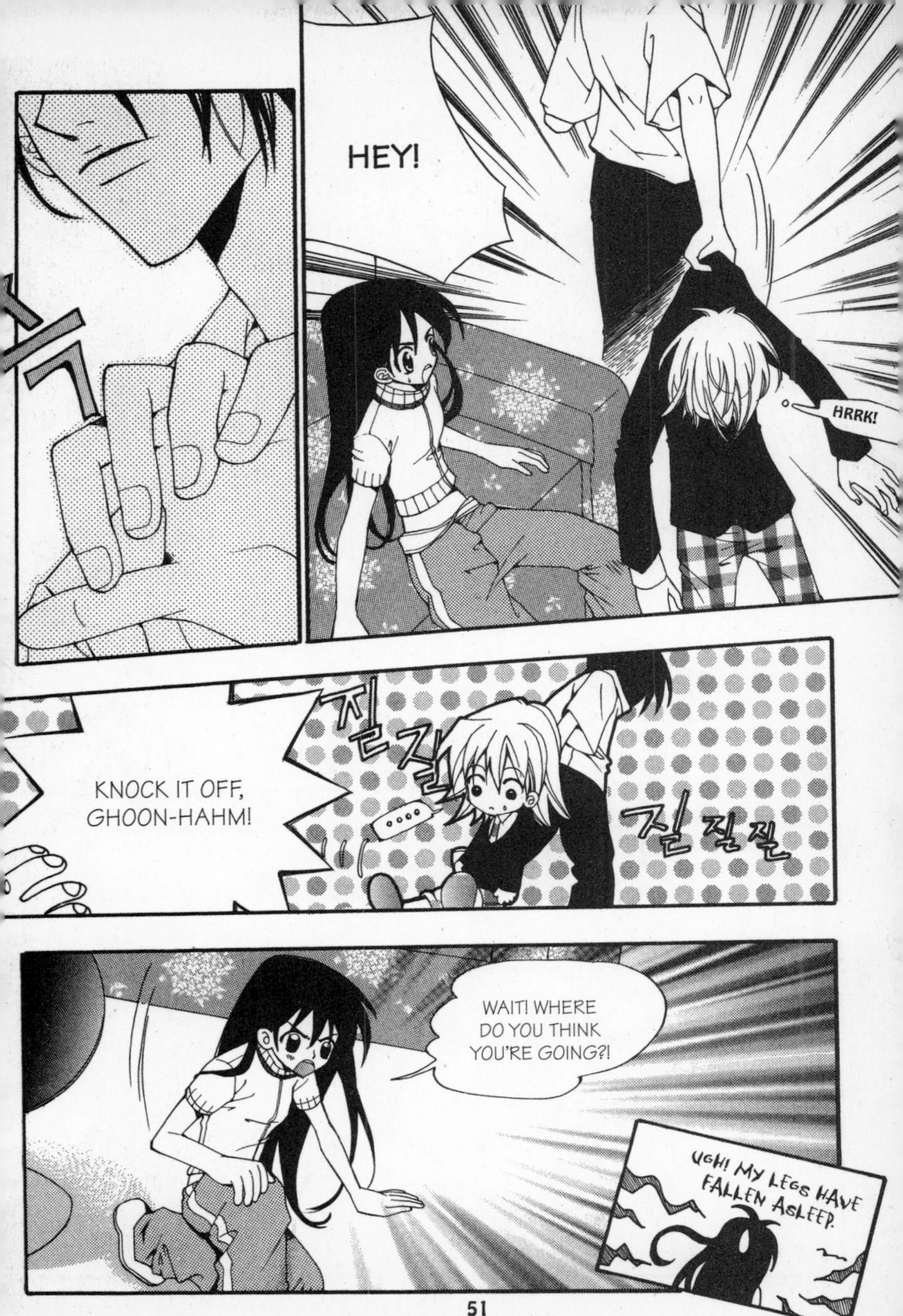
HEY!
HRRK!
KNOCK IT OFF, GHOON-HAHM!
질질
....
질질질
WAIT! WHERE DO YOU THINK YOU'RE GOING?!
UGH! MY LEGS HAVE FALLEN ASLEEP.

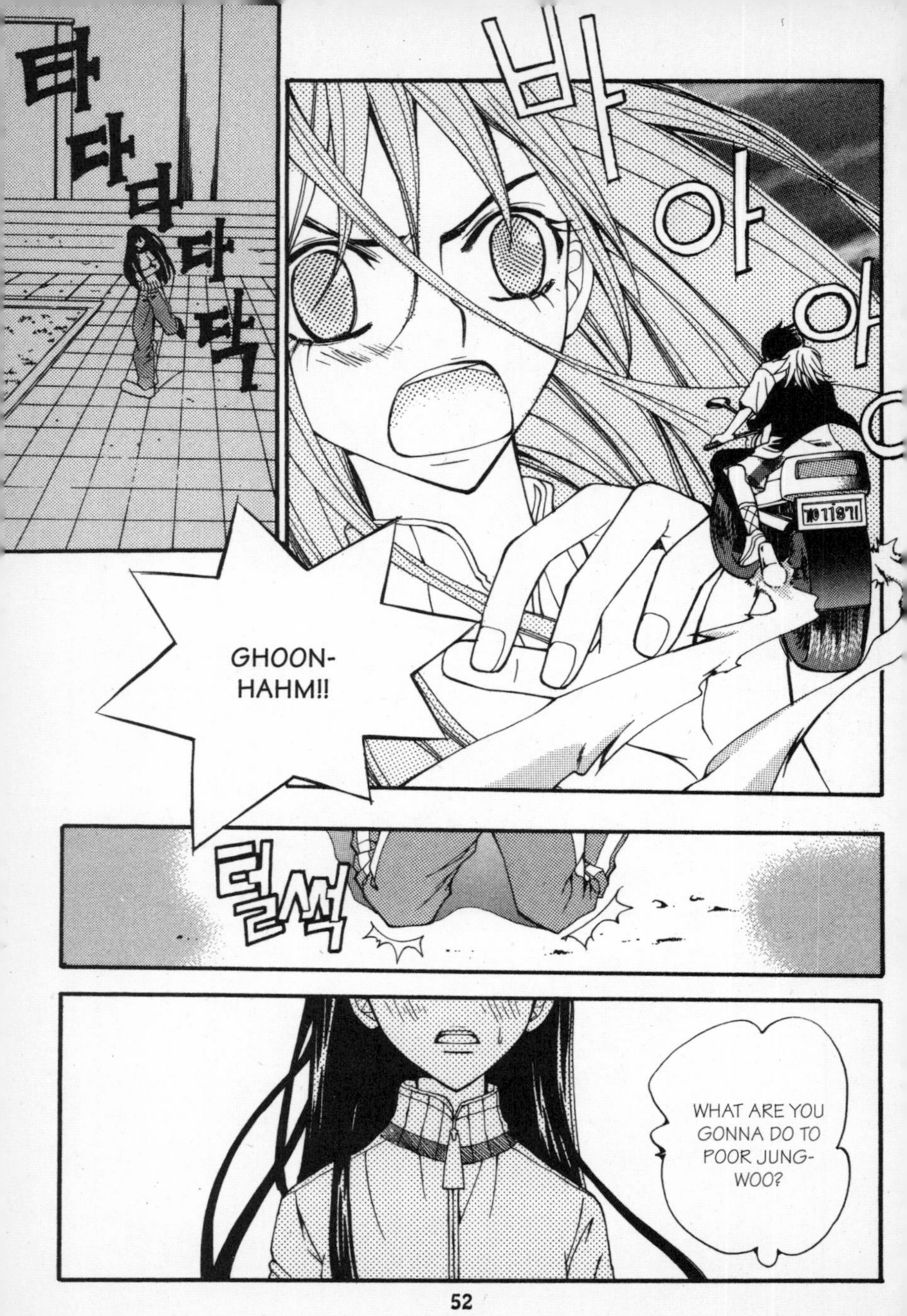
타다다다닥
바아아
GHOON-HAHM!!
털썩
WHAT ARE YOU GONNA DO TO POOR JUNG-WOO?

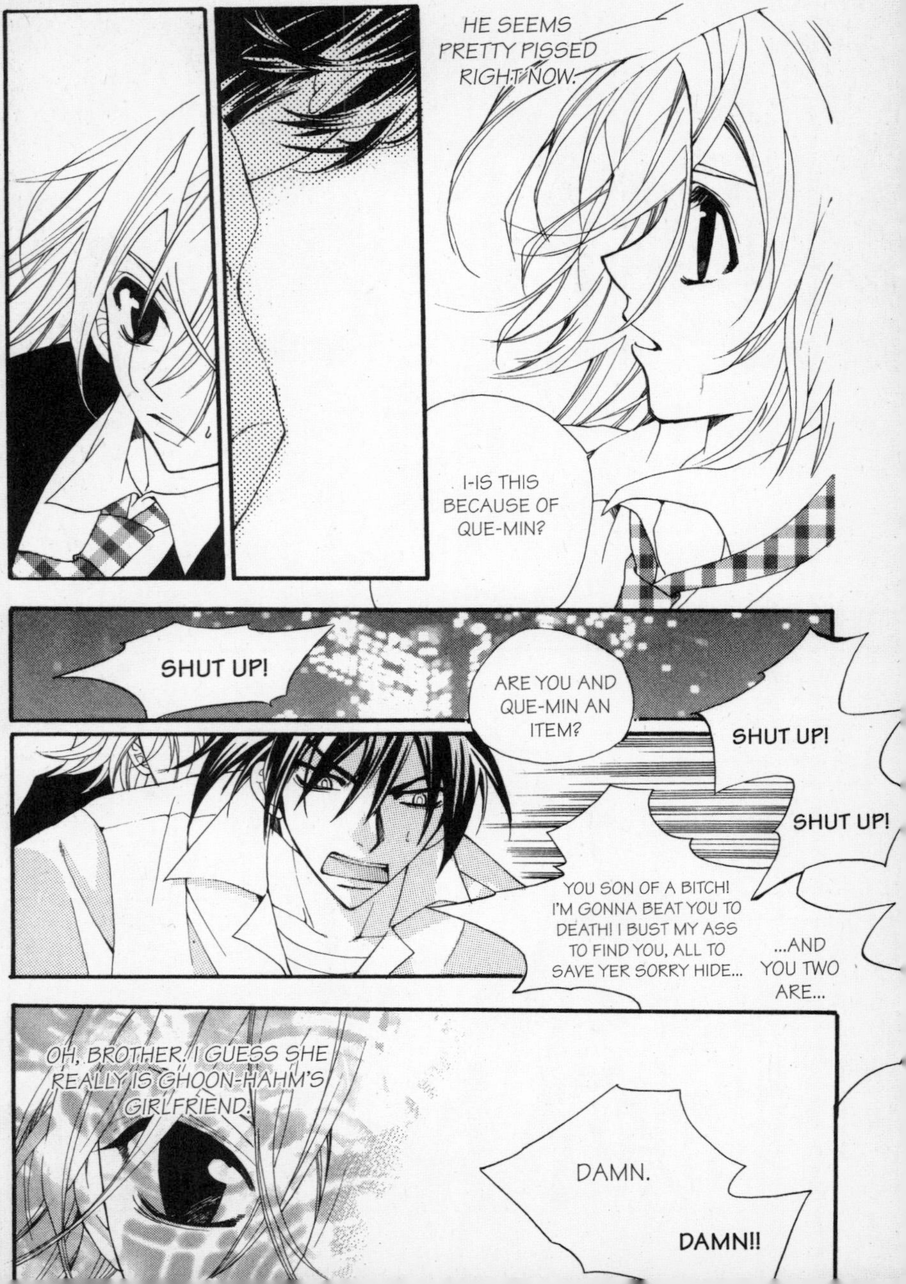
HE SEEMS PRETTY PISSED RIGHT NOW.
I-IS THIS BECAUSE OF QUE-MIN?
SHUT UP!
ARE YOU AND QUE-MIN AN ITEM?
SHUT UP!
SHUT UP!
YOU SON OF A BITCH! I'M GONNA BEAT YOU TO DEATH! I BUST MY ASS TO FIND YOU, ALL TO SAVE YER SORRY HIDE...
...AND YOU TWO ARE...
OH, BROTHER. I GUESS SHE REALLY IS GHOON-HAHM'S GIRLFRIEND.
DAMN.
DAMN!!

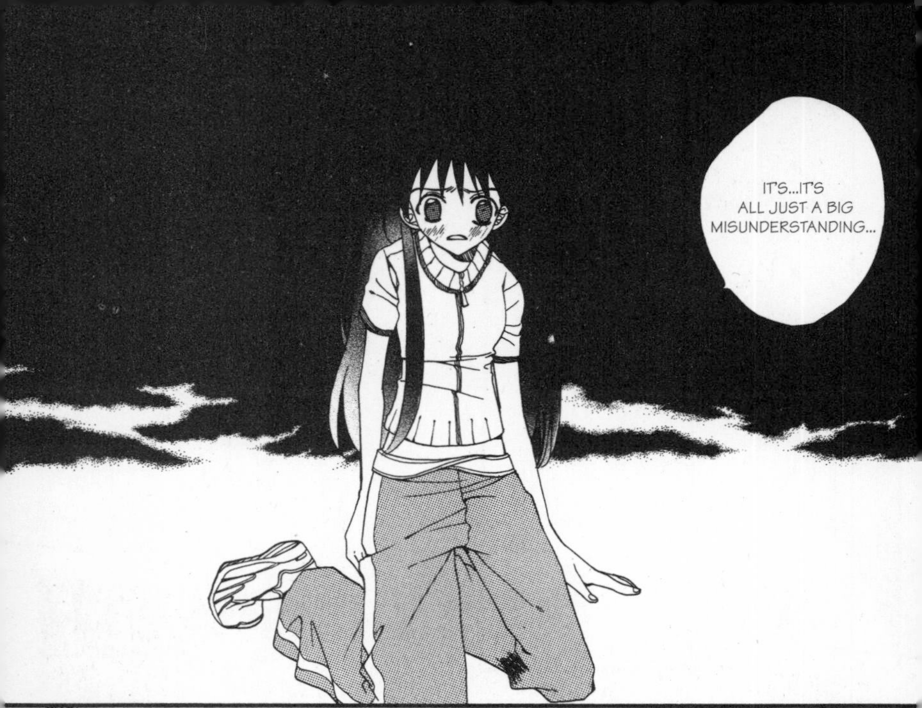
IT'S...IT'S ALL JUST A BIG MISUNDERSTANDING...
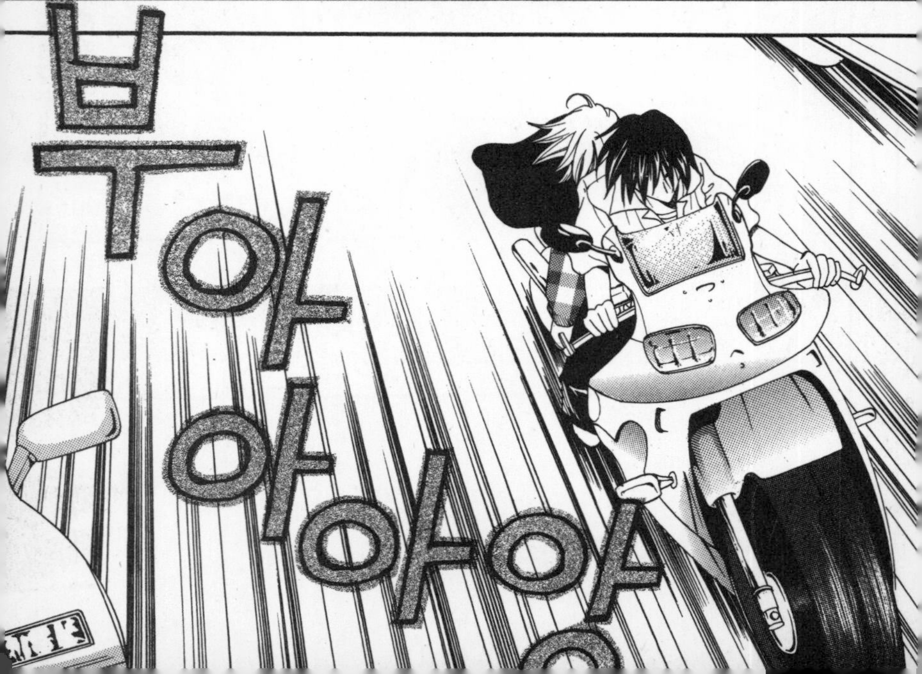

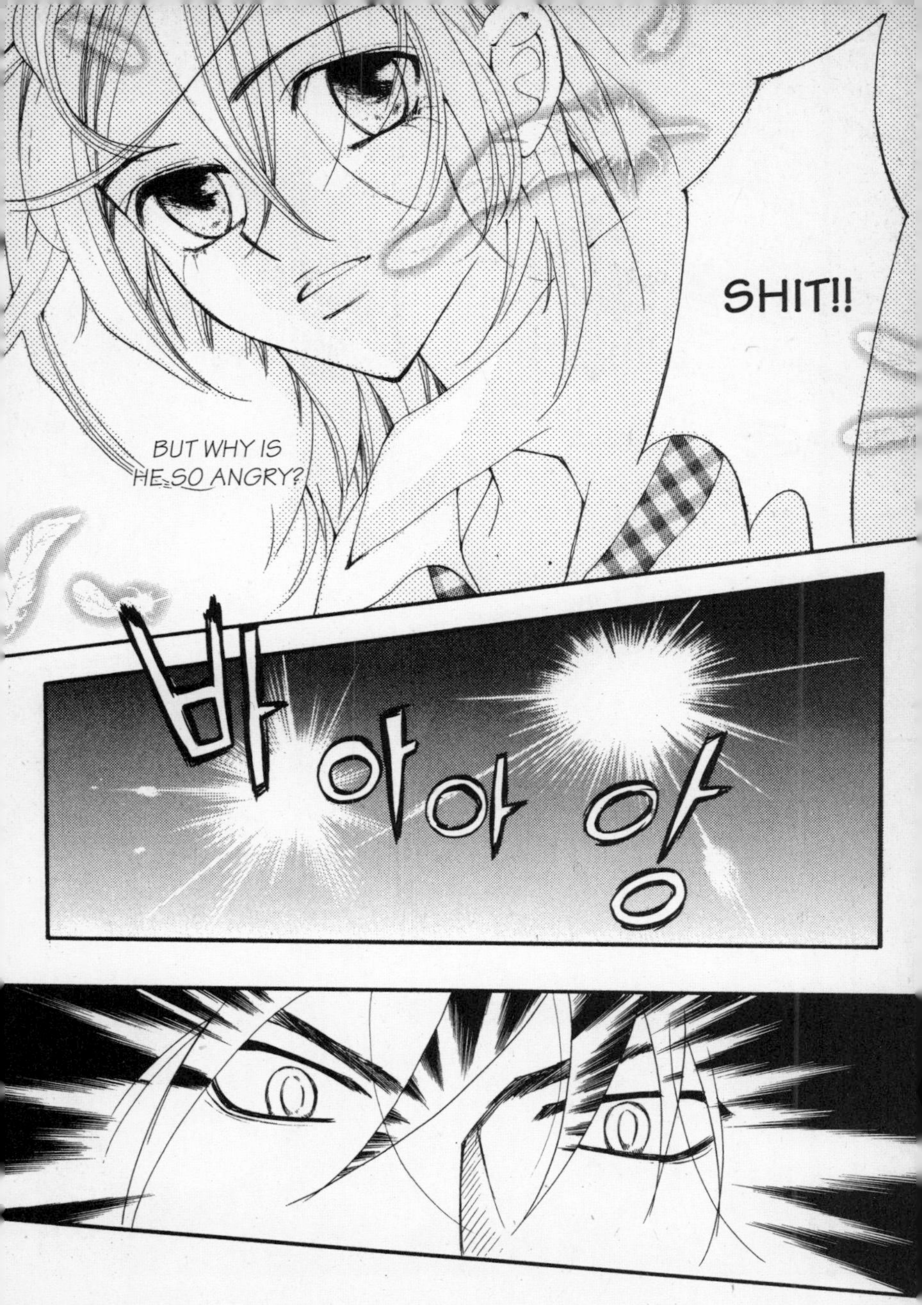
BUT WHY IS HE SO ANGRY?
SHIT!!
바아아앙

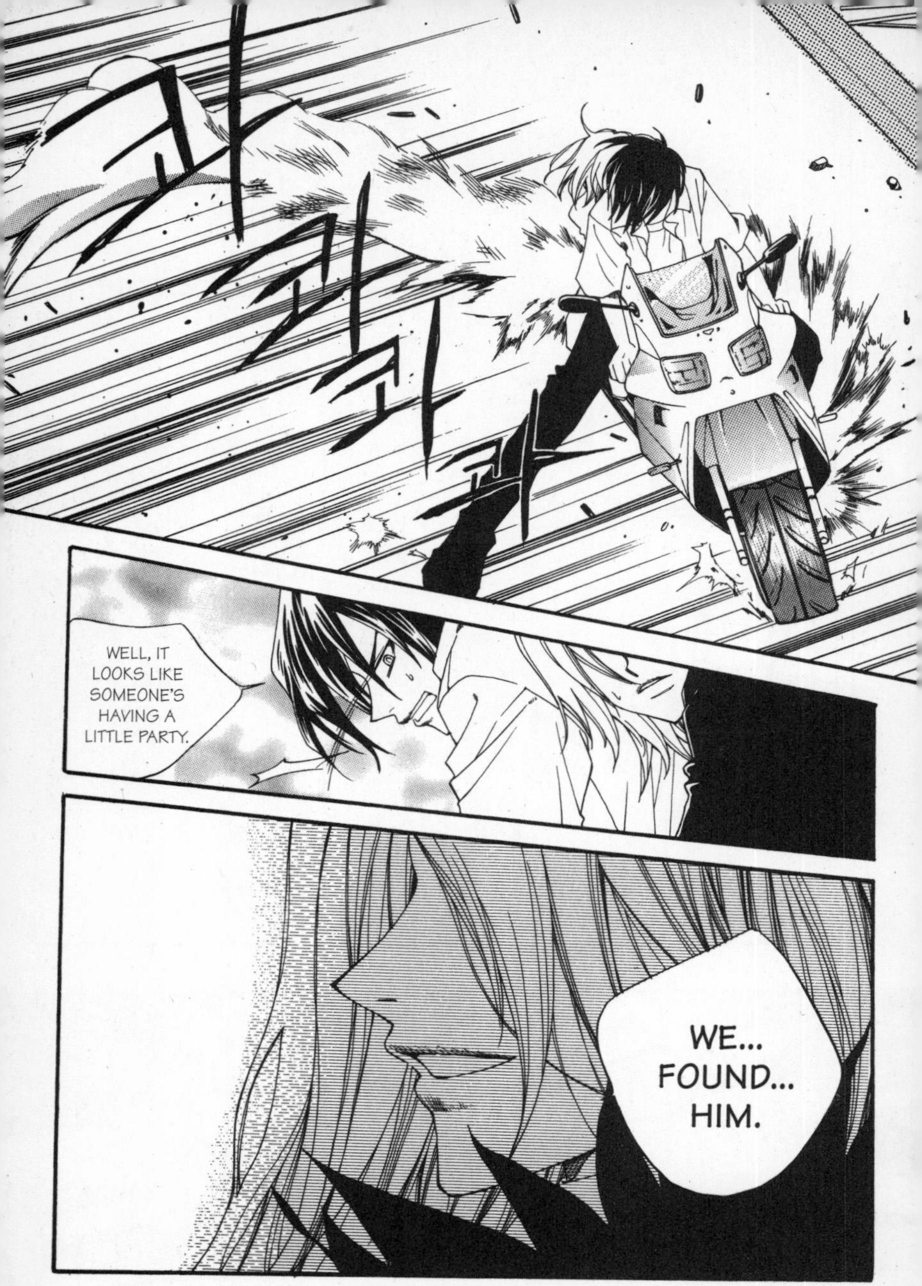
WELL, IT LOOKS LIKE SOMEONE'S HAVING A LITTLE PARTY.
WE... FOUND... HIM.

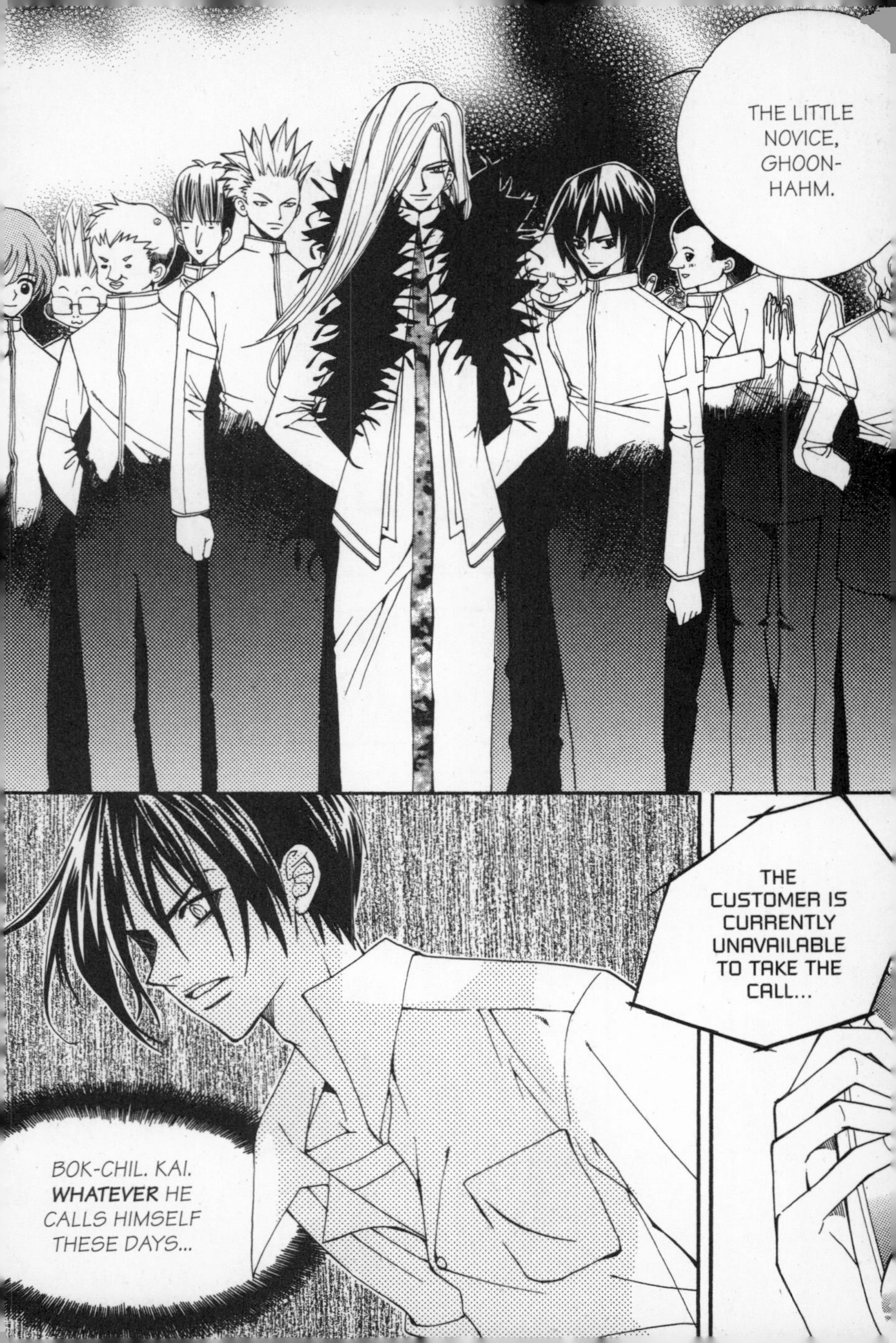
THE LITTLE NOVICE, GHOON-HAHM.
BOK-CHIL. KAI. WHATEVER HE CALLS HIMSELF THESE DAYS...
THE CUSTOMER IS CURRENTLY UNAVAILABLE TO TAKE THE CALL...

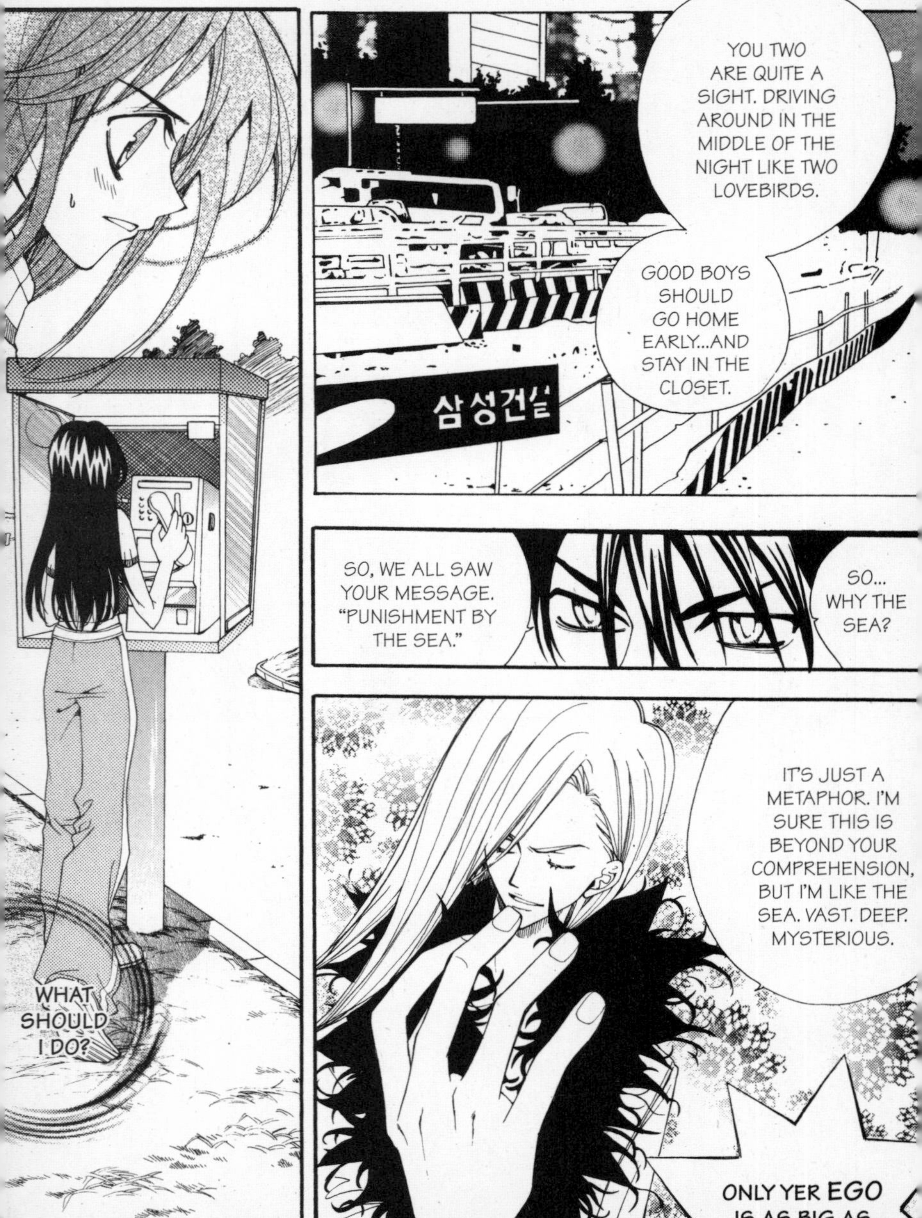

WHAT SHOULD I DO?
YOU TWO ARE QUITE A SIGHT. DRIVING AROUND IN THE MIDDLE OF THE NIGHT LIKE TWO LOVEBIRDS.
GOOD BOYS SHOULD GO HOME EARLY...AND STAY IN THE CLOSET.
삼성건설
SO, WE ALL SAW YOUR MESSAGE. "PUNISHMENT BY THE SEA."
SO... WHY THE SEA?
IT'S JUST A METAPHOR. I'M SURE THIS IS BEYOND YOUR COMPREHENSION, BUT I'M LIKE THE SEA. VAST. DEEP. MYSTERIOUS.
ONLY YER EGO IS AS BIG AS THE OCEAN!

SURE, YOU KICKED OUR COLLECTIVE ASS IN MIDDLE SCHOOL...

...BUT WE'RE NOT KIDS ANYMORE.

TRUST ME, WE'LL PLOW THROUGH YOU AND CRUSH THAT LITTLE PRINCE YOU'RE PROTECTING.

· · · ·

IS THAT **FEAR** I DETECT IN YOUR VOICE?

WHAT PRINCE?! YOU CAN HAVE HIM!

SMILE

REALLY?

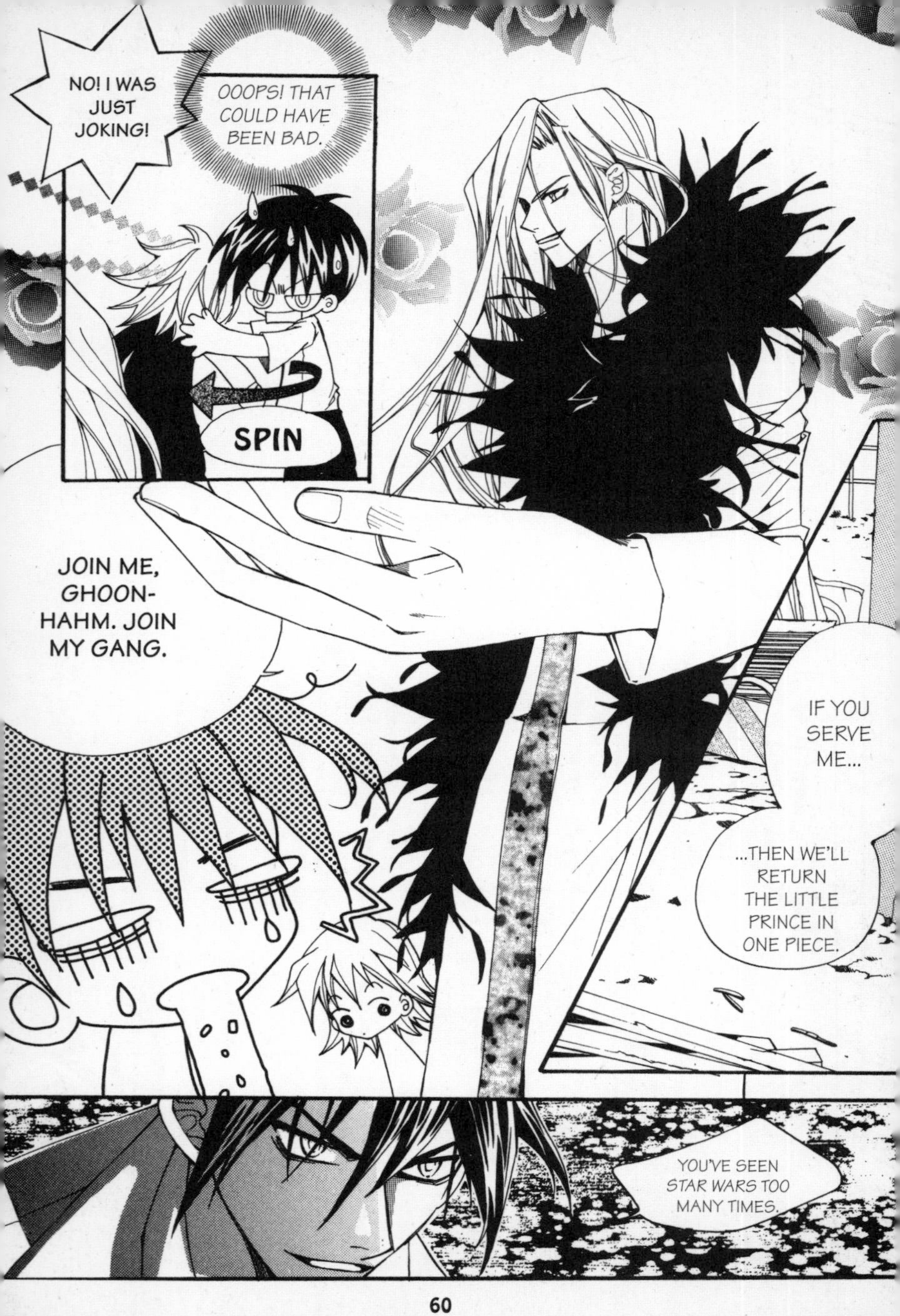
NO! I WAS JUST JOKING!
OOOPS! THAT COULD HAVE BEEN BAD.
SPIN
JOIN ME, GHOON-HAHM. JOIN MY GANG.
IF YOU SERVE ME...
...THEN WE'LL RETURN THE LITTLE PRINCE IN ONE PIECE.
YOU'VE SEEN STAR WARS TOO MANY TIMES.

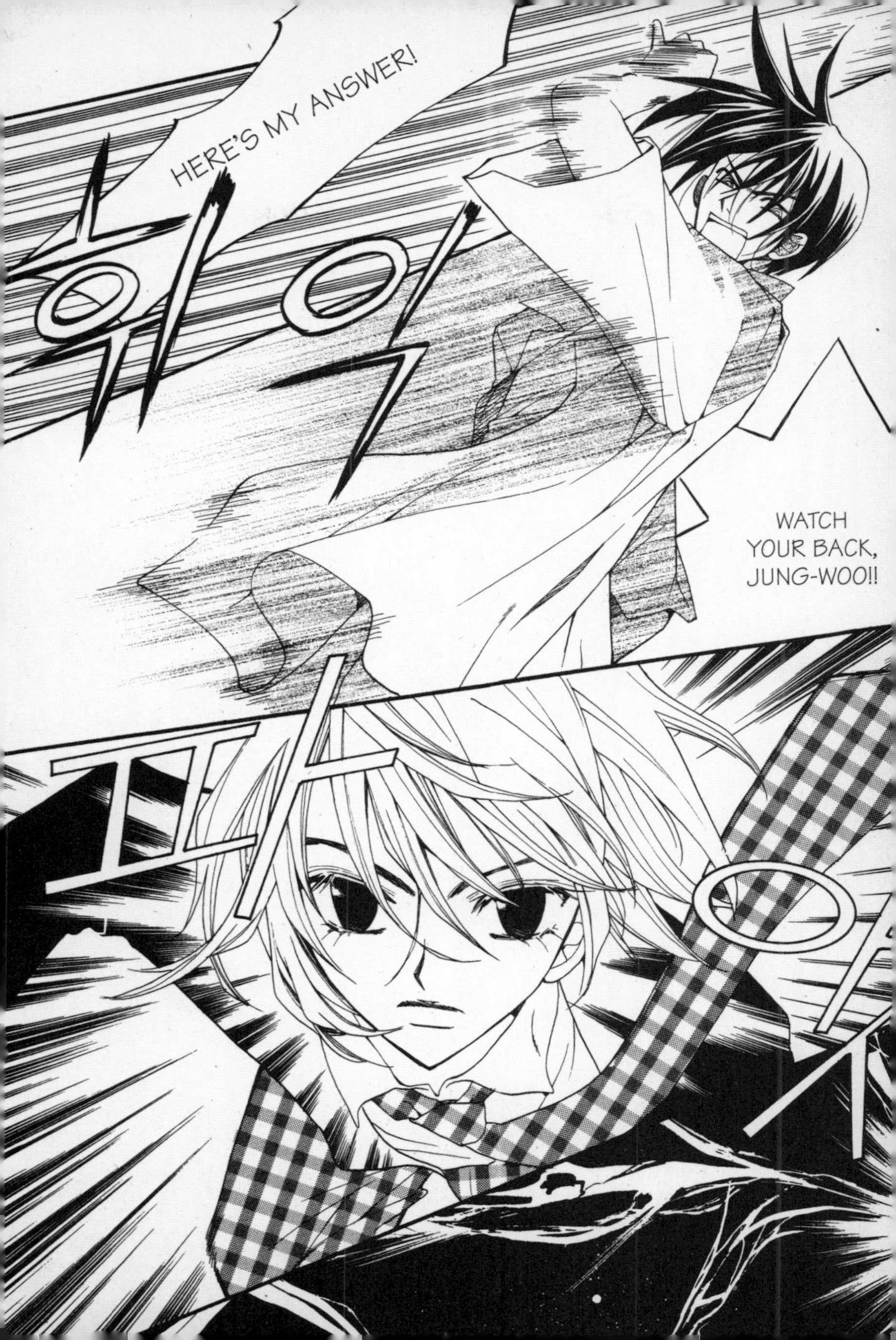
HERE'S MY ANSWER!
휘익
WATCH YOUR BACK, JUNG-WOO!!

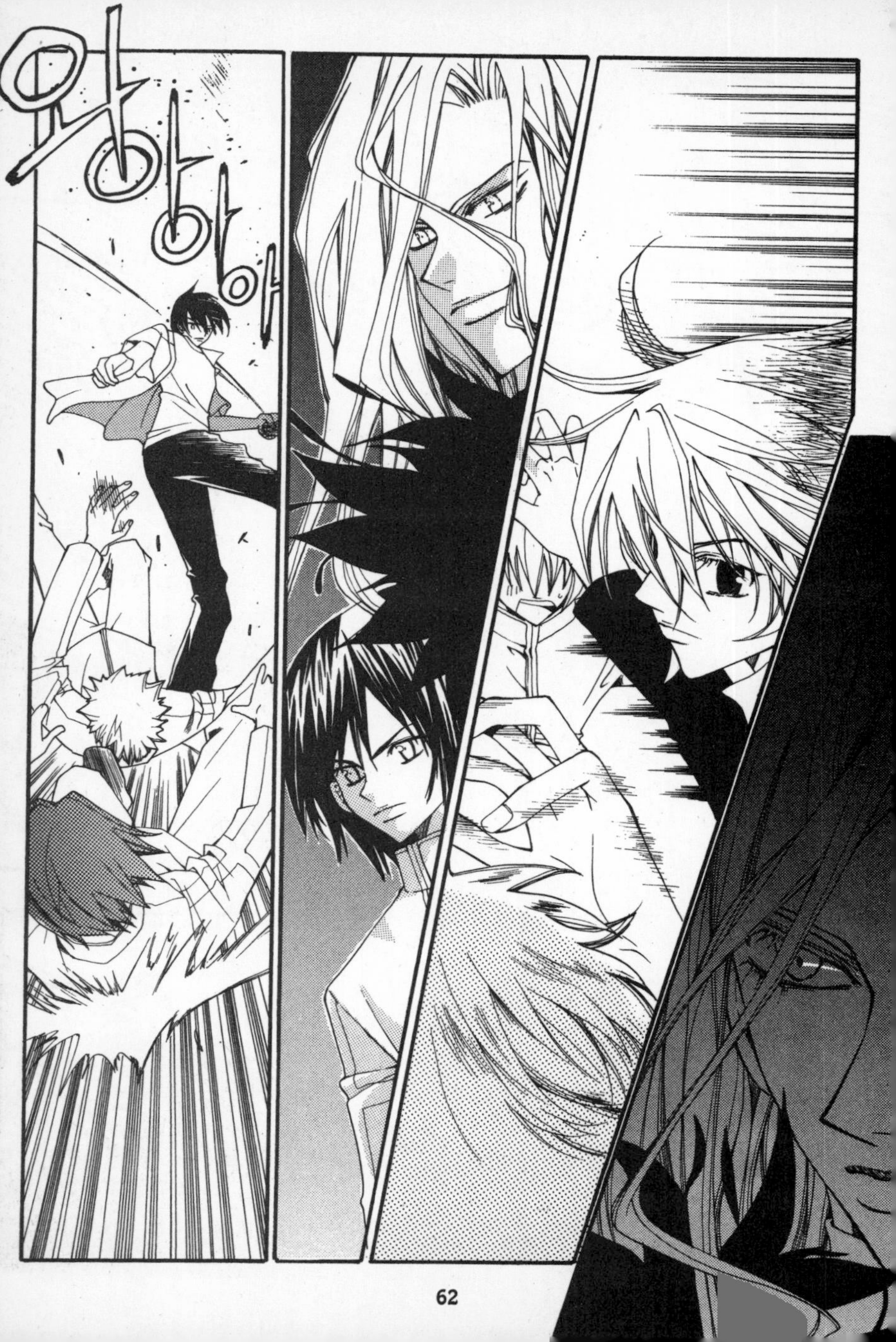
와아아아

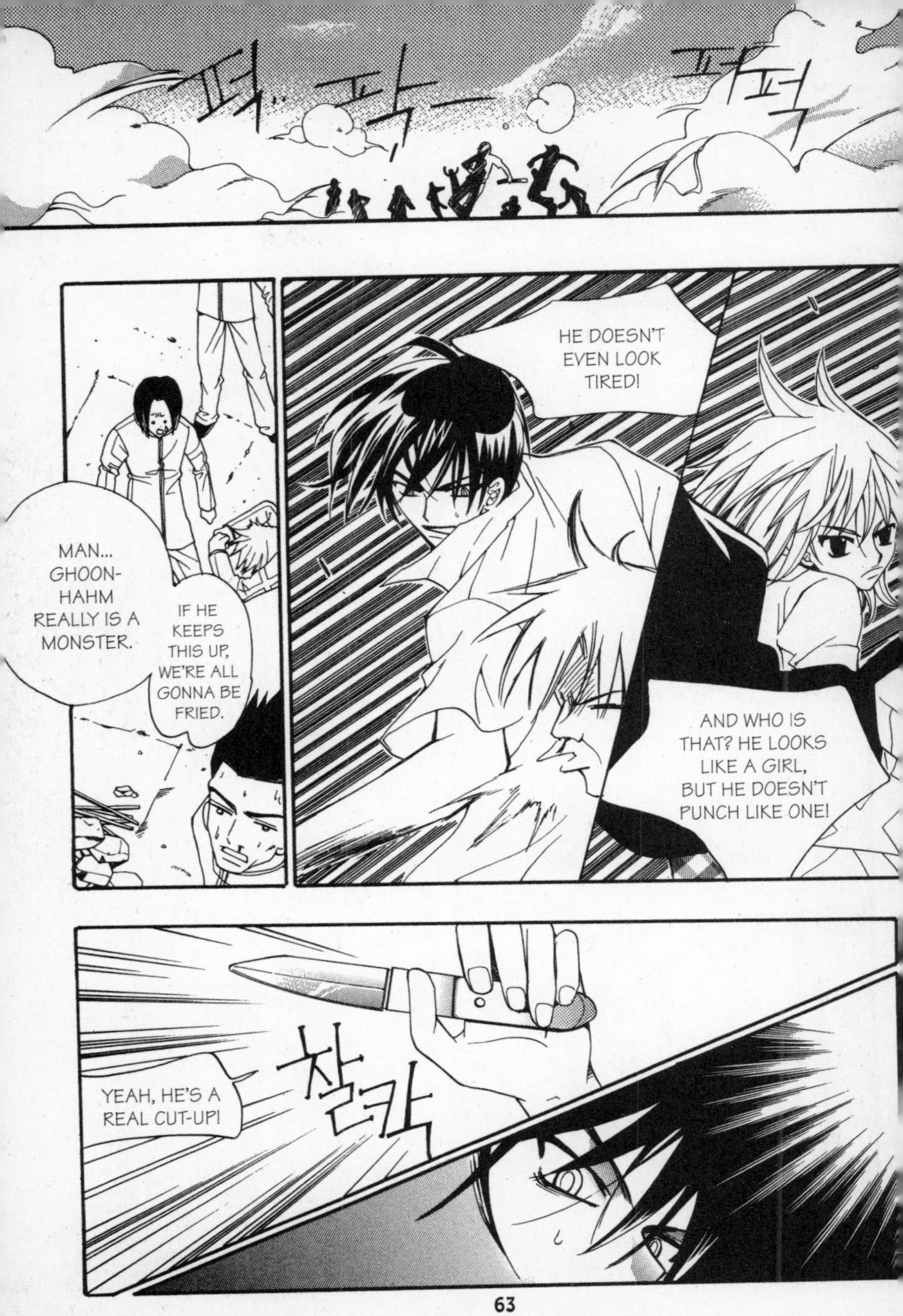
퍽.. 퍽ㅡ
퍼퍽
MAN... GHOON-HAHM REALLY IS A MONSTER.
IF HE KEEPS THIS UP, WE'RE ALL GONNA BE FRIED.
HE DOESN'T EVEN LOOK TIRED!
AND WHO IS THAT? HE LOOKS LIKE A GIRL, BUT HE DOESN'T PUNCH LIKE ONE!
YEAH, HE'S A REAL CUT-UP!
찰칵

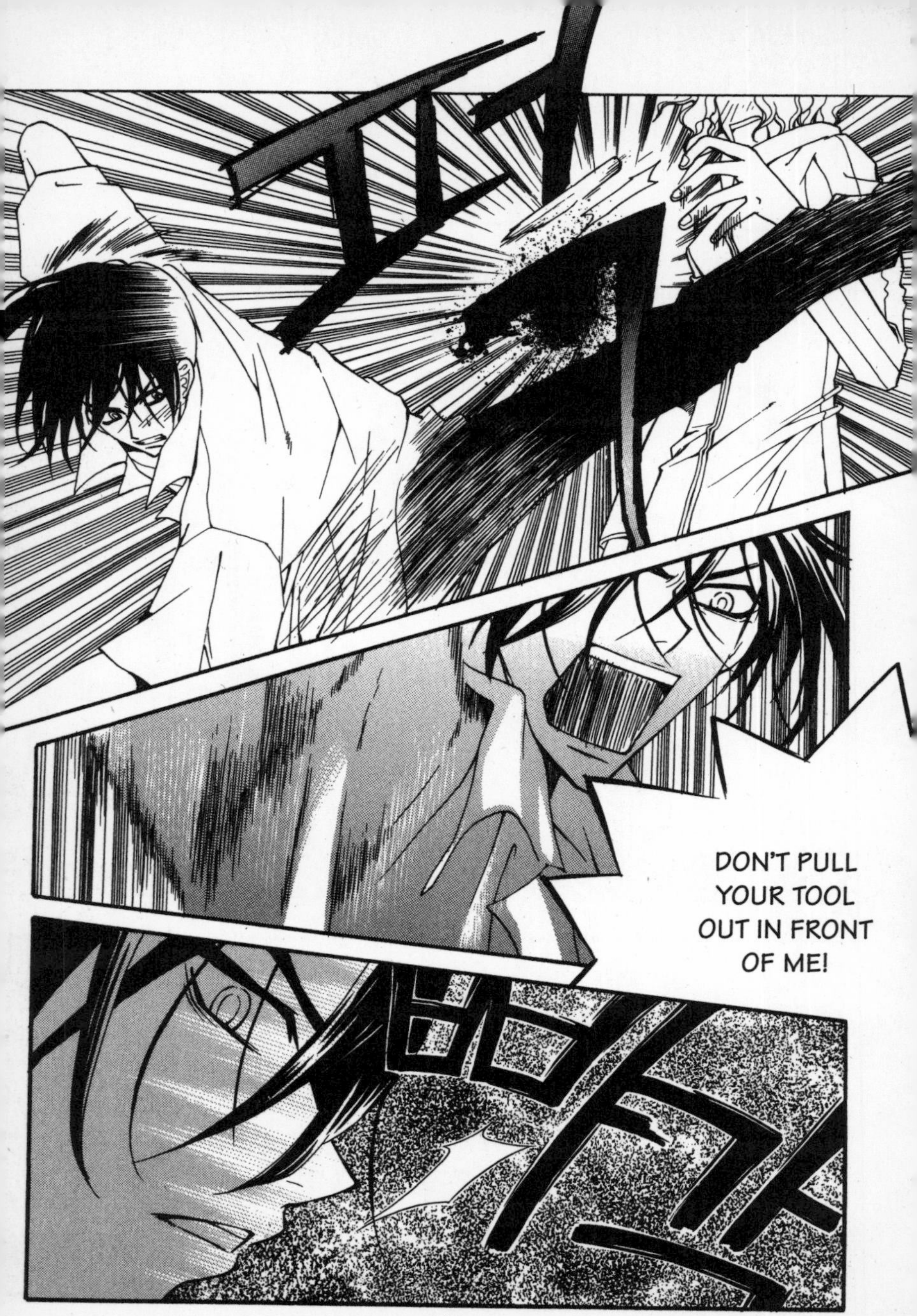
DON'T PULL YOUR TOOL OUT IN FRONT OF ME!

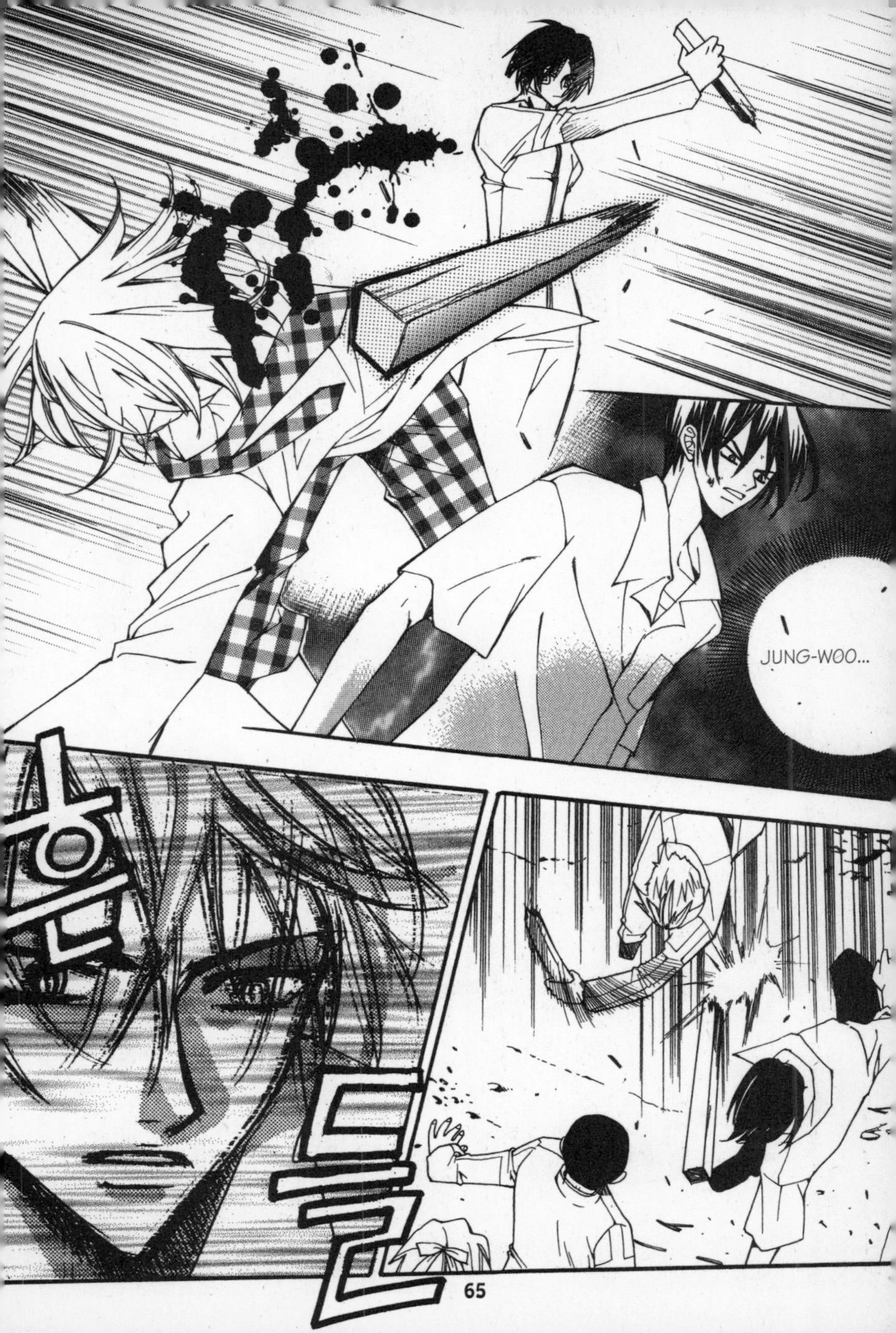
JUNG-WOO...

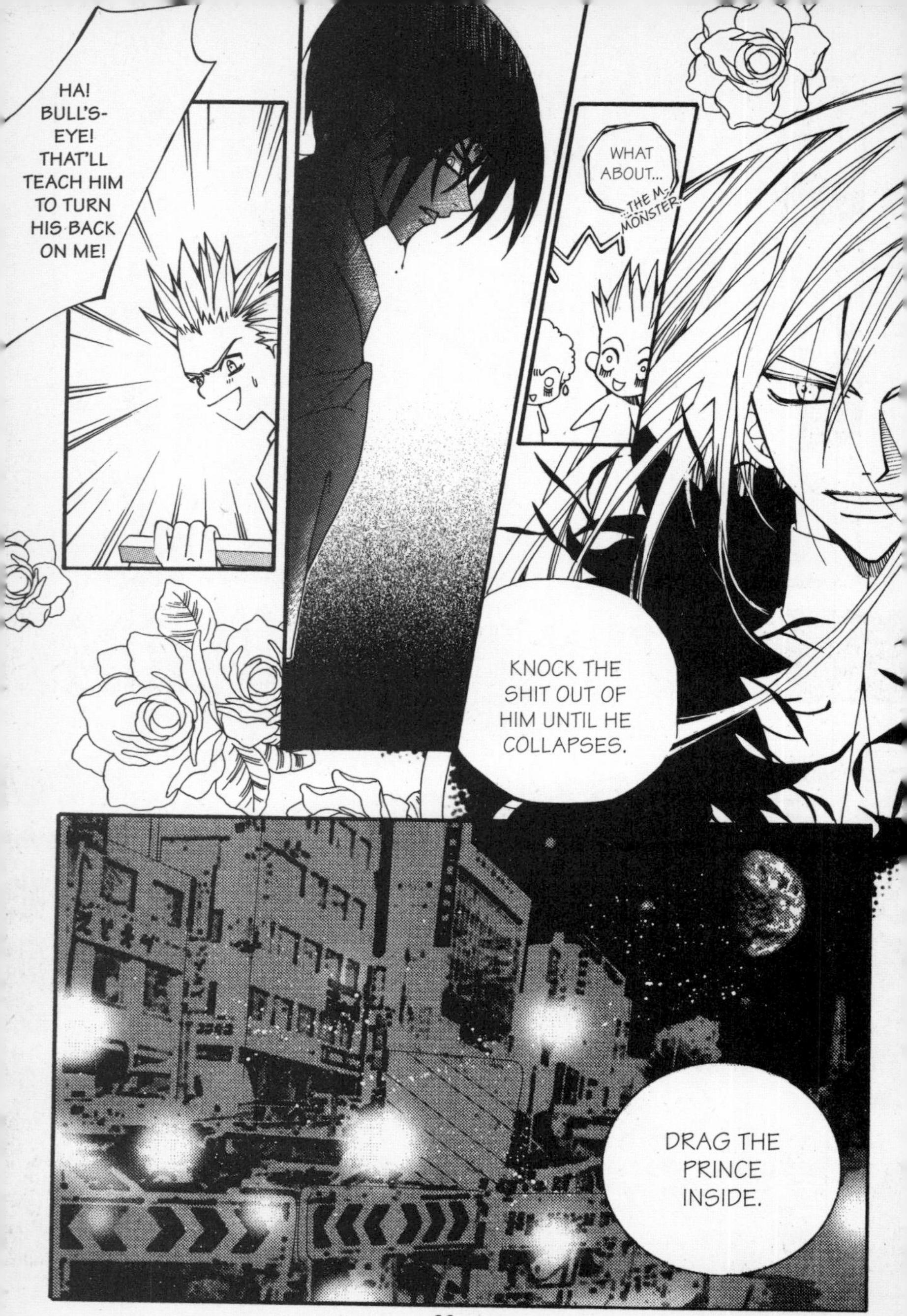
HA! BULL'S-EYE! THAT'LL TEACH HIM TO TURN HIS BACK ON ME!
WHAT ABOUT...
...THE M-MONSTER
KNOCK THE SHIT OUT OF HIM UNTIL HE COLLAPSES.
DRAG THE PRINCE INSIDE.

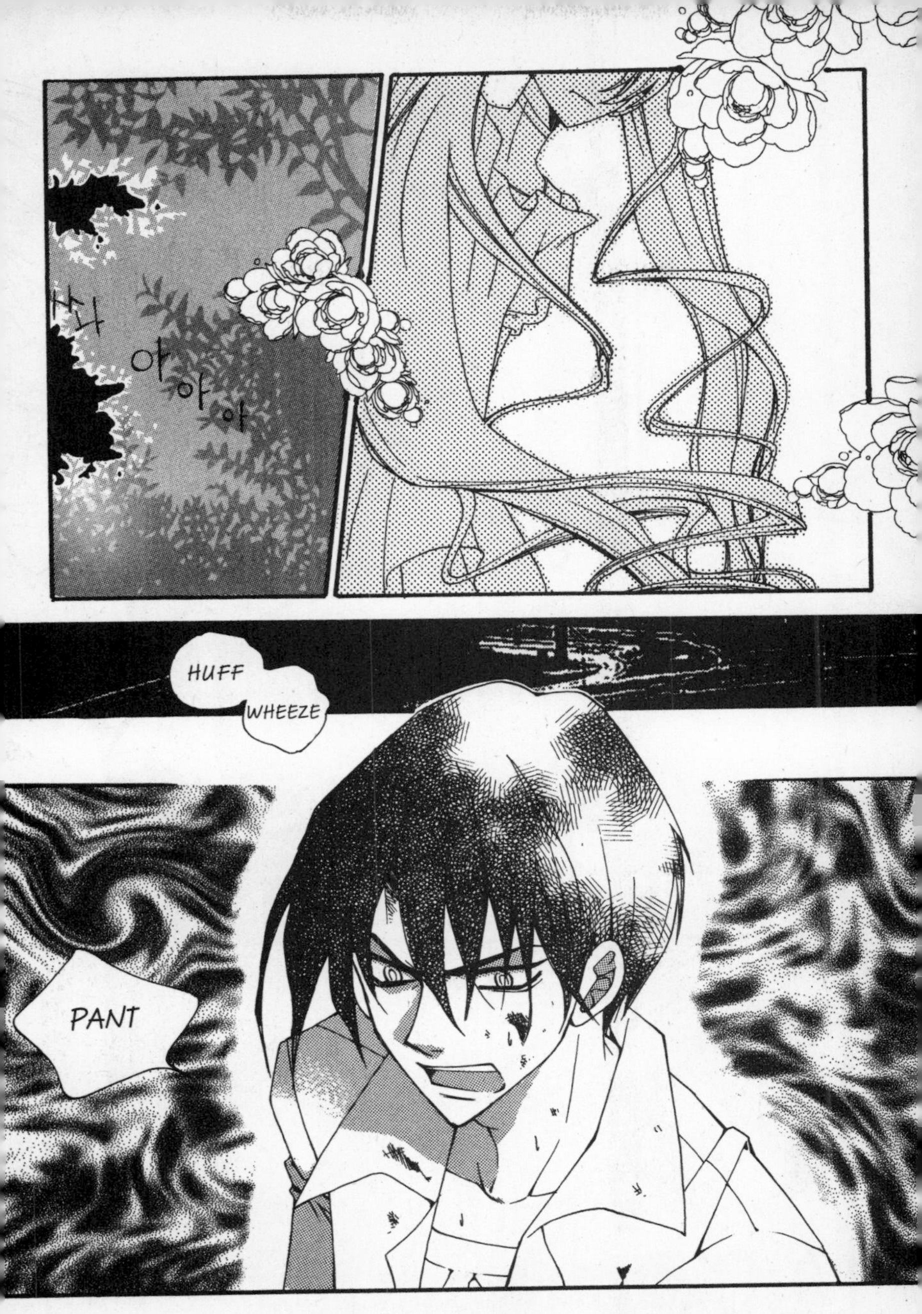
쏴아아아
HUFF
WHEEZE
PANT

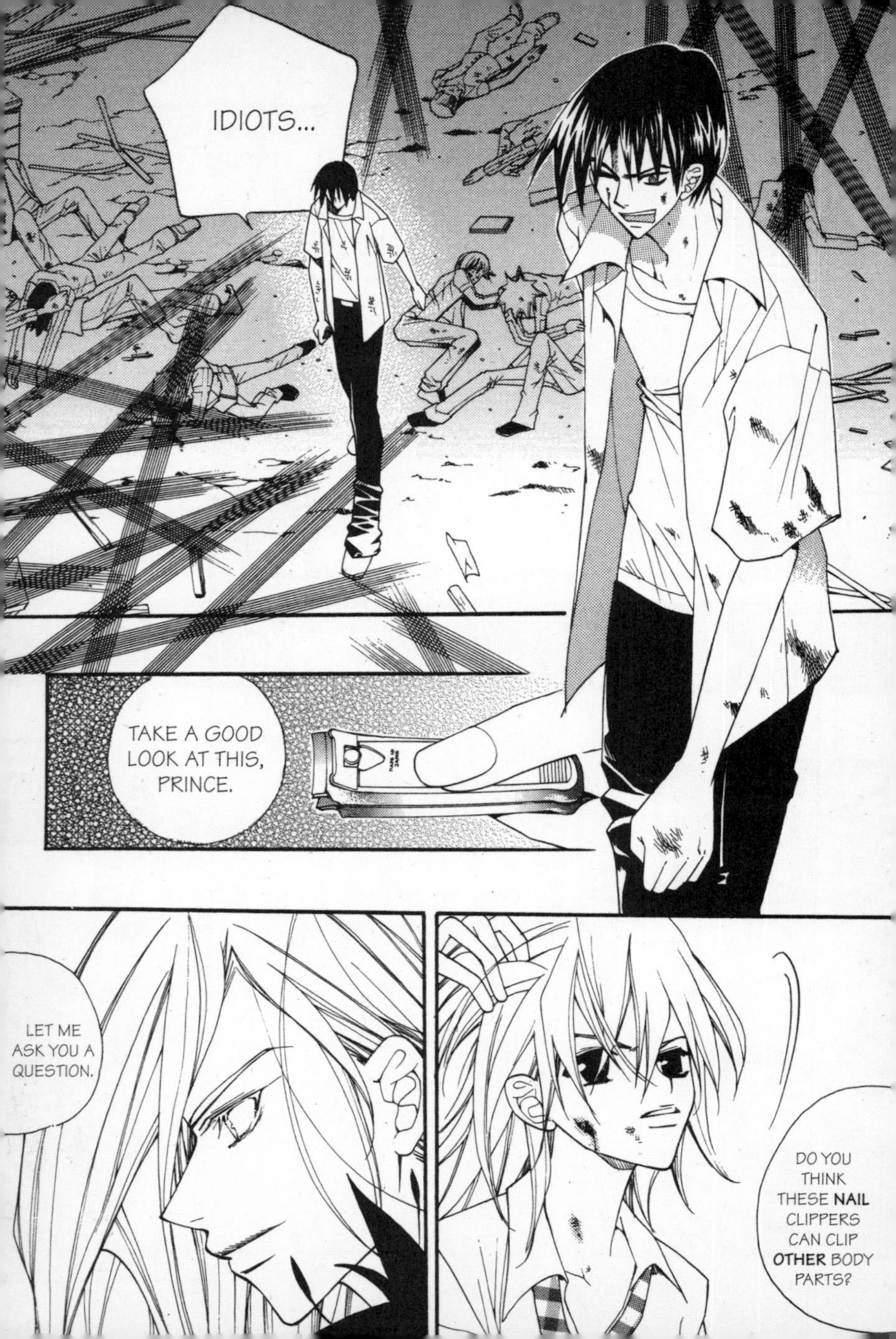
IDIOTS...
TAKE A *GOOD* LOOK AT THIS, PRINCE.
LET ME ASK YOU A QUESTION.
DO YOU THINK THESE **NAIL** CLIPPERS CAN CLIP **OTHER** BODY PARTS?

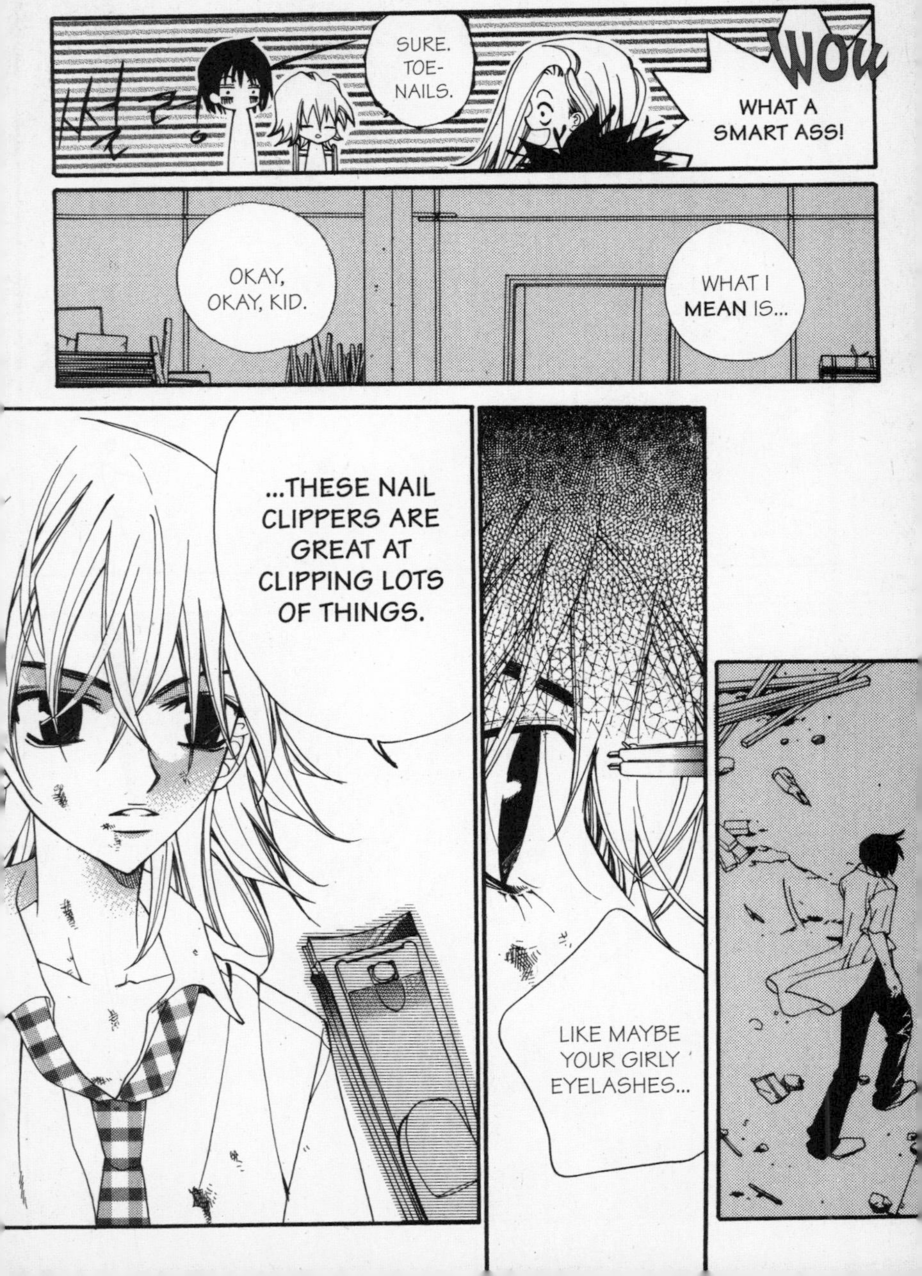
SURE. TOE-NAILS.
WOW
WHAT A SMART ASS!
OKAY, OKAY, KID.
WHAT I MEAN IS...
...THESE NAIL CLIPPERS ARE GREAT AT CLIPPING LOTS OF THINGS.
LIKE MAYBE YOUR GIRLY EYELASHES...

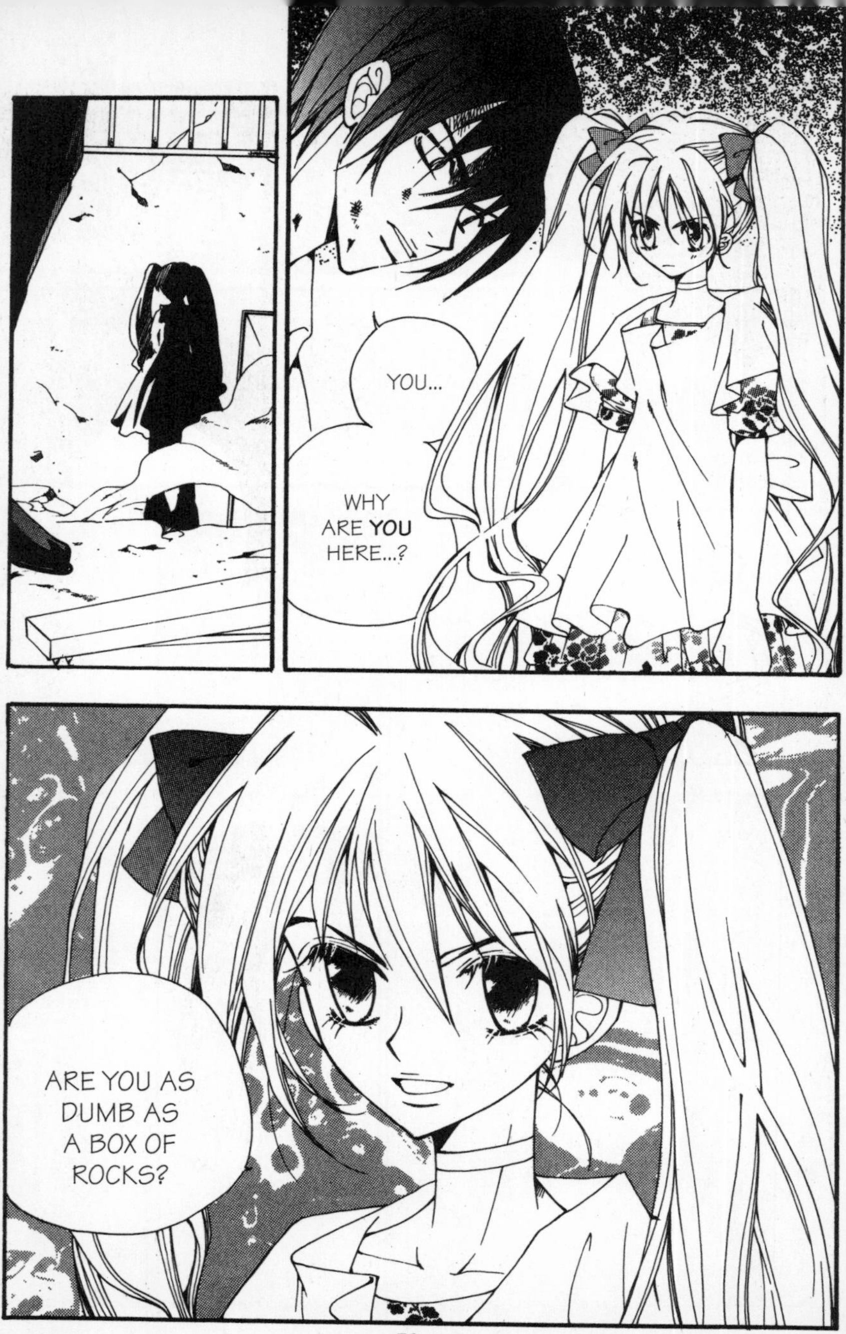
YOU...
WHY ARE **YOU** HERE...?
ARE YOU AS DUMB AS A BOX OF ROCKS?

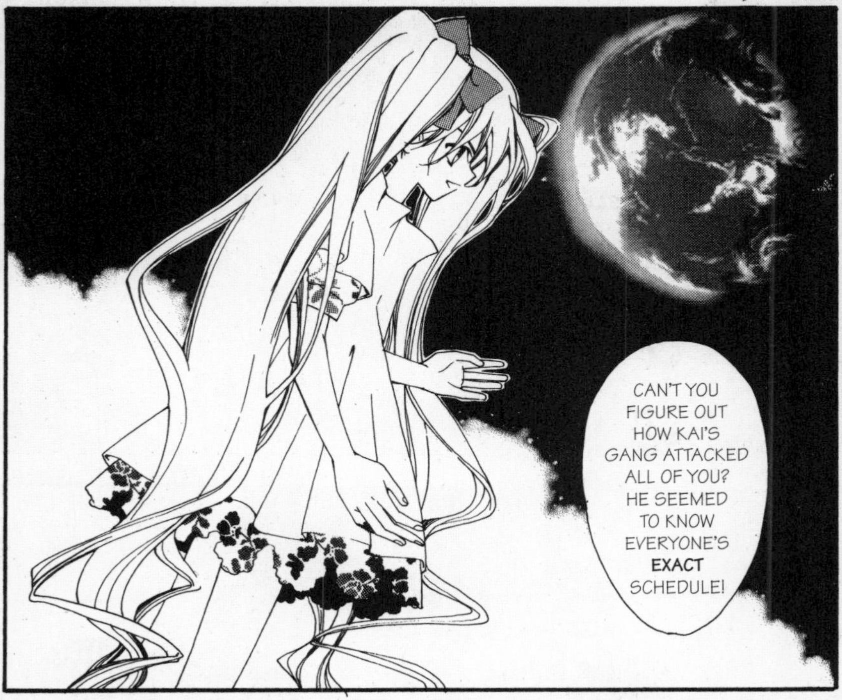
CAN'T YOU FIGURE OUT HOW KAI'S GANG ATTACKED ALL OF YOU? HE SEEMED TO KNOW EVERYONE'S **EXACT** SCHEDULE!

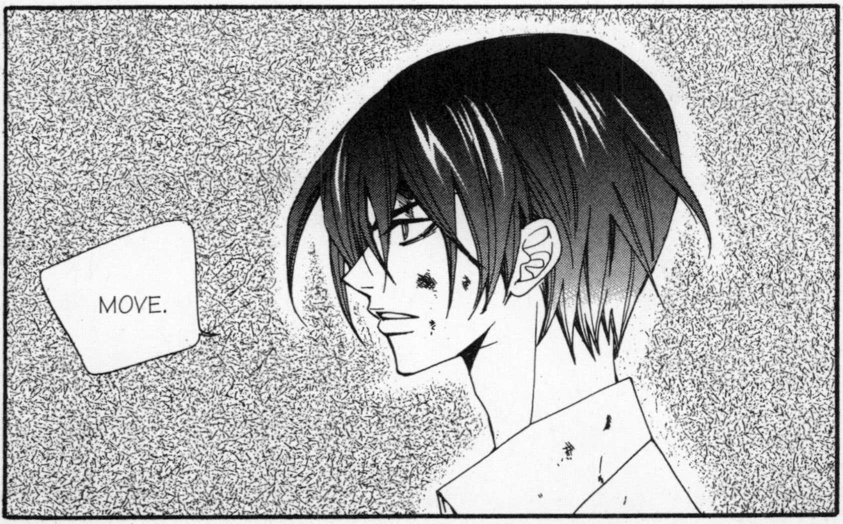
MOVE.

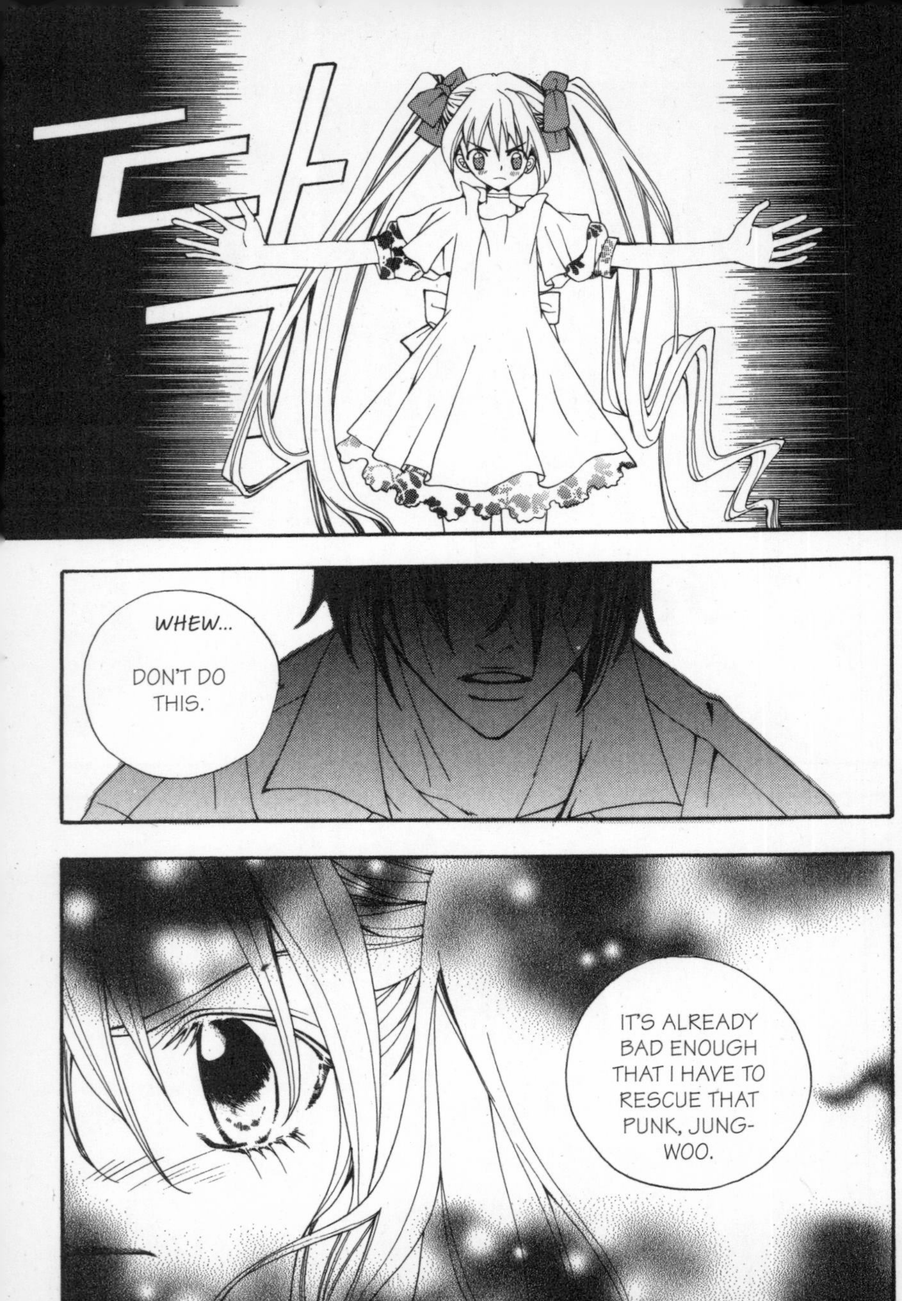
WHEW...
DON'T DO THIS.
IT'S ALREADY BAD ENOUGH THAT I HAVE TO RESCUE THAT PUNK, JUNG-WOO.

K2 Kill me Kiss me

BORN TO MUSIC
oops

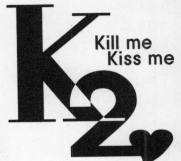

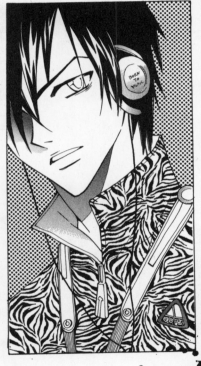

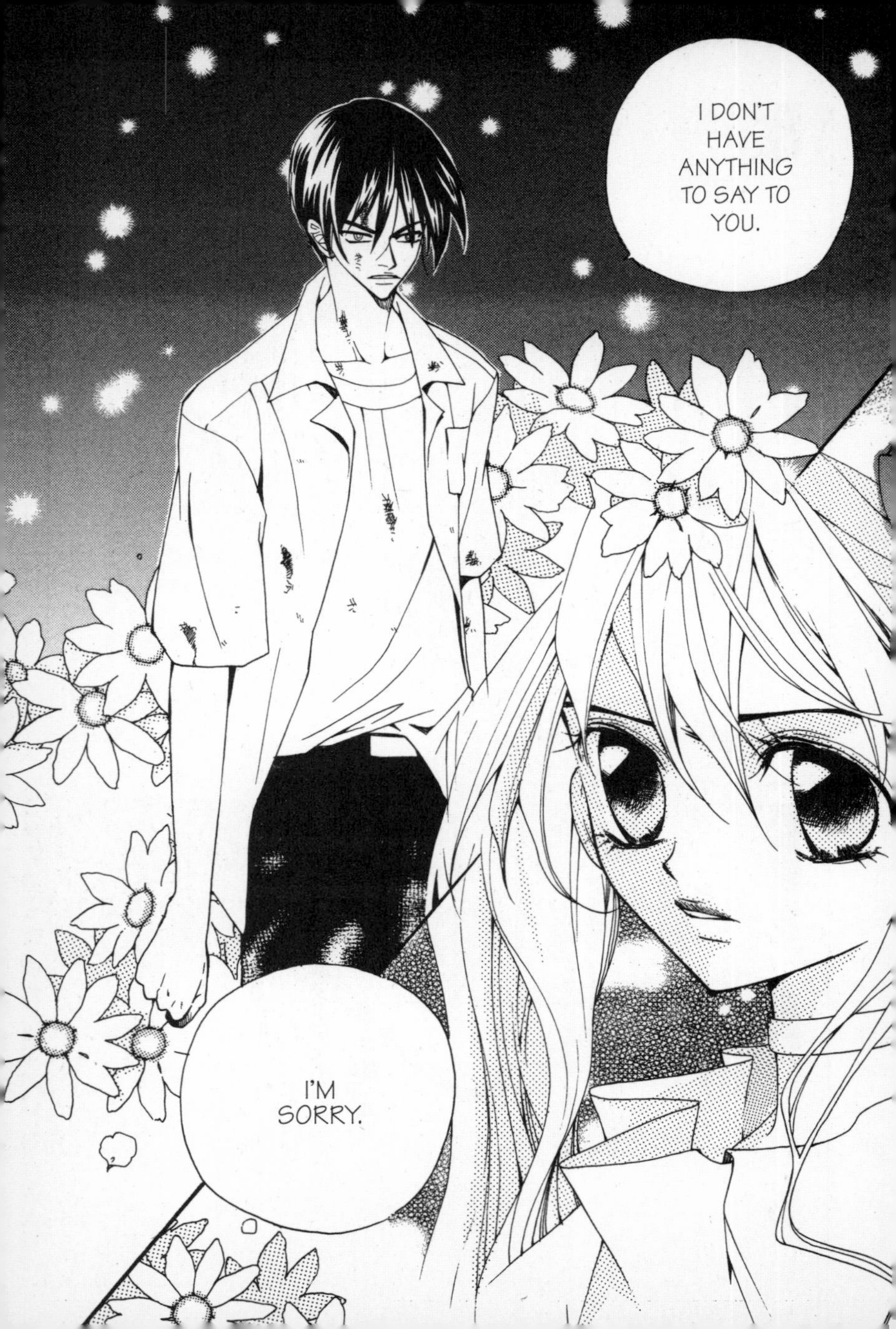
I DON'T HAVE ANYTHING TO SAY TO YOU.
I'M SORRY.

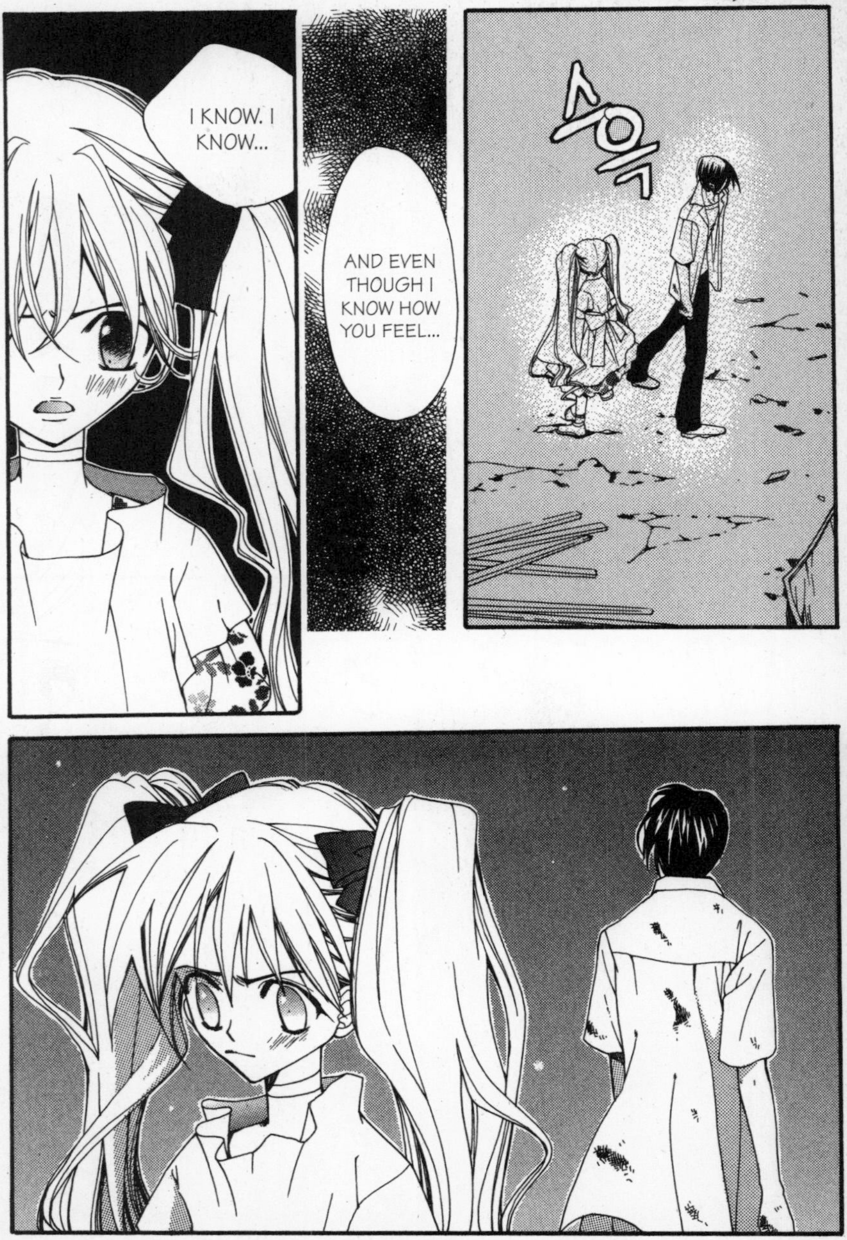
I KNOW. I KNOW...
AND EVEN THOUGH I KNOW HOW YOU FEEL...

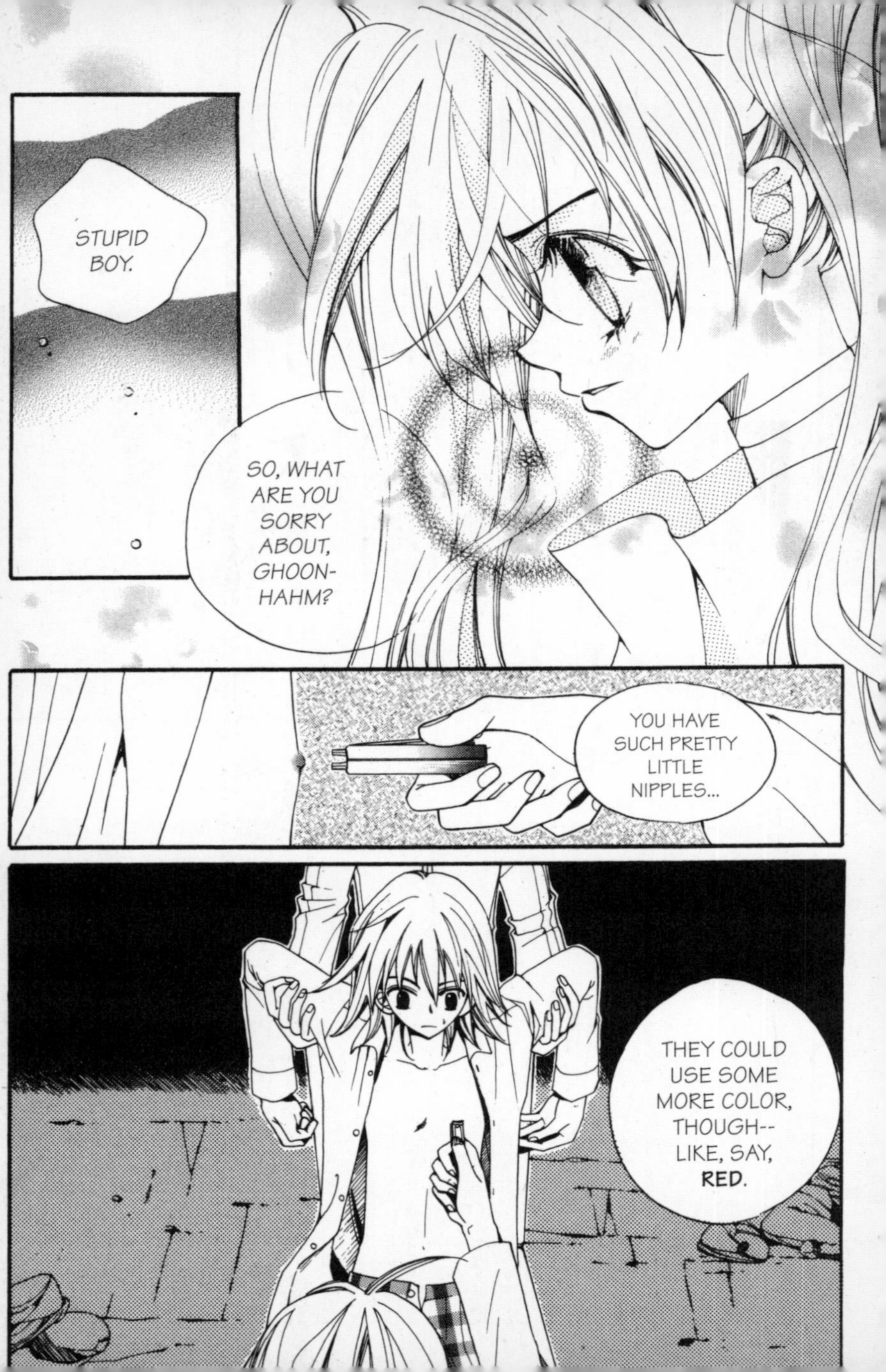
STUPID BOY.
SO, WHAT ARE YOU SORRY ABOUT, GHOON-HAHM?
YOU HAVE SUCH PRETTY LITTLE NIPPLES...
THEY COULD USE SOME MORE COLOR, THOUGH-- LIKE, SAY, **RED**.

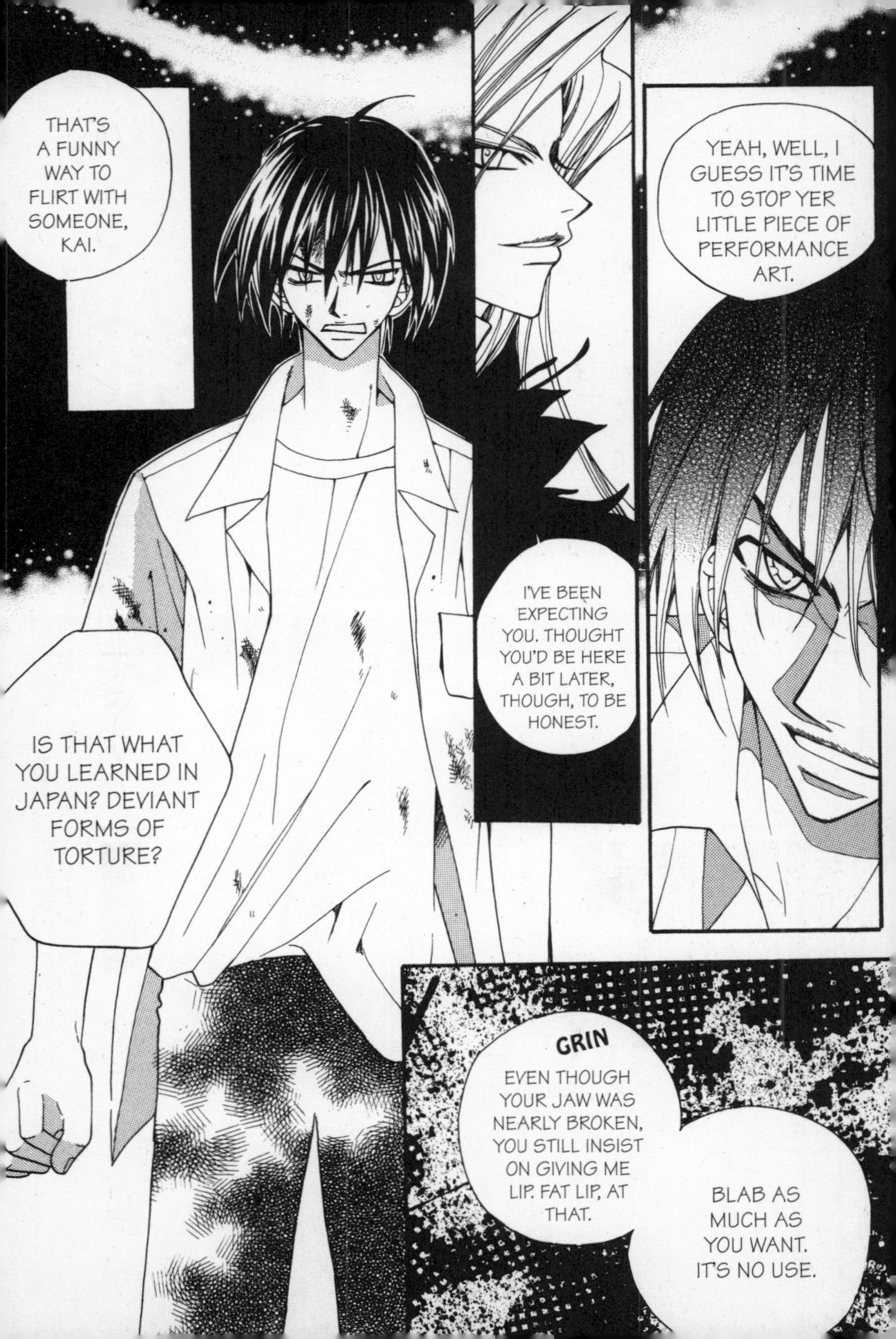
THAT'S A FUNNY WAY TO FLIRT WITH SOMEONE, KAI.
IS THAT WHAT YOU LEARNED IN JAPAN? DEVIANT FORMS OF TORTURE?
I'VE BEEN EXPECTING YOU. THOUGHT YOU'D BE HERE A BIT LATER, THOUGH, TO BE HONEST.
YEAH, WELL, I GUESS IT'S TIME TO STOP YER LITTLE PIECE OF PERFORMANCE ART.
GRIN
EVEN THOUGH YOUR JAW WAS NEARLY BROKEN, YOU STILL INSIST ON GIVING ME LIP. FAT LIP, AT THAT.
BLAB AS MUCH AS YOU WANT. IT'S NO USE.

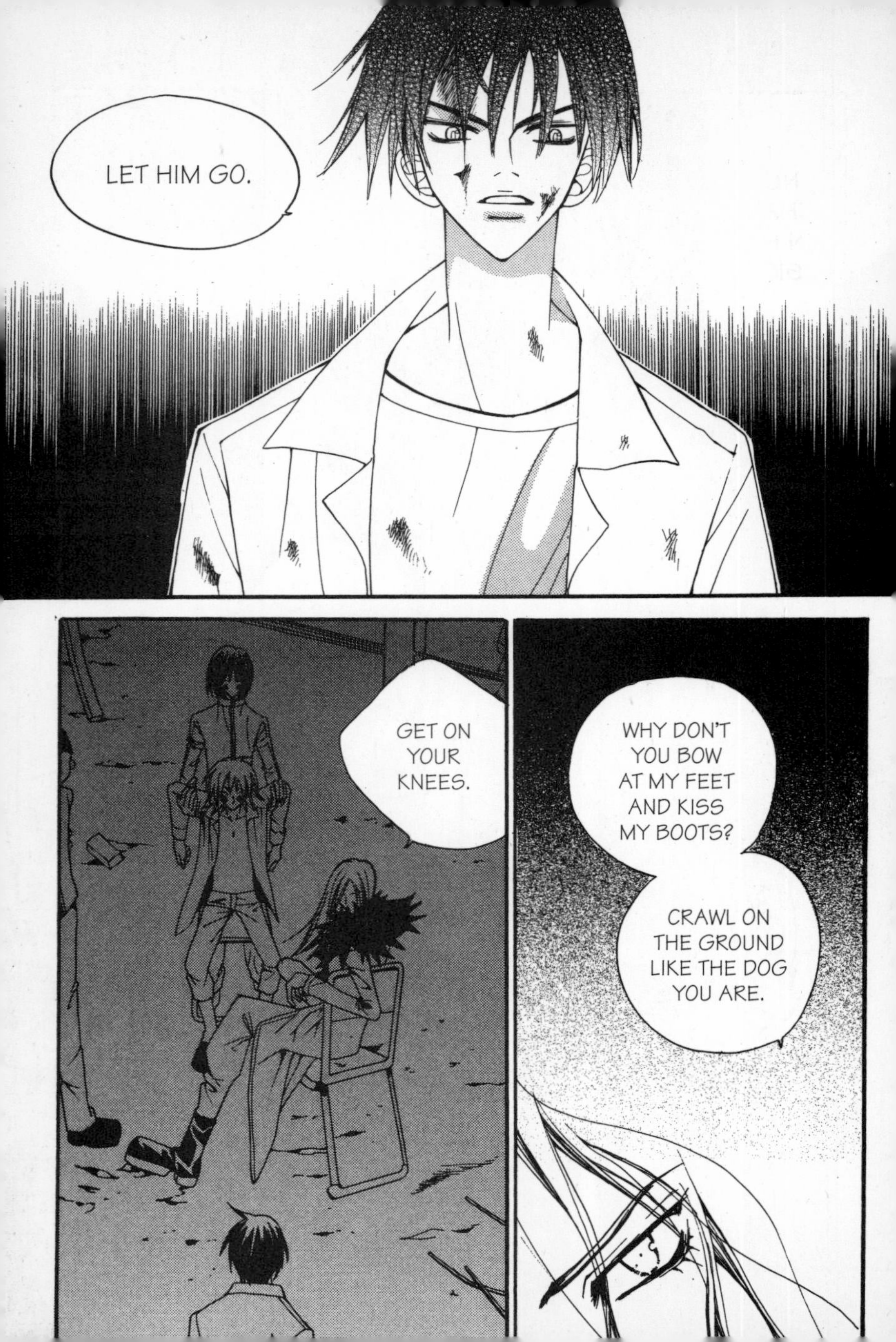
LET HIM GO.
GET ON YOUR KNEES.
WHY DON'T YOU BOW AT MY FEET AND KISS MY BOOTS?
CRAWL ON THE GROUND LIKE THE DOG YOU ARE.

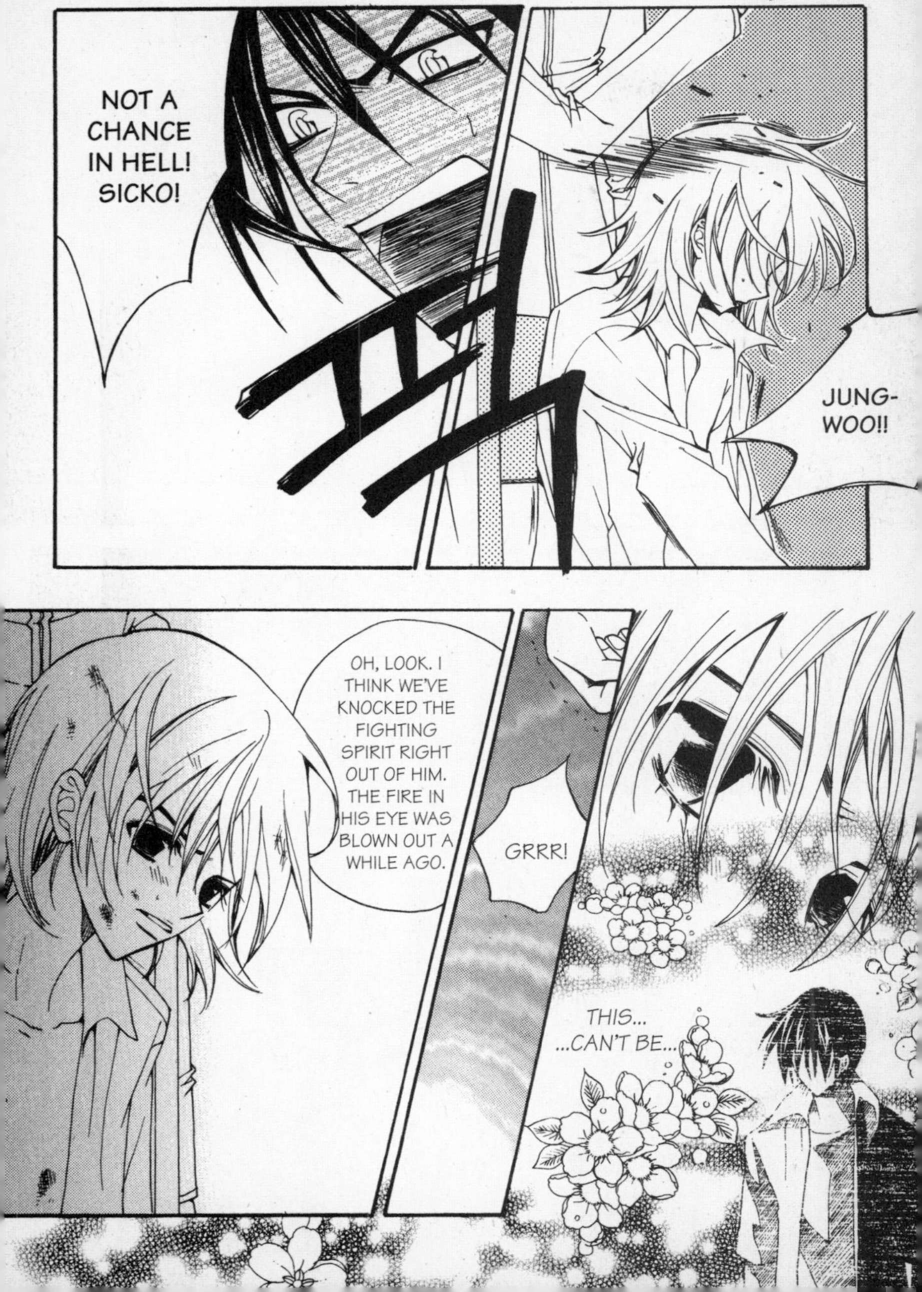
NOT A CHANCE IN HELL! SICKO!
JUNG-WOO!!
OH, LOOK. I THINK WE'VE KNOCKED THE FIGHTING SPIRIT RIGHT OUT OF HIM. THE FIRE IN HIS EYE WAS BLOWN OUT A WHILE AGO.
GRRR!
THIS... ...CAN'T BE...

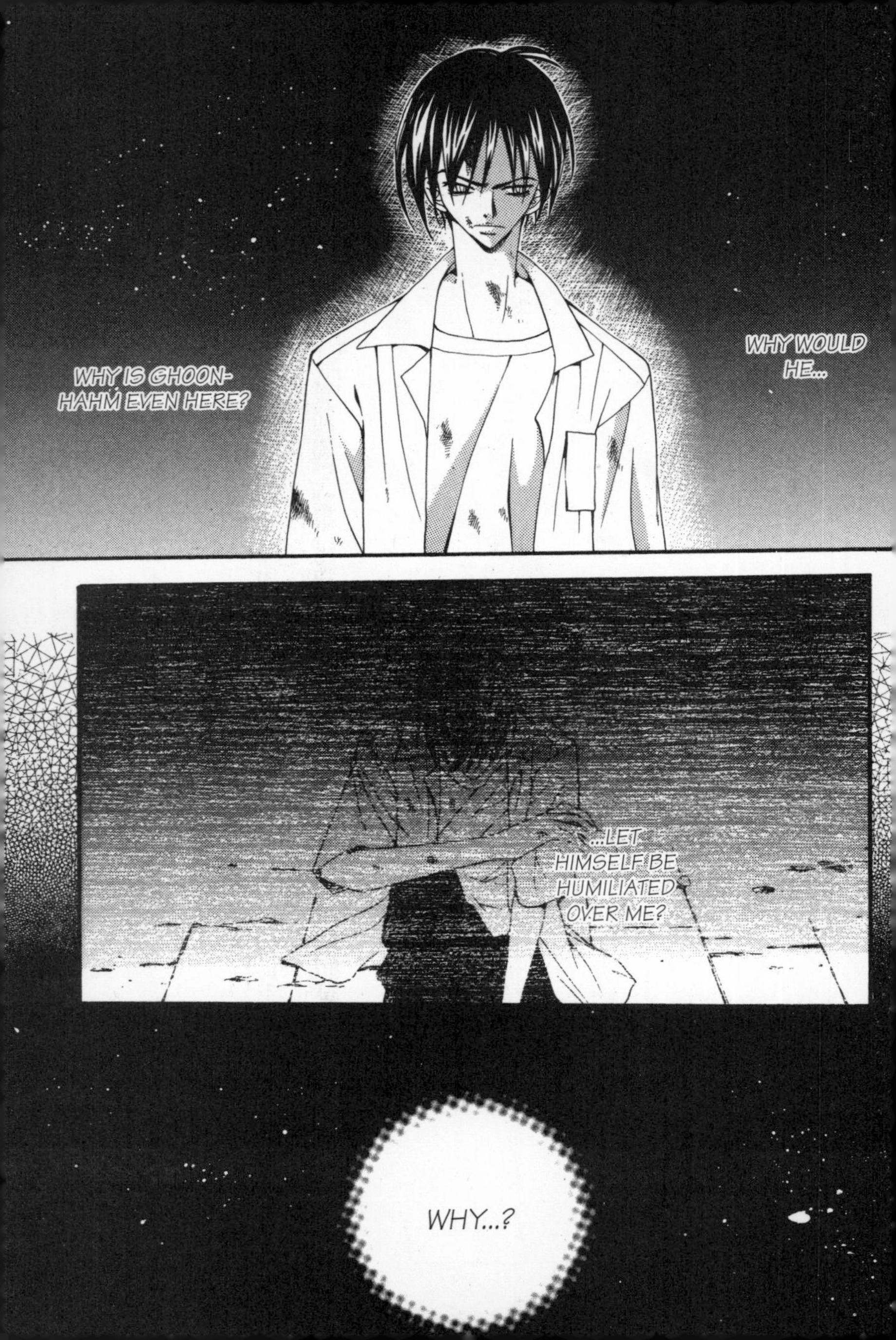
WHY IS GHOON-HAHM EVEN HERE?
WHY WOULD HE...
...LET HIMSELF BE HUMILIATED OVER ME?
WHY...?

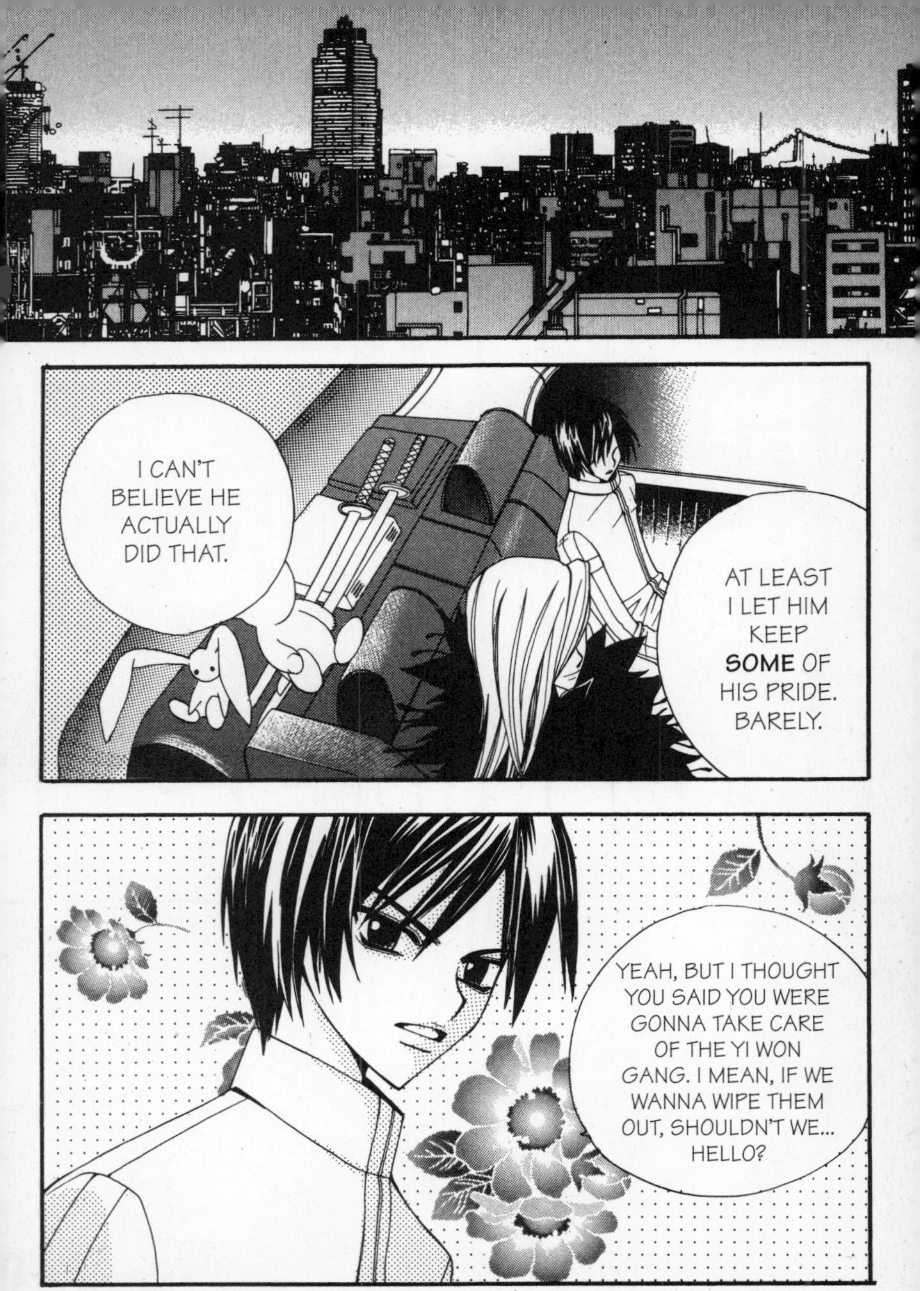
I CAN'T BELIEVE HE ACTUALLY DID THAT.
AT LEAST I LET HIM KEEP **SOME** OF HIS PRIDE. BARELY.
YEAH, BUT I THOUGHT YOU SAID YOU WERE GONNA TAKE CARE OF THE YI WON GANG. I MEAN, IF WE WANNA WIPE THEM OUT, SHOULDN'T WE... HELLO?

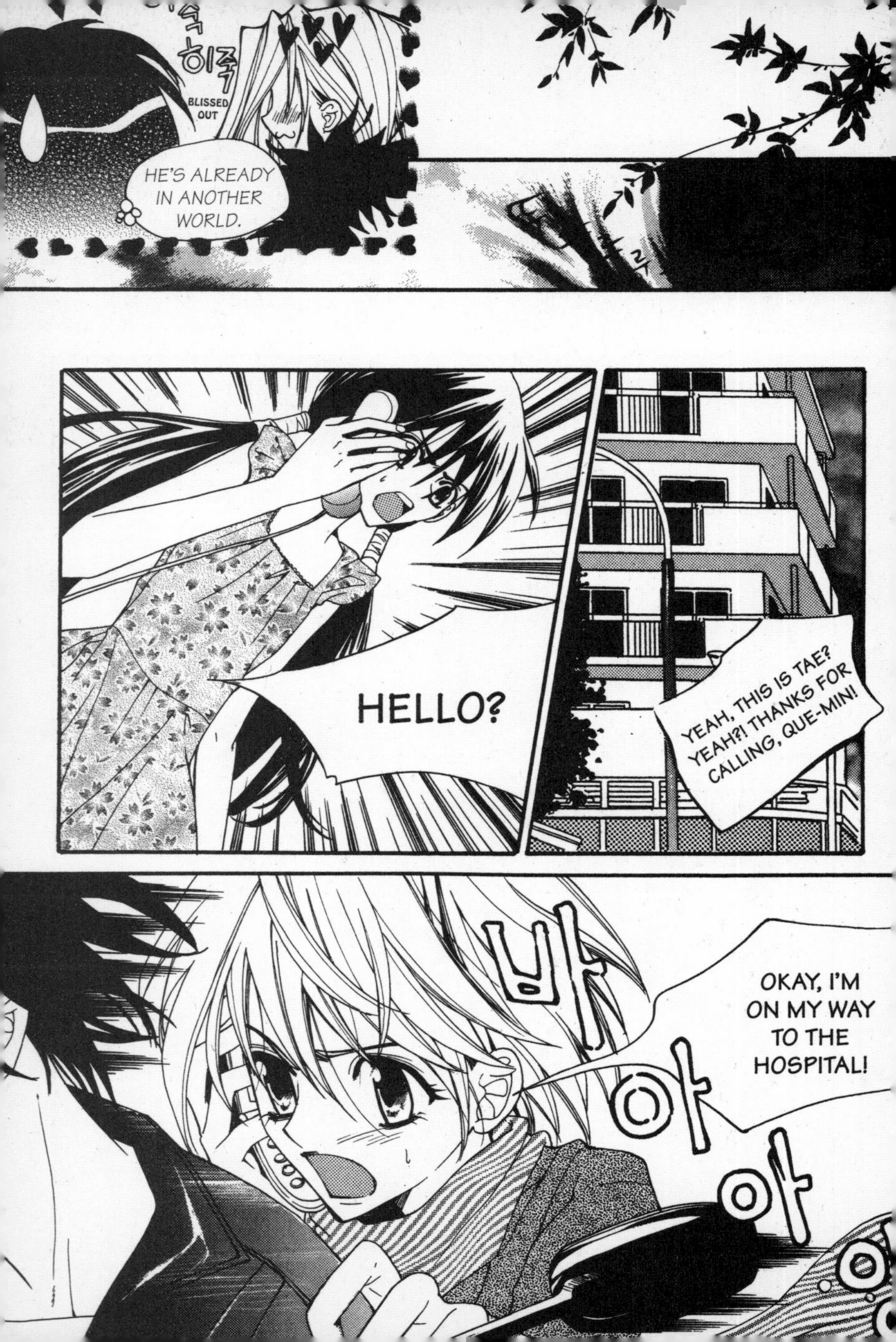
히죽
BLISSED OUT
HE'S ALREADY IN ANOTHER WORLD.
HELLO?
YEAH, THIS IS TAE? YEAH?! THANKS FOR CALLING, QUE-MIN!
OKAY, I'M ON MY WAY TO THE HOSPITAL!

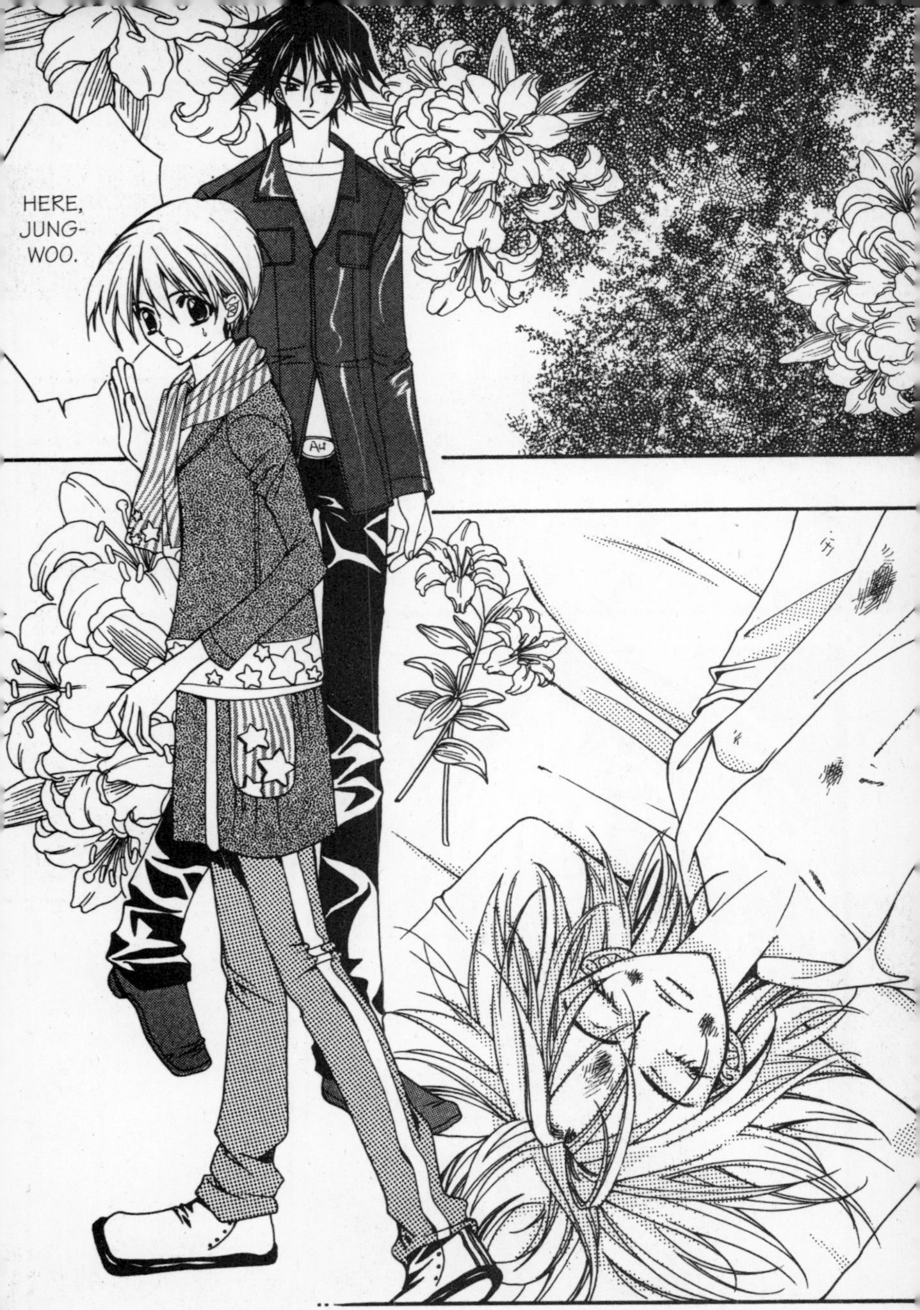
HERE, JUNG-WOO.

THERE IS A SEVERE GASH ON THE BACK OF HIS SKULL. IT'S AN IMPACT WOUND.

IT SEEMS HE WAS HIT WITH A WEAPON SEVERAL TIMES.

WHEN WILL HE LEARN TO STOP FIGHTING?!

TAE, STOP IT! HE'S ALREADY HURT ENOUGH!

POW

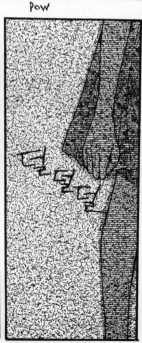

SHAKE SHAKE

SHAKE SHAKE SHAKE

84

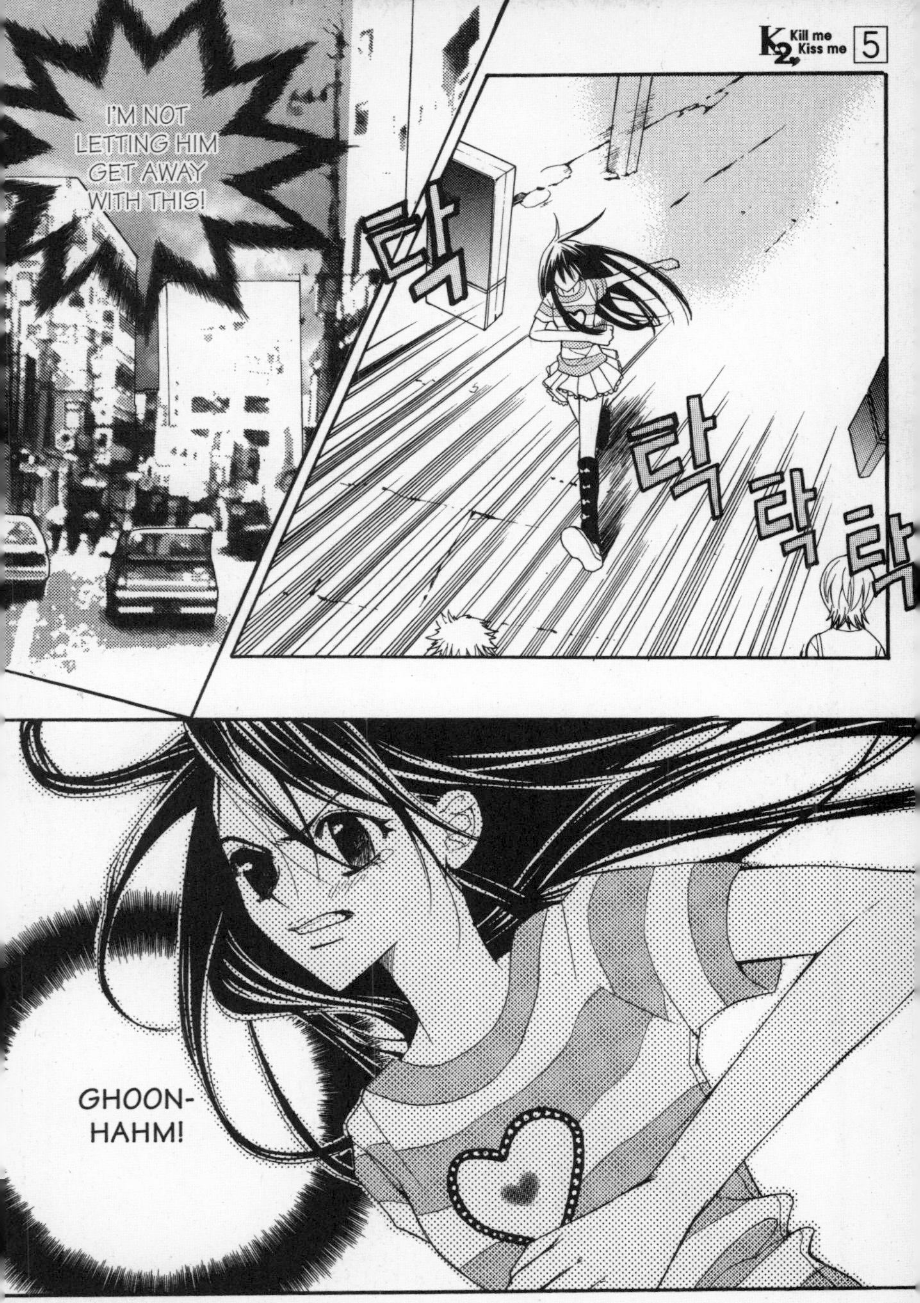
I'M NOT LETTING HIM GET AWAY WITH THIS!
탁
탁
탁
탁
GHOON-HAHM!

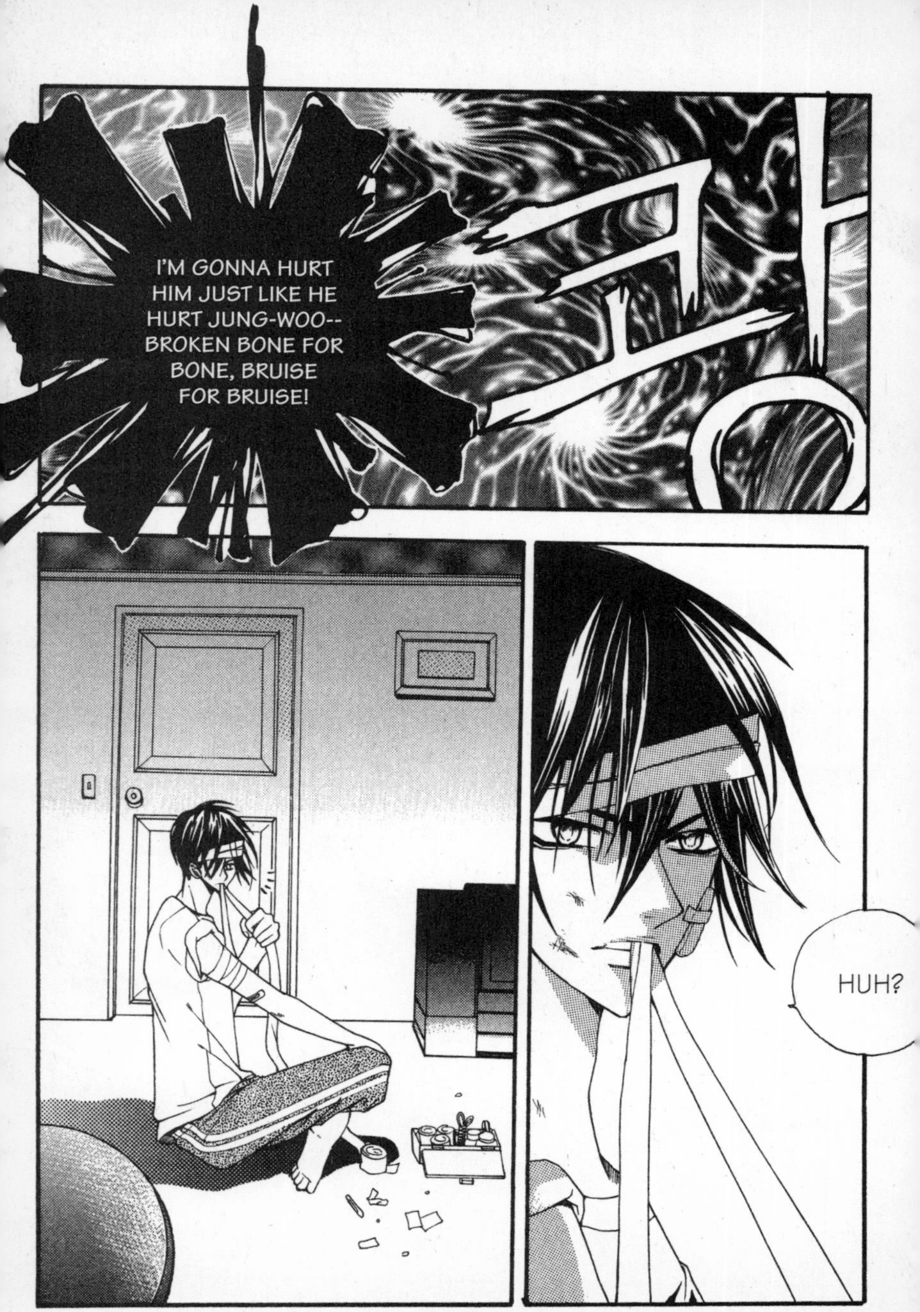
I'M GONNA HURT HIM JUST LIKE HE HURT JUNG-WOO-- BROKEN BONE FOR BONE, BRUISE FOR BRUISE!
HUH?

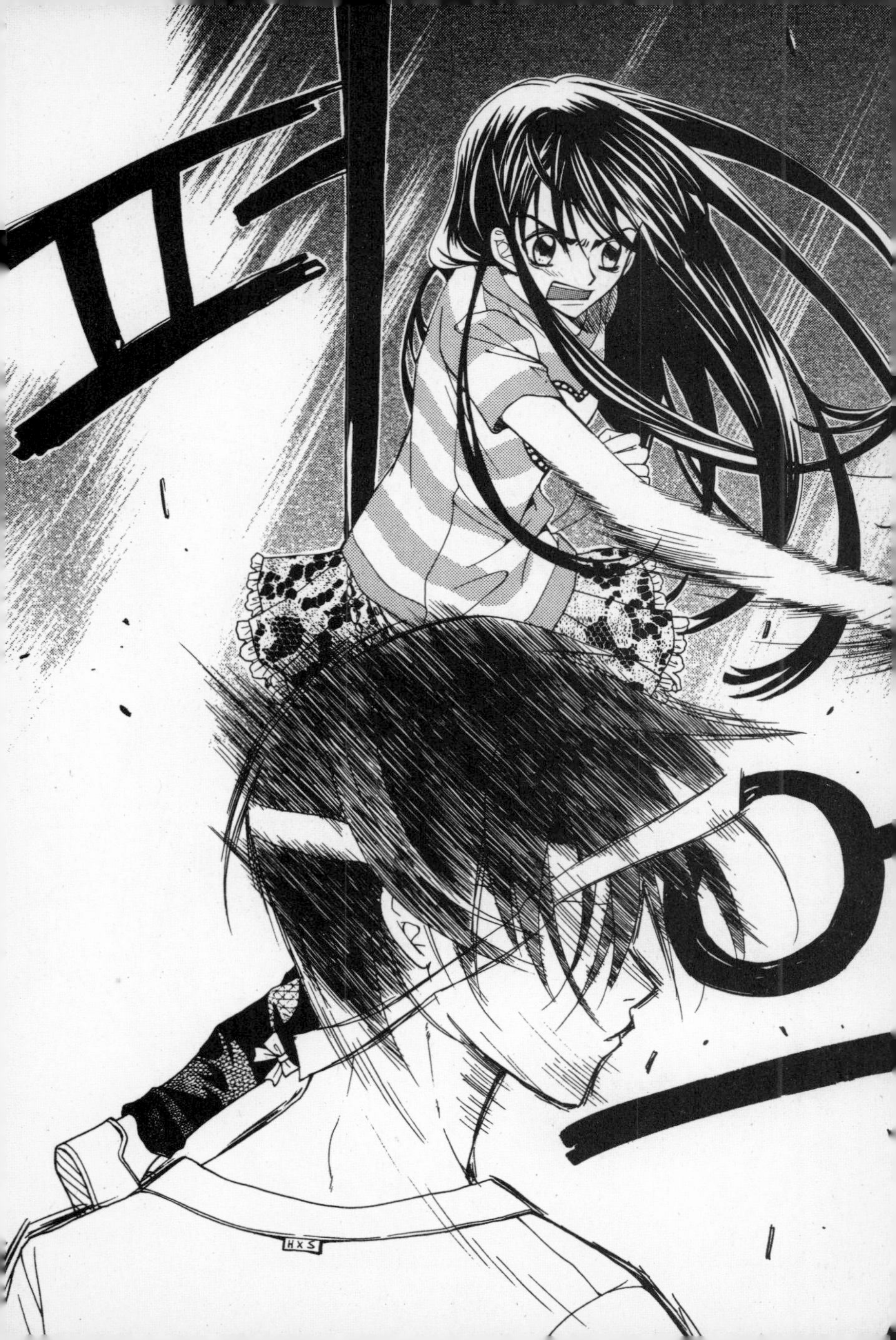

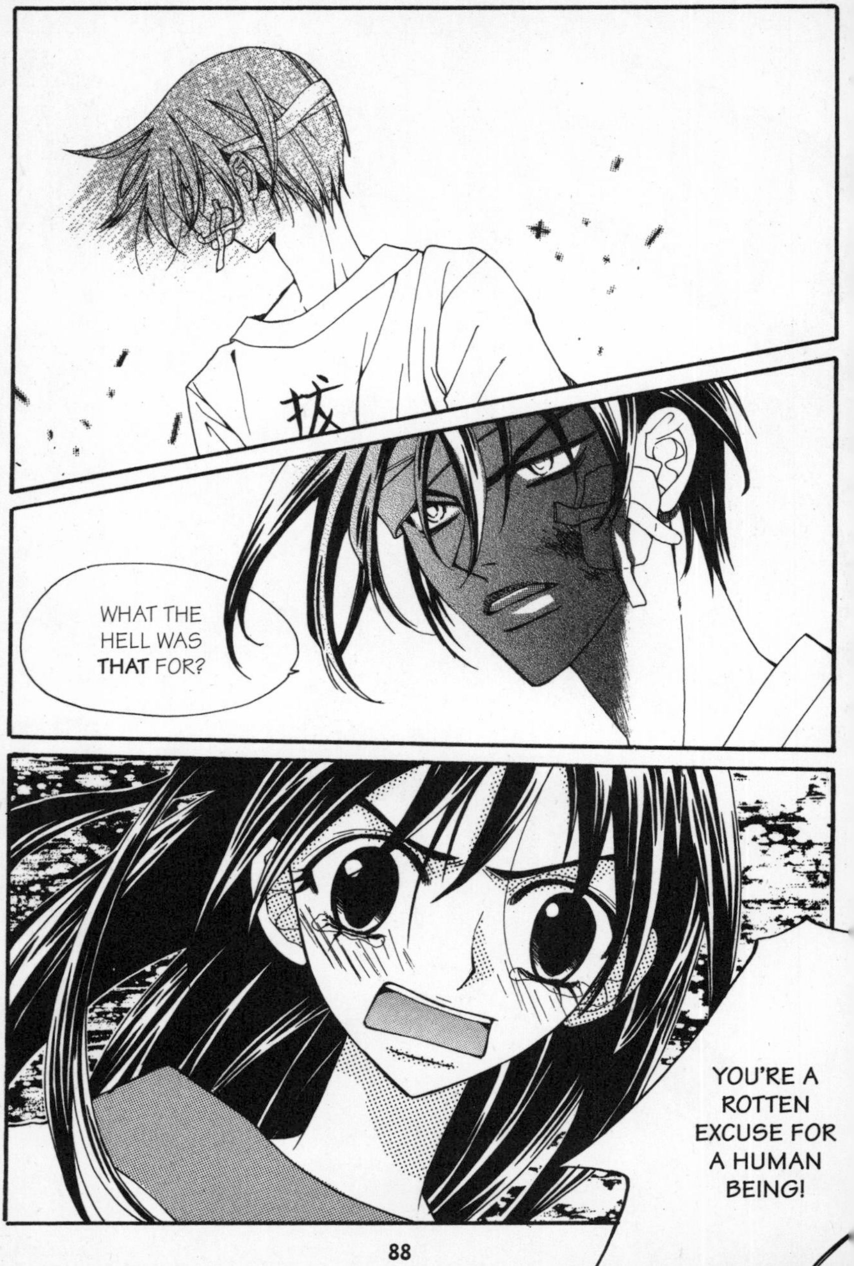
WHAT THE HELL WAS **THAT** FOR?
YOU'RE A ROTTEN EXCUSE FOR A HUMAN BEING!

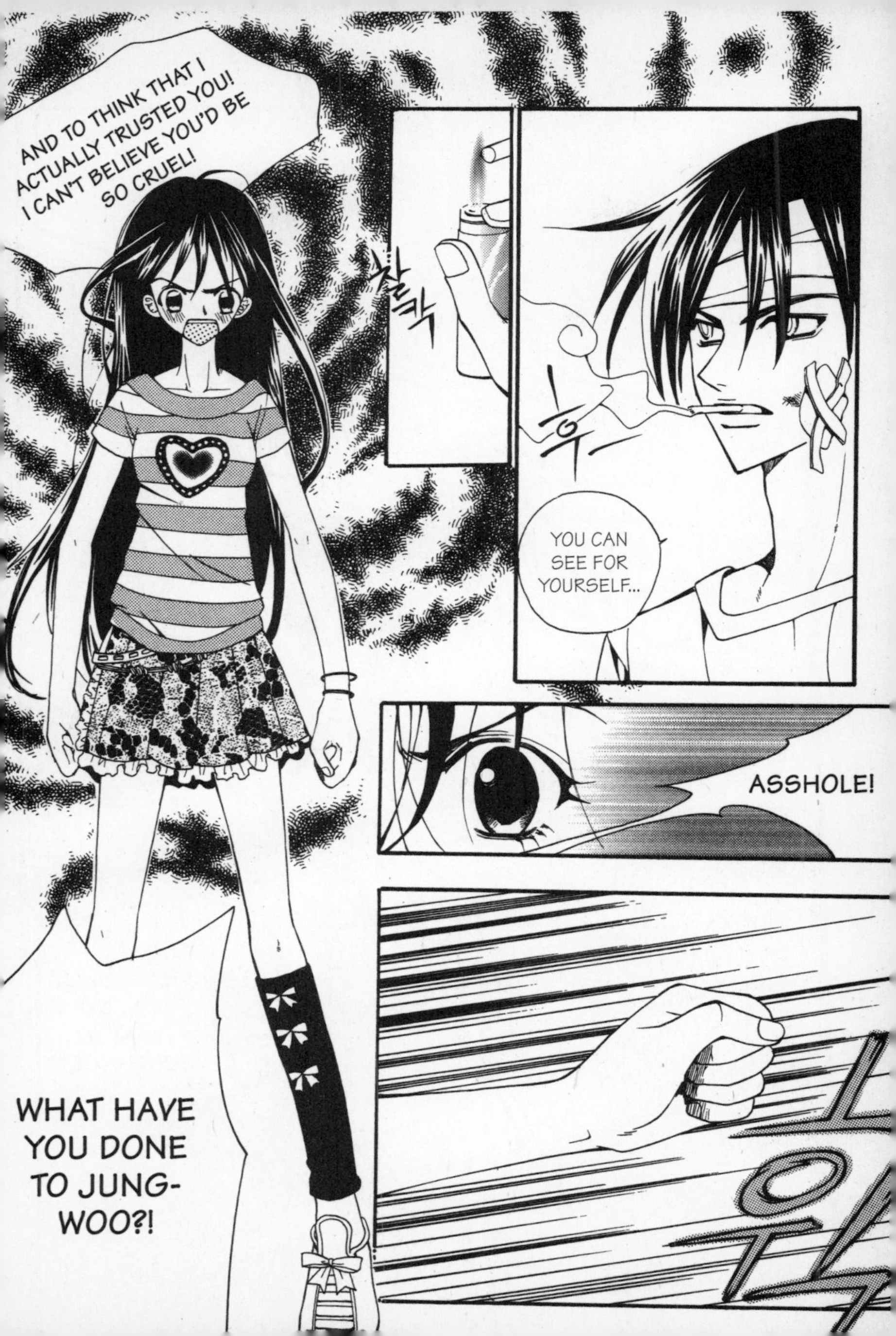
AND TO THINK THAT I ACTUALLY TRUSTED YOU! I CAN'T BELIEVE YOU'D BE SO CRUEL!
WHAT HAVE YOU DONE TO JUNG-WOO?!
찰칵
YOU CAN SEE FOR YOURSELF...
ASSHOLE!

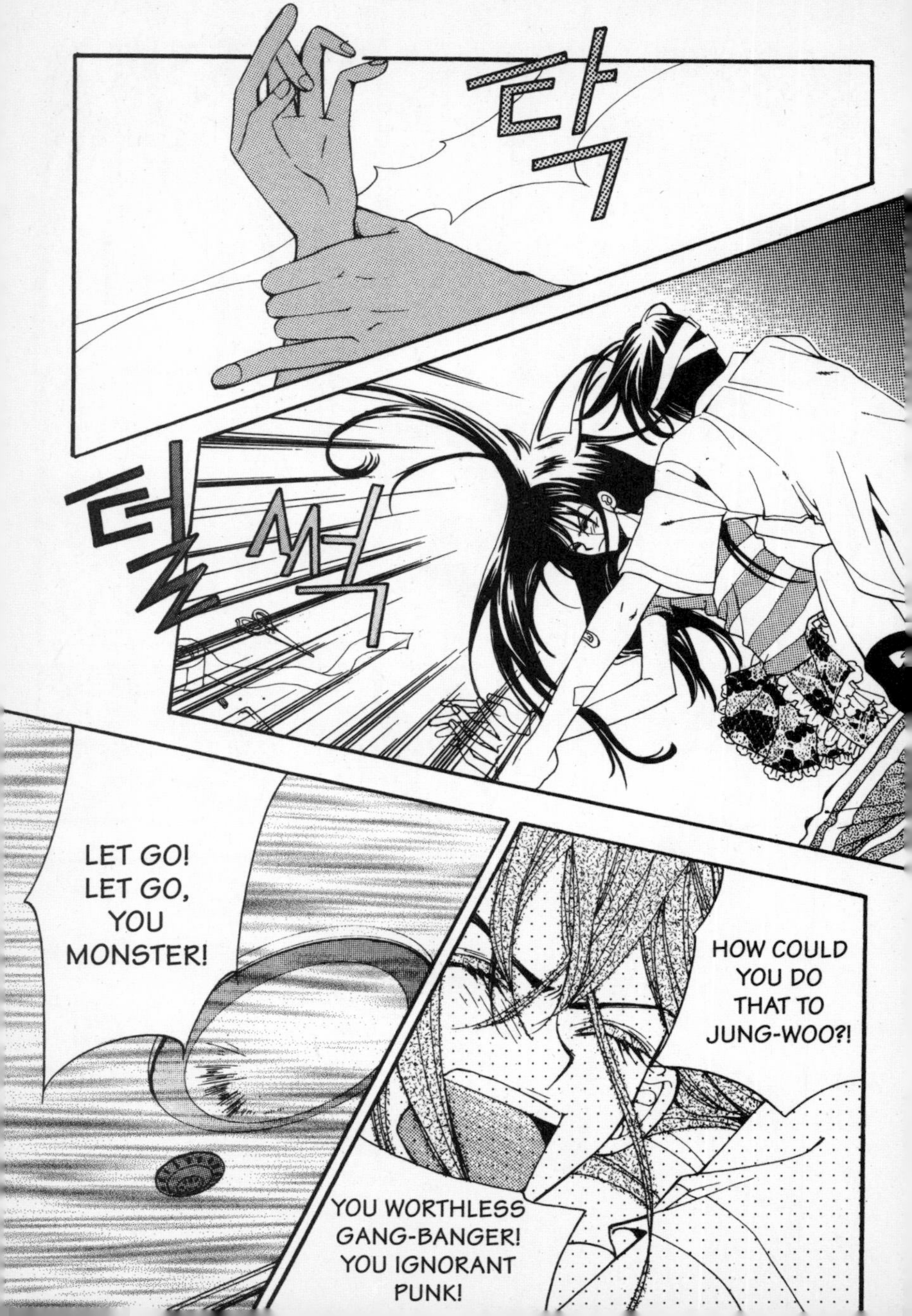
탁
덥썩
LET GO! LET GO, YOU MONSTER!
HOW COULD YOU DO THAT TO JUNG-WOO?!
YOU WORTHLESS GANG-BANGER! YOU IGNORANT PUNK!

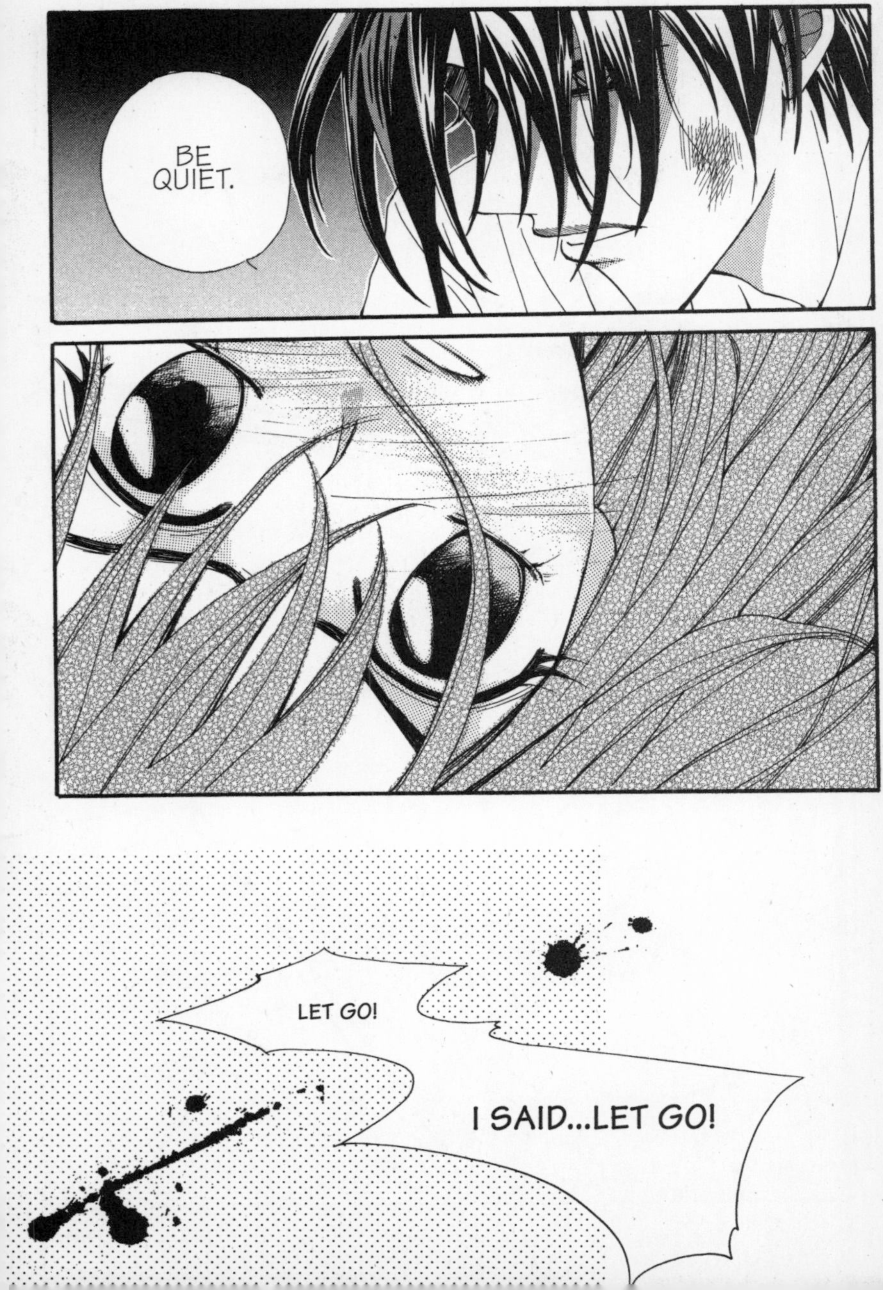
BE QUIET.
LET GO!
I SAID...LET GO!

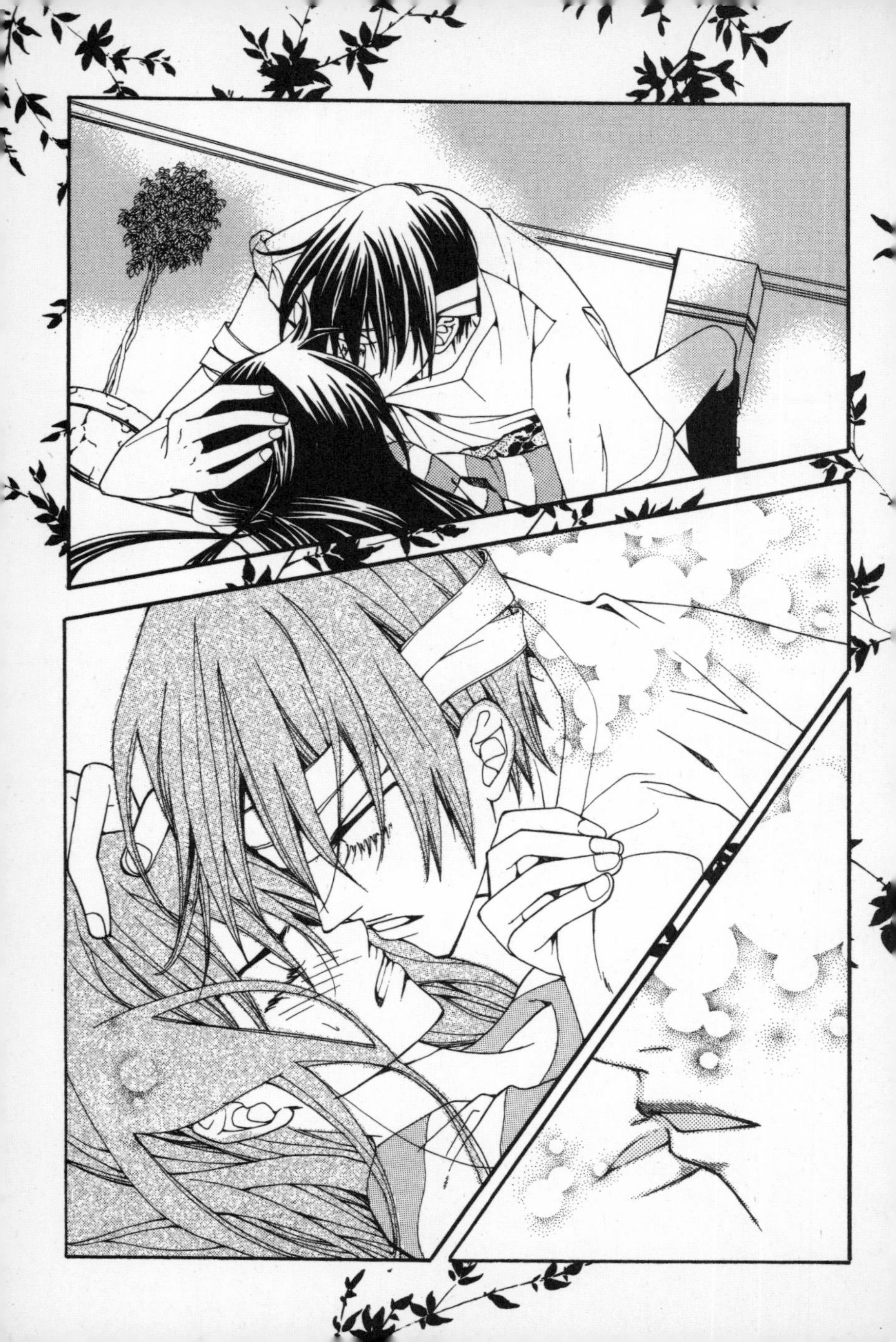

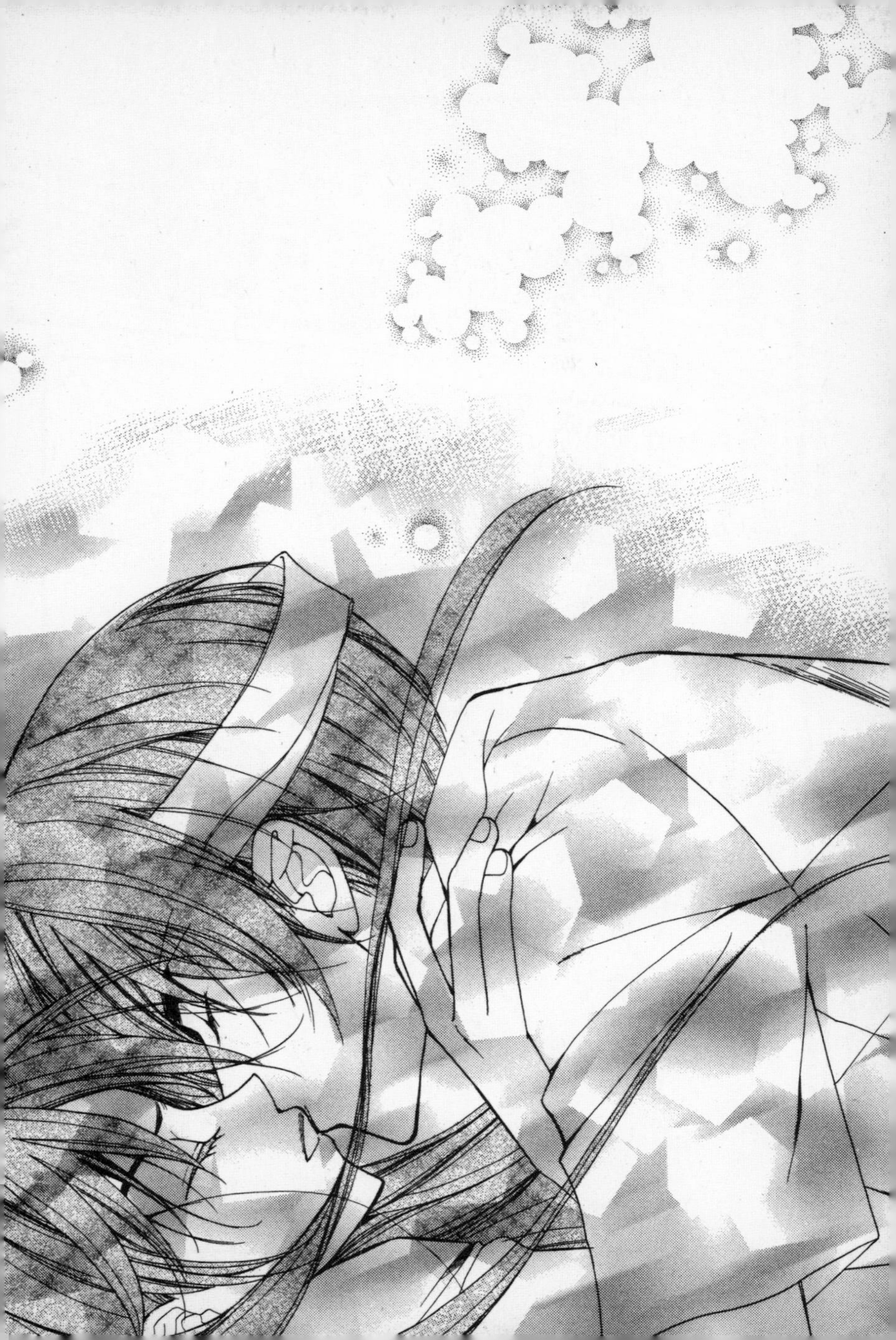

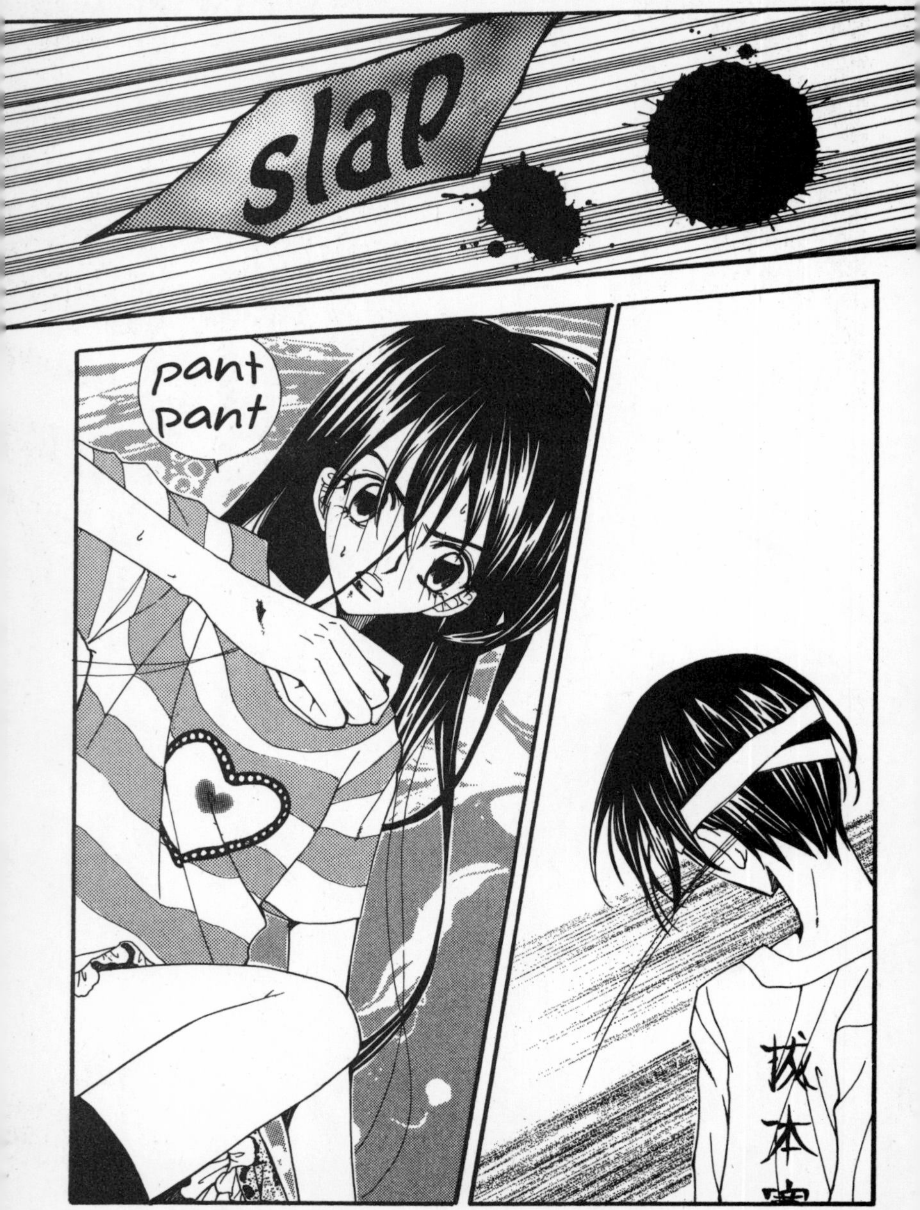
slap
pant pant

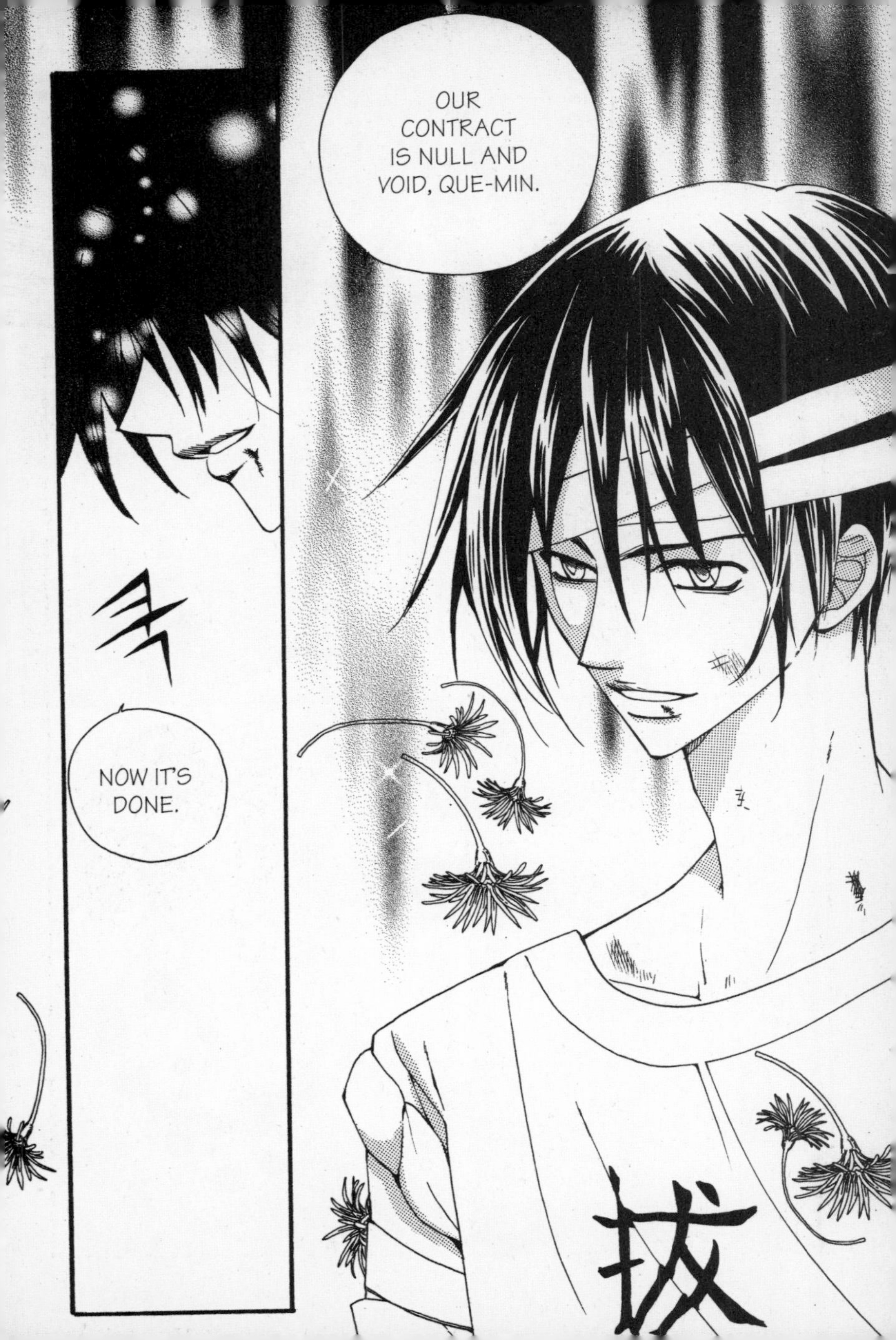
NOW IT'S DONE.
OUR CONTRACT IS NULL AND VOID, QUE-MIN.
抜

HIS KISS...
TASTED LIKE
CIGARETTES
AND BLOOD...

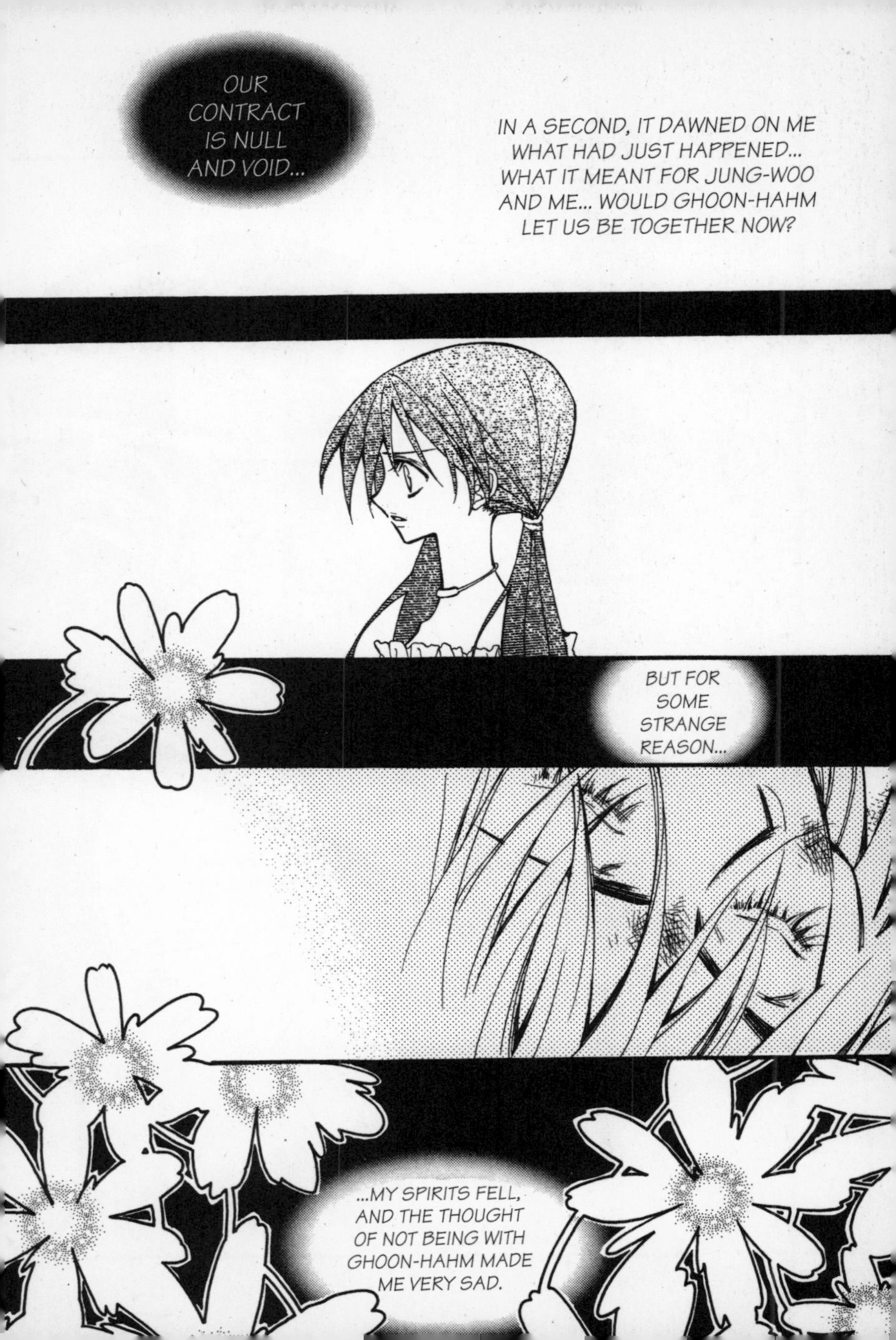
OUR CONTRACT IS NULL AND VOID...
IN A SECOND, IT DAWNED ON ME WHAT HAD JUST HAPPENED... WHAT IT MEANT FOR JUNG-WOO AND ME... WOULD GHOON-HAHM LET US BE TOGETHER NOW?
BUT FOR SOME STRANGE REASON...
...MY SPIRITS FELL, AND THE THOUGHT OF NOT BEING WITH GHOON-HAHM MADE ME VERY SAD.

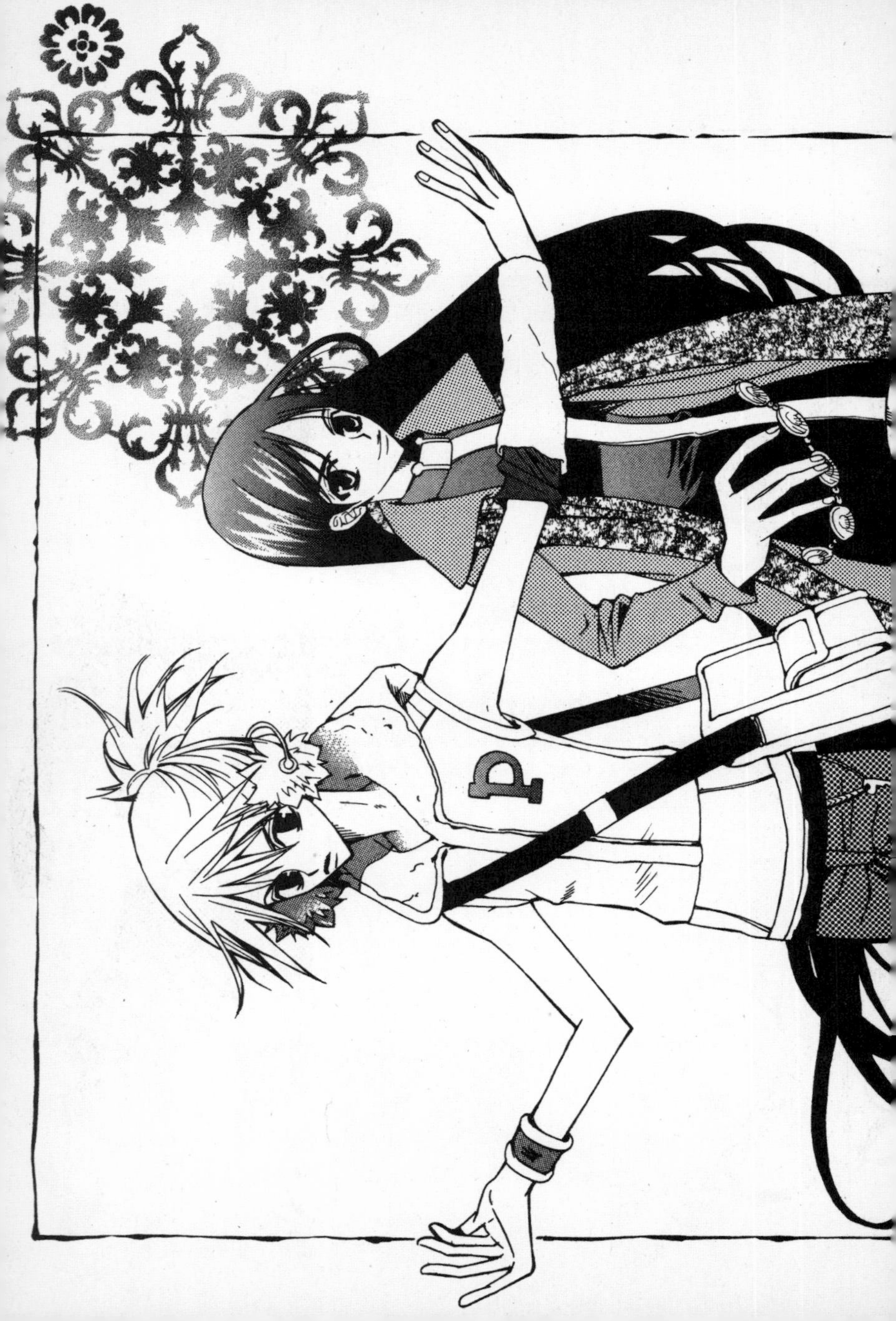

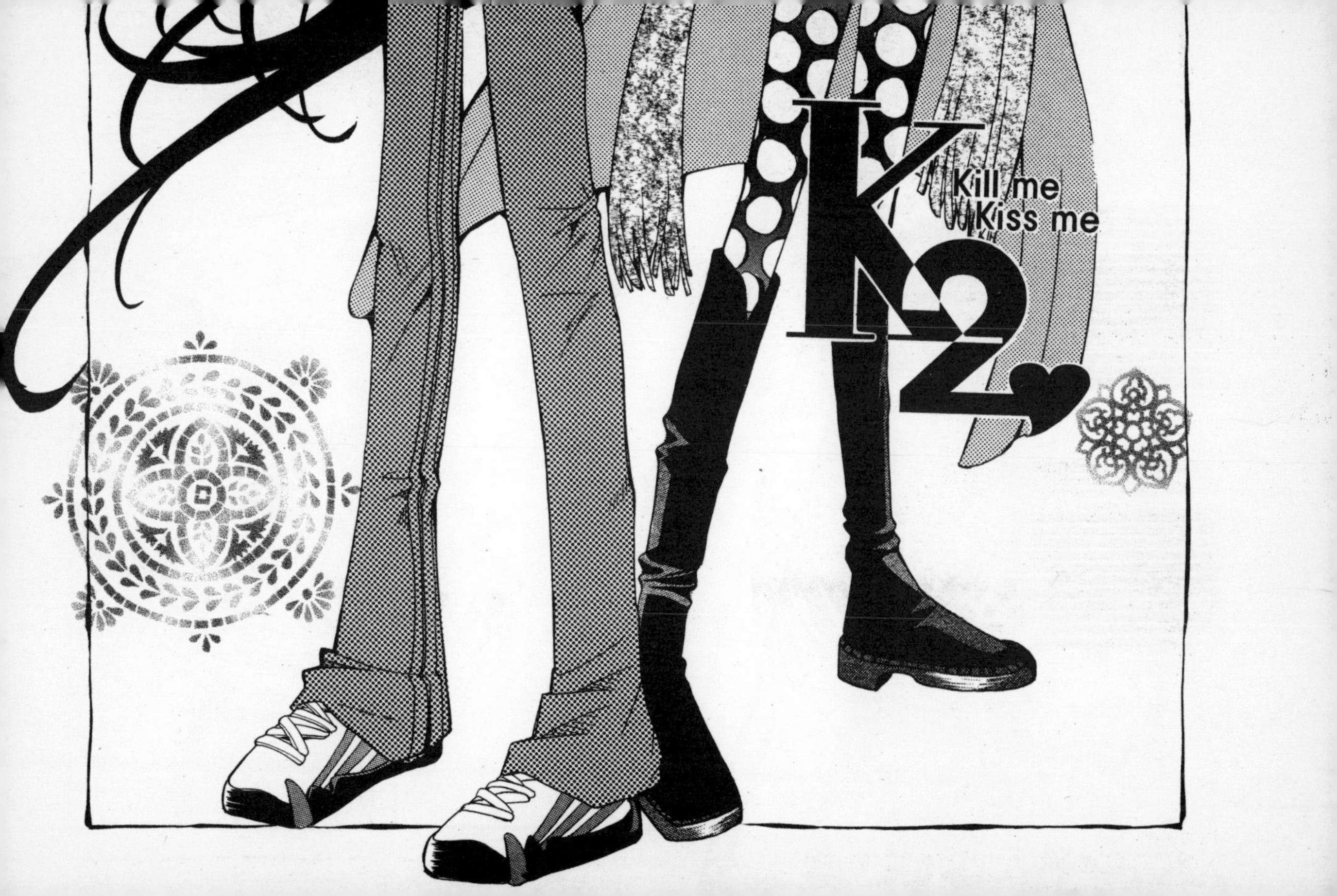
K2
Kill me
Kiss me

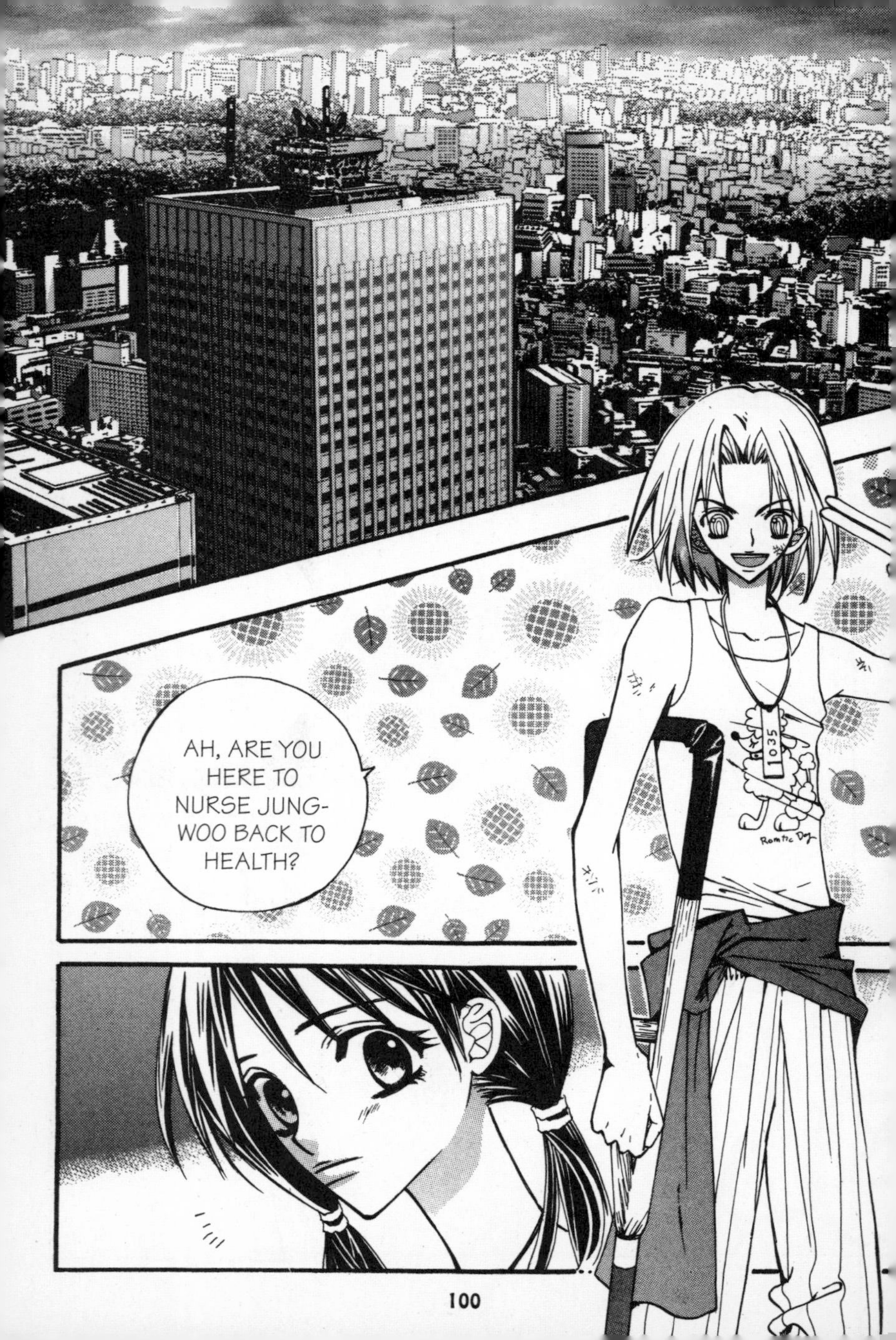
AH, ARE YOU HERE TO NURSE JUNG-WOO BACK TO HEALTH?
1035
Romtic Dog

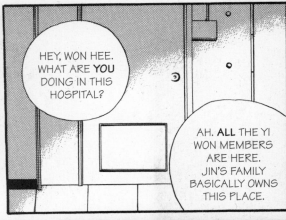

HEY, WON HEE. WHAT ARE **YOU** DOING IN THIS HOSPITAL?

AH. **ALL** THE YI WON MEMBERS ARE HERE. JIN'S FAMILY BASICALLY OWNS THIS PLACE.

KAI'S GUYS REALLY GOT US. EVEN GHOON-HAHM AND JUNG-WOO.

KAI'S GANG?

HUH?

YOU...

...DIDN'T KNOW?

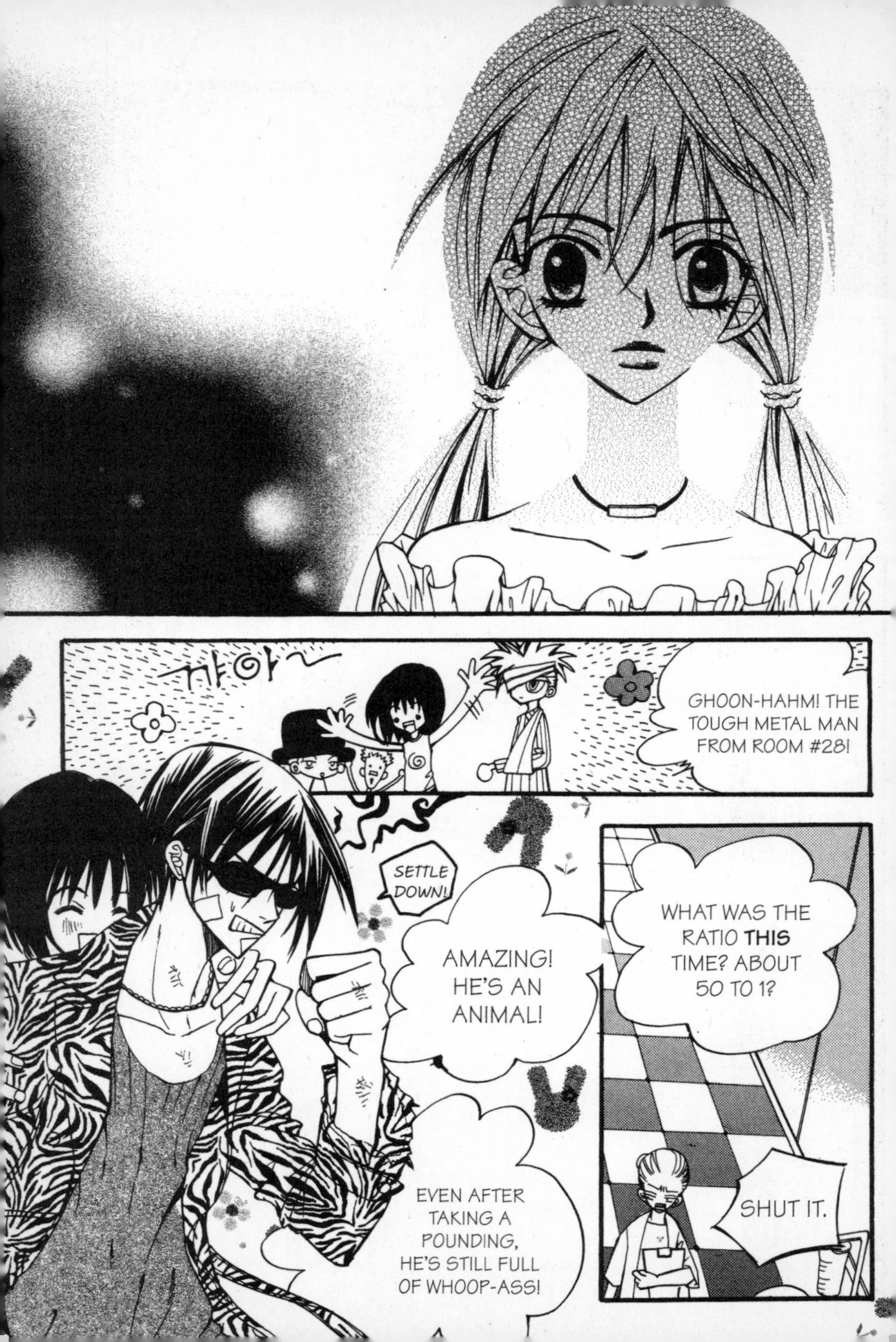
꺄아~
GHOON-HAHM! THE TOUGH METAL MAN FROM ROOM #28!
SETTLE DOWN!
AMAZING! HE'S AN ANIMAL!
EVEN AFTER TAKING A POUNDING, HE'S STILL FULL OF WHOOP-ASS!
WHAT WAS THE RATIO **THIS** TIME? ABOUT 50 TO 1?
SHUT IT.

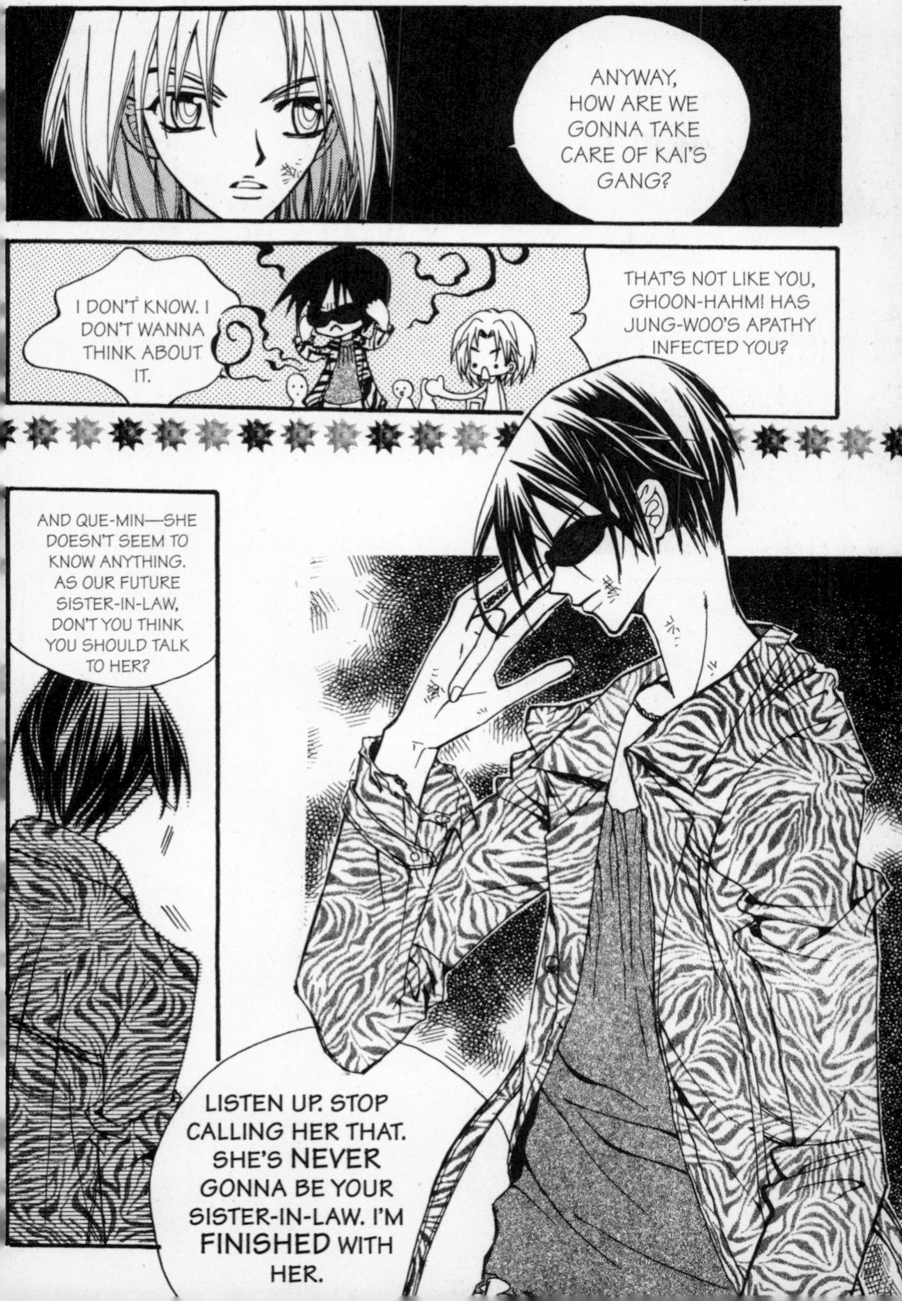
ANYWAY, HOW ARE WE GONNA TAKE CARE OF KAI'S GANG?
I DON'T KNOW. I DON'T WANNA THINK ABOUT IT.
THAT'S NOT LIKE YOU, GHOON-HAHM! HAS JUNG-WOO'S APATHY INFECTED YOU?
AND QUE-MIN—SHE DOESN'T SEEM TO KNOW ANYTHING. AS OUR FUTURE SISTER-IN-LAW, DON'T YOU THINK YOU SHOULD TALK TO HER?
LISTEN UP. STOP CALLING HER THAT. SHE'S NEVER GONNA BE YOUR SISTER-IN-LAW. I'M FINISHED WITH HER.

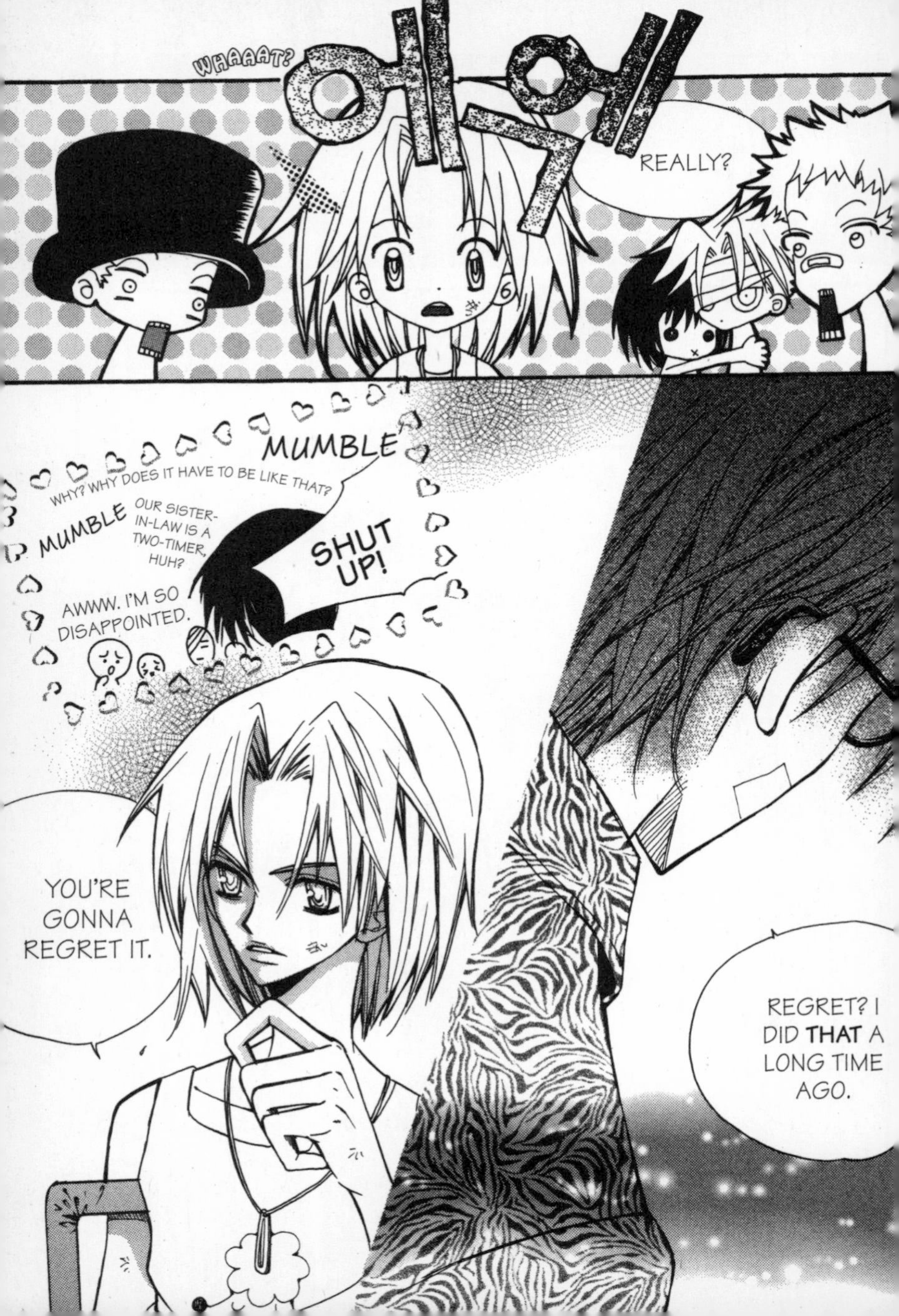
WHAAAT?
REALLY?
MUMBLE
WHY? WHY DOES IT HAVE TO BE LIKE THAT?
MUMBLE
OUR SISTER-IN-LAW IS A TWO-TIMER, HUH?
AWWW. I'M SO DISAPPOINTED.
SHUT UP!
YOU'RE GONNA REGRET IT.
REGRET? I DID **THAT** A LONG TIME AGO.

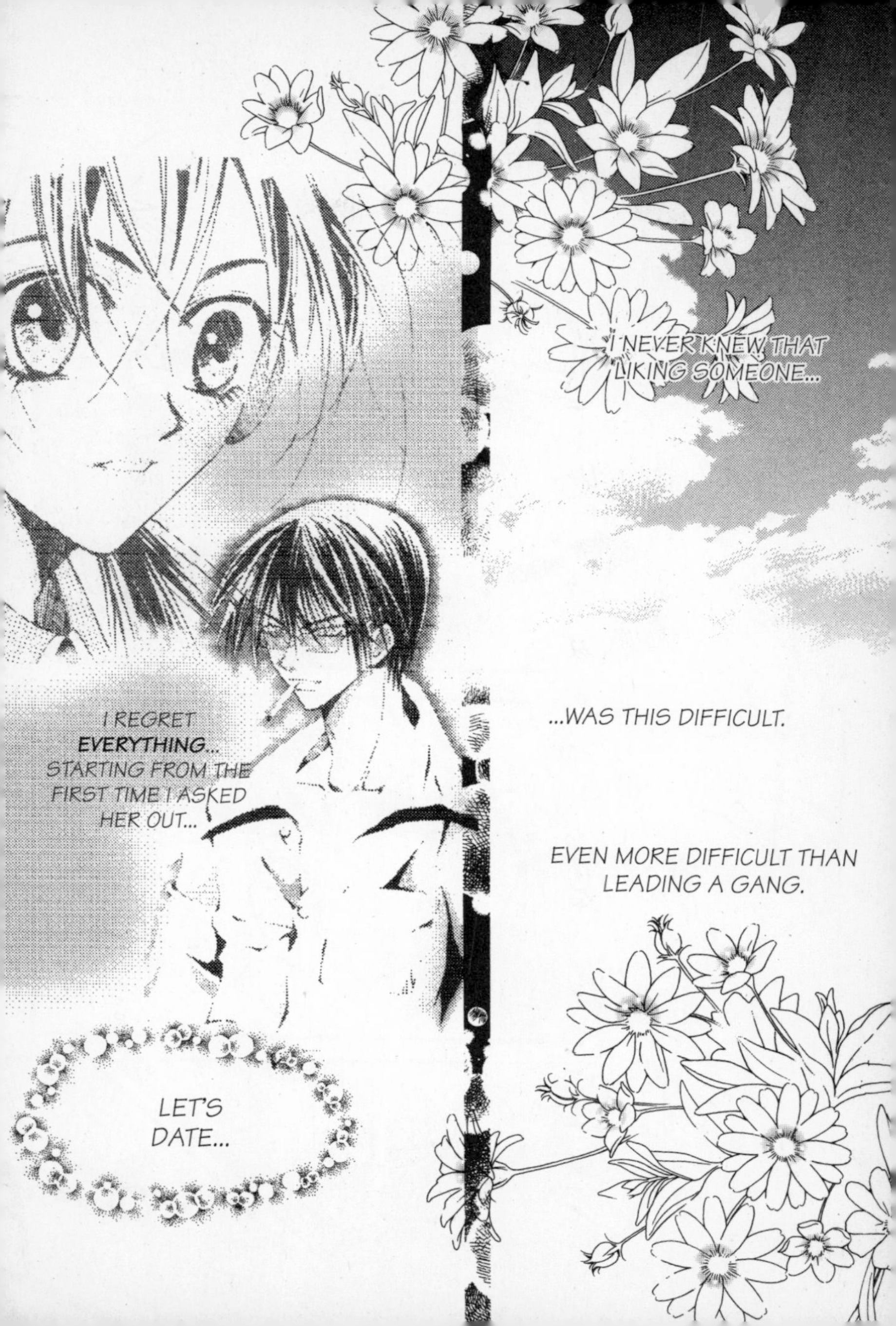
I REGRET EVERYTHING... STARTING FROM THE FIRST TIME I ASKED HER OUT...
LET'S DATE...
I NEVER KNEW THAT LIKING SOMEONE...
...WAS THIS DIFFICULT.
EVEN MORE DIFFICULT THAN LEADING A GANG.

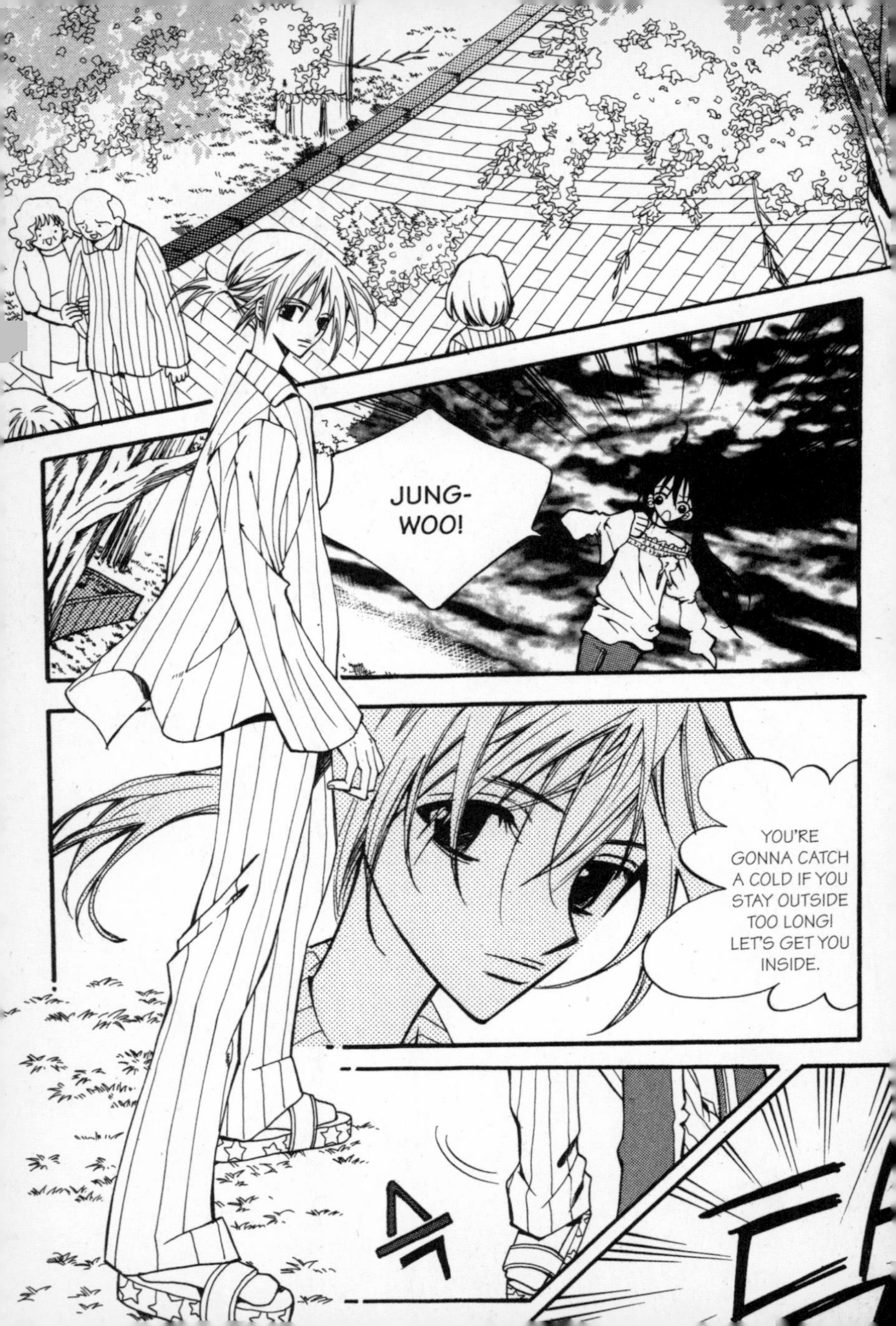
JUNG-
WOO!
YOU'RE
GONNA CATCH
A COLD IF YOU
STAY OUTSIDE
TOO LONG!
LET'S GET YOU
INSIDE.

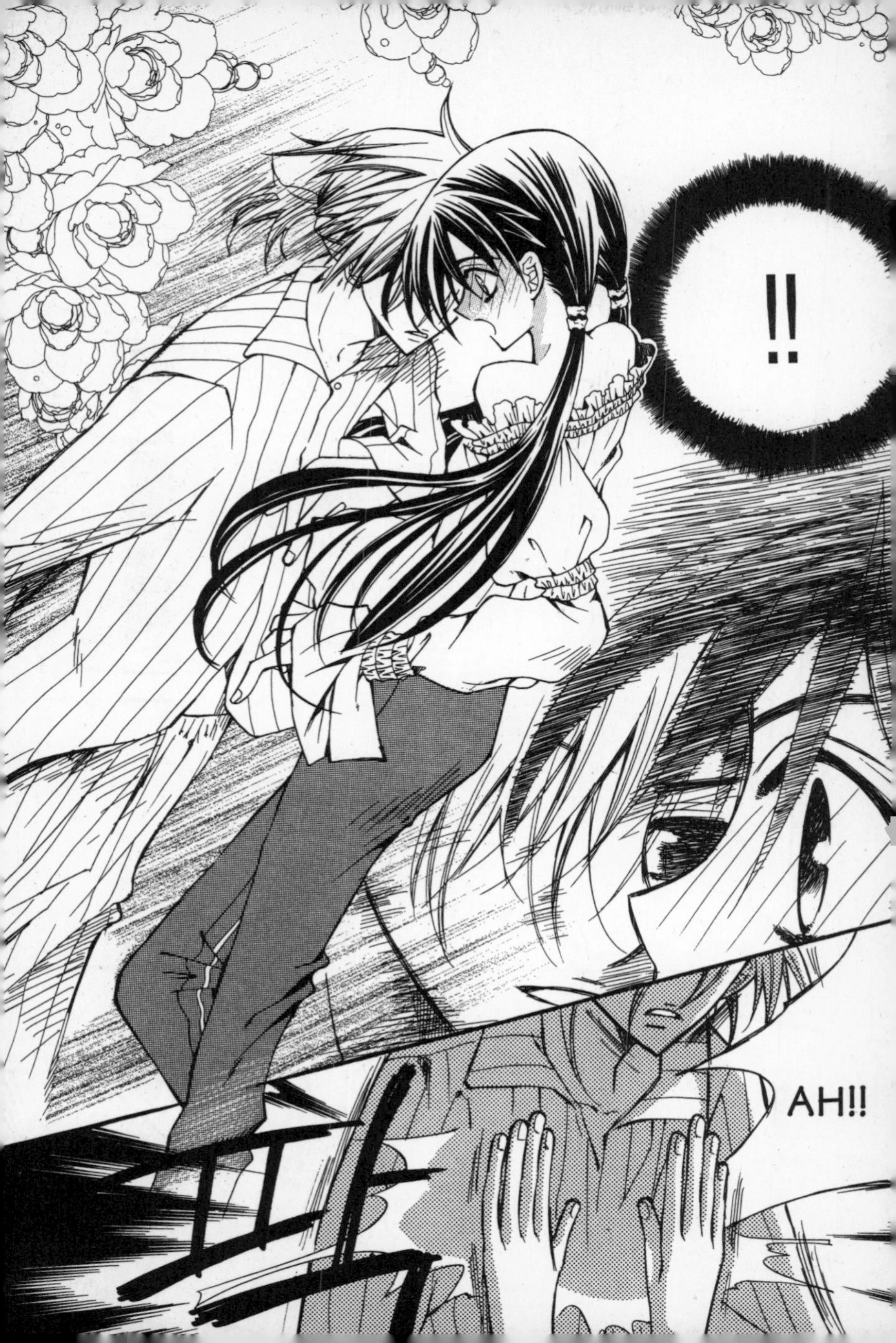
!!
AH!!

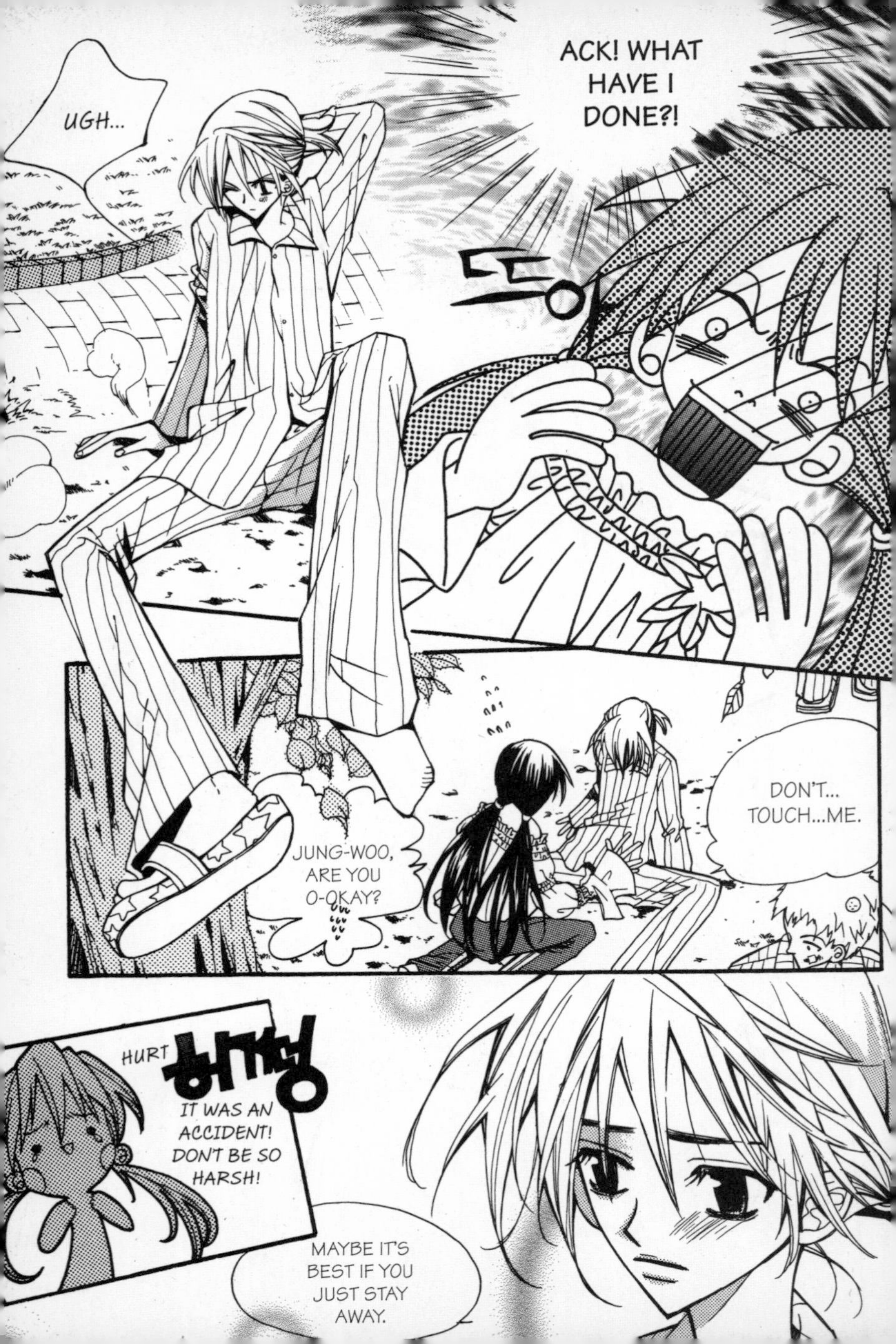
UGH...
ACK! WHAT HAVE I DONE?!
JUNG-WOO, ARE YOU O-OKAY?
DON'T... TOUCH...ME.
HURT
IT WAS AN ACCIDENT! DON'T BE SO HARSH!
MAYBE IT'S BEST IF YOU JUST STAY AWAY.

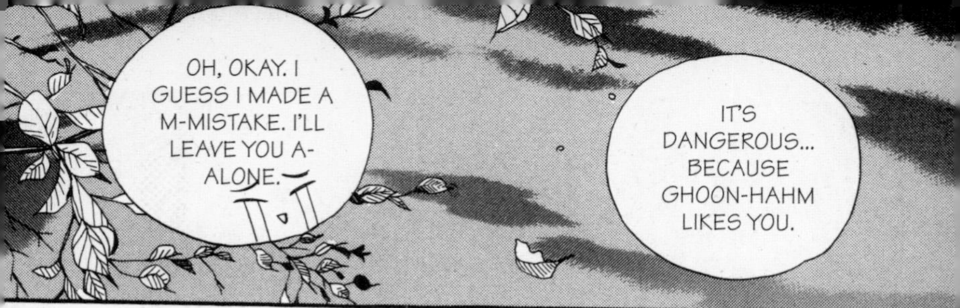
OH, OKAY. I GUESS I MADE A M-MISTAKE. I'LL LEAVE YOU A-ALONE.
IT'S DANGEROUS... BECAUSE GHOON-HAHM LIKES YOU.
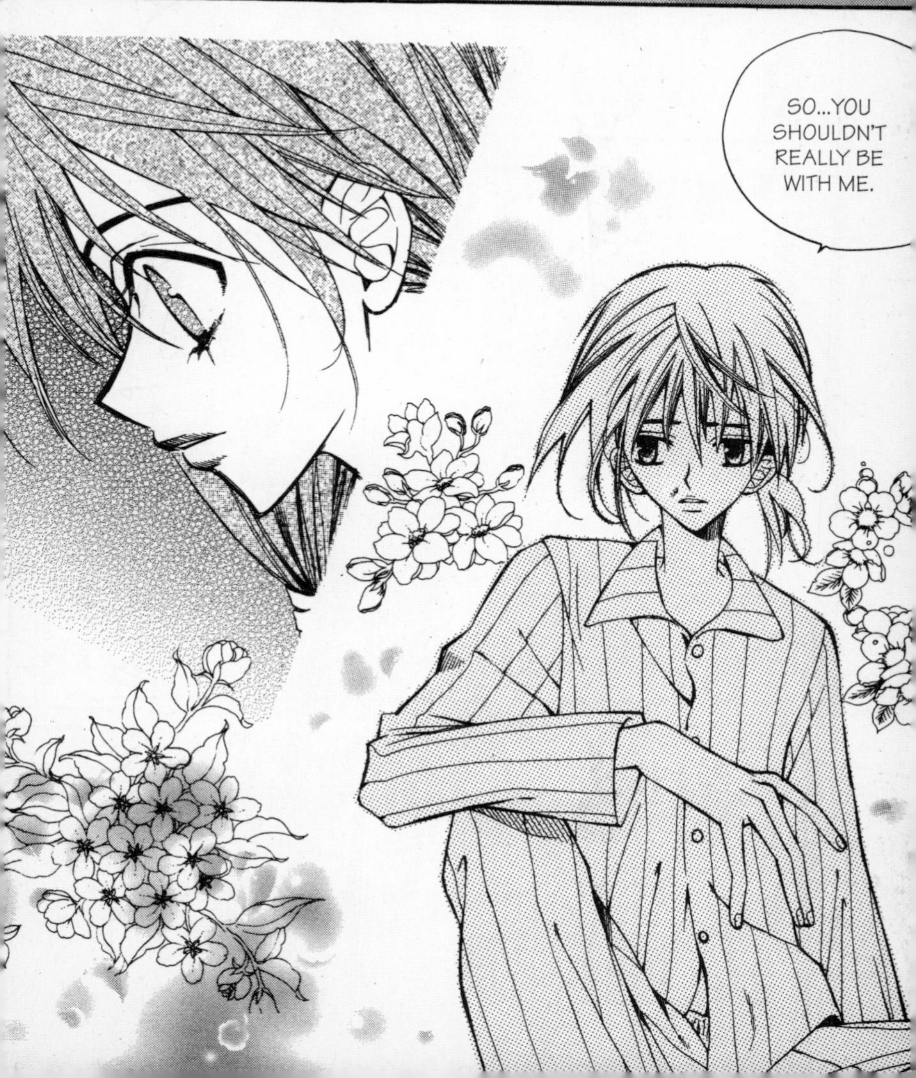
SO...YOU SHOULDN'T REALLY BE WITH ME.

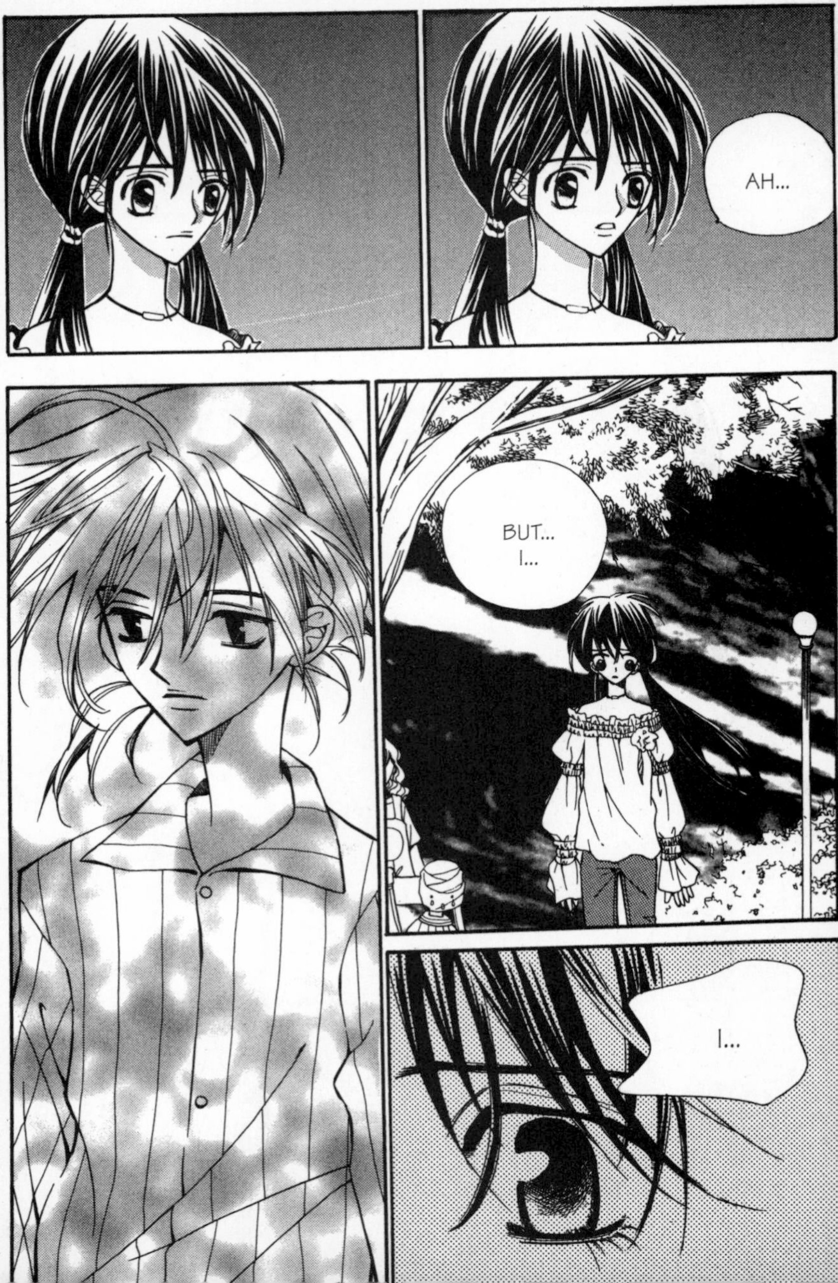
AH...
BUT...
I...
I...

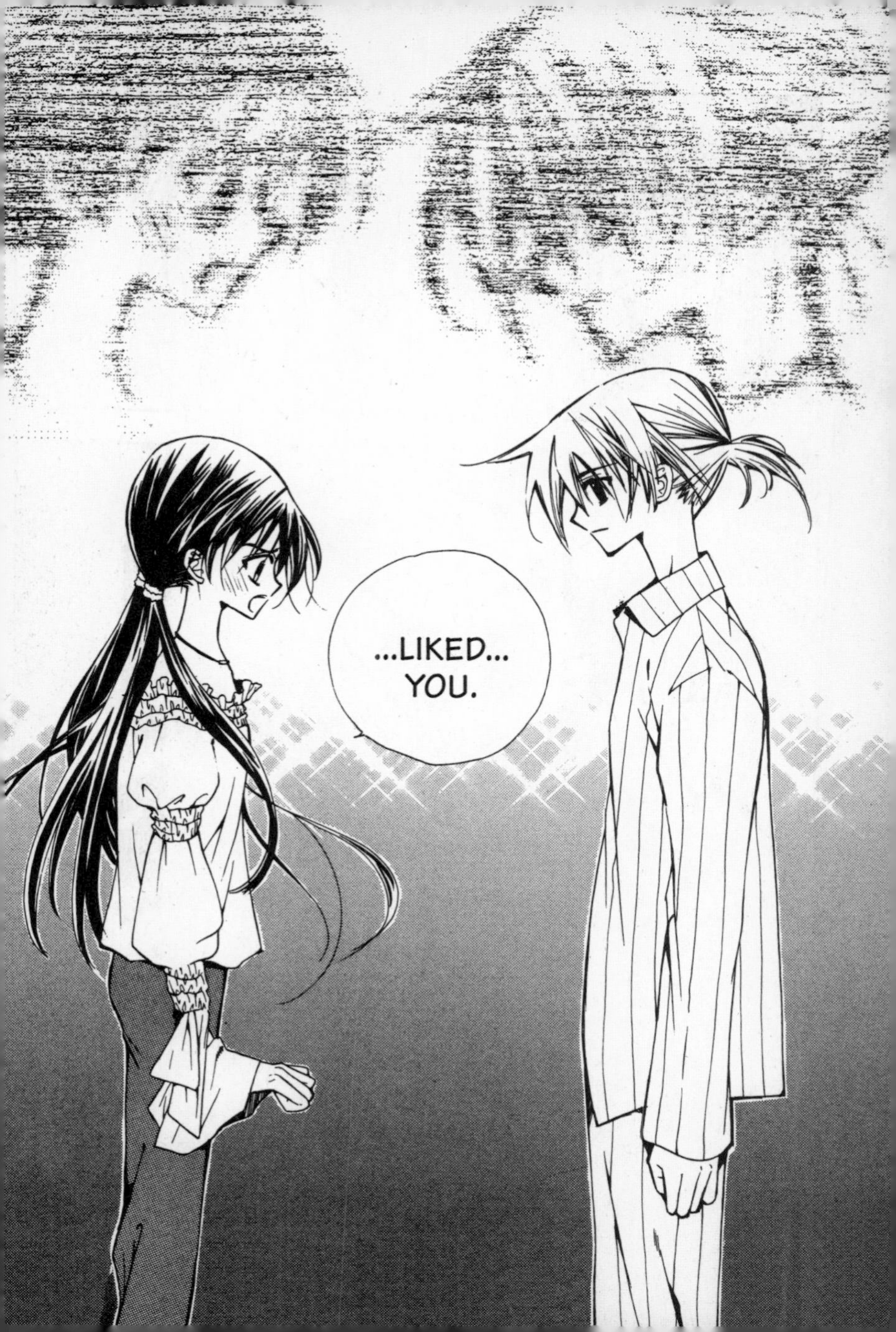
...LIKED... YOU.

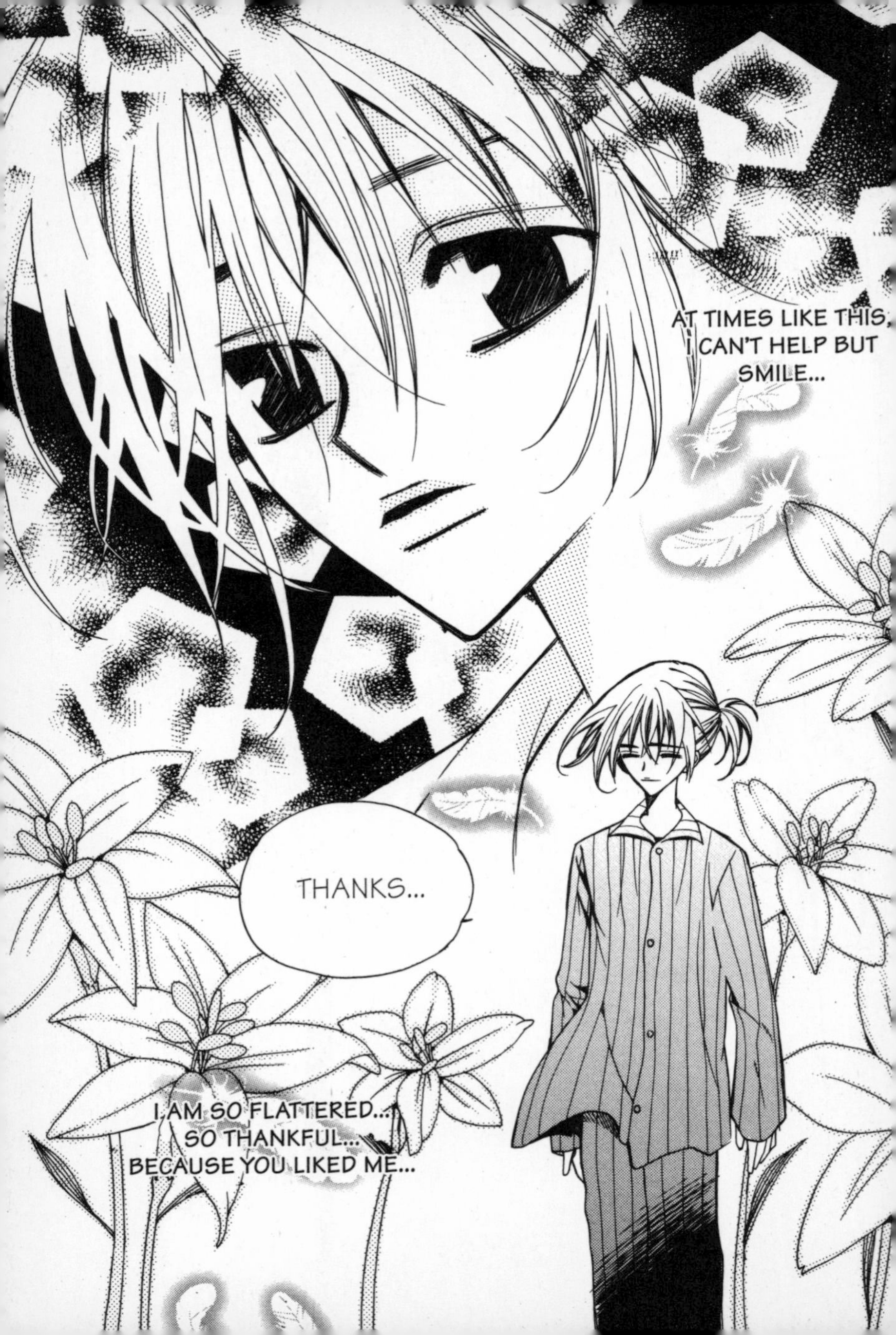
AT TIMES LIKE THIS, I CAN'T HELP BUT SMILE...
THANKS...
I AM SO FLATTERED... SO THANKFUL... BECAUSE YOU LIKED ME...

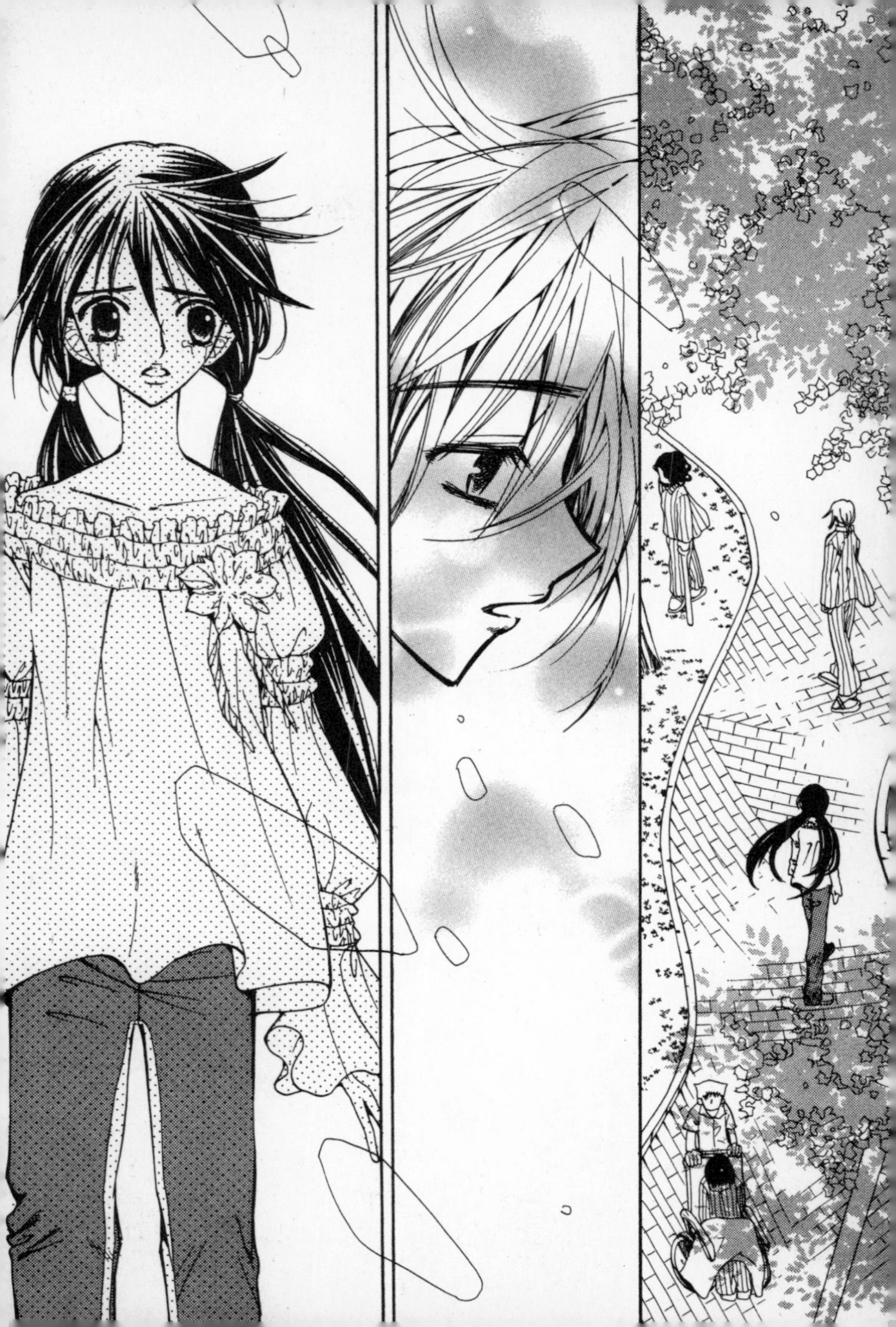

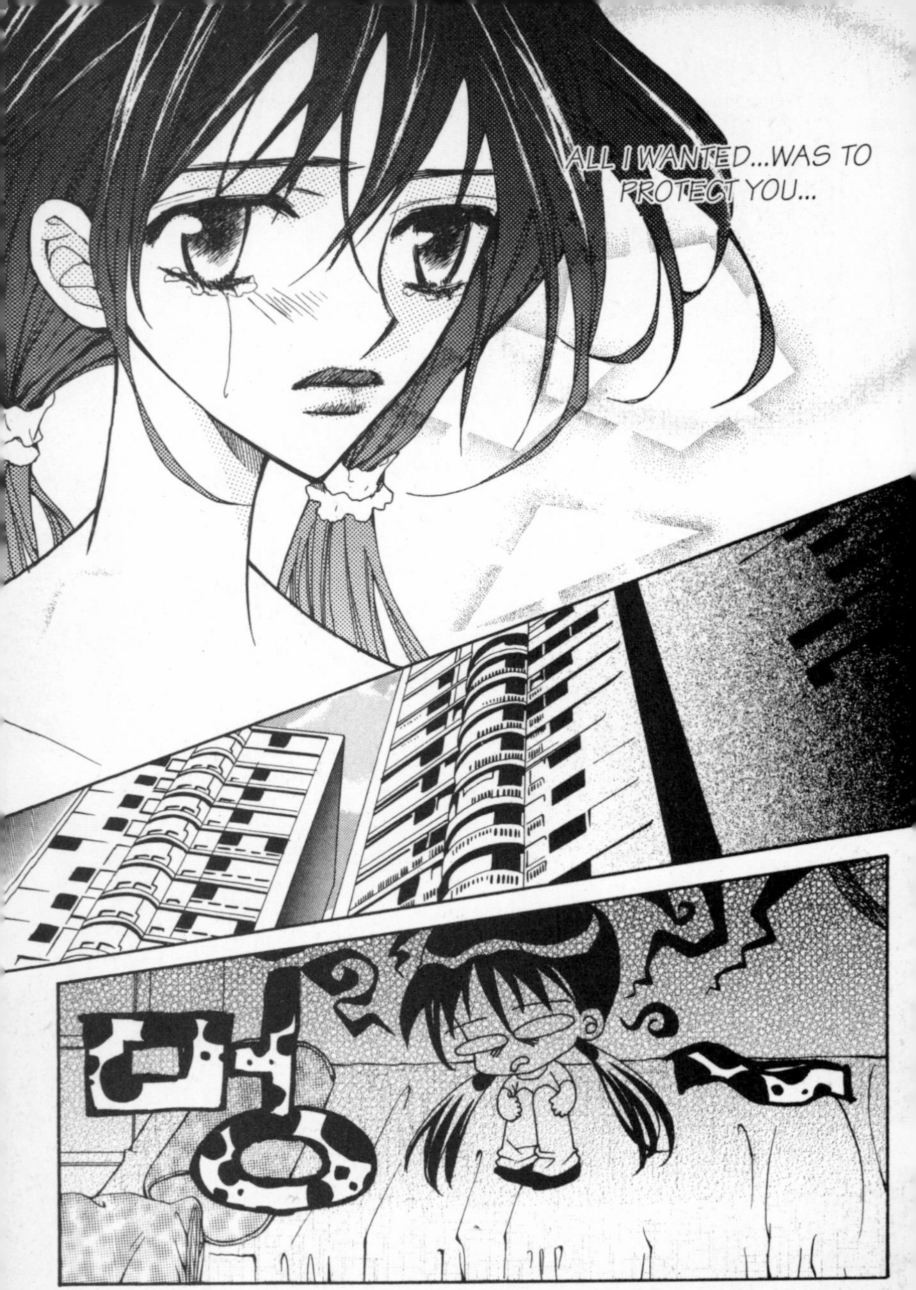
ALL I WANTED...WAS TO PROTECT YOU...

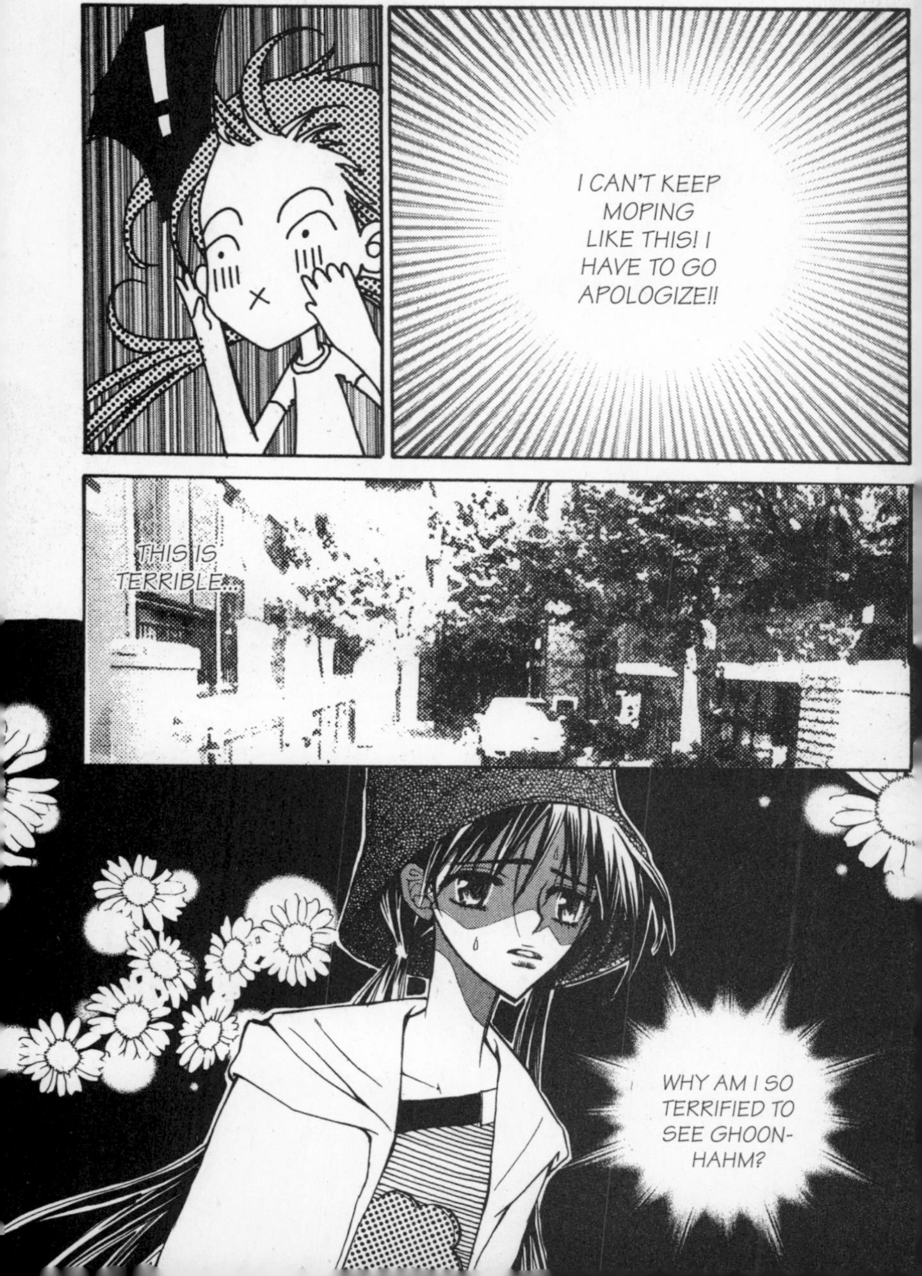
!
I CAN'T KEEP MOPING LIKE THIS! I HAVE TO GO APOLOGIZE!!
THIS IS TERRIBLE...
WHY AM I SO TERRIFIED TO SEE GHOON-HAHM?

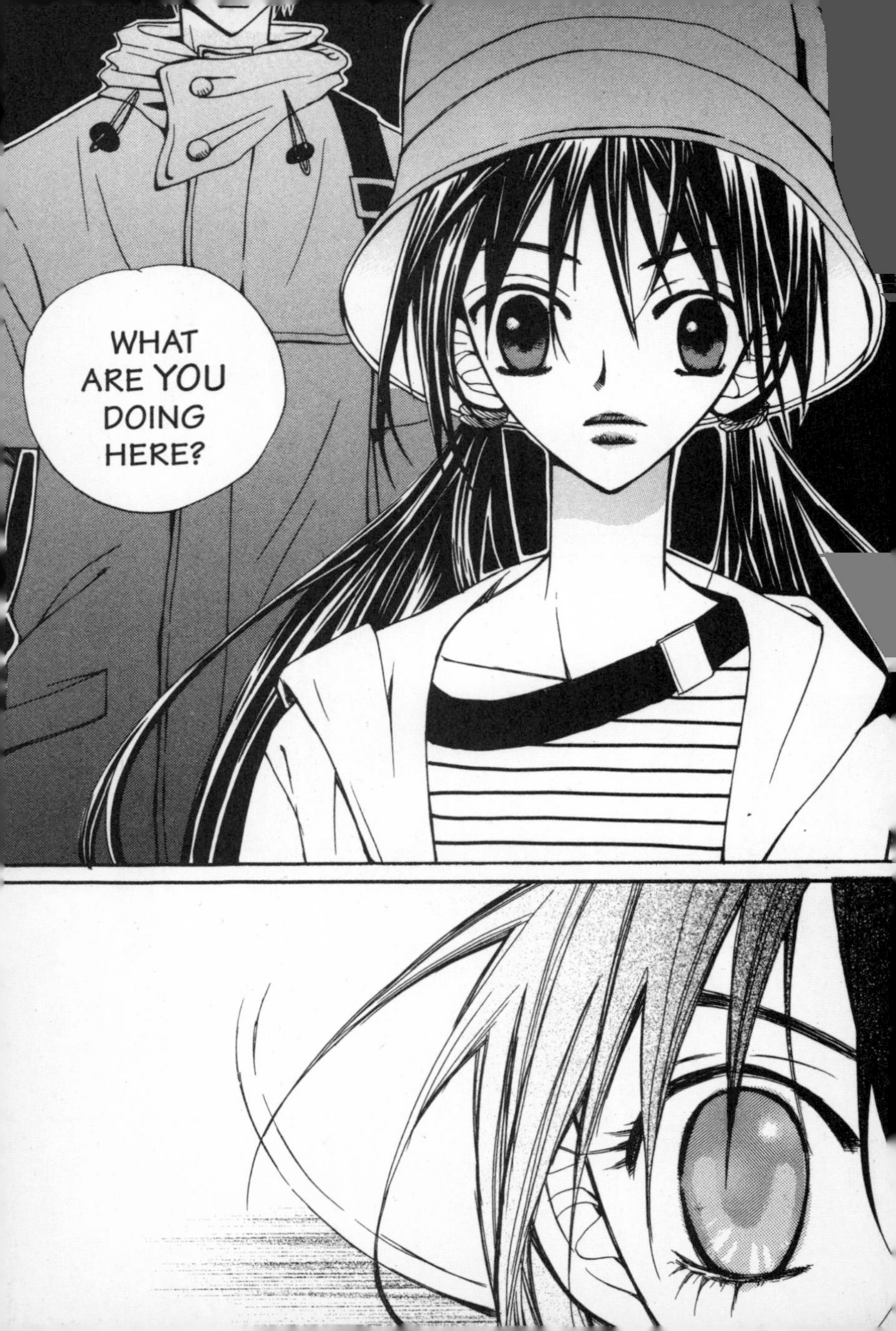
WHAT ARE YOU DOING HERE?

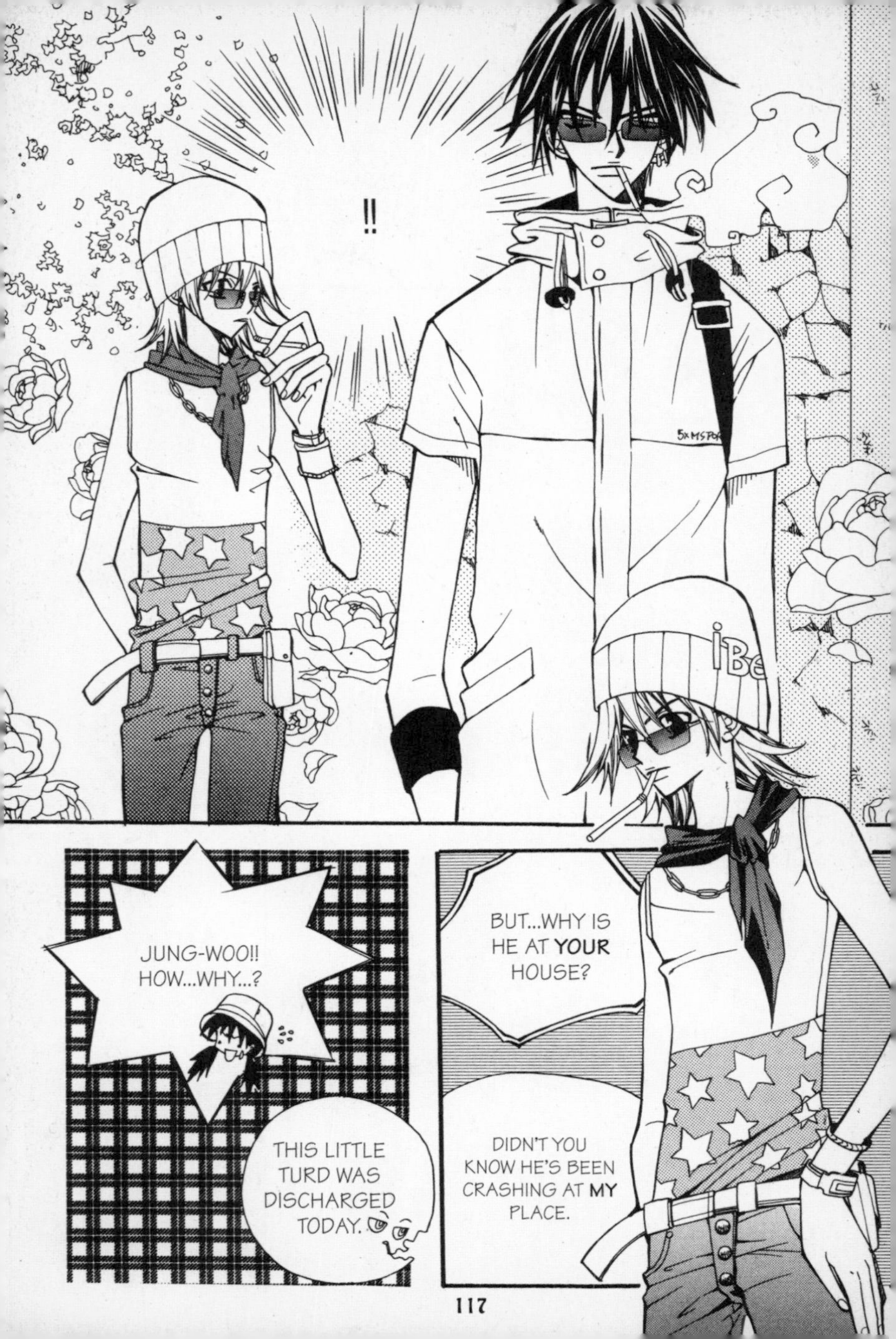
!!
JUNG-WOO!! HOW...WHY...?
THIS LITTLE TURD WAS DISCHARGED TODAY.
BUT...WHY IS HE AT **YOUR** HOUSE?
DIDN'T YOU KNOW HE'S BEEN CRASHING AT **MY** PLACE.

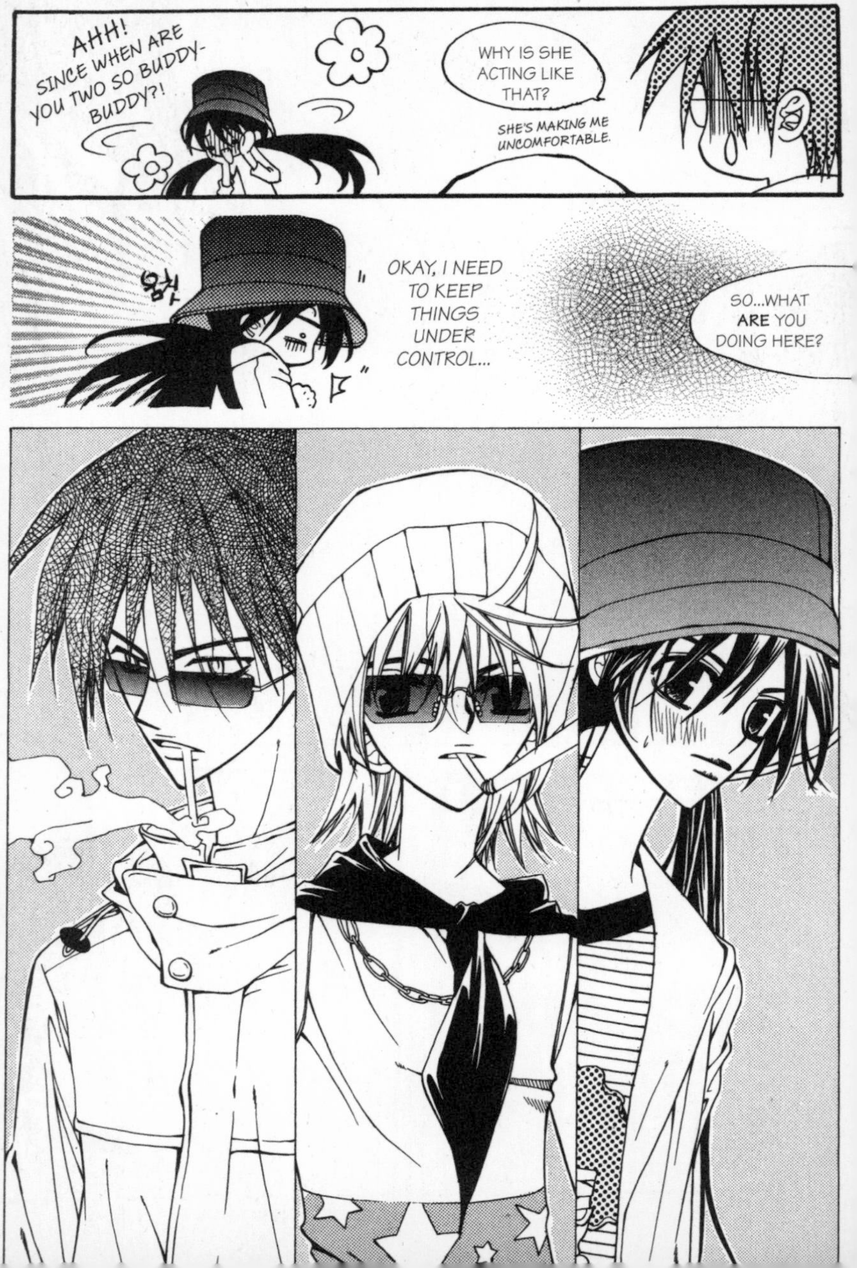

AHH! SINCE WHEN ARE YOU TWO SO BUDDY-BUDDY?!
WHY IS SHE ACTING LIKE THAT?
SHE'S MAKING ME UNCOMFORTABLE.
움찔
OKAY, I NEED TO KEEP THINGS UNDER CONTROL...
SO...WHAT **ARE** YOU DOING HERE?

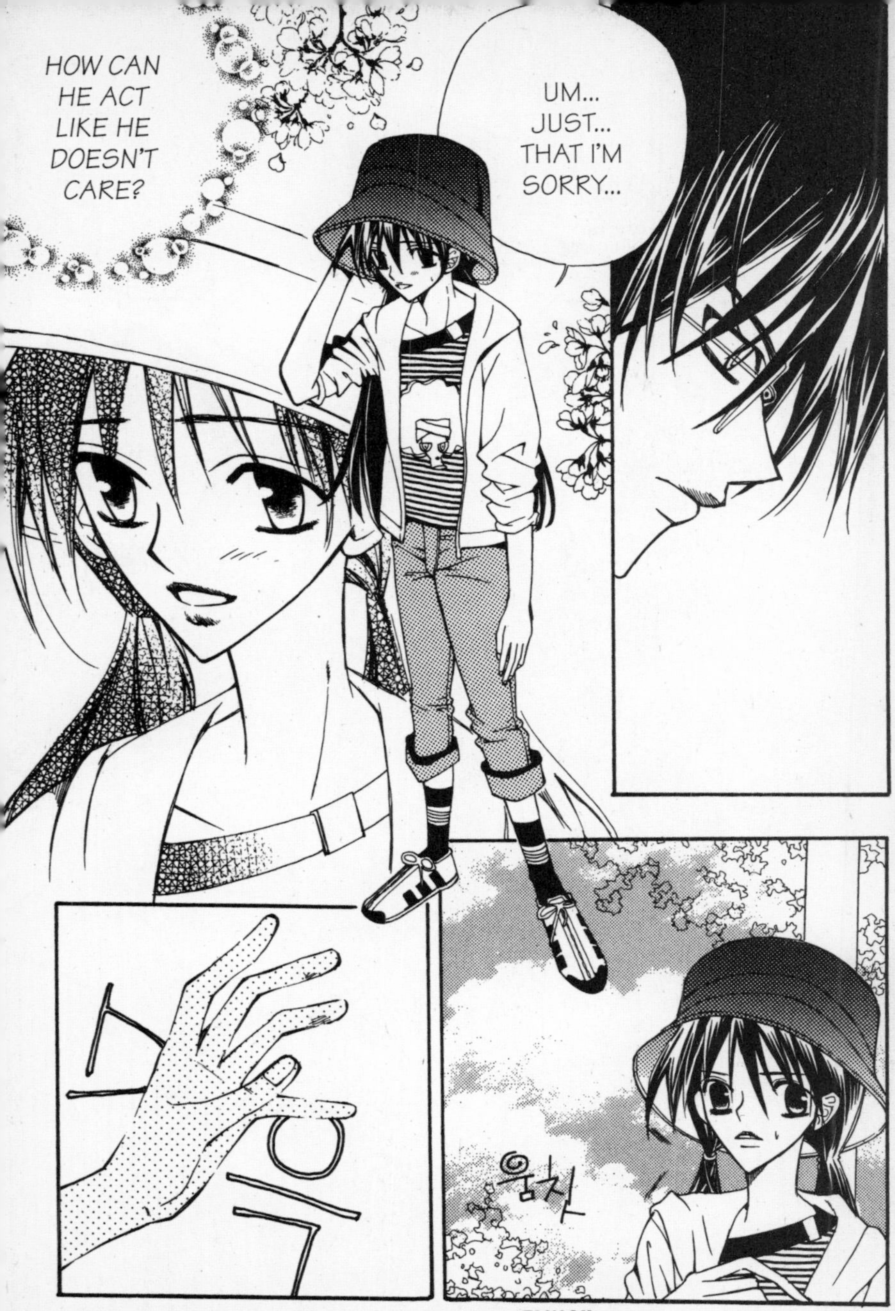
HOW CAN HE ACT LIKE HE DOESN'T CARE?
UM... JUST... THAT I'M SORRY...
움찔

FLINCH

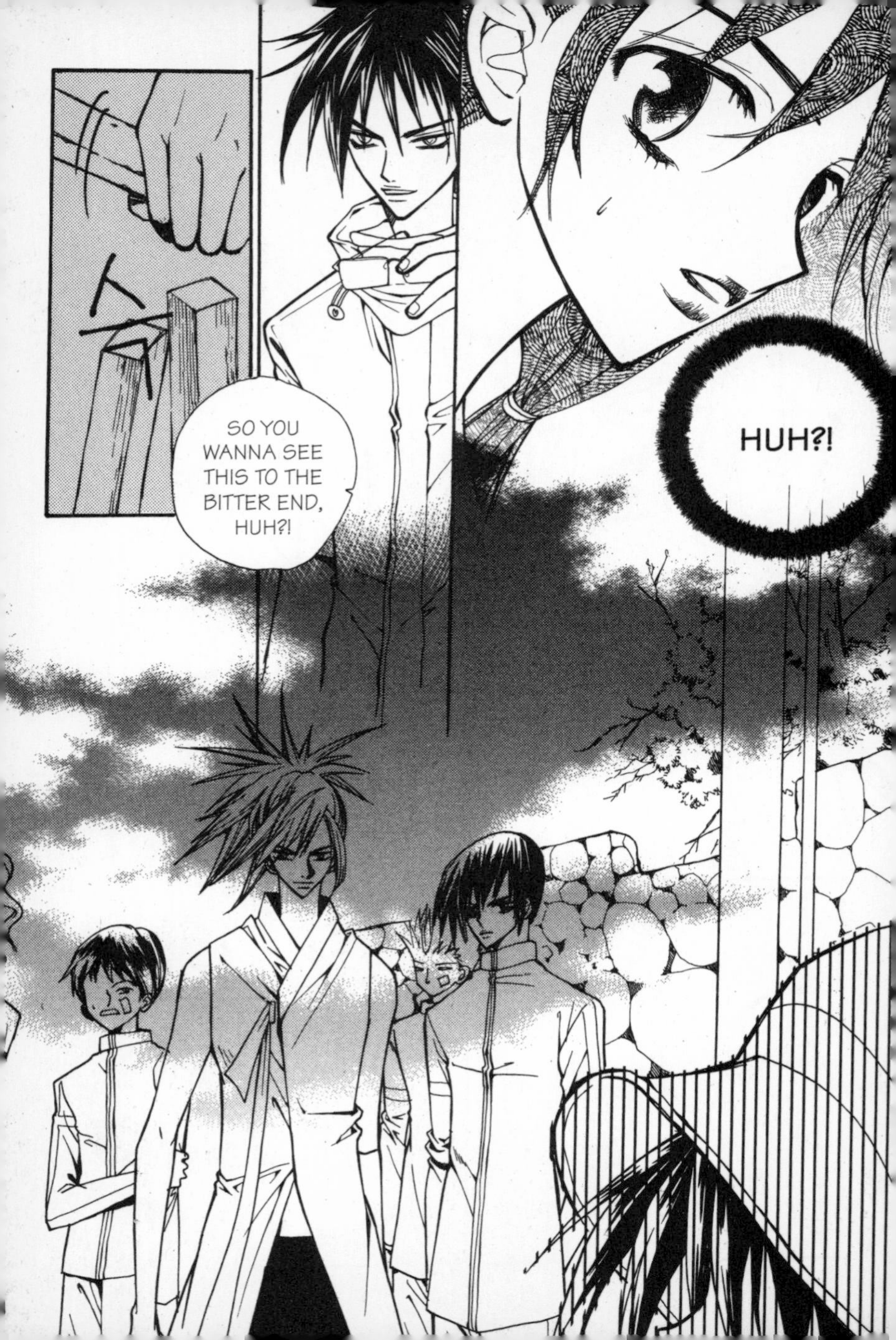
SO YOU WANNA SEE THIS TO THE BITTER END, HUH?!
HUH?!

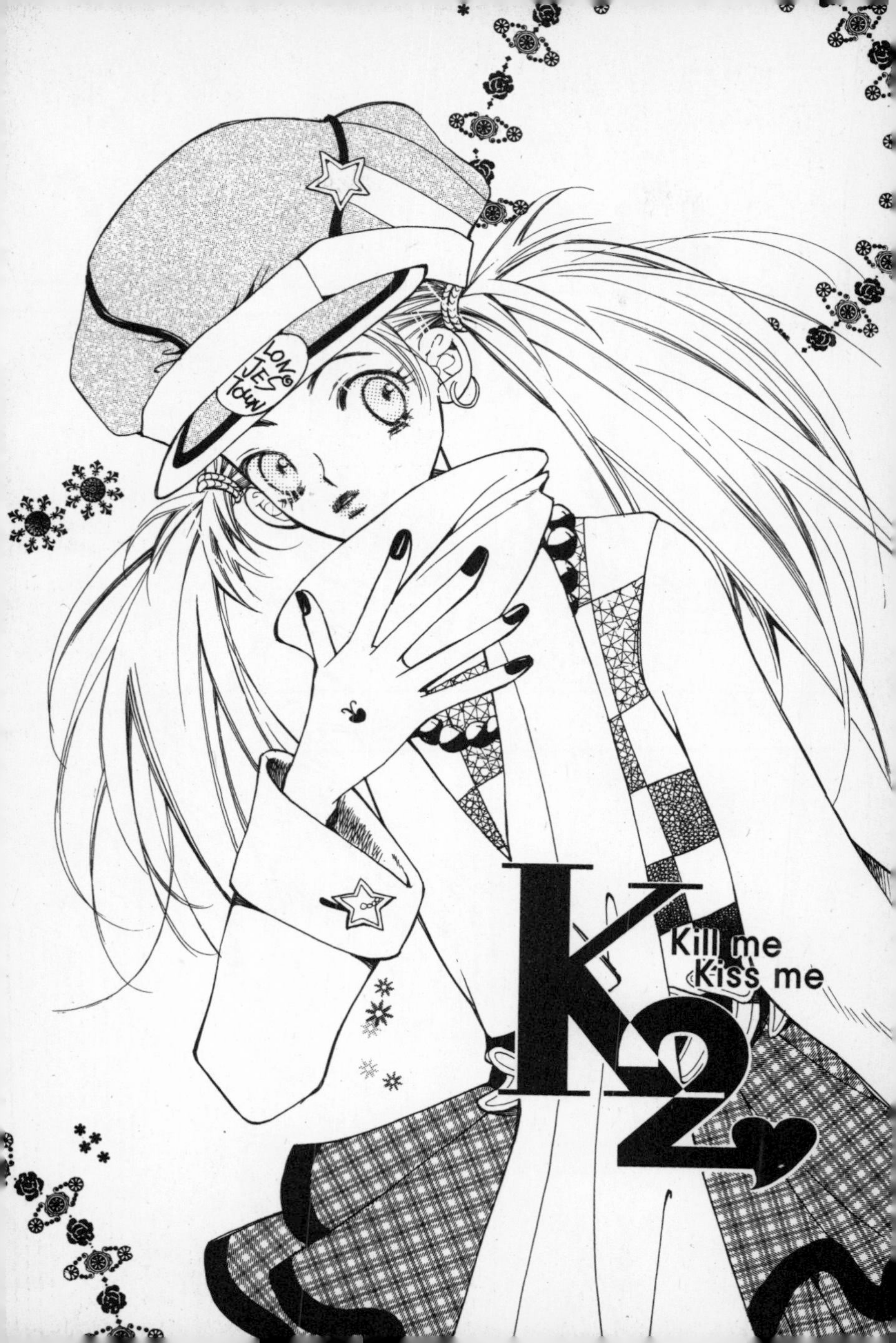
K2
Kill me
Kiss me

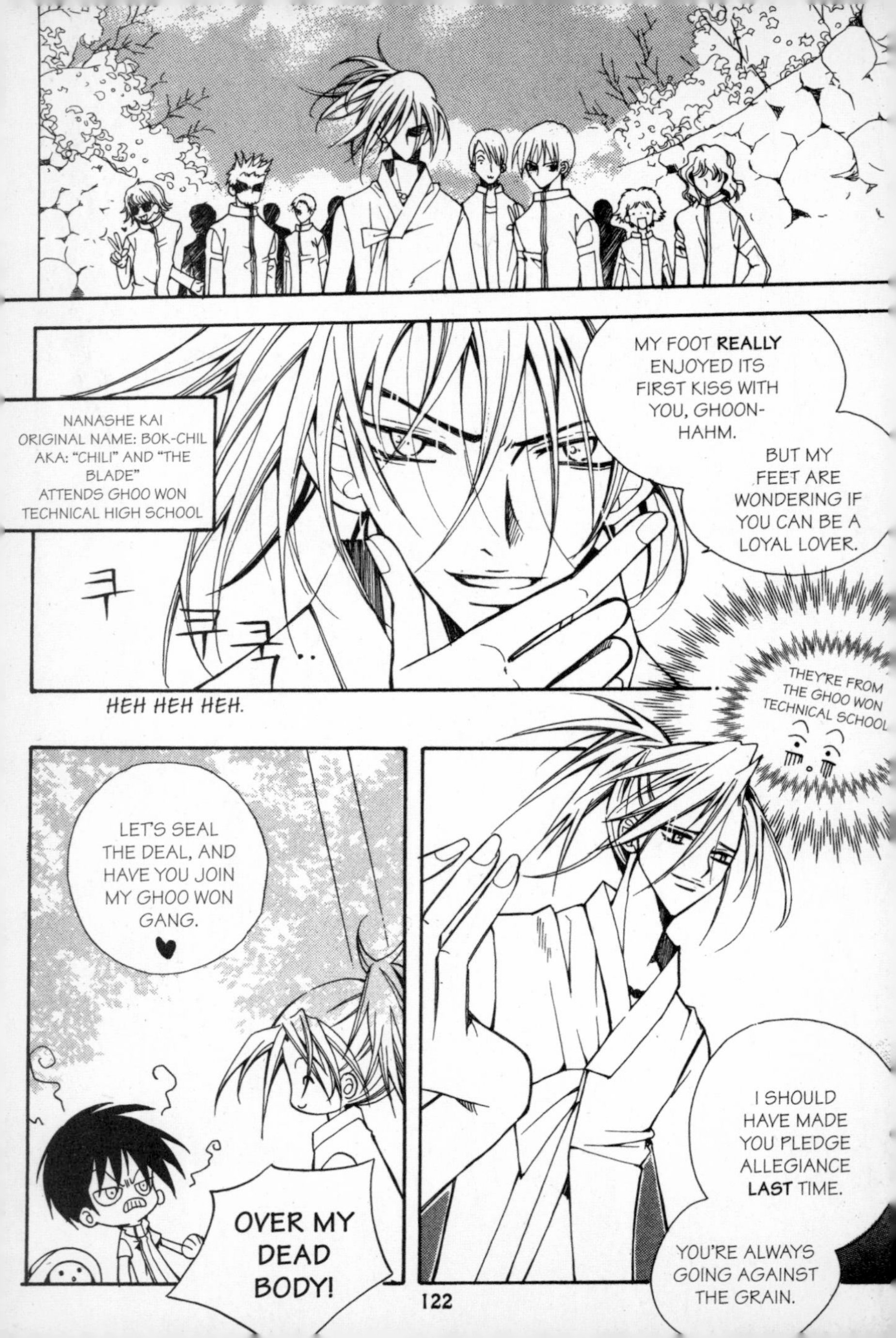
NANASHE KAI
ORIGINAL NAME: BOK-CHIL
AKA: "CHILI" AND "THE BLADE"
ATTENDS GHOO WON TECHNICAL HIGH SCHOOL
크 크크..
MY FOOT **REALLY** ENJOYED ITS FIRST KISS WITH YOU, GHOON-HAHM.
BUT MY FEET ARE WONDERING IF YOU CAN BE A LOYAL LOVER.
HEH HEH HEH.
LET'S SEAL THE DEAL, AND HAVE YOU JOIN MY GHOO WON GANG.
OVER MY DEAD BODY!
THEY'RE FROM THE GHOO WON TECHNICAL SCHOOL
I SHOULD HAVE MADE YOU PLEDGE ALLEGIANCE **LAST** TIME.
YOU'RE ALWAYS GOING AGAINST THE GRAIN.

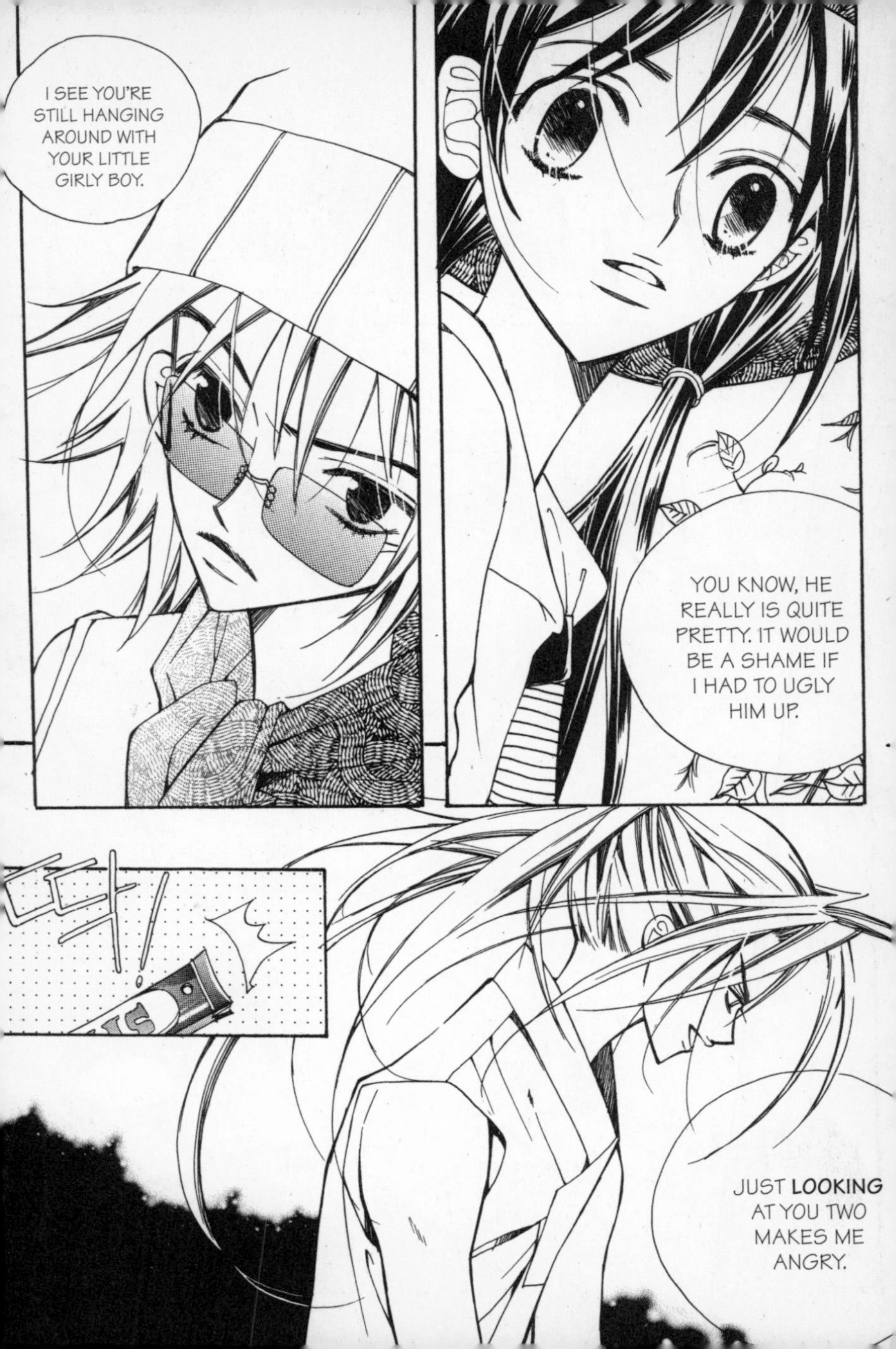
I SEE YOU'RE STILL HANGING AROUND WITH YOUR LITTLE GIRLY BOY.
YOU KNOW, HE REALLY IS QUITE PRETTY. IT WOULD BE A SHAME IF I HAD TO UGLY HIM UP.
JUST **LOOKING** AT YOU TWO MAKES ME ANGRY.

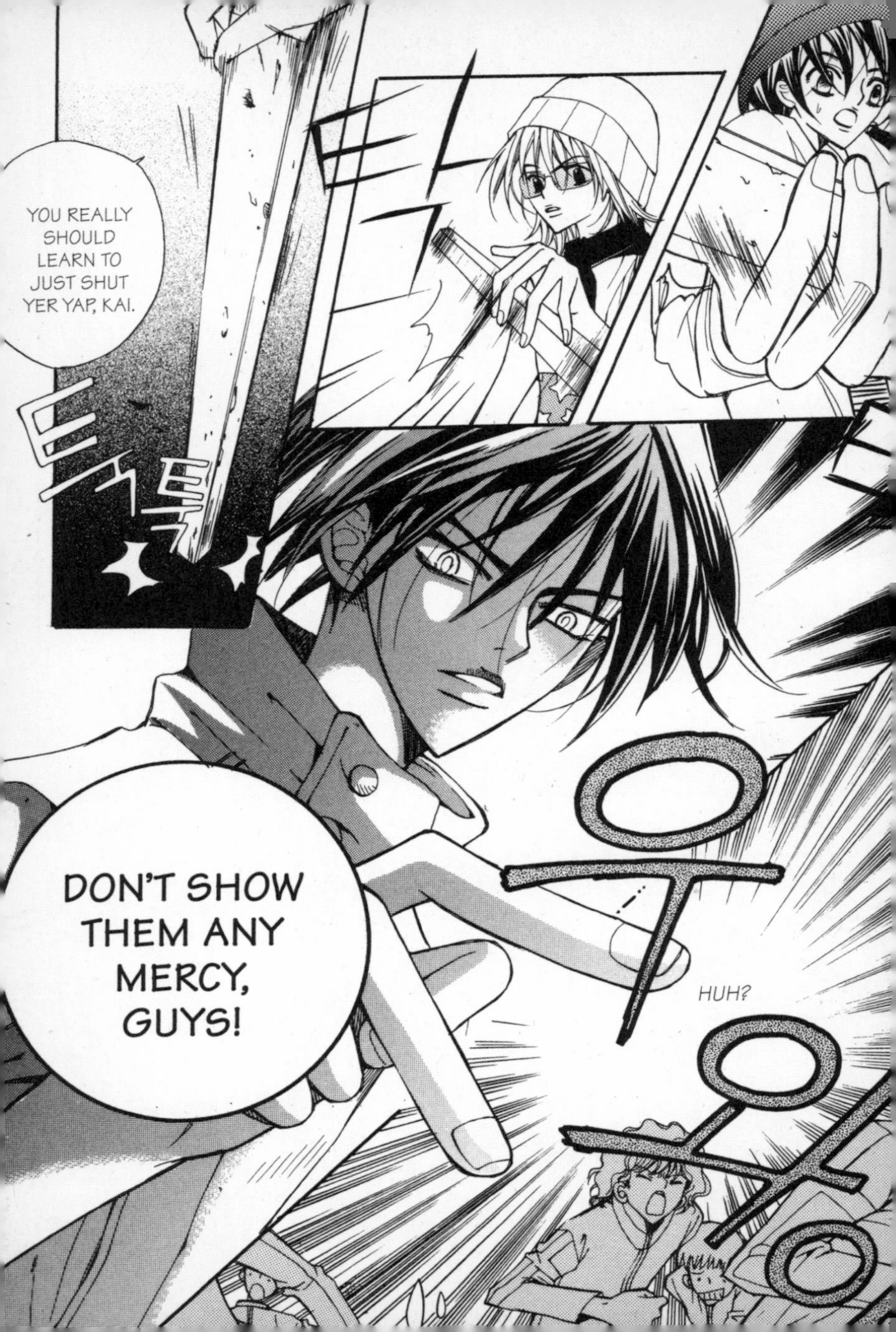
YOU REALLY SHOULD LEARN TO JUST SHUT YER YAP, KAI.
DON'T SHOW THEM ANY MERCY, GUYS!
HUH?

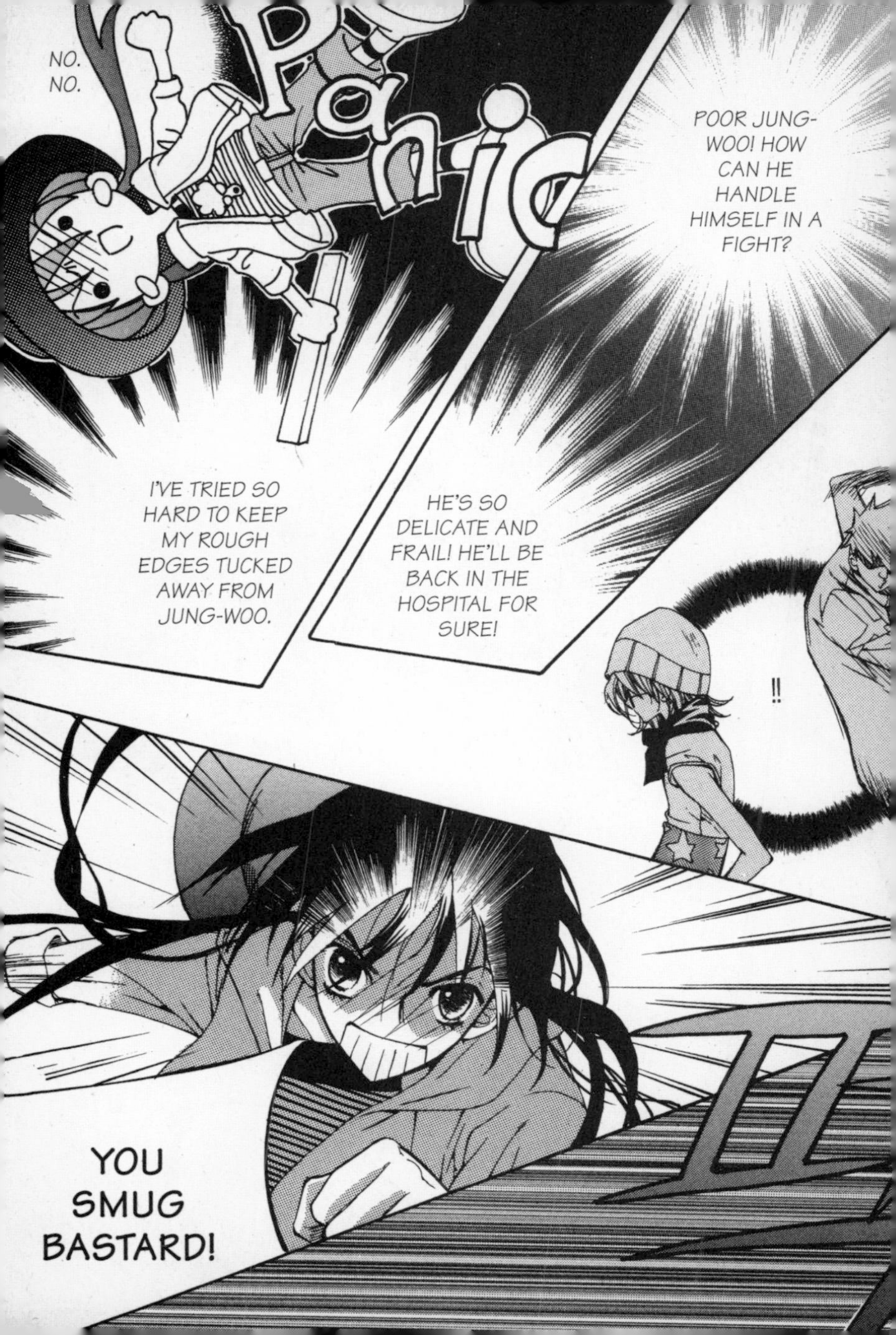
NO.
NO.
Panic
POOR JUNG-WOO! HOW CAN HE HANDLE HIMSELF IN A FIGHT?
I'VE TRIED SO HARD TO KEEP MY ROUGH EDGES TUCKED AWAY FROM JUNG-WOO.
HE'S SO DELICATE AND FRAIL! HE'LL BE BACK IN THE HOSPITAL FOR SURE!
!!
YOU SMUG BASTARD!

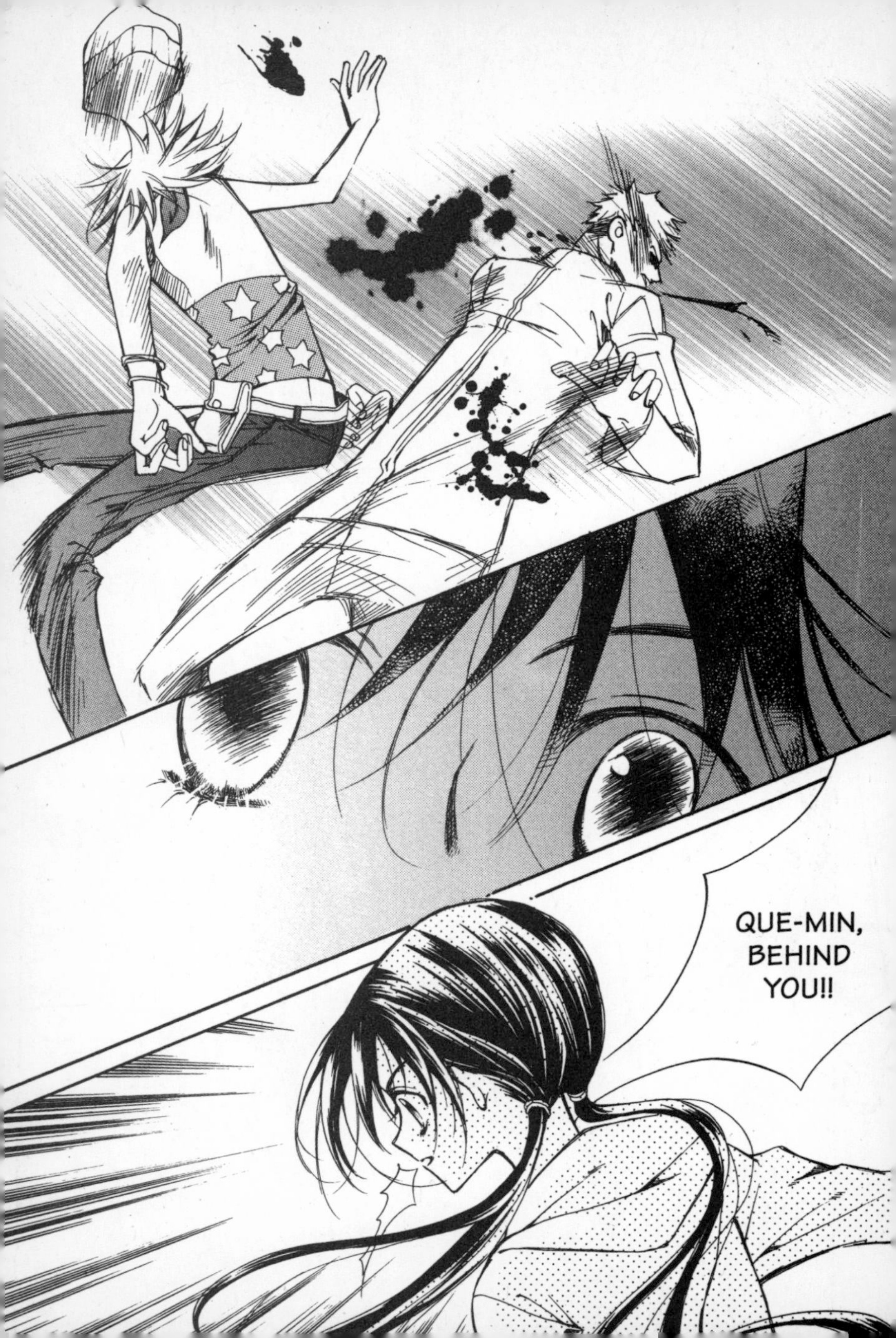
QUE-MIN, BEHIND YOU!!

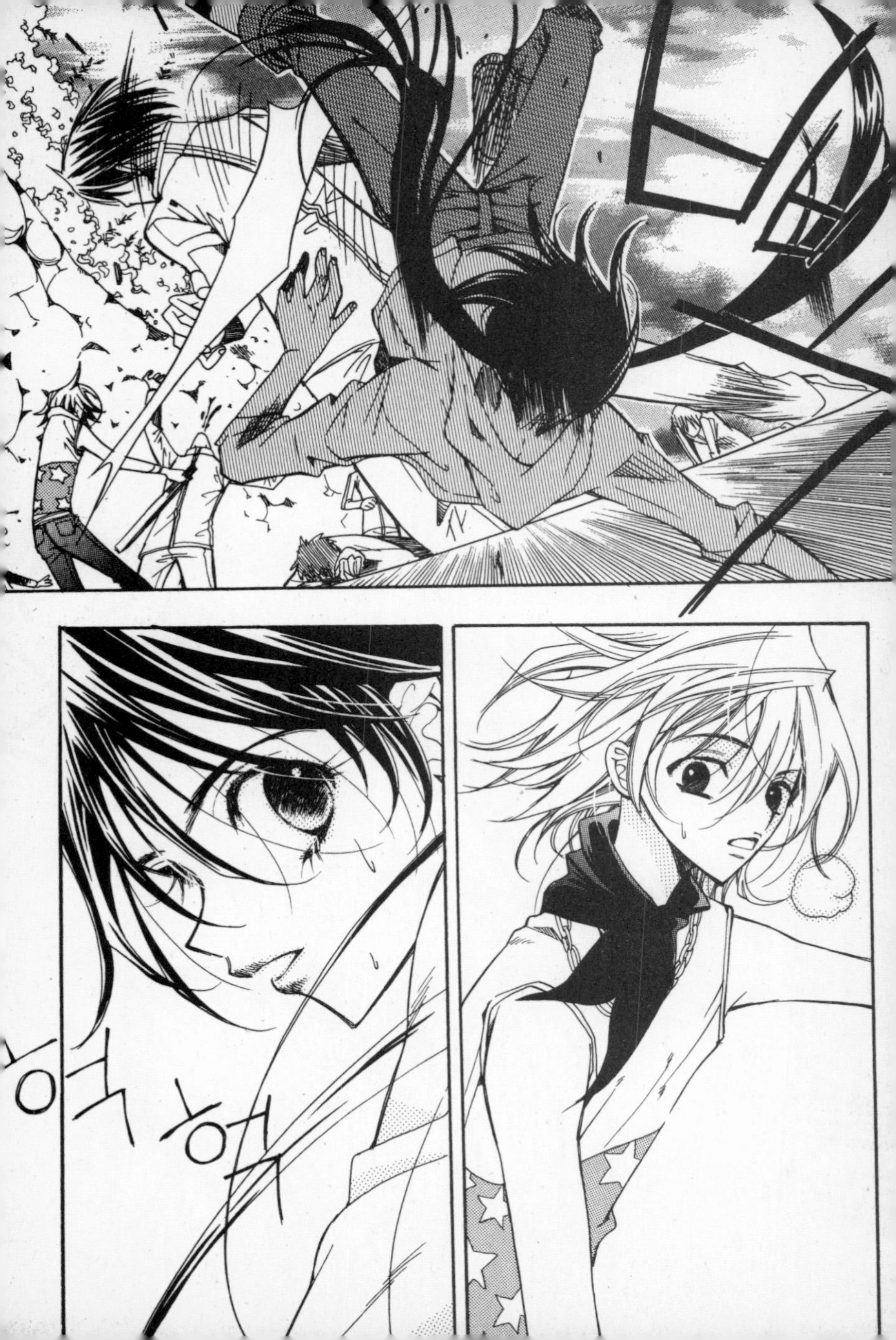
헉 헉

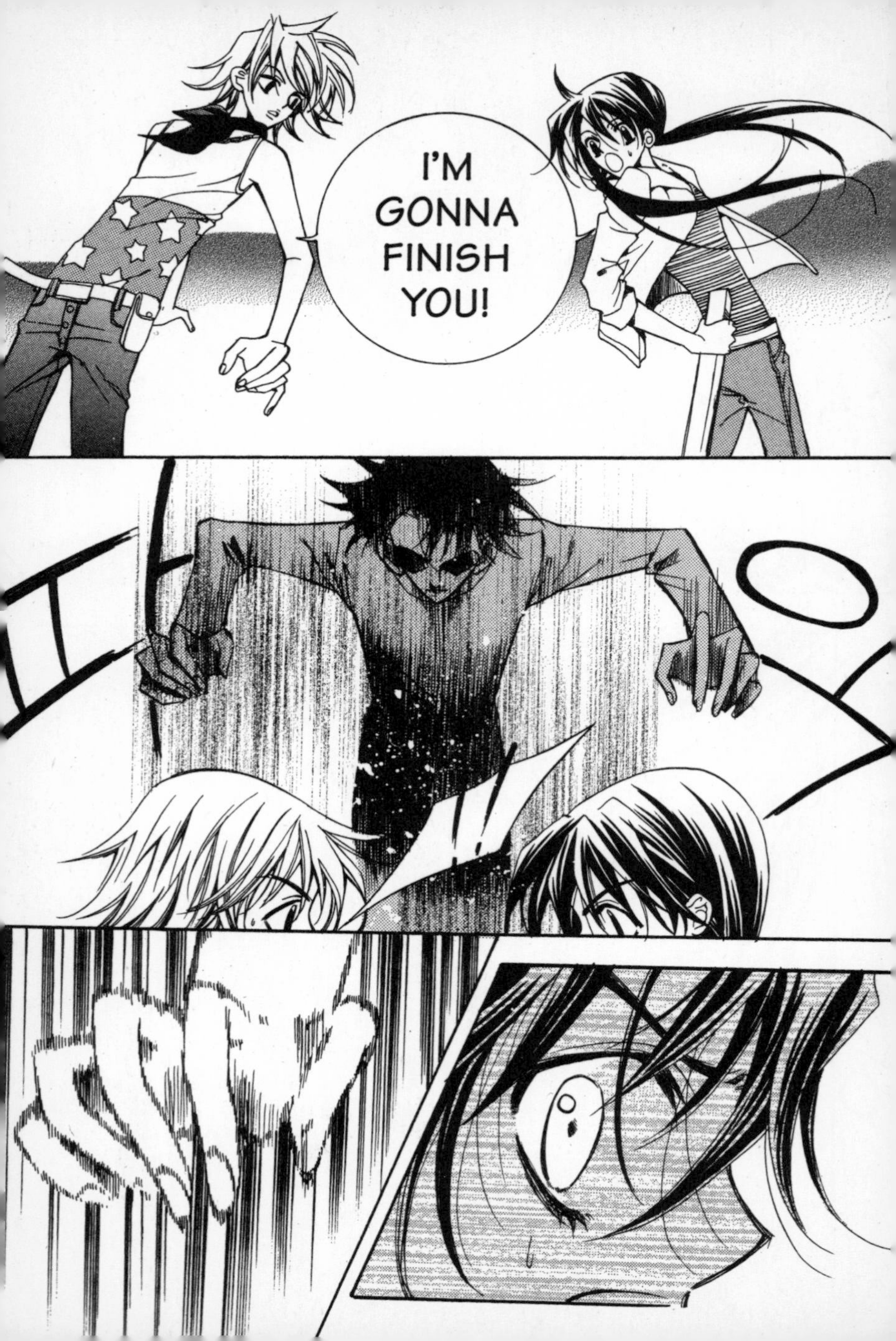
I'M GONNA FINISH YOU!

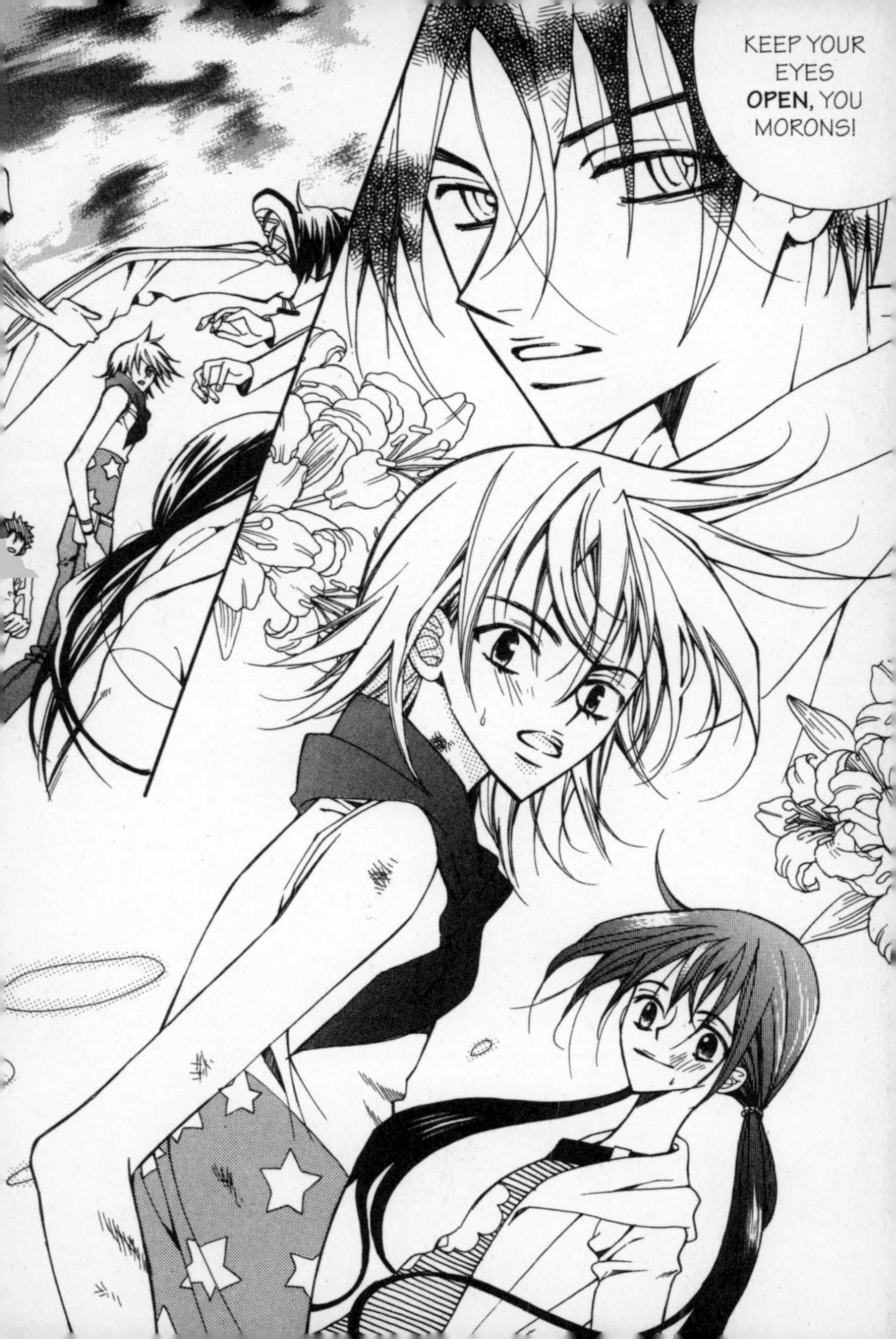
KEEP YOUR EYES **OPEN,** YOU MORONS!

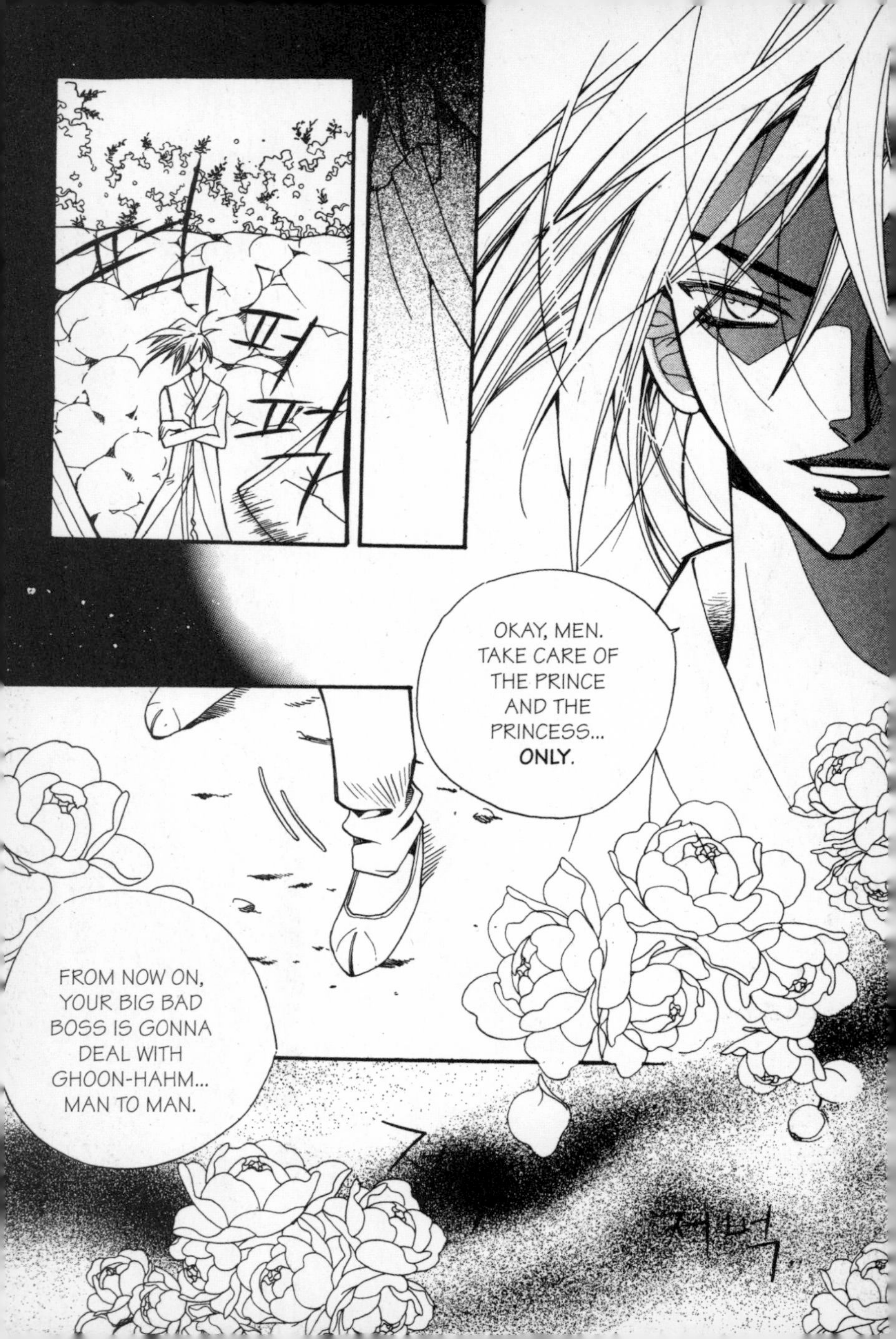
OKAY, MEN. TAKE CARE OF THE PRINCE AND THE PRINCESS... **ONLY**.
FROM NOW ON, YOUR BIG BAD BOSS IS GONNA DEAL WITH GHOON-HAHM... MAN TO MAN.

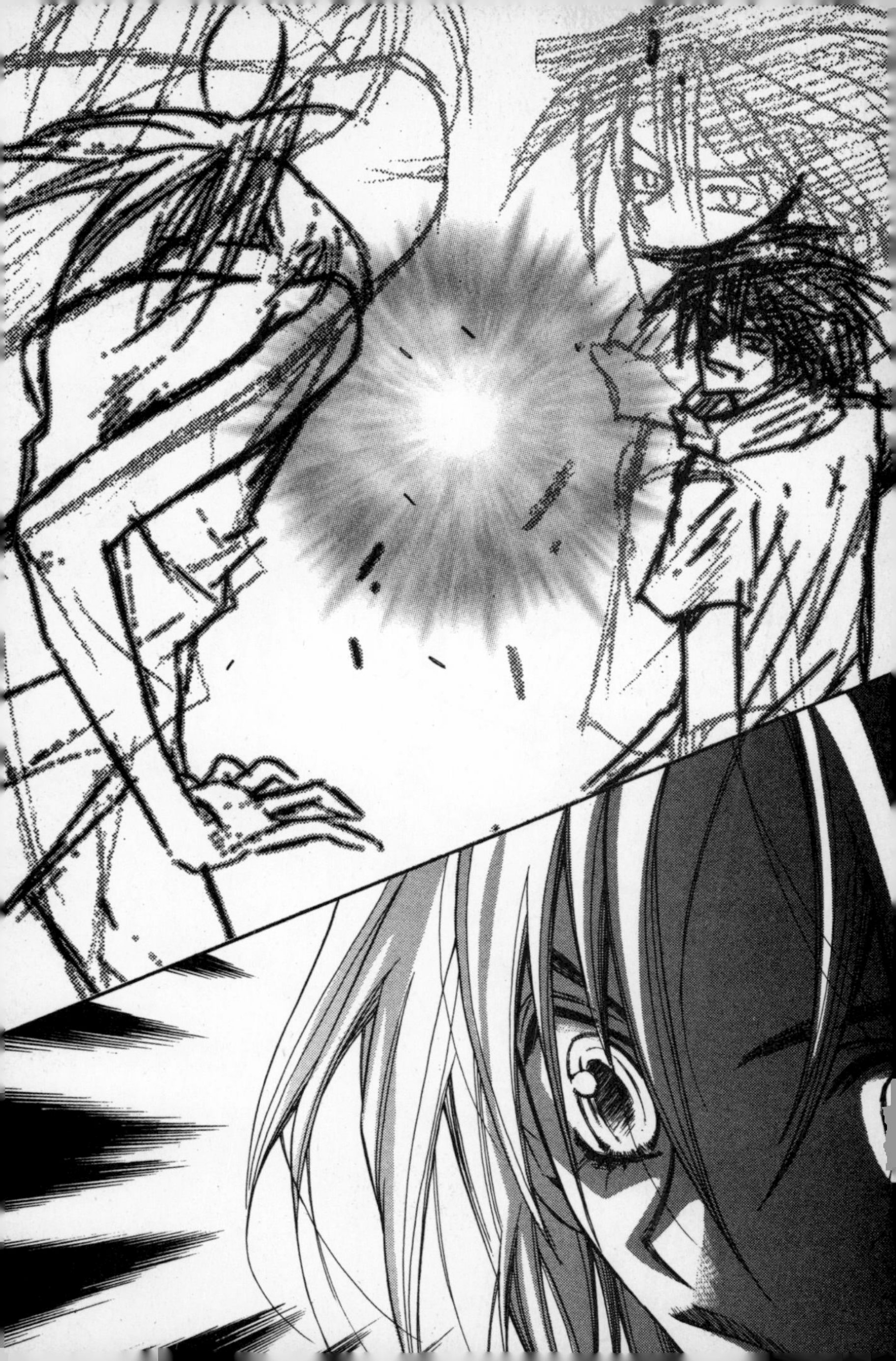

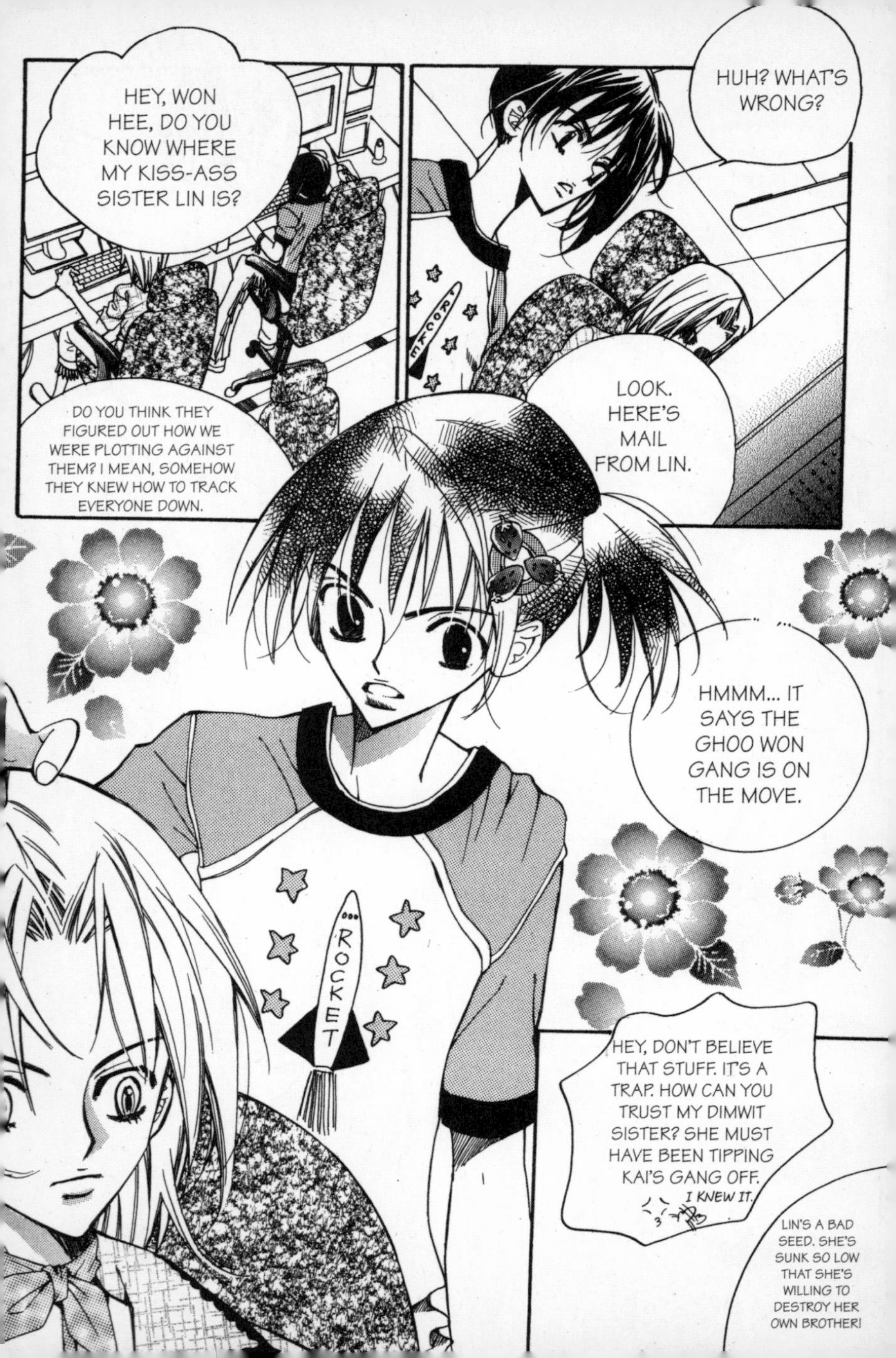
HEY, WON HEE, DO YOU KNOW WHERE MY KISS-ASS SISTER LIN IS?
DO YOU THINK THEY FIGURED OUT HOW WE WERE PLOTTING AGAINST THEM? I MEAN, SOMEHOW THEY KNEW HOW TO TRACK EVERYONE DOWN.
HUH? WHAT'S WRONG?
LOOK. HERE'S MAIL FROM LIN.
ROCKET
...
HMMM... IT SAYS THE GHOO WON GANG IS ON THE MOVE.
HEY, DON'T BELIEVE THAT STUFF. IT'S A TRAP. HOW CAN YOU TRUST MY DIMWIT SISTER? SHE MUST HAVE BEEN TIPPING KAI'S GANG OFF.
I KNEW IT.
LIN'S A BAD SEED. SHE'S SUNK SO LOW THAT SHE'S WILLING TO DESTROY HER OWN BROTHER!

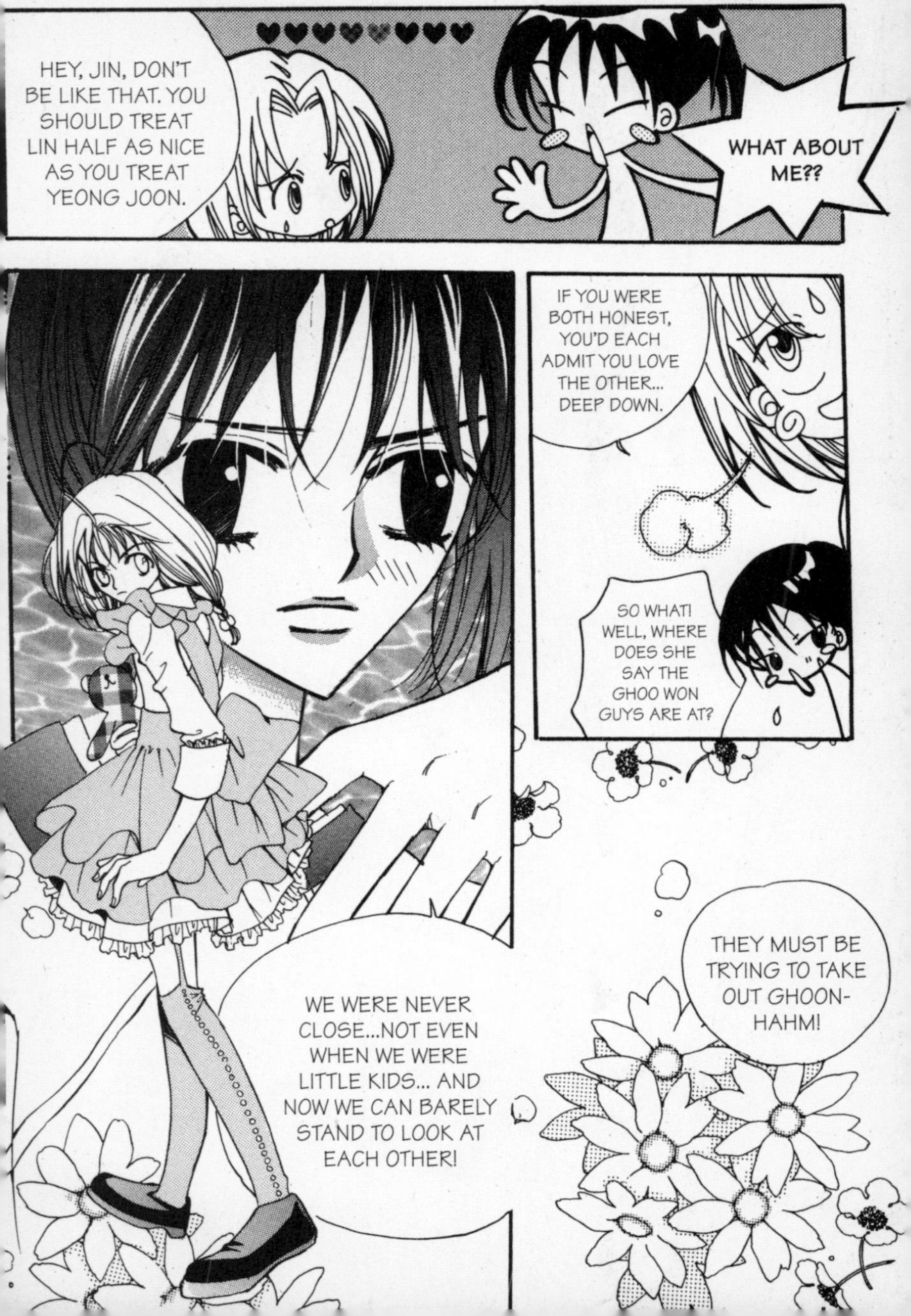
HEY, JIN, DON'T BE LIKE THAT. YOU SHOULD TREAT LIN HALF AS NICE AS YOU TREAT YEONG JOON.
WHAT ABOUT ME??
WE WERE NEVER CLOSE...NOT EVEN WHEN WE WERE LITTLE KIDS... AND NOW WE CAN BARELY STAND TO LOOK AT EACH OTHER!
IF YOU WERE BOTH HONEST, YOU'D EACH ADMIT YOU LOVE THE OTHER... DEEP DOWN.
SO WHAT! WELL, WHERE DOES SHE SAY THE GHOO WON GUYS ARE AT?
THEY MUST BE TRYING TO TAKE OUT GHOON-HAHM!

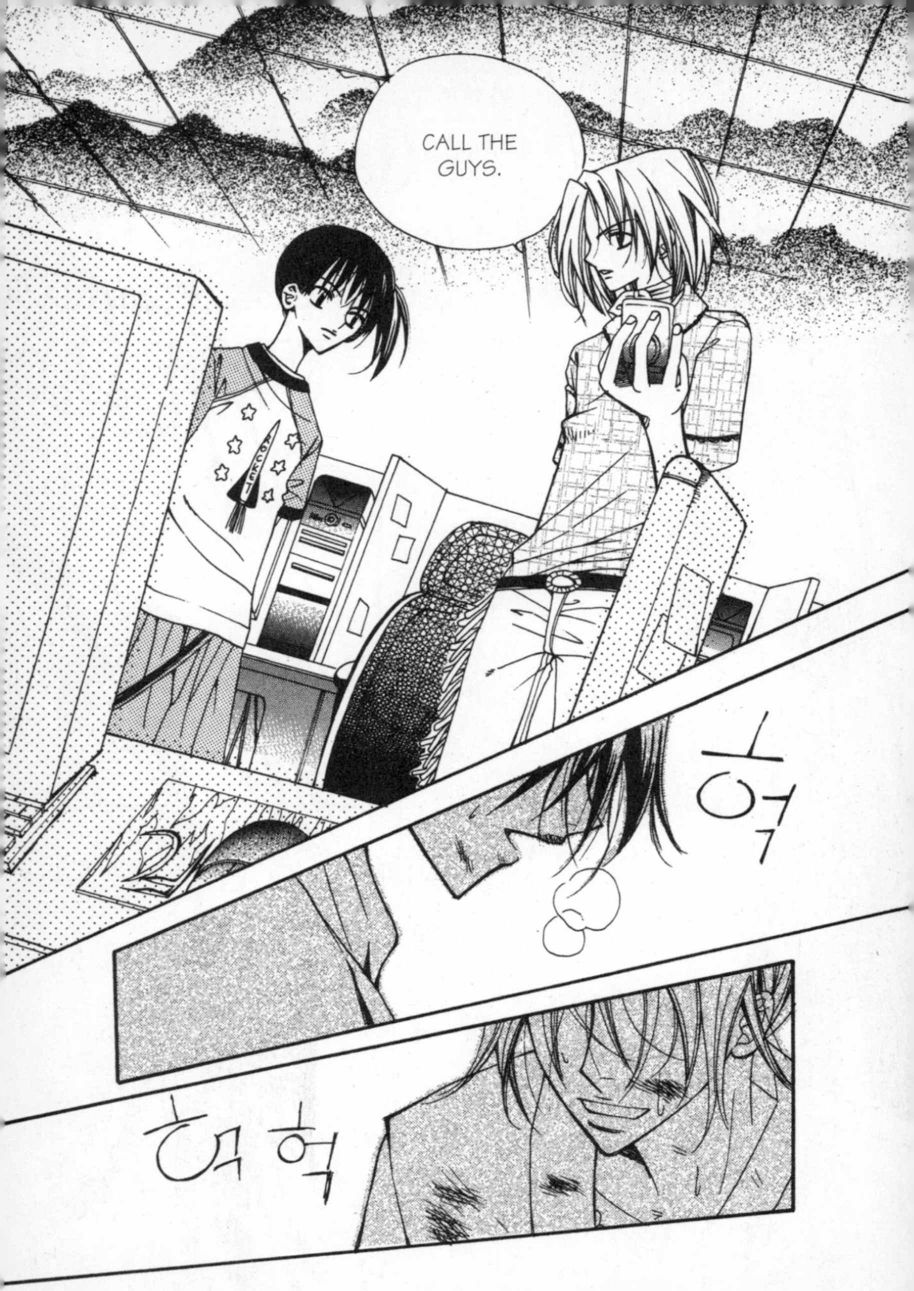
CALL THE GUYS.
헉
헉 헉

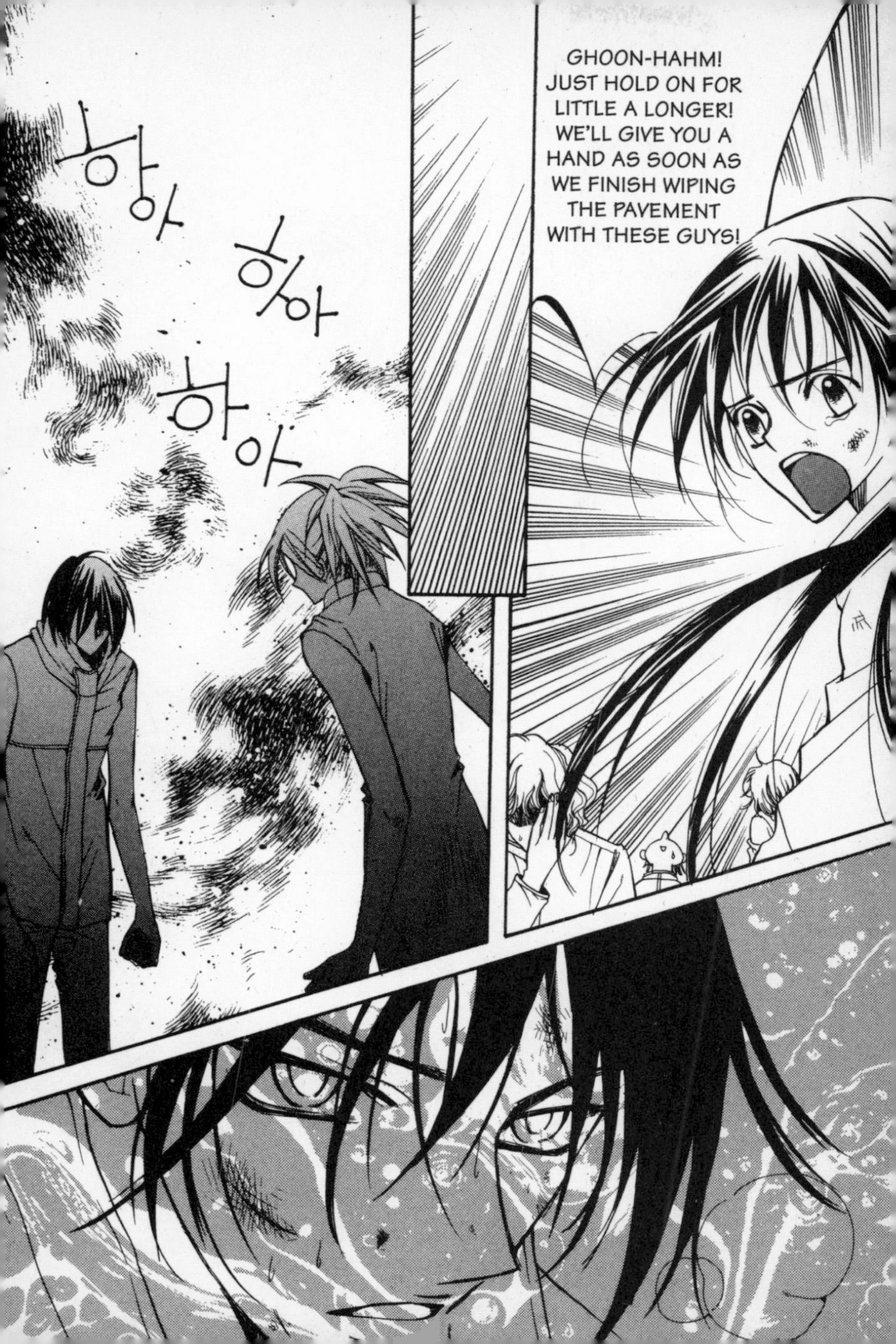
하아 하아 하아
GHOON-HAHM! JUST HOLD ON FOR LITTLE A LONGER! WE'LL GIVE YOU A HAND AS SOON AS WE FINISH WIPING THE PAVEMENT WITH THESE GUYS!

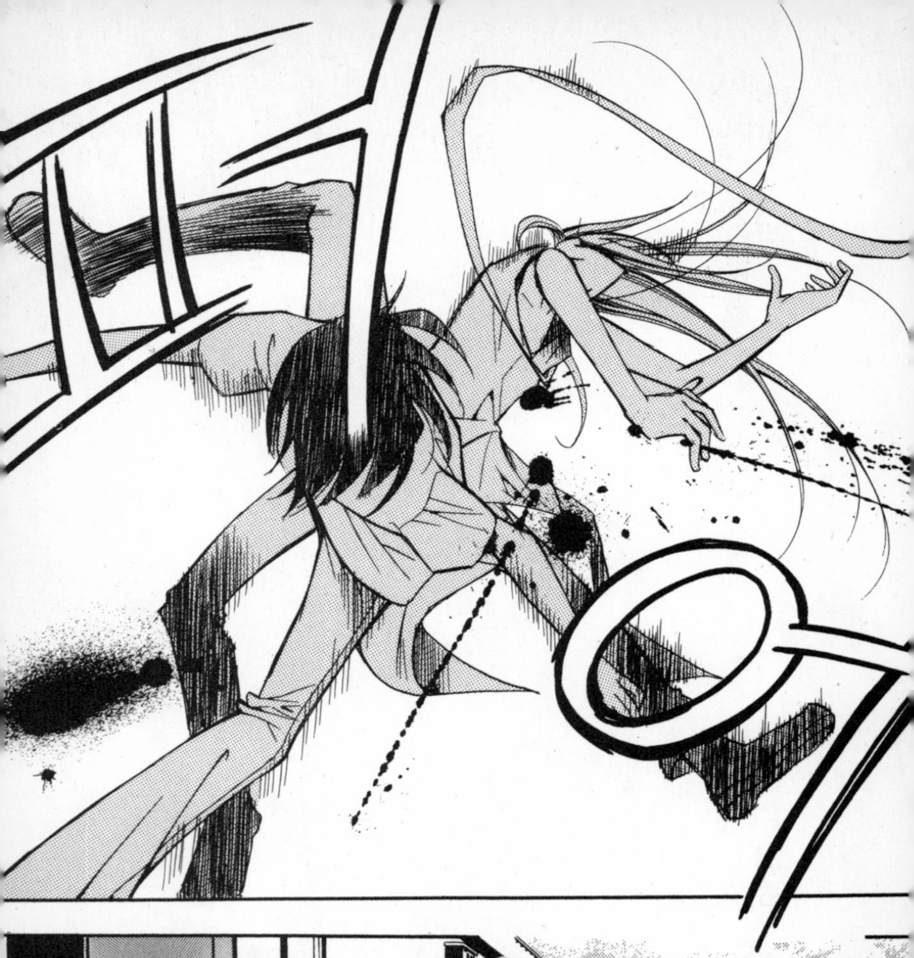
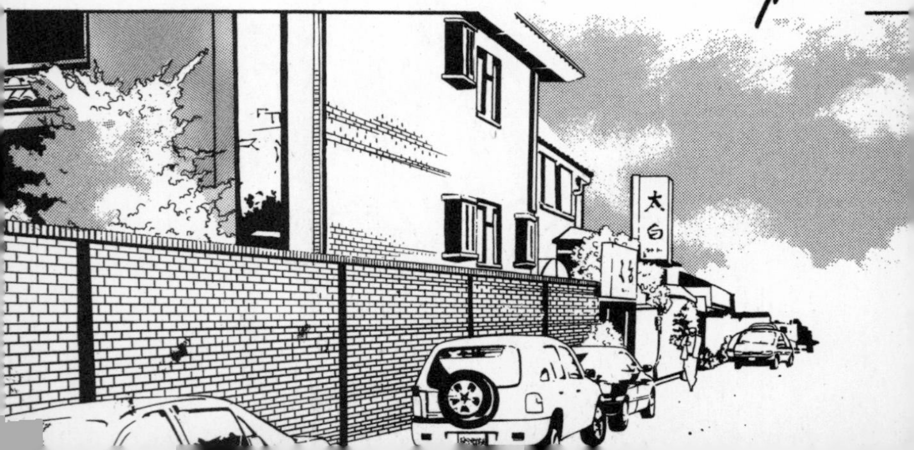
太白

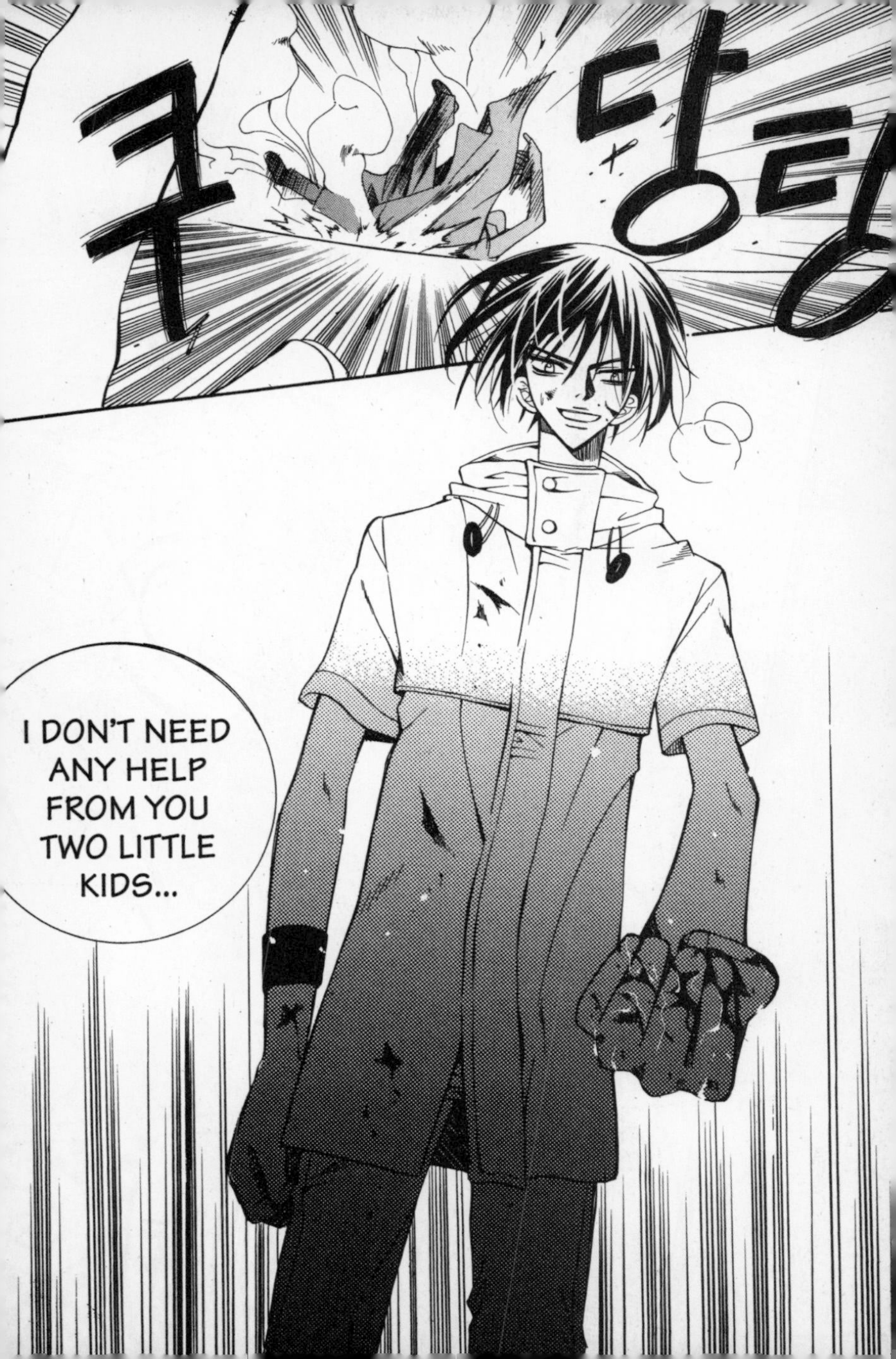
쿠당탕
I DON'T NEED ANY HELP FROM YOU TWO LITTLE KIDS...

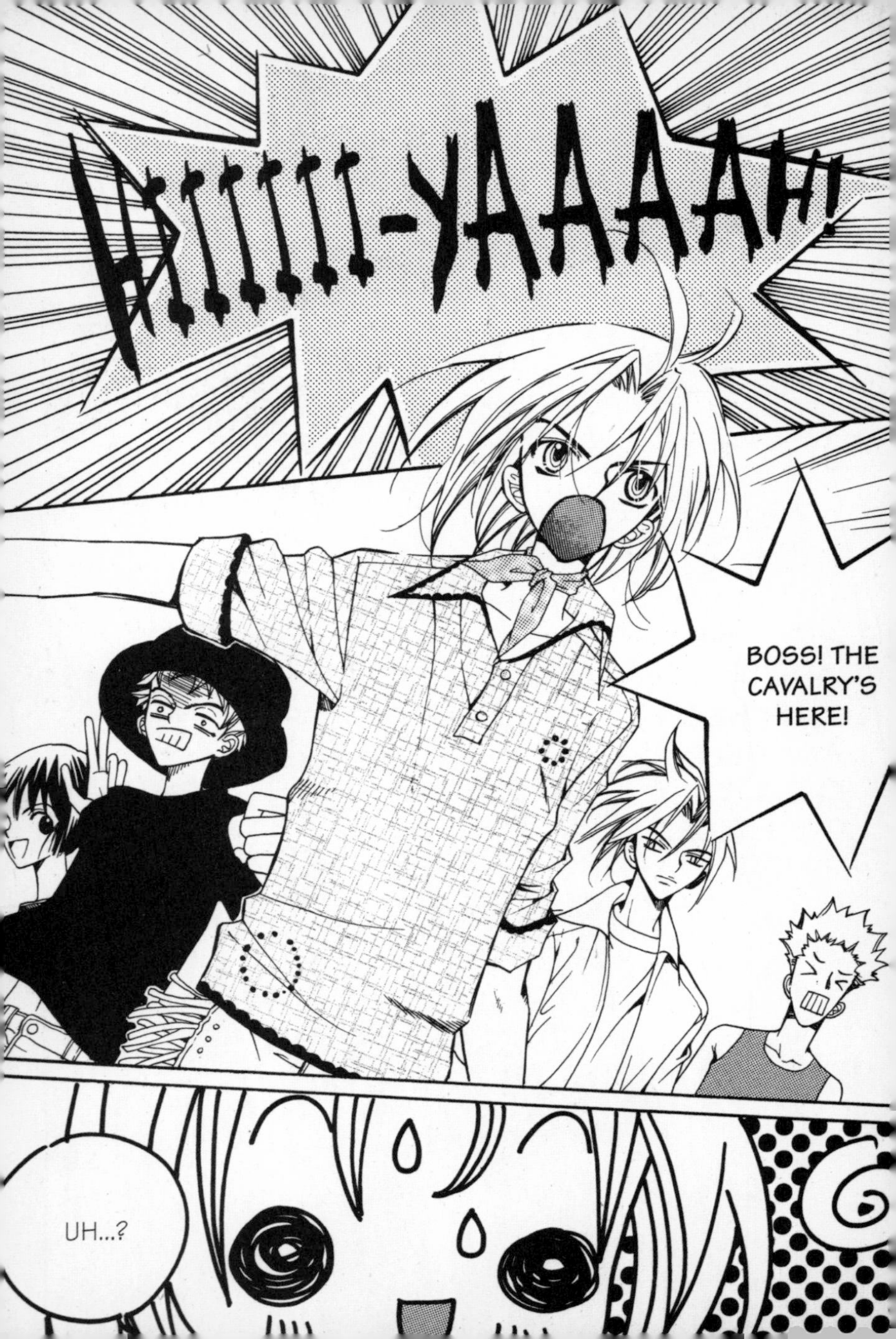
HIIIIII-YAAAAH!
BOSS! THE CAVALRY'S HERE!
UH...?

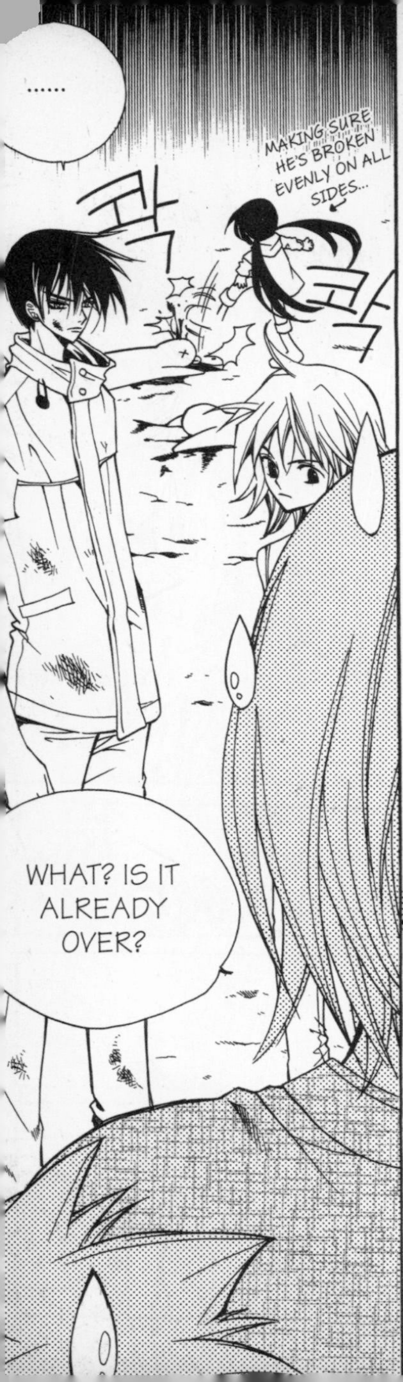
......
MAKING SURE HE'S BROKEN EVENLY ON ALL SIDES...
WHAT? IS IT ALREADY OVER?

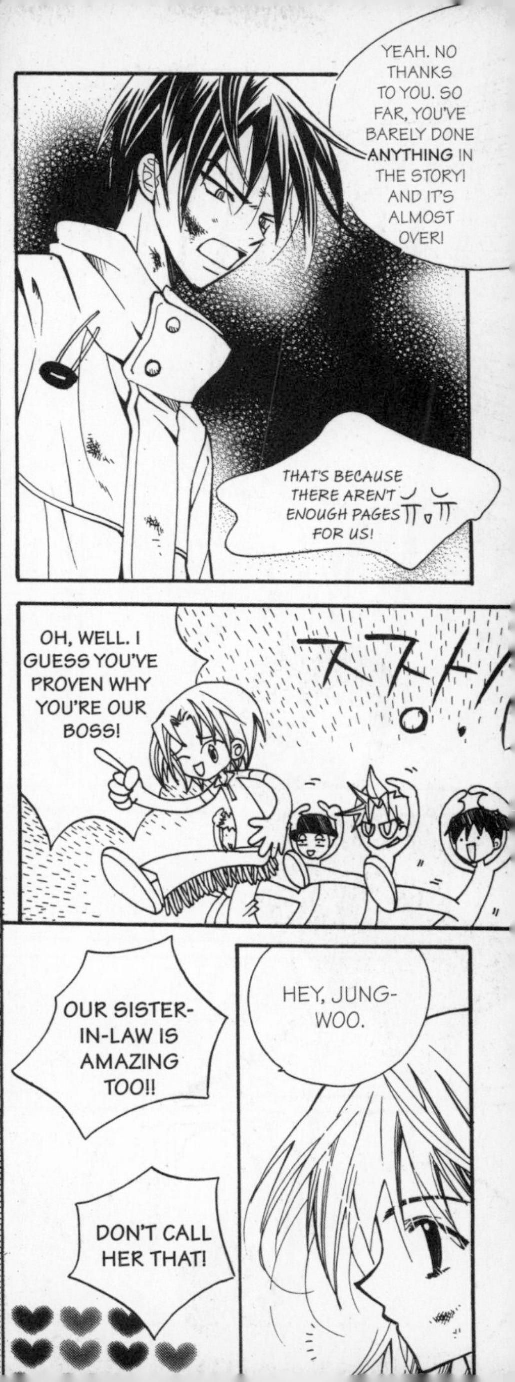
YEAH. NO THANKS TO YOU. SO FAR, YOU'VE BARELY DONE **ANYTHING** IN THE STORY! AND IT'S ALMOST OVER!
THAT'S BECAUSE THERE AREN'T ENOUGH PAGES FOR US!
OH, WELL. I GUESS YOU'VE PROVEN WHY YOU'RE OUR BOSS!
OUR SISTER-IN-LAW IS AMAZING TOO!!
DON'T CALL HER THAT!
HEY, JUNG-WOO.

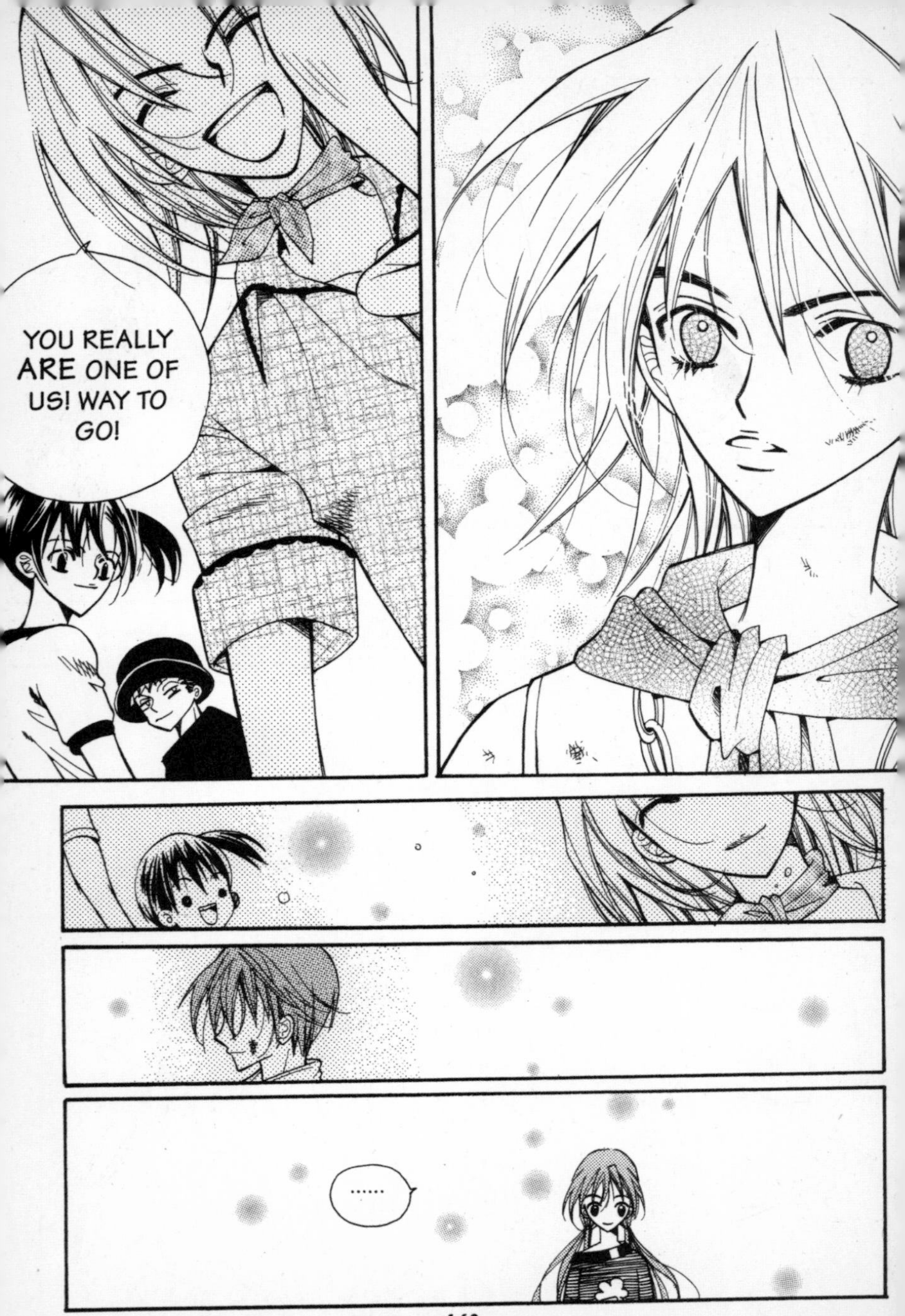
YOU REALLY ARE ONE OF US! WAY TO GO!
......

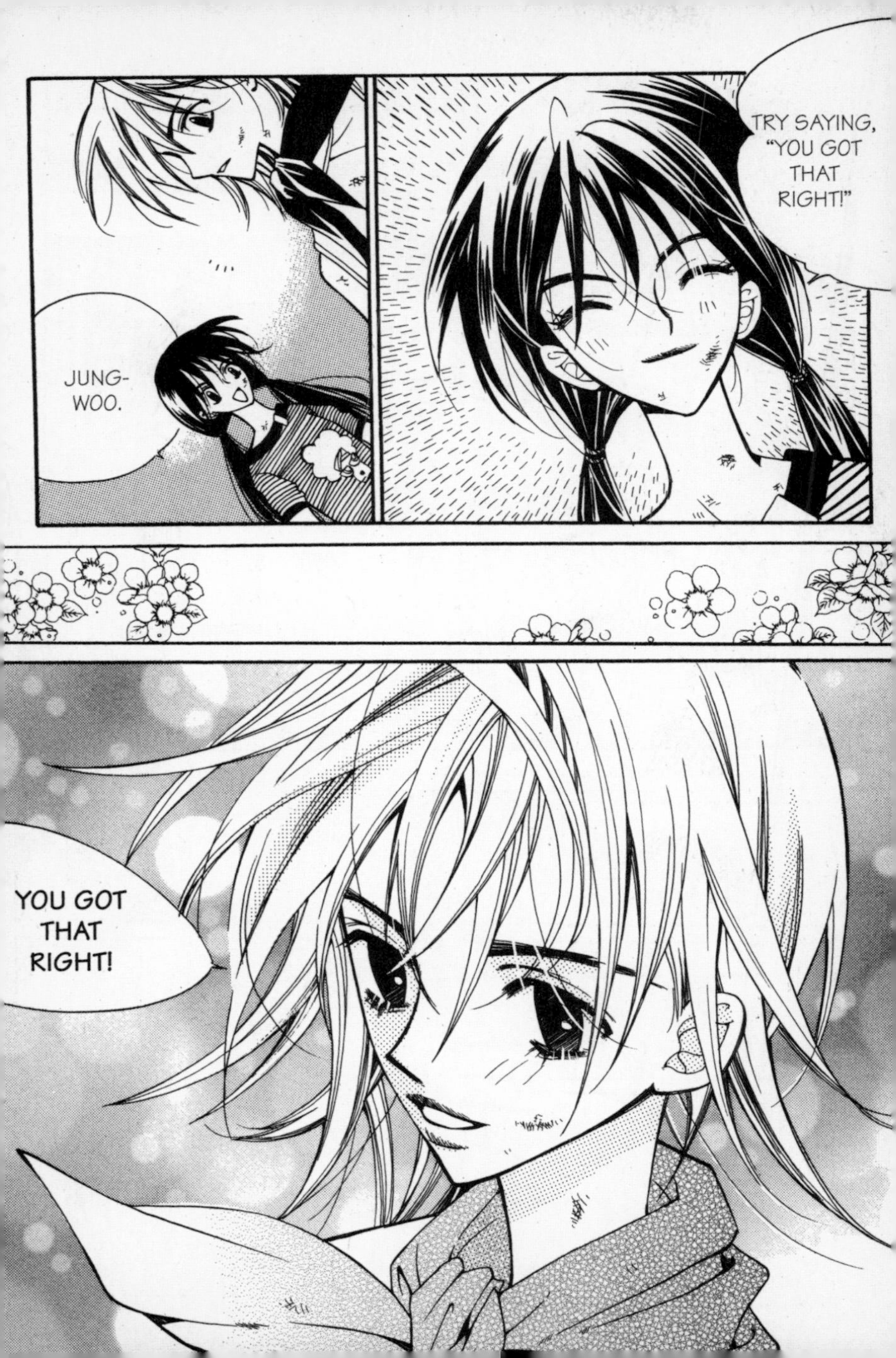
JUNG-WOO.
TRY SAYING, "YOU GOT THAT RIGHT!"
YOU GOT THAT RIGHT!

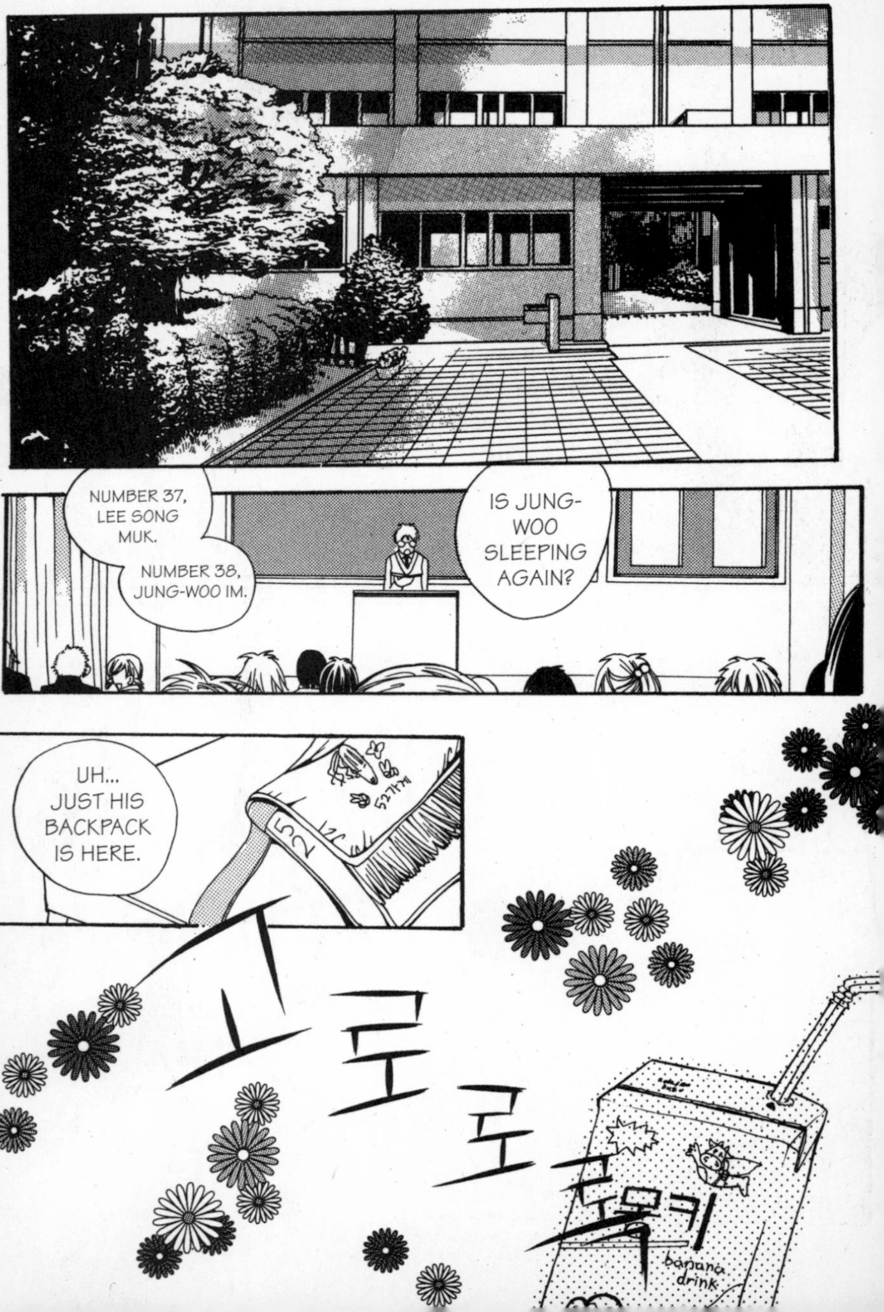

NUMBER 37, LEE SONG MUK.
NUMBER 38, JUNG-WOO IM.
IS JUNG-WOO SLEEPING AGAIN?
UH... JUST HIS BACKPACK IS HERE.
banana drink

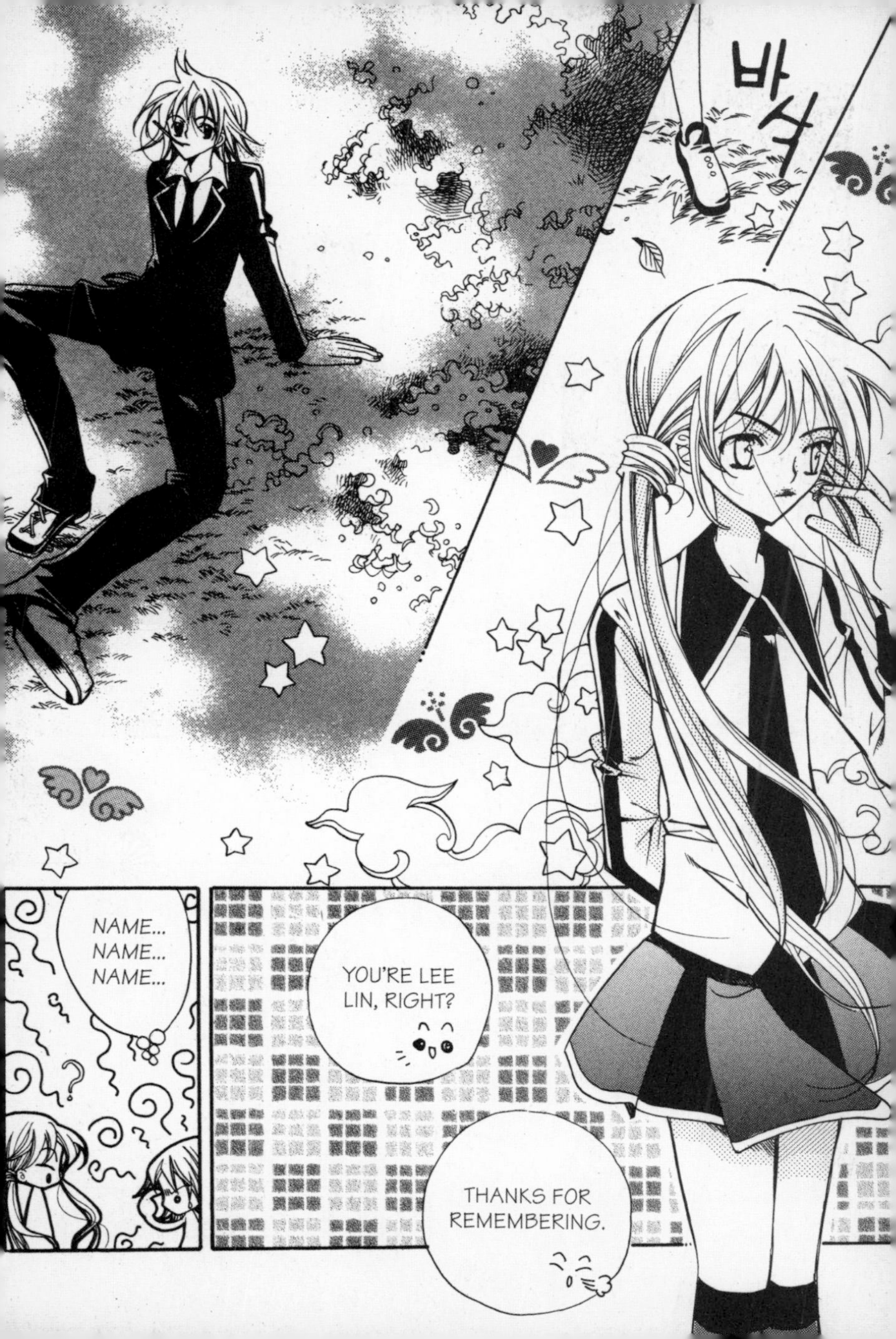
바삭
NAME... NAME... NAME...
YOU'RE LEE LIN, RIGHT?
THANKS FOR REMEMBERING.

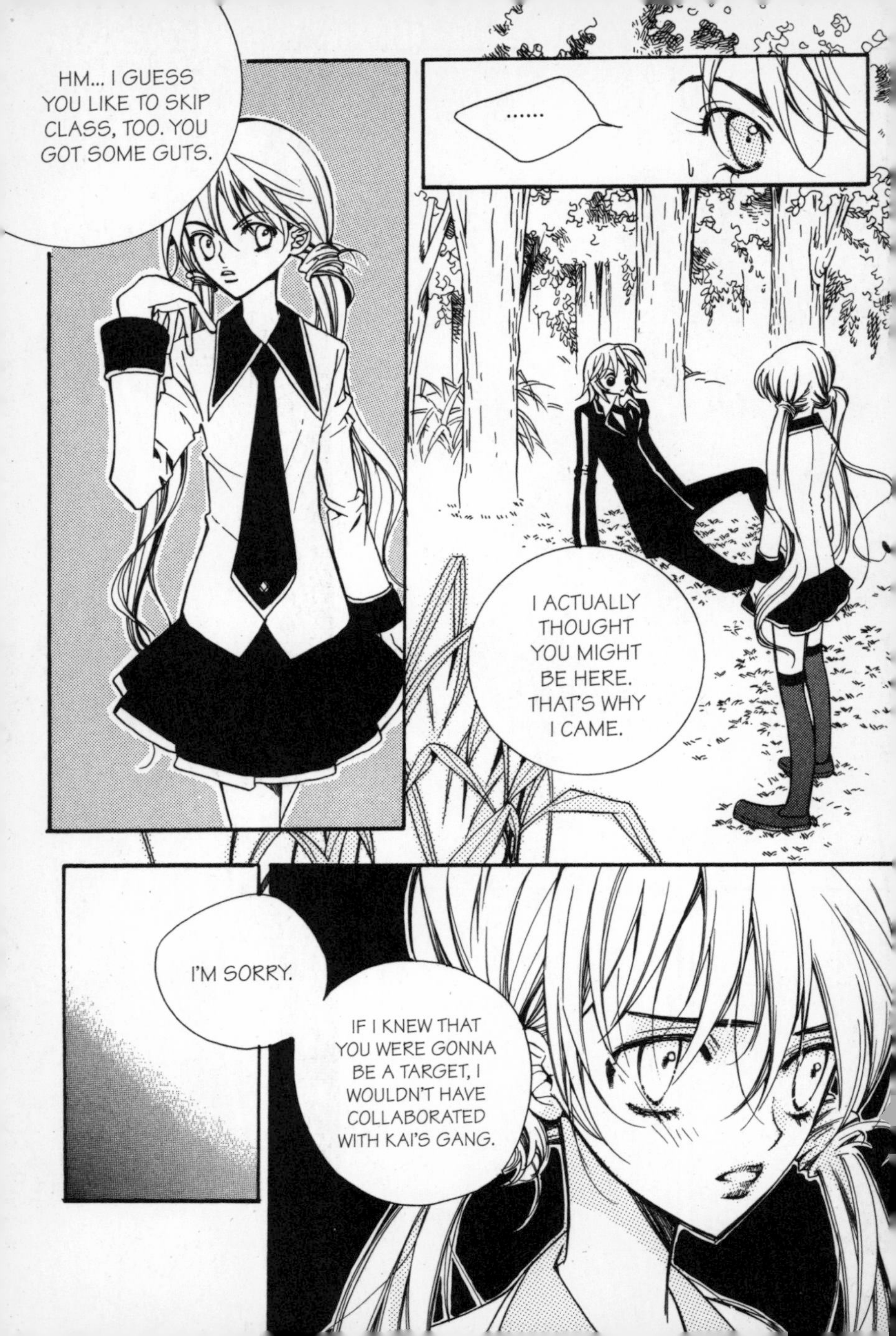
HM... I GUESS YOU LIKE TO SKIP CLASS, TOO. YOU GOT SOME GUTS.
......
I ACTUALLY THOUGHT YOU MIGHT BE HERE. THAT'S WHY I CAME.
I'M SORRY.
IF I KNEW THAT YOU WERE GONNA BE A TARGET, I WOULDN'T HAVE COLLABORATED WITH KAI'S GANG.

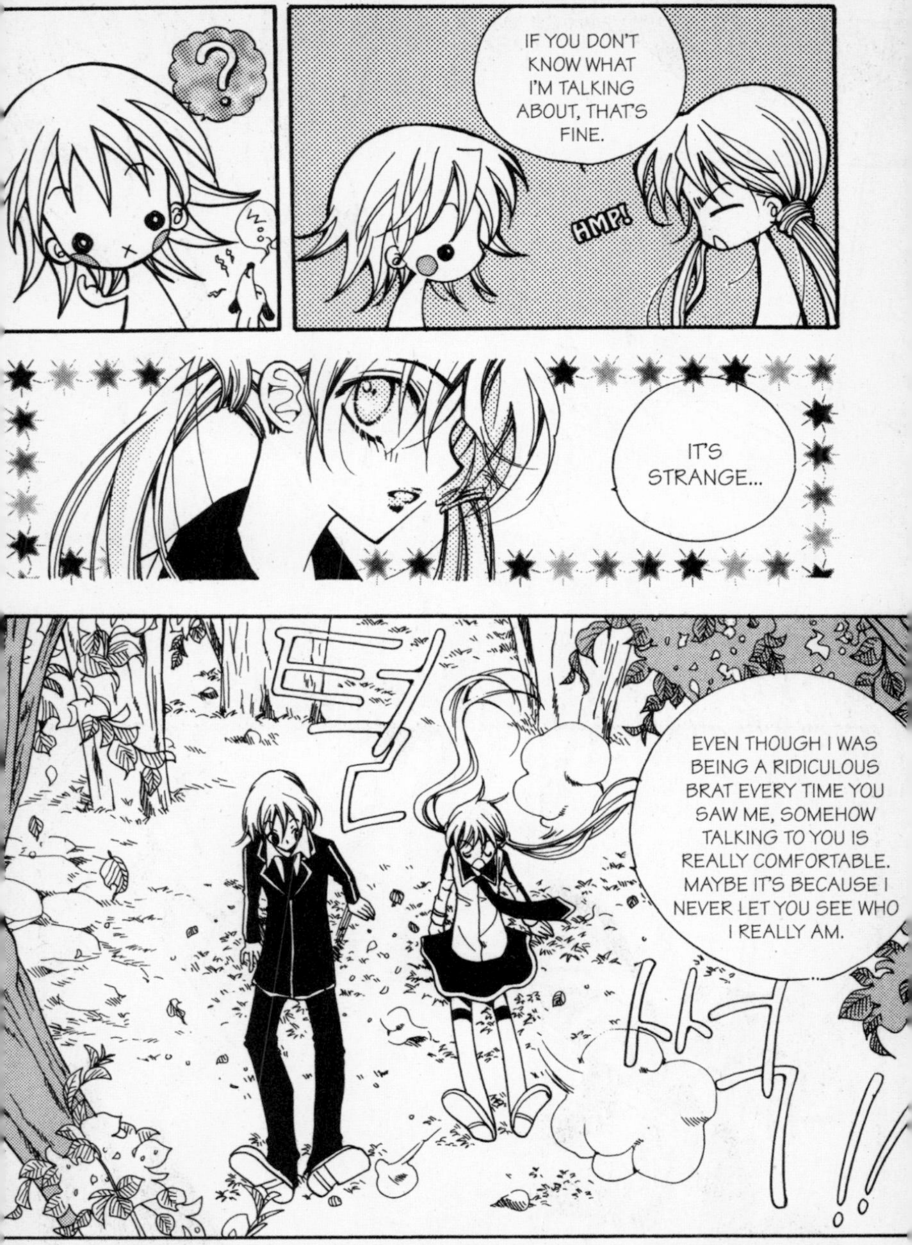
IF YOU DON'T KNOW WHAT I'M TALKING ABOUT, THAT'S FINE.
HMP!
IT'S STRANGE...
EVEN THOUGH I WAS BEING A RIDICULOUS BRAT EVERY TIME YOU SAW ME, SOMEHOW TALKING TO YOU IS REALLY COMFORTABLE. MAYBE IT'S BECAUSE I NEVER LET YOU SEE WHO I REALLY AM.

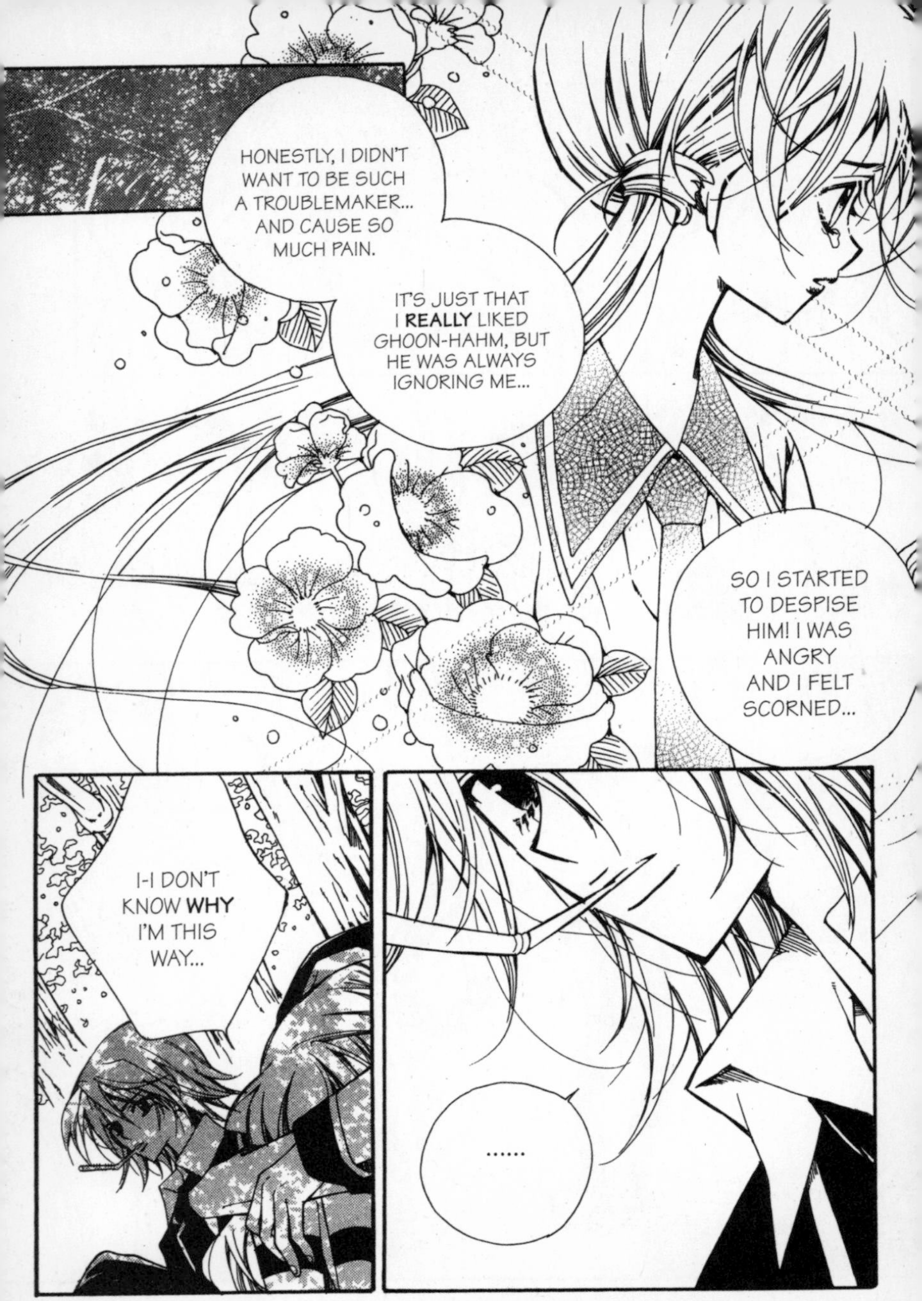
HONESTLY, I DIDN'T WANT TO BE SUCH A TROUBLEMAKER... AND CAUSE SO MUCH PAIN.
IT'S JUST THAT I **REALLY** LIKED GHOON-HAHM, BUT HE WAS ALWAYS IGNORING ME...
SO I STARTED TO DESPISE HIM! I WAS ANGRY AND I FELT SCORNED...
I-I DON'T KNOW **WHY** I'M THIS WAY...
......

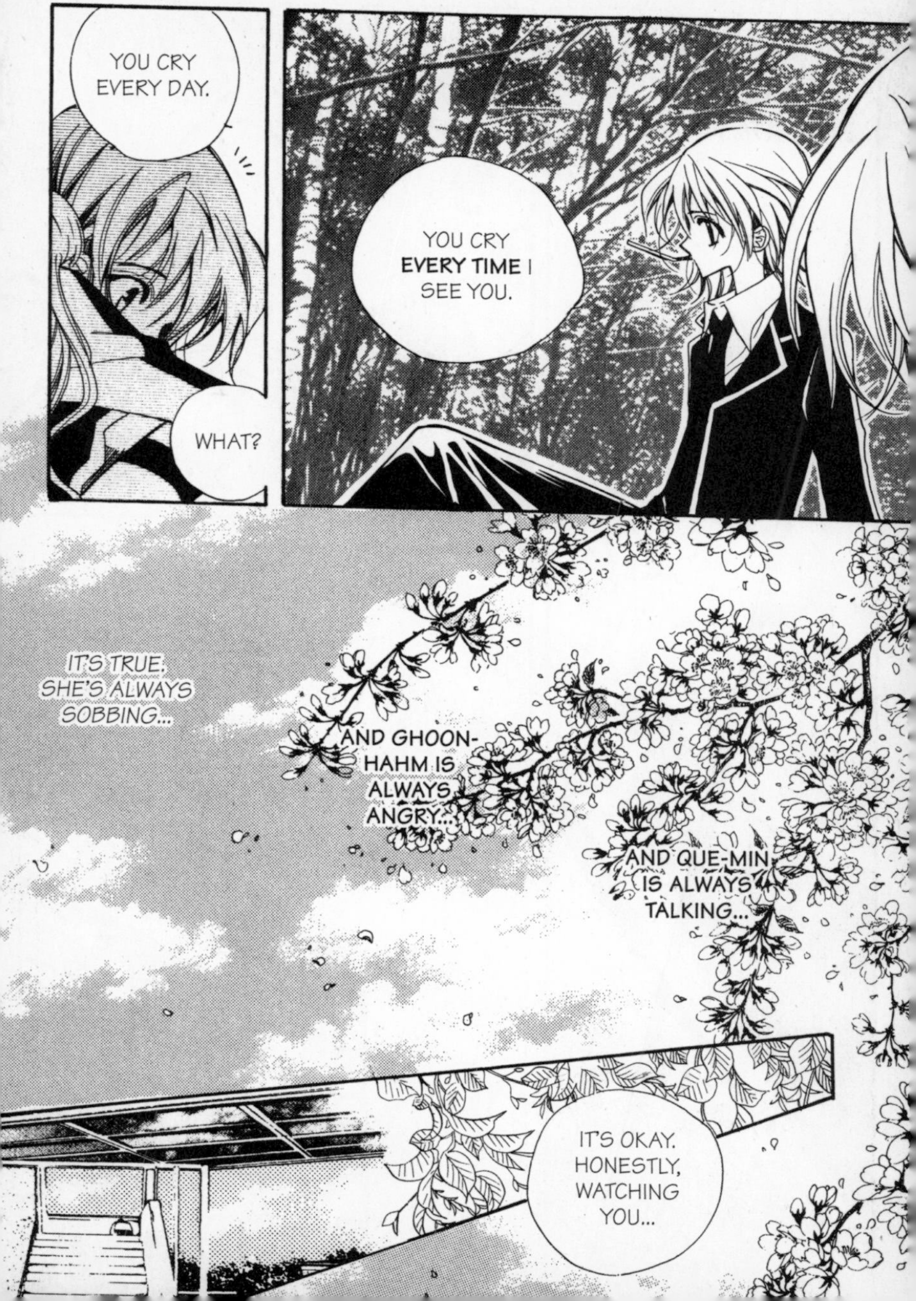
YOU CRY EVERY DAY.
WHAT?
YOU CRY EVERY TIME I SEE YOU.
IT'S TRUE. SHE'S ALWAYS SOBBING...
AND GHOON-HAHM IS ALWAYS ANGRY...
AND QUE-MIN IS ALWAYS TALKING...
IT'S OKAY. HONESTLY, WATCHING YOU...

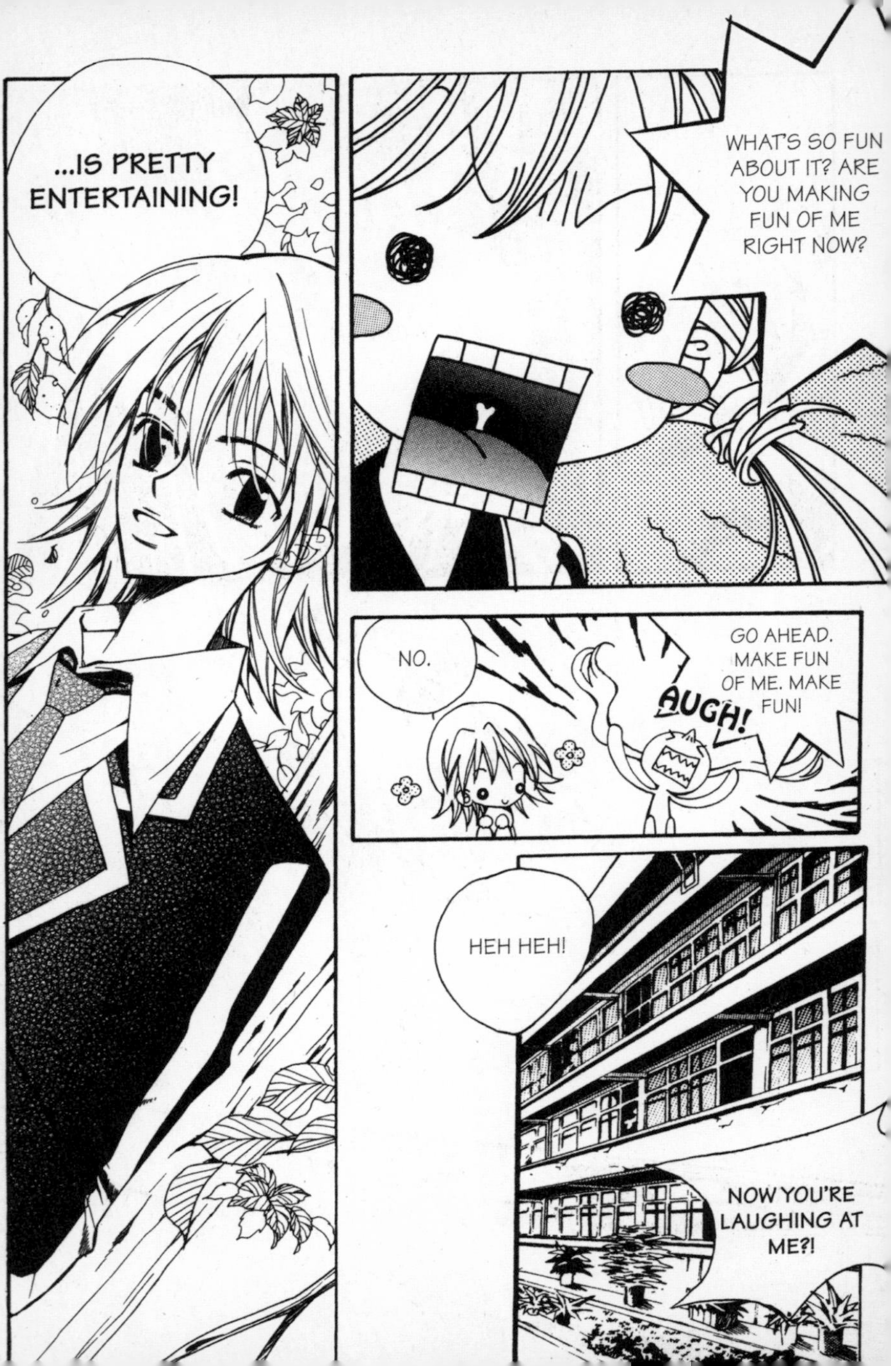
...IS PRETTY ENTERTAINING!
WHAT'S SO FUN ABOUT IT? ARE YOU MAKING FUN OF ME RIGHT NOW?
NO.
AUGH!
GO AHEAD. MAKE FUN OF ME. MAKE FUN!
HEH HEH!
NOW YOU'RE LAUGHING AT ME?!

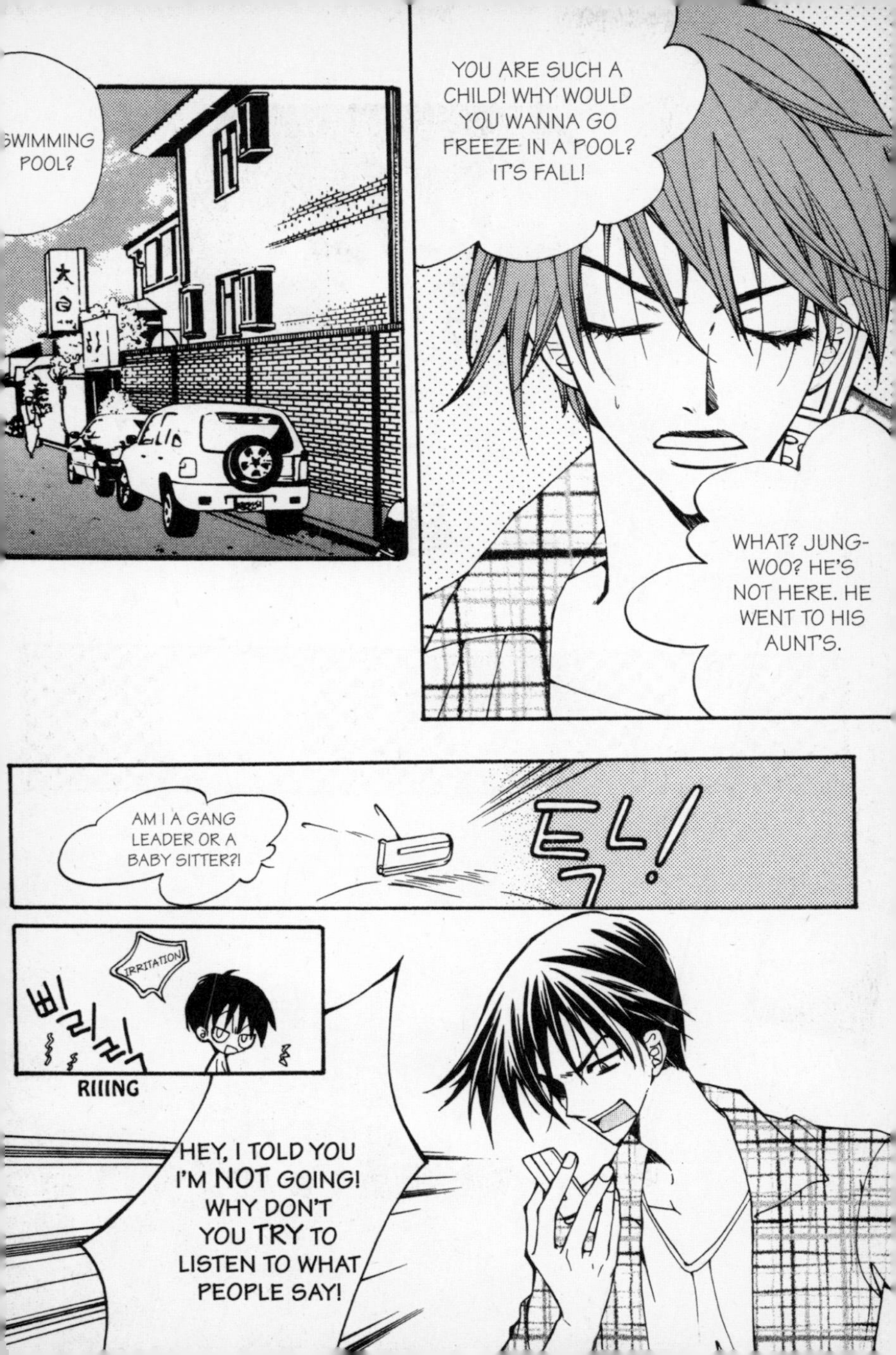
SWIMMING POOL?
YOU ARE SUCH A CHILD! WHY WOULD YOU WANNA GO FREEZE IN A POOL? IT'S FALL!
WHAT? JUNG-WOO? HE'S NOT HERE. HE WENT TO HIS AUNT'S.
AM I A GANG LEADER OR A BABY SITTER?!
툭!
IRRITATION
삐리릭
RIIING
HEY, I TOLD YOU I'M NOT GOING! WHY DON'T YOU TRY TO LISTEN TO WHAT PEOPLE SAY!

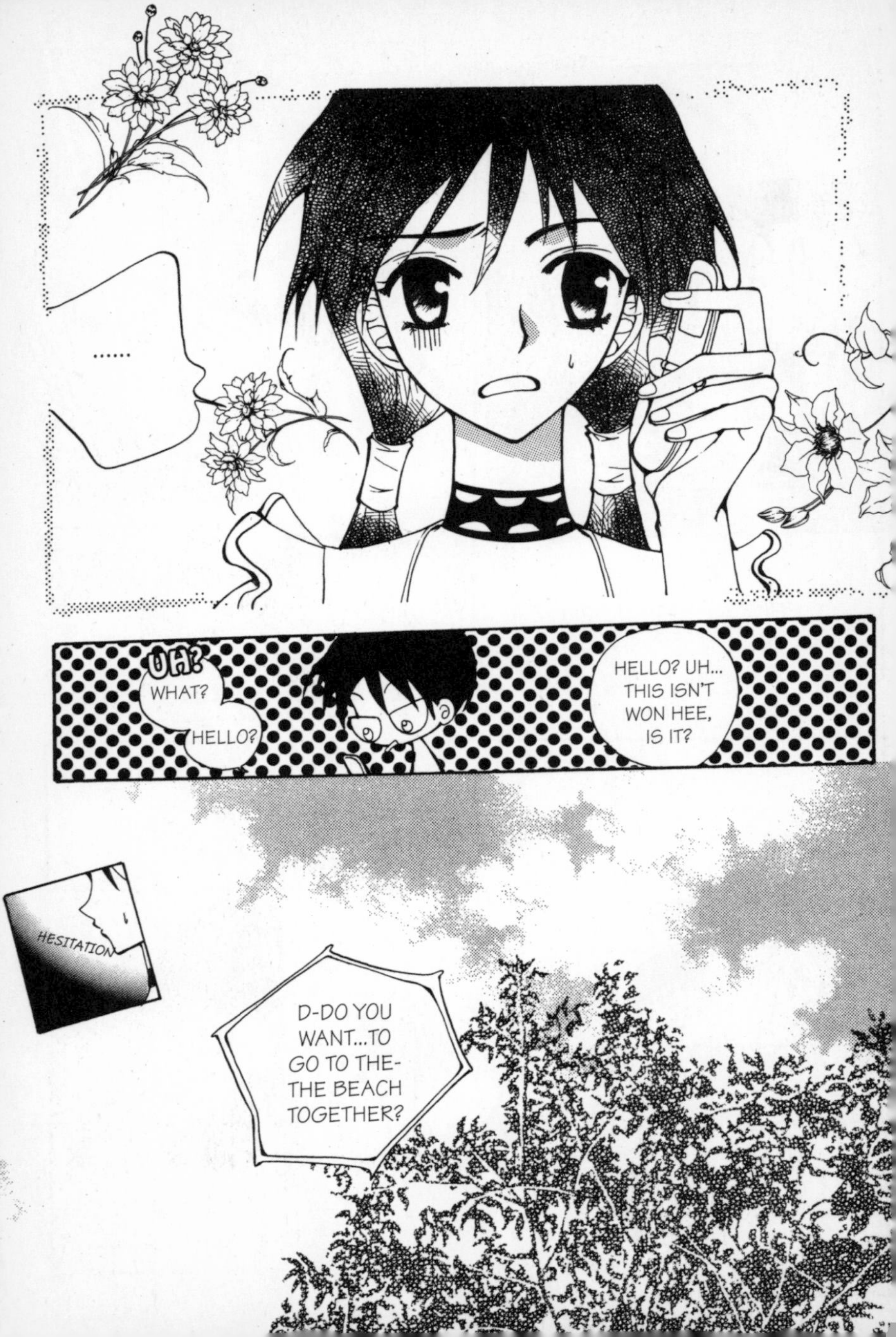
......
UH?
WHAT?
HELLO?
HELLO? UH... THIS ISN'T WON HEE, IS IT?
HESITATION
D-DO YOU WANT...TO GO TO THE- THE BEACH TOGETHER?

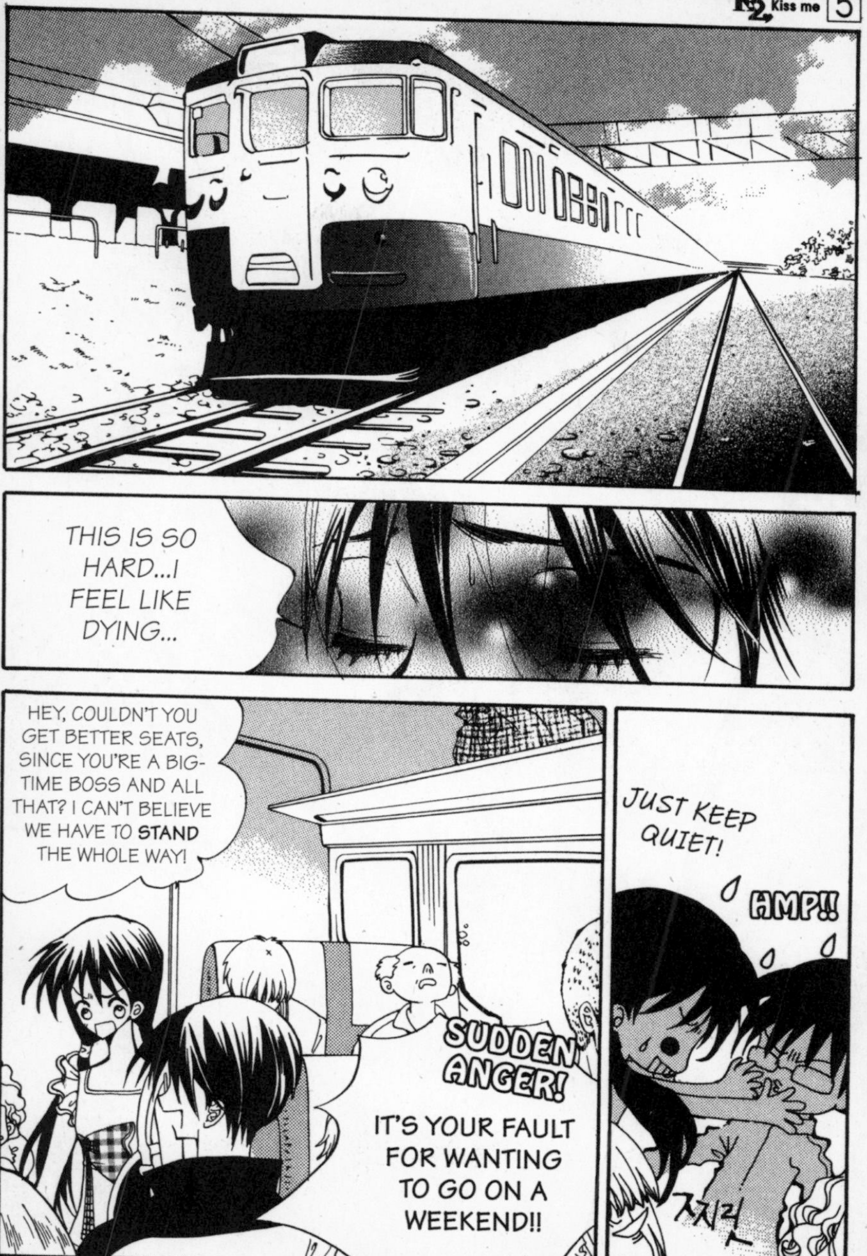
THIS IS SO HARD...I FEEL LIKE DYING...
HEY, COULDN'T YOU GET BETTER SEATS, SINCE YOU'RE A BIG-TIME BOSS AND ALL THAT? I CAN'T BELIEVE WE HAVE TO **STAND** THE WHOLE WAY!
SUDDEN ANGER!
IT'S YOUR FAULT FOR WANTING TO GO ON A WEEKEND!!
JUST KEEP QUIET!
HMP!!
STARE

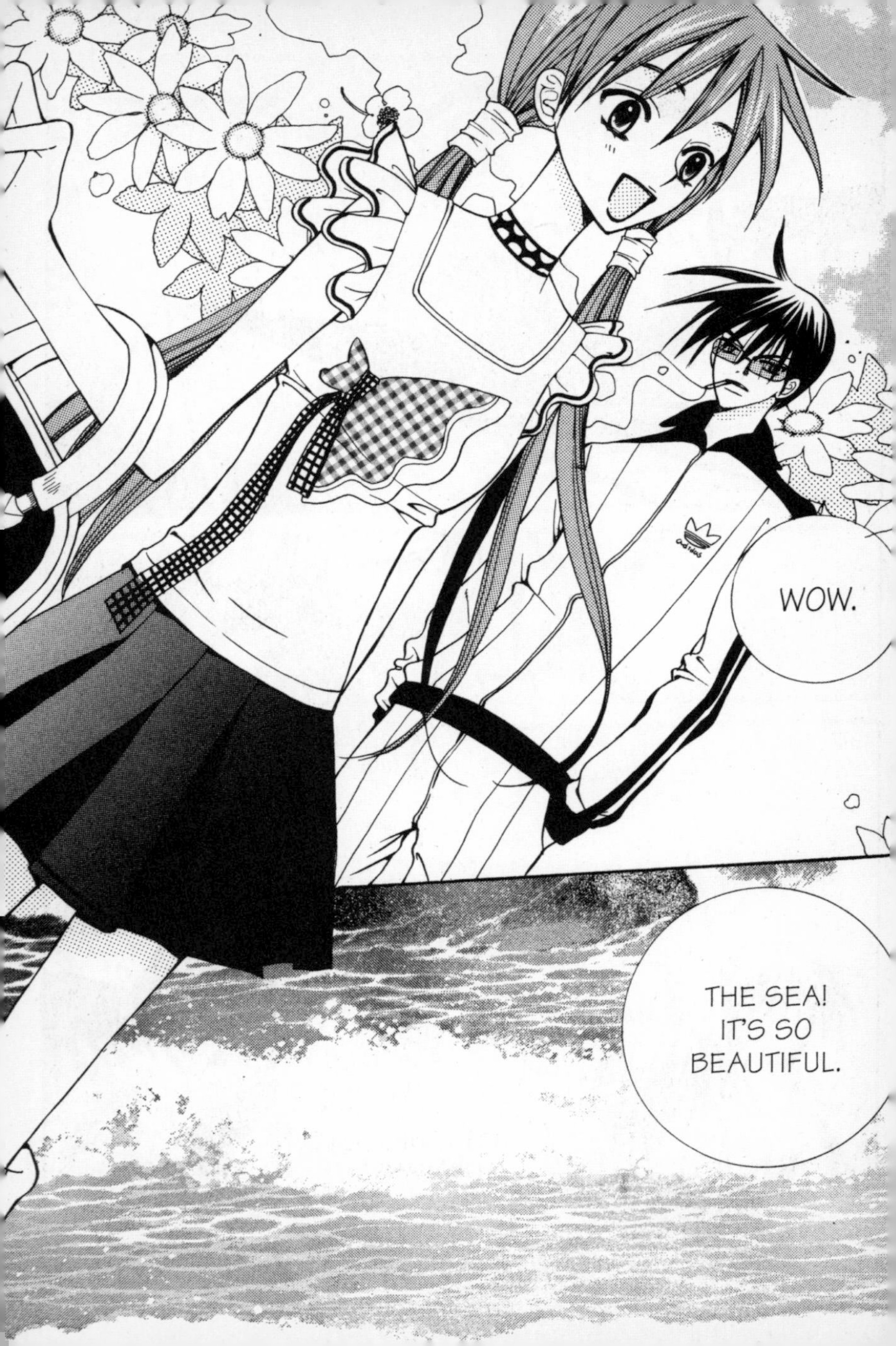
WOW.
THE SEA! IT'S SO BEAUTIFUL.

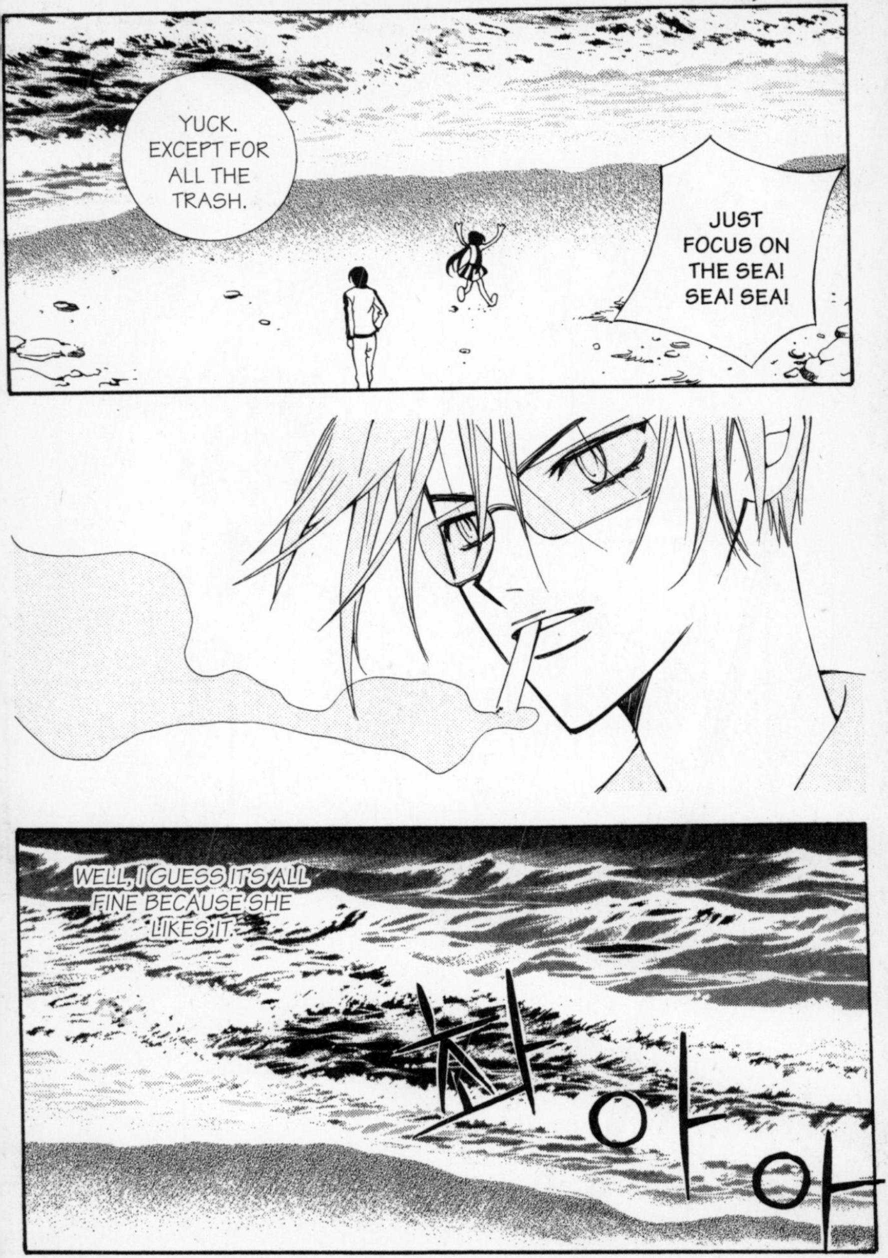
YUCK. EXCEPT FOR ALL THE TRASH.
JUST FOCUS ON THE SEA! SEA! SEA!
WELL, I GUESS ITS ALL FINE BECAUSE SHE LIKES IT.
쏴아아아

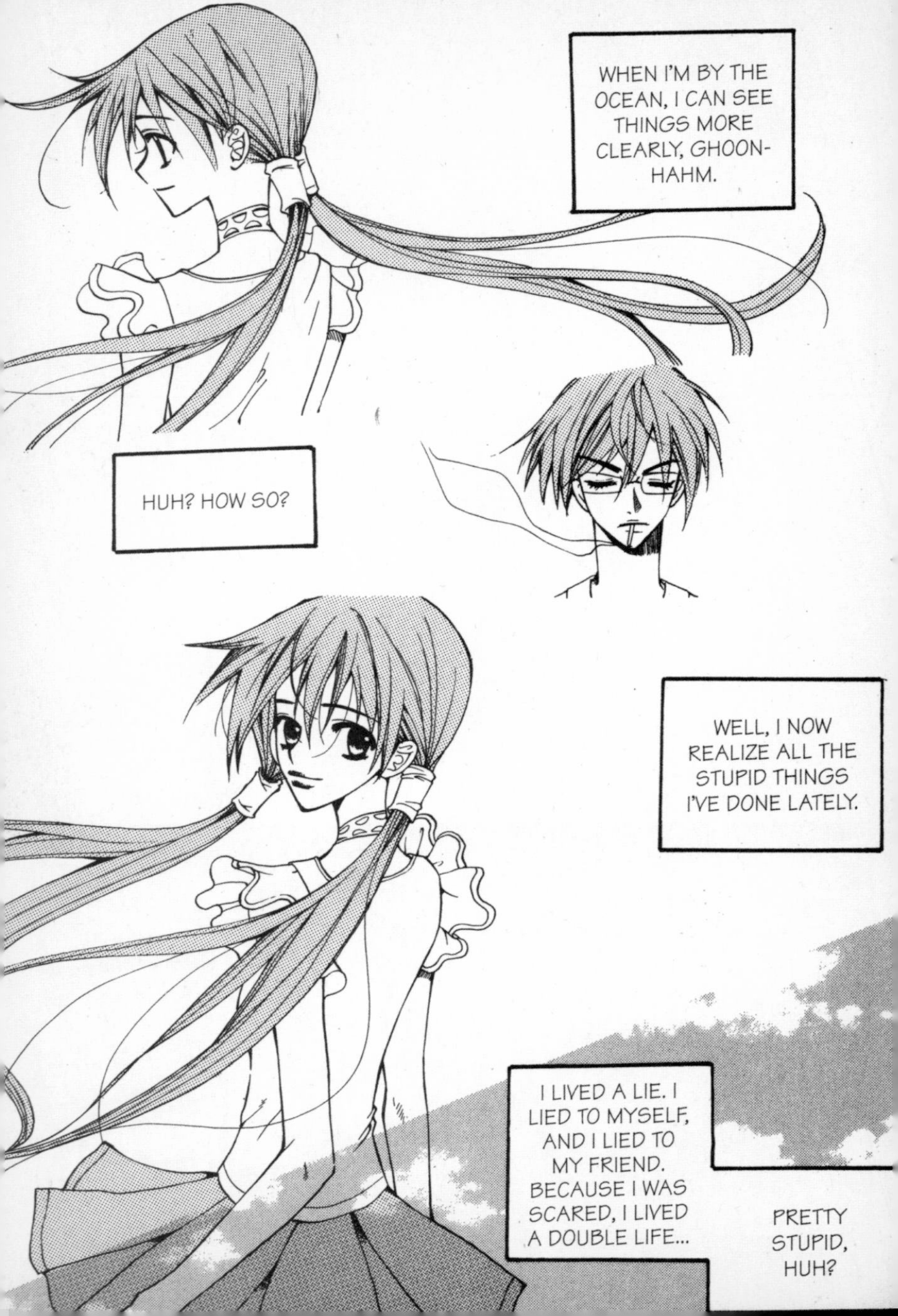
WHEN I'M BY THE OCEAN, I CAN SEE THINGS MORE CLEARLY, GHOON-HAHM.
HUH? HOW SO?
WELL, I NOW REALIZE ALL THE STUPID THINGS I'VE DONE LATELY.
I LIVED A LIE. I LIED TO MYSELF, AND I LIED TO MY FRIEND. BECAUSE I WAS SCARED, I LIVED A DOUBLE LIFE...
PRETTY STUPID, HUH?

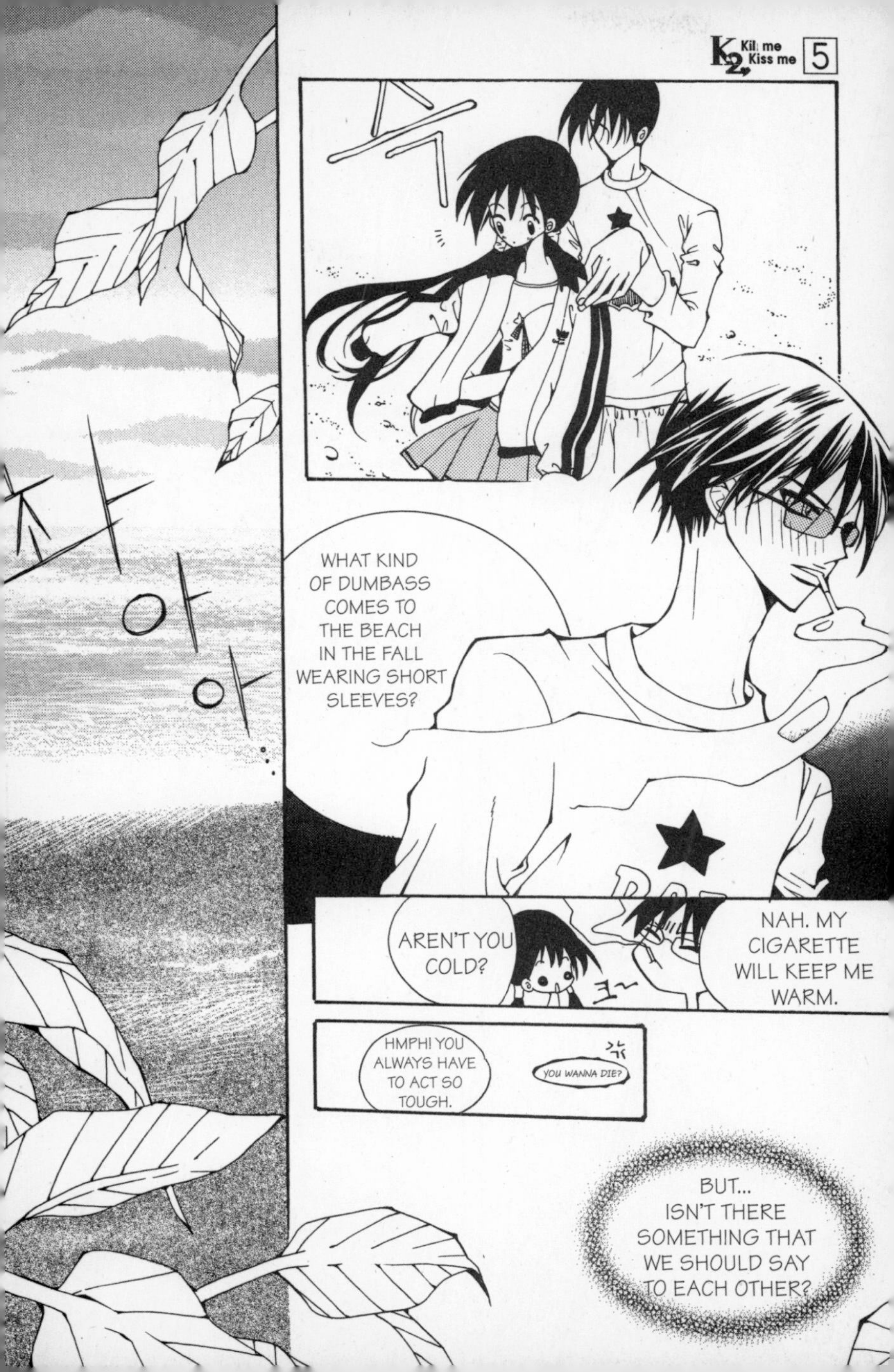
쏴아아
WHAT KIND OF DUMBASS COMES TO THE BEACH IN THE FALL WEARING SHORT SLEEVES?
AREN'T YOU COLD?
NAH. MY CIGARETTE WILL KEEP ME WARM.
HMPH! YOU ALWAYS HAVE TO ACT SO TOUGH.
YOU WANNA DIE?
BUT... ISN'T THERE SOMETHING THAT WE SHOULD SAY TO EACH OTHER?

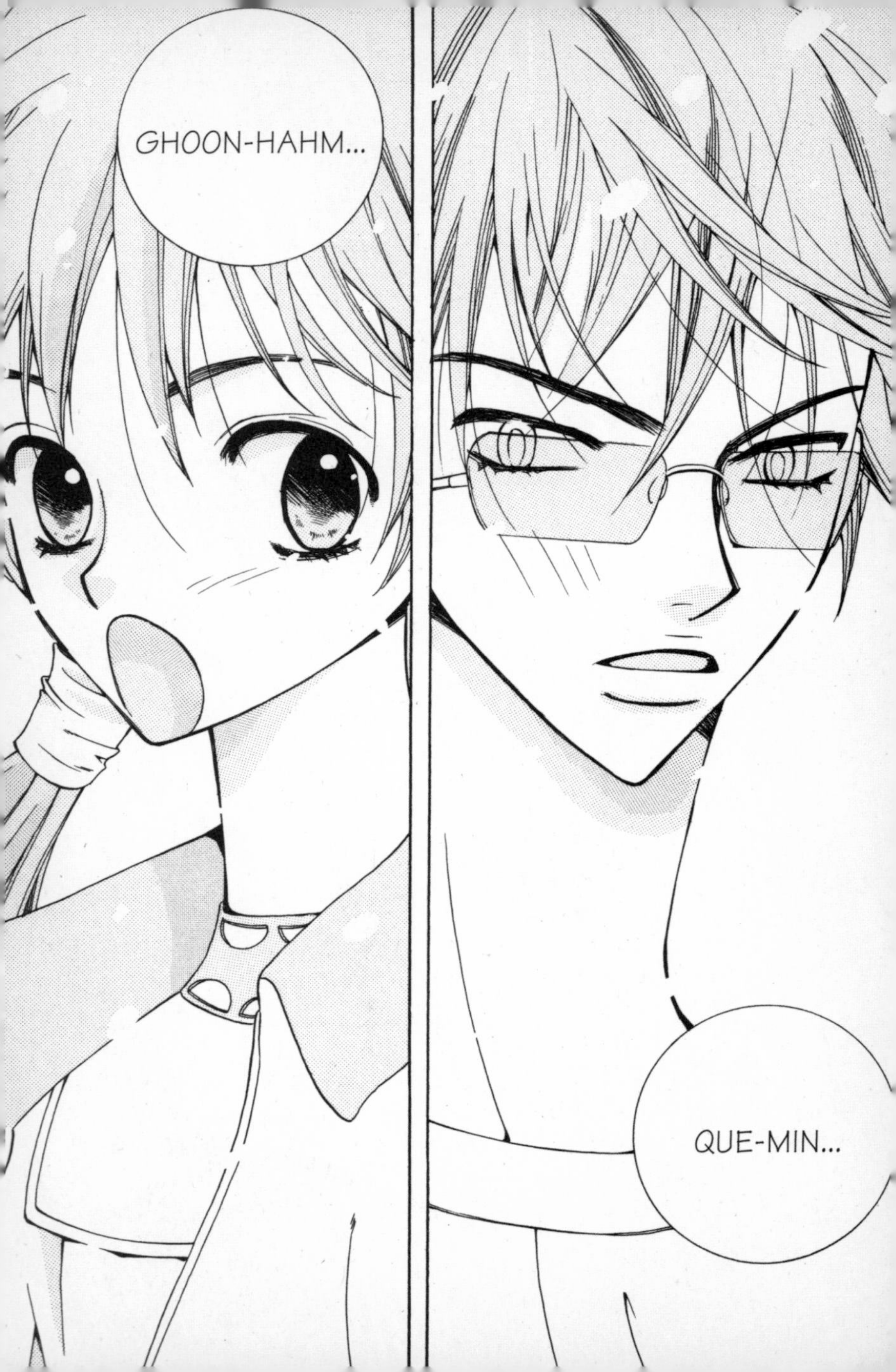
GHOON-HAHM...
QUE-MIN...

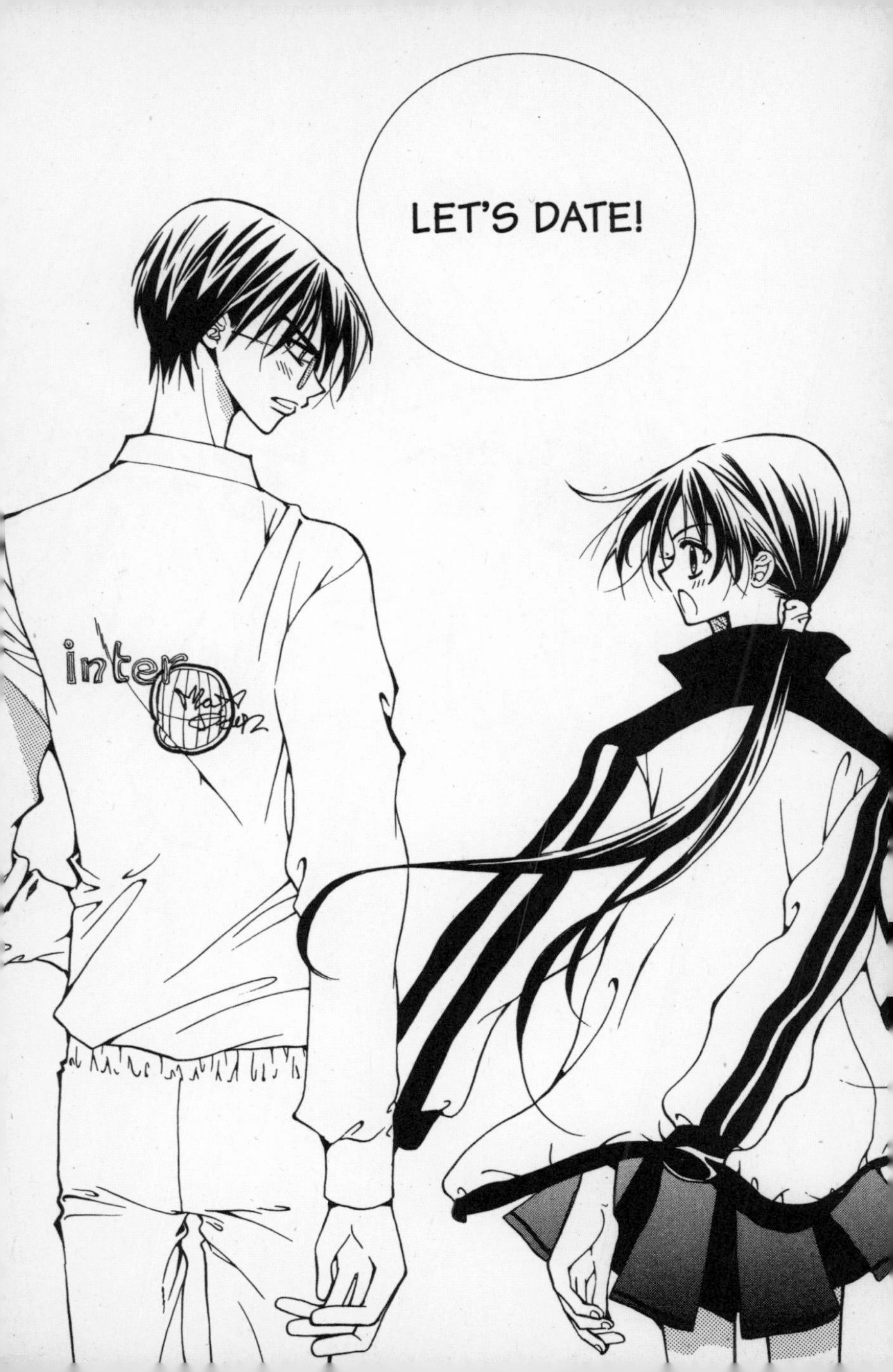
LET'S DATE!
inter

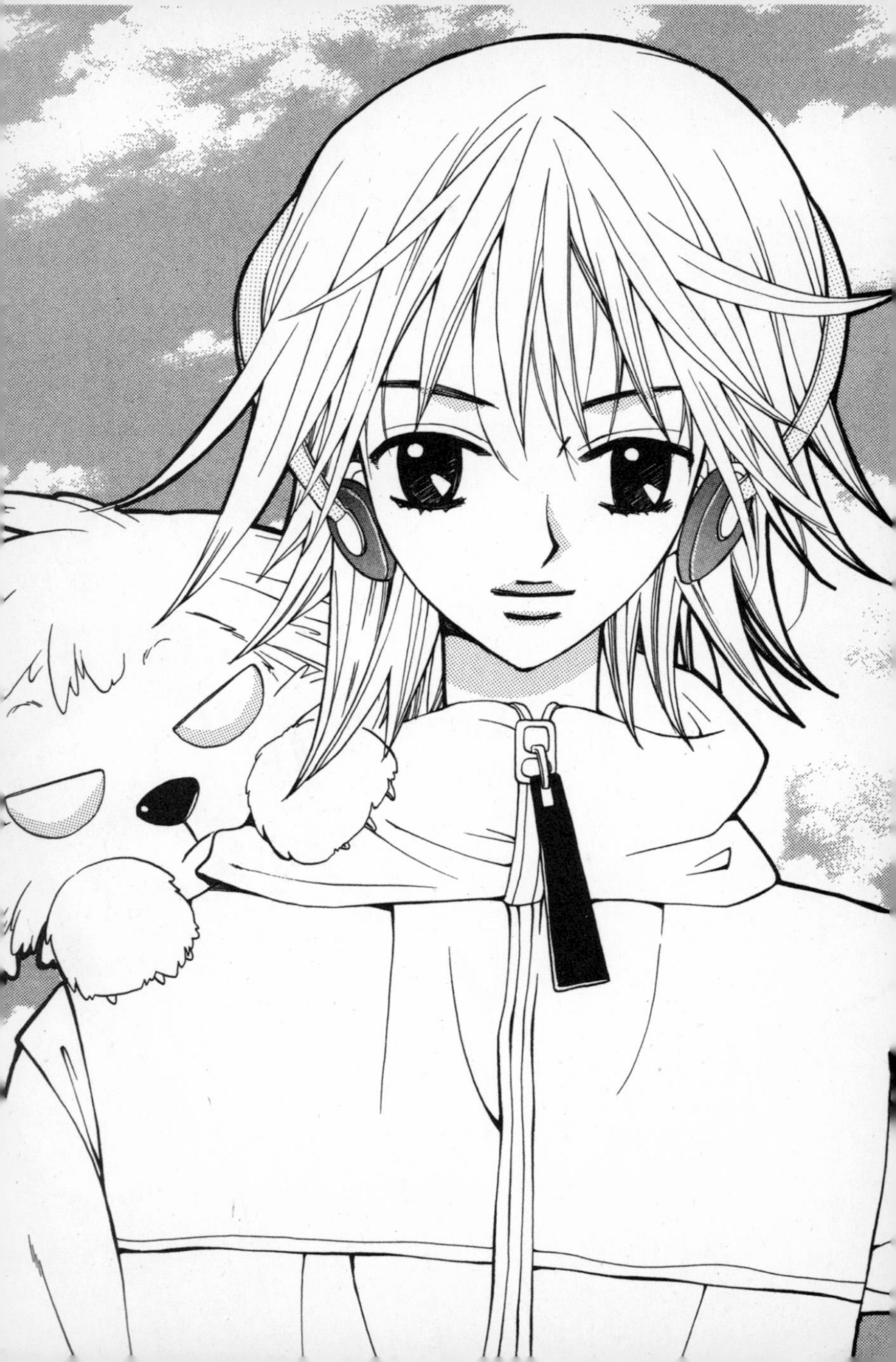

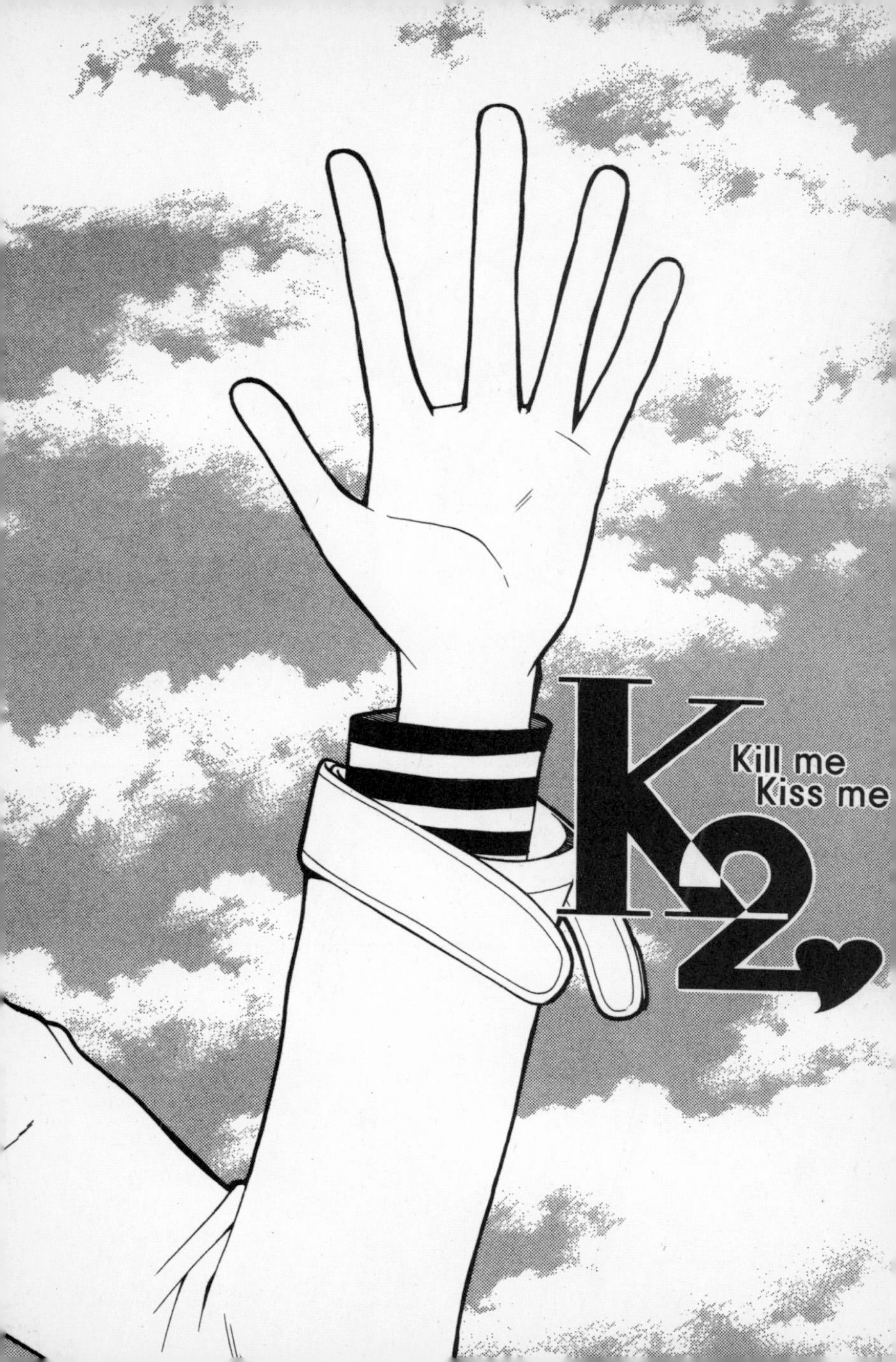
K2
Kill me
Kiss me

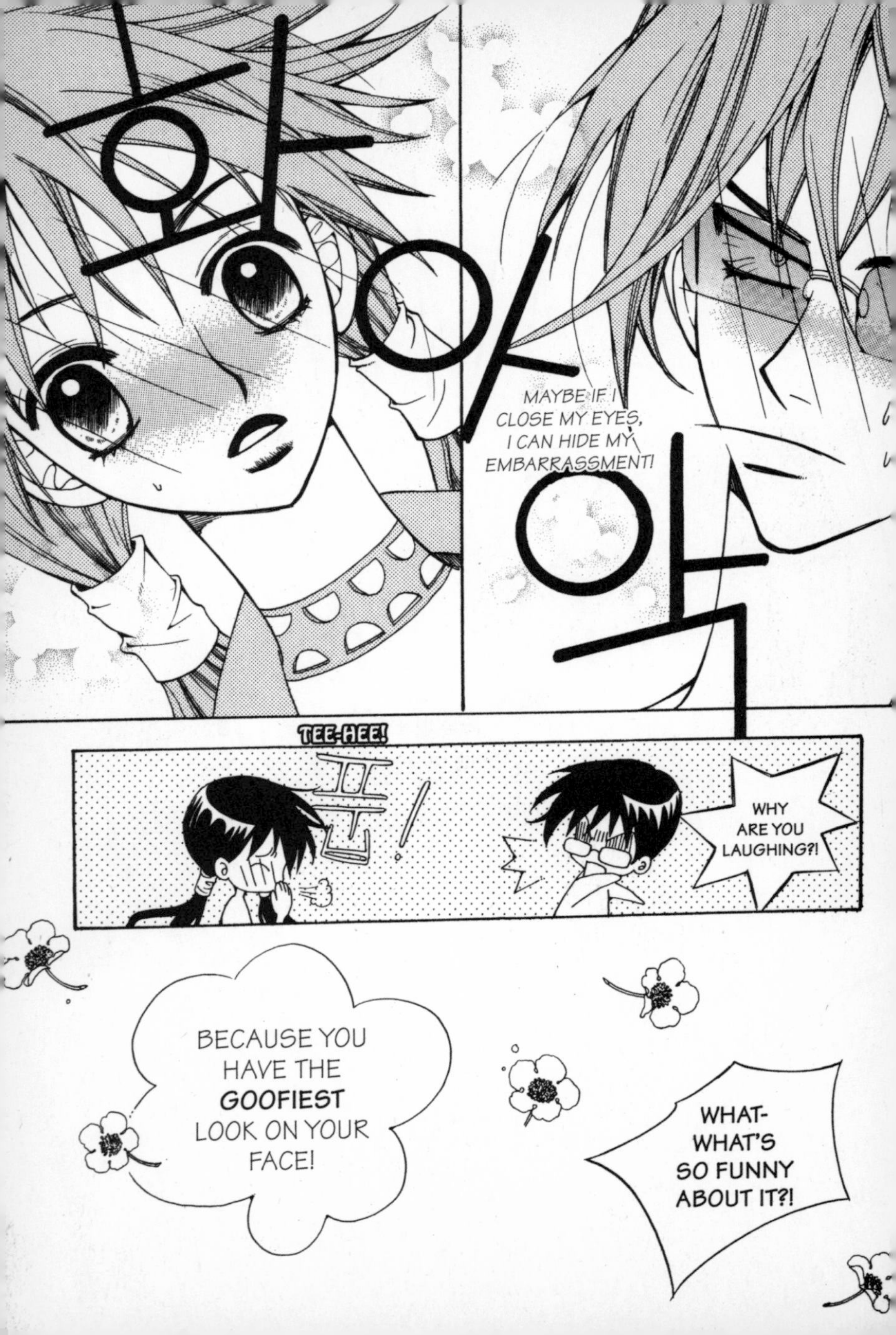
MAYBE IF I CLOSE MY EYES, I CAN HIDE MY EMBARRASSMENT!
TEE-HEE!
WHY ARE YOU LAUGHING?!
BECAUSE YOU HAVE THE GOOFIEST LOOK ON YOUR FACE!
WHAT-WHAT'S SO FUNNY ABOUT IT?!

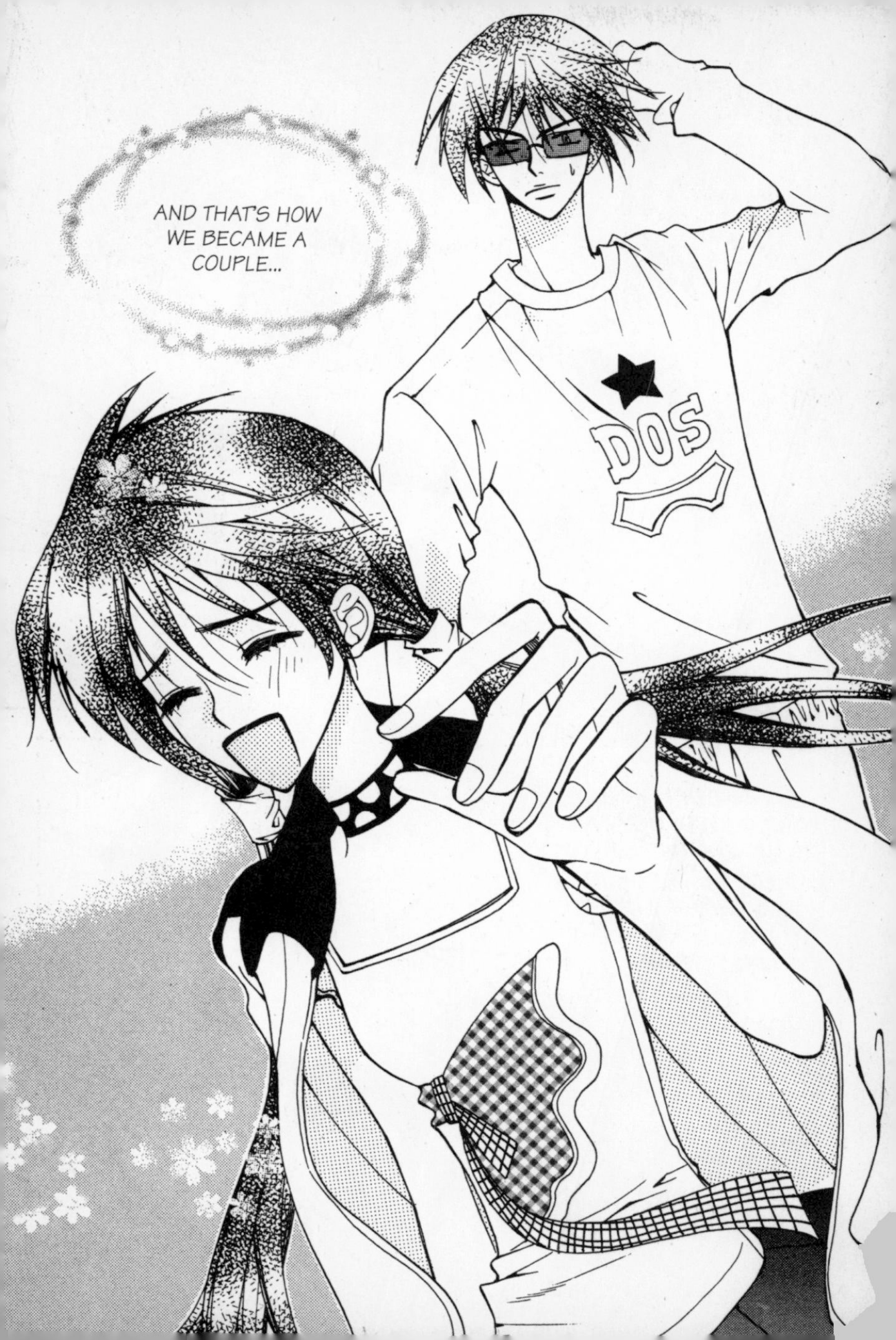
AND THAT'S HOW WE BECAME A COUPLE...
DOS

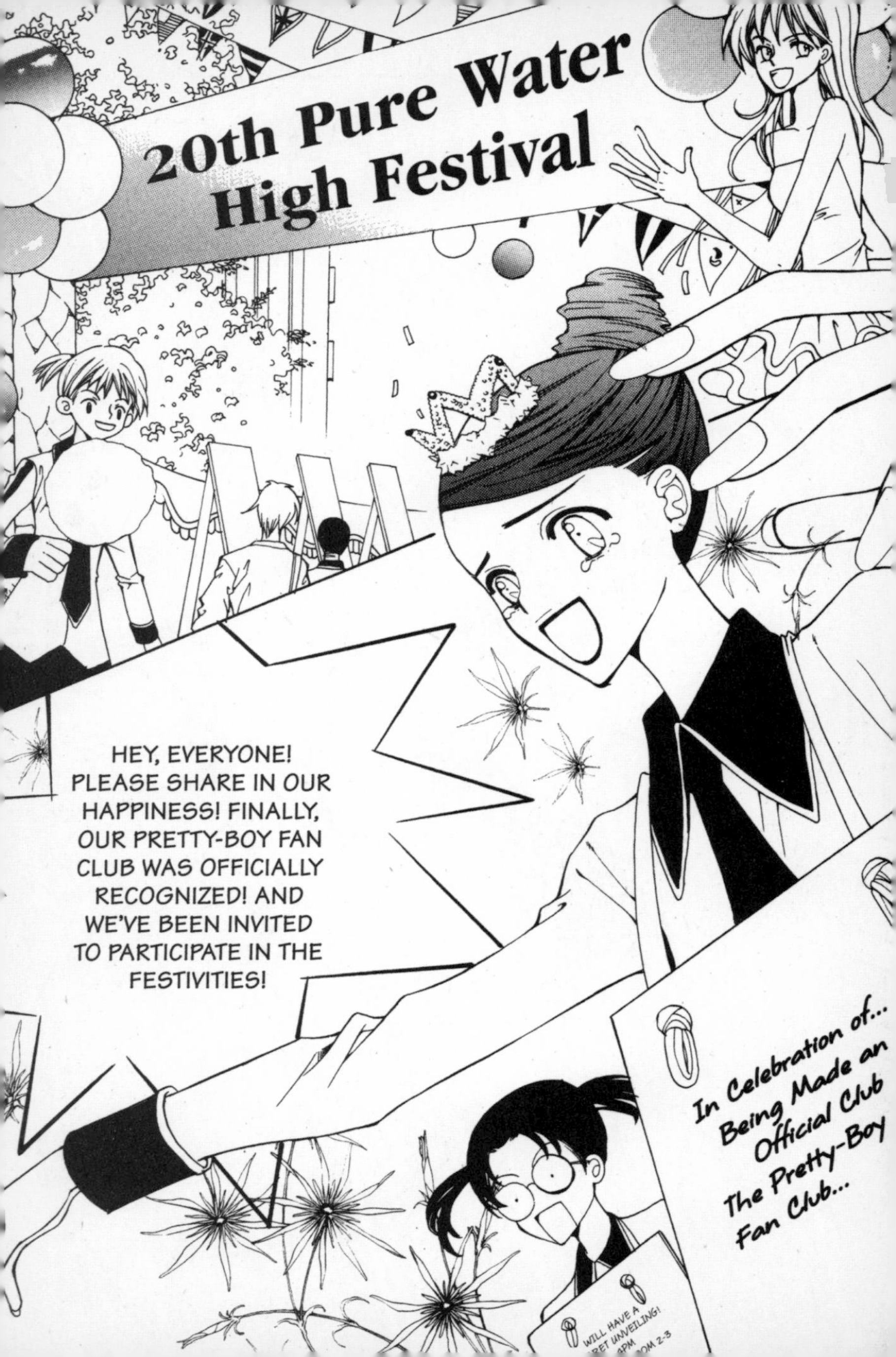
20th Pure Water High Festival
HEY, EVERYONE! PLEASE SHARE IN OUR HAPPINESS! FINALLY, OUR PRETTY-BOY FAN CLUB WAS OFFICIALLY RECOGNIZED! AND WE'VE BEEN INVITED TO PARTICIPATE IN THE FESTIVITIES!
In Celebration of... Being Made an Official Club The Pretty-Boy Fan Club...

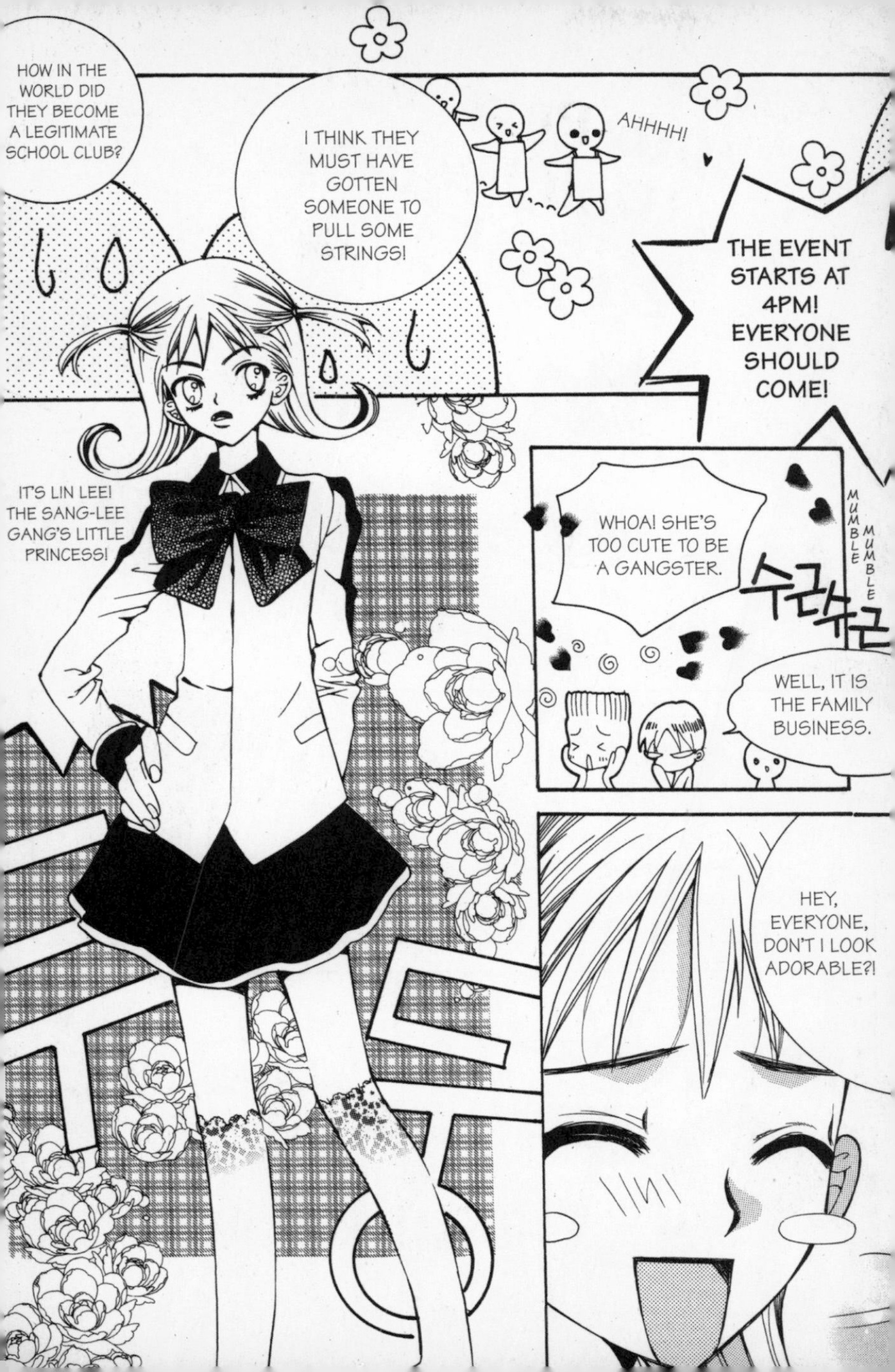
HOW IN THE WORLD DID THEY BECOME A LEGITIMATE SCHOOL CLUB?
I THINK THEY MUST HAVE GOTTEN SOMEONE TO PULL SOME STRINGS!
AHHHH!
THE EVENT STARTS AT 4PM! EVERYONE SHOULD COME!
IT'S LIN LEE! THE SANG-LEE GANG'S LITTLE PRINCESS!
WHOA! SHE'S TOO CUTE TO BE A GANGSTER.
MUMBLE MUMBLE
수군수군
WELL, IT IS THE FAMILY BUSINESS.
HEY, EVERYONE, DON'T I LOOK ADORABLE?!

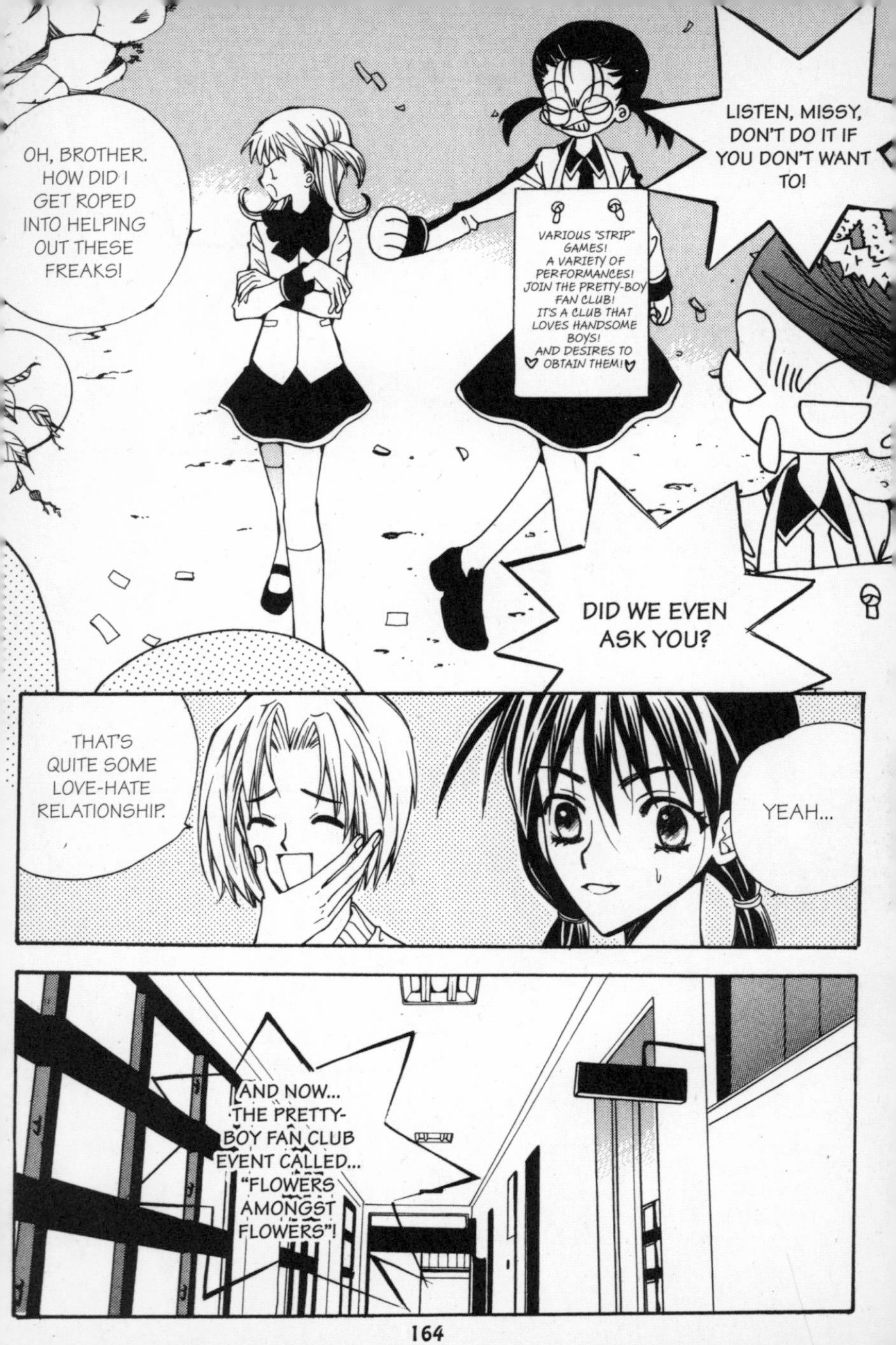
OH, BROTHER. HOW DID I GET ROPED INTO HELPING OUT THESE FREAKS!
VARIOUS "STRIP" GAMES! A VARIETY OF PERFORMANCES! JOIN THE PRETTY-BOY FAN CLUB! IT'S A CLUB THAT LOVES HANDSOME BOYS! AND DESIRES TO OBTAIN THEM!
LISTEN, MISSY, DON'T DO IT IF YOU DON'T WANT TO!
DID WE EVEN ASK YOU?
THAT'S QUITE SOME LOVE-HATE RELATIONSHIP.
YEAH...
AND NOW... THE PRETTY-BOY FAN CLUB EVENT CALLED... "FLOWERS AMONGST FLOWERS"!

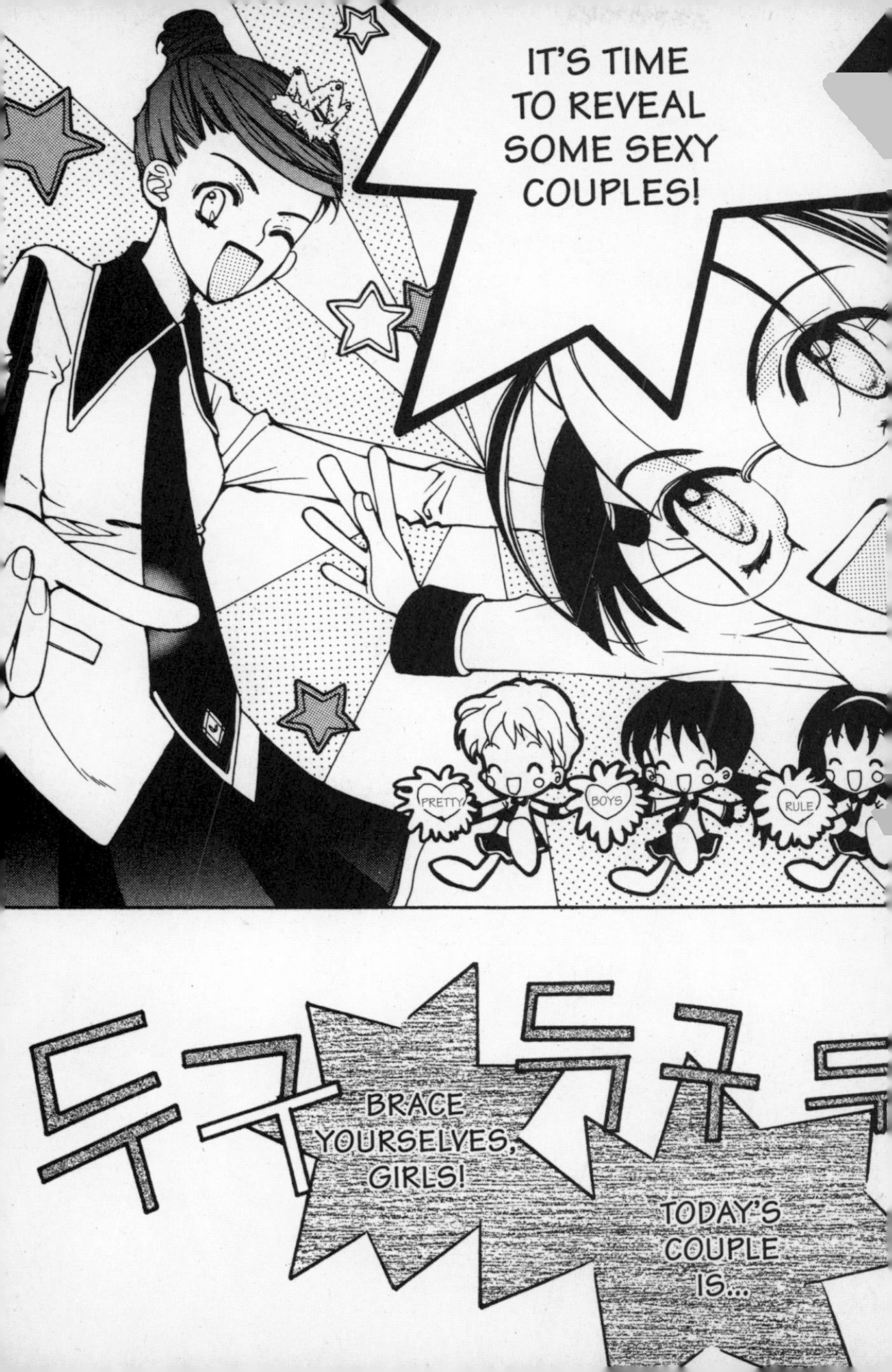
IT'S TIME TO REVEAL SOME SEXY COUPLES!
PRETTY
BOYS
RULE
BRACE YOURSELVES, GIRLS!
TODAY'S COUPLE IS...

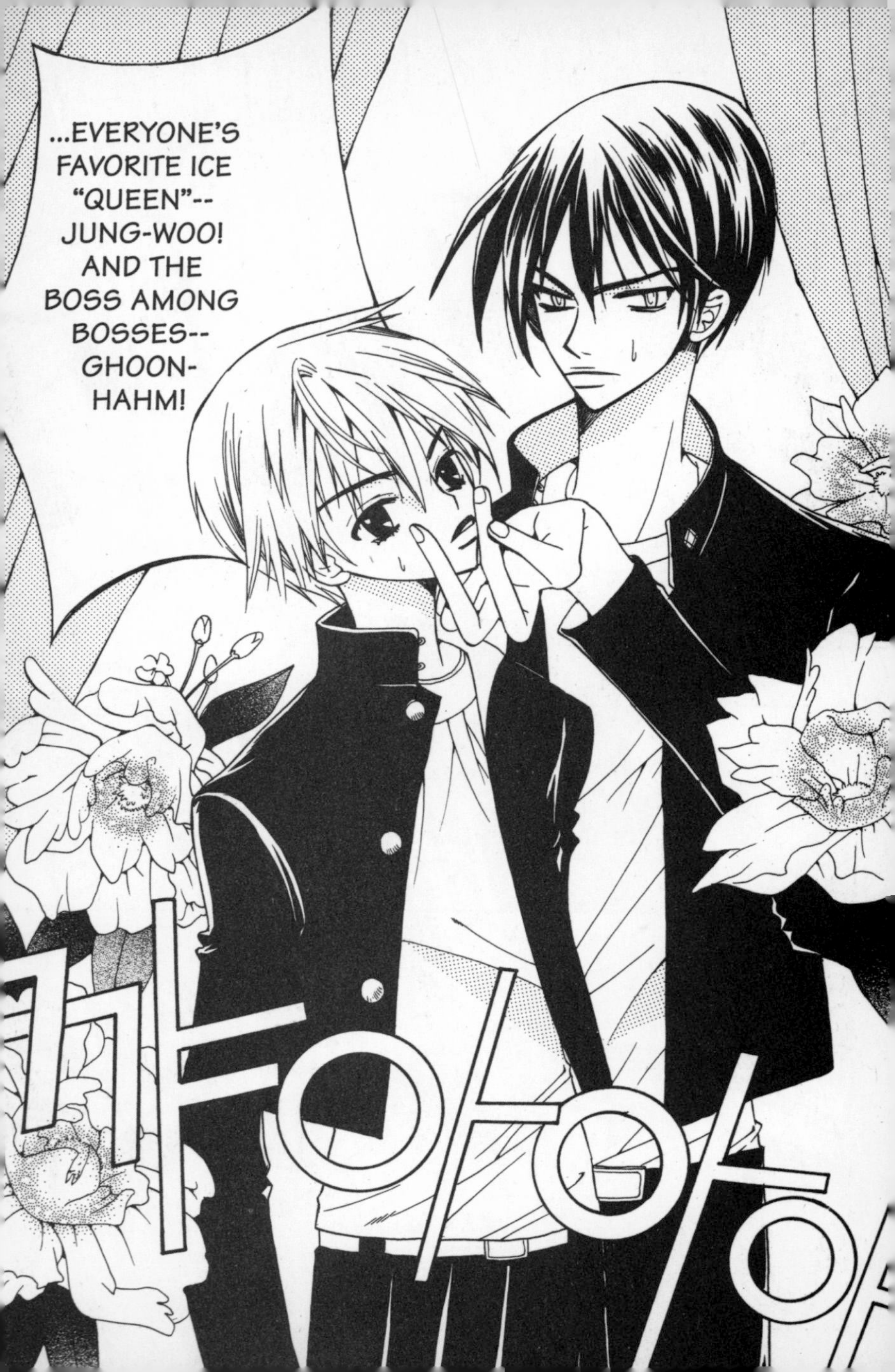
...EVERYONE'S FAVORITE ICE "QUEEN"-- JUNG-WOO! AND THE BOSS AMONG BOSSES-- GHOON-HAHM!

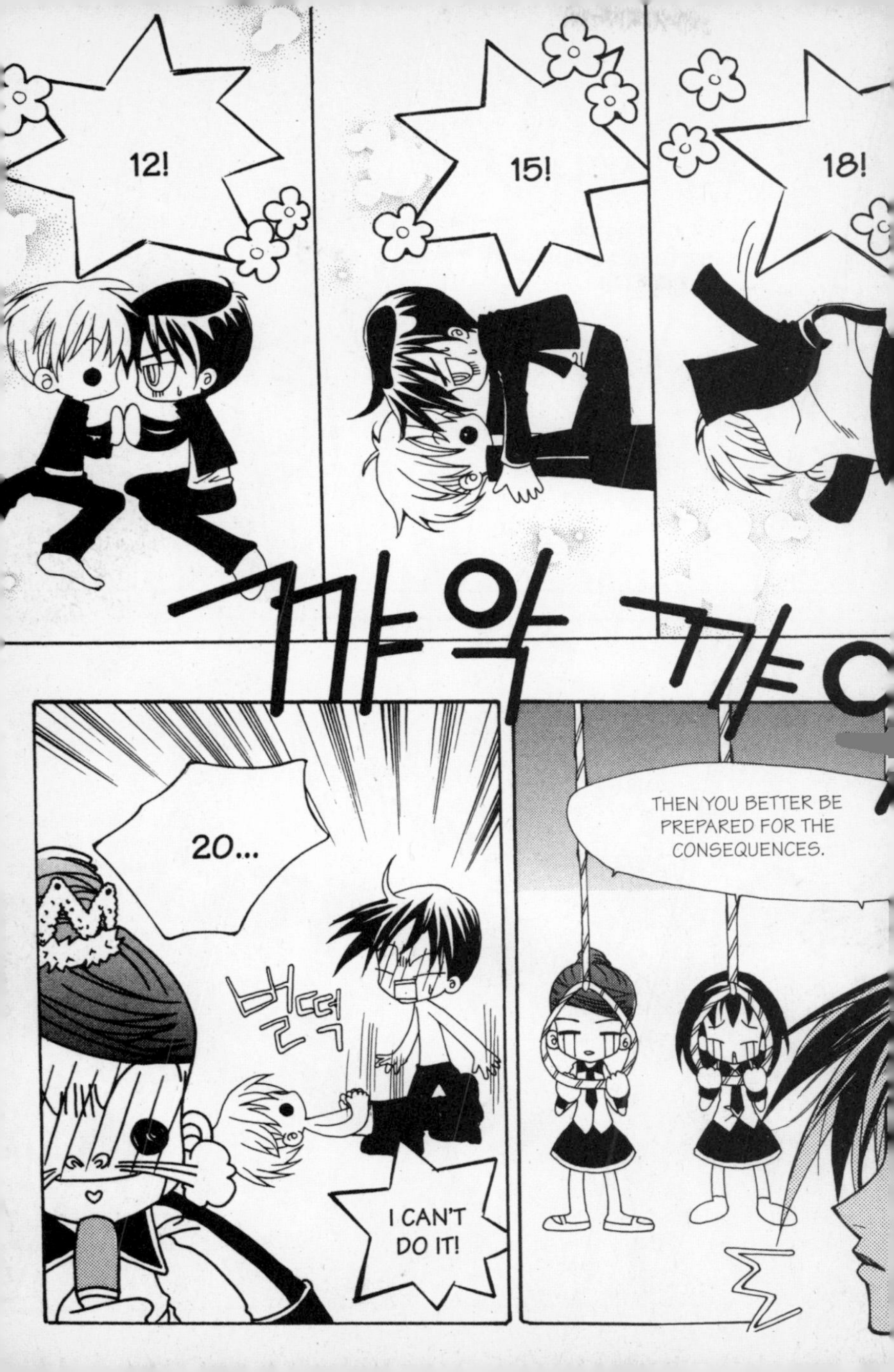
12!
15!
18!
20...
벌떡
I CAN'T DO IT!
THEN YOU BETTER BE PREPARED FOR THE CONSEQUENCES.

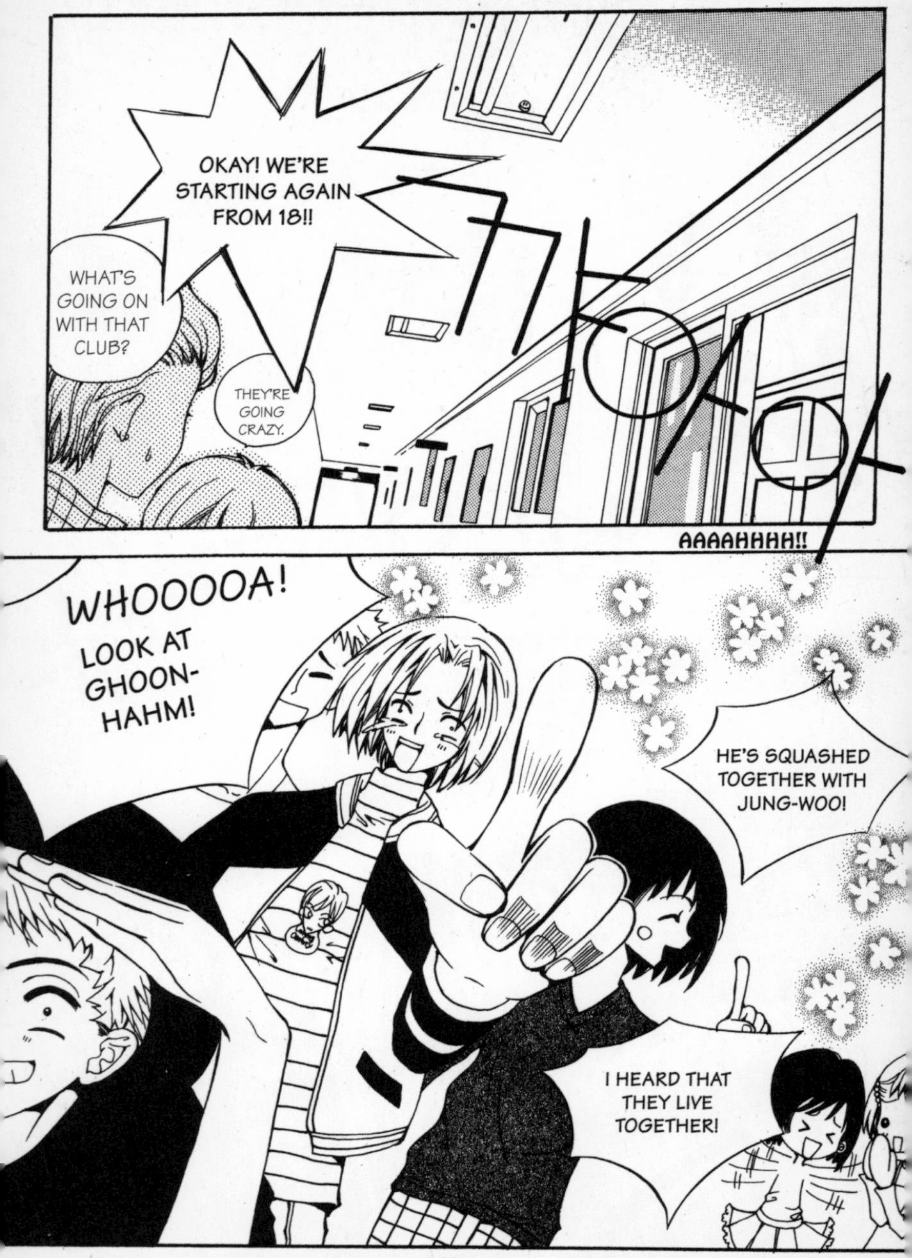
OKAY! WE'RE STARTING AGAIN FROM 18!!
WHAT'S GOING ON WITH THAT CLUB?
THEY'RE GOING CRAZY.
AAAAHHHH!!
WHOOOOA!
LOOK AT GHOON-HAHM!
HE'S SQUASHED TOGETHER WITH JUNG-WOO!
I HEARD THAT THEY LIVE TOGETHER!

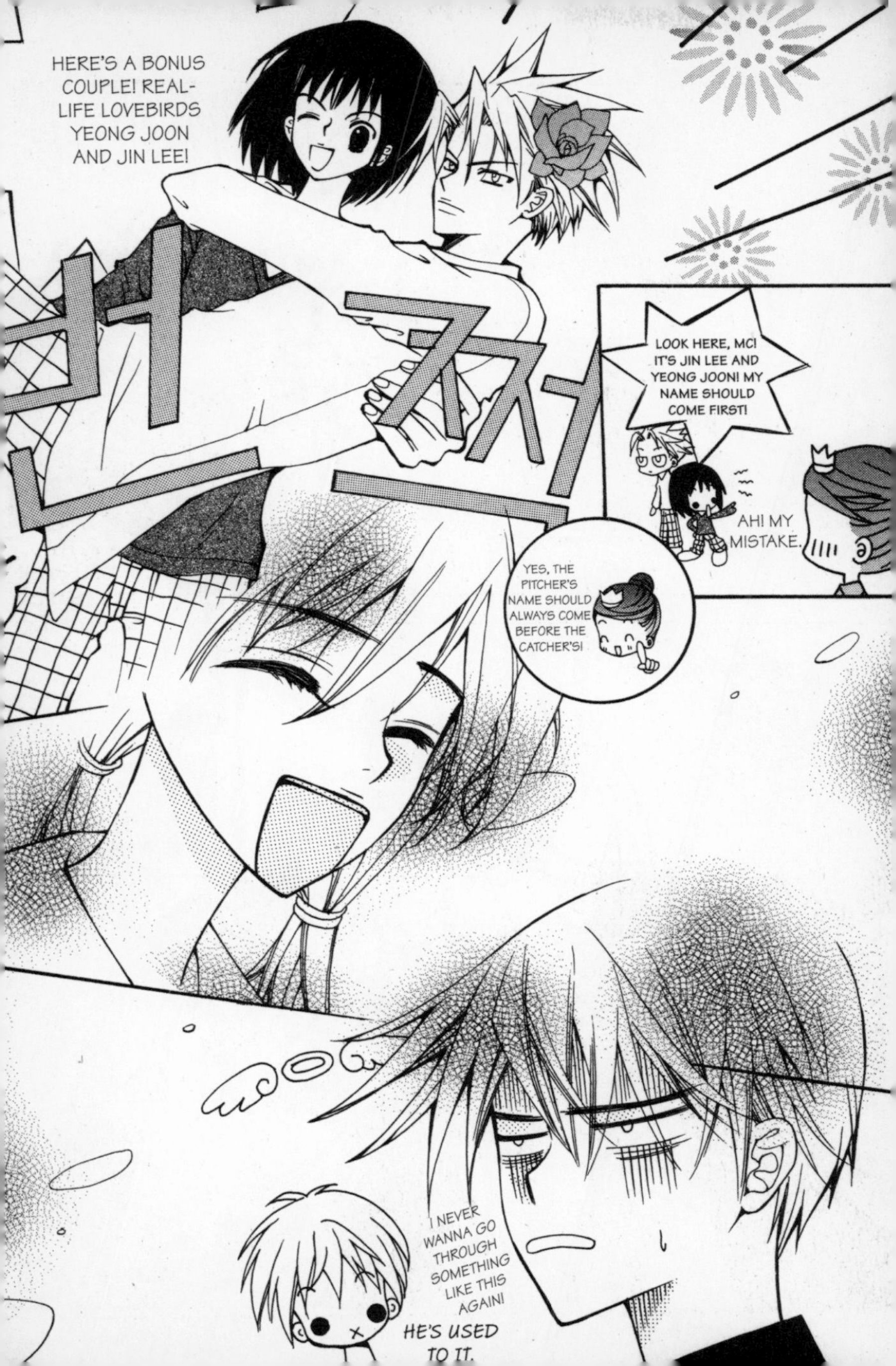
HERE'S A BONUS COUPLE! REAL-LIFE LOVEBIRDS YEONG JOON AND JIN LEE!
LOOK HERE, MC! IT'S JIN LEE AND YEONG JOON! MY NAME SHOULD COME FIRST!
AH! MY MISTAKE.
YES, THE PITCHER'S NAME SHOULD ALWAYS COME BEFORE THE CATCHER'S!
I NEVER WANNA GO THROUGH SOMETHING LIKE THIS AGAIN!
HE'S USED TO IT.

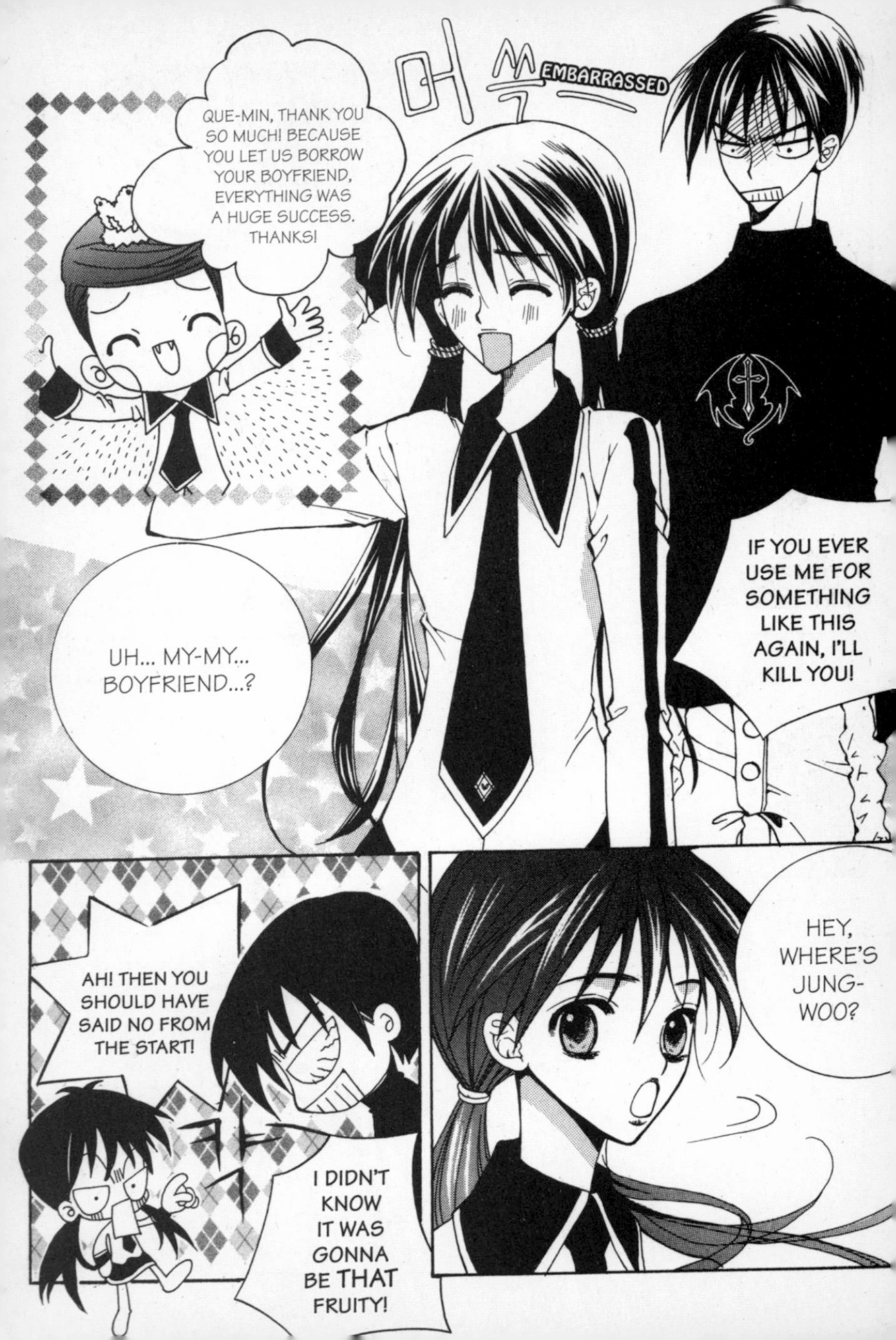
QUE-MIN, THANK YOU SO MUCH! BECAUSE YOU LET US BORROW YOUR BOYFRIEND, EVERYTHING WAS A HUGE SUCCESS. THANKS!
EMBARRASSED
UH... MY-MY... BOYFRIEND...?
IF YOU EVER USE ME FOR SOMETHING LIKE THIS AGAIN, I'LL KILL YOU!
AH! THEN YOU SHOULD HAVE SAID NO FROM THE START!
I DIDN'T KNOW IT WAS GONNA BE THAT FRUITY!
HEY, WHERE'S JUNG-WOO?

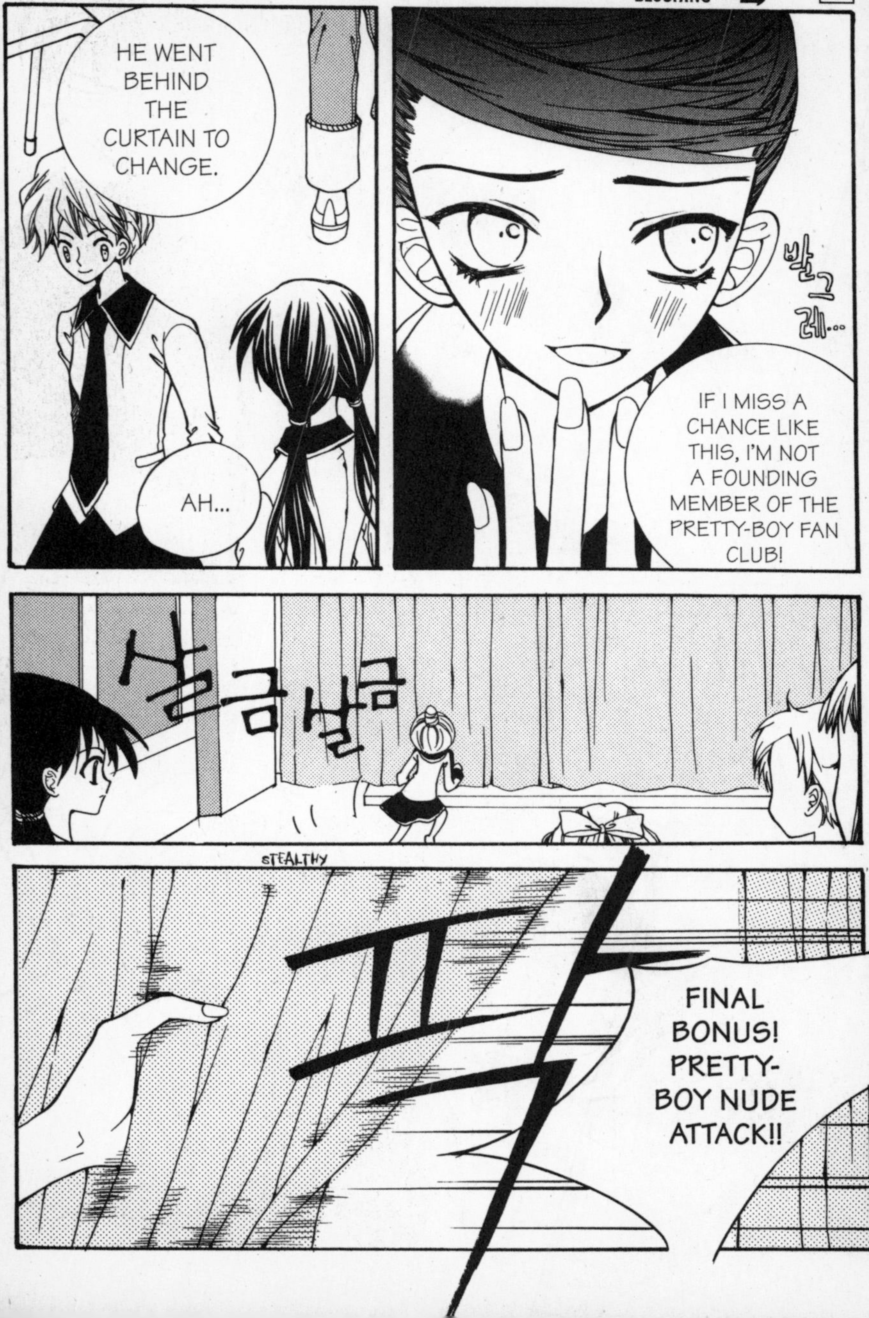
HE WENT BEHIND THE CURTAIN TO CHANGE.
AH...
발그레...
IF I MISS A CHANCE LIKE THIS, I'M NOT A FOUNDING MEMBER OF THE PRETTY-BOY FAN CLUB!
살금살금
STEALTHY
팍
FINAL BONUS! PRETTY-BOY NUDE ATTACK!!

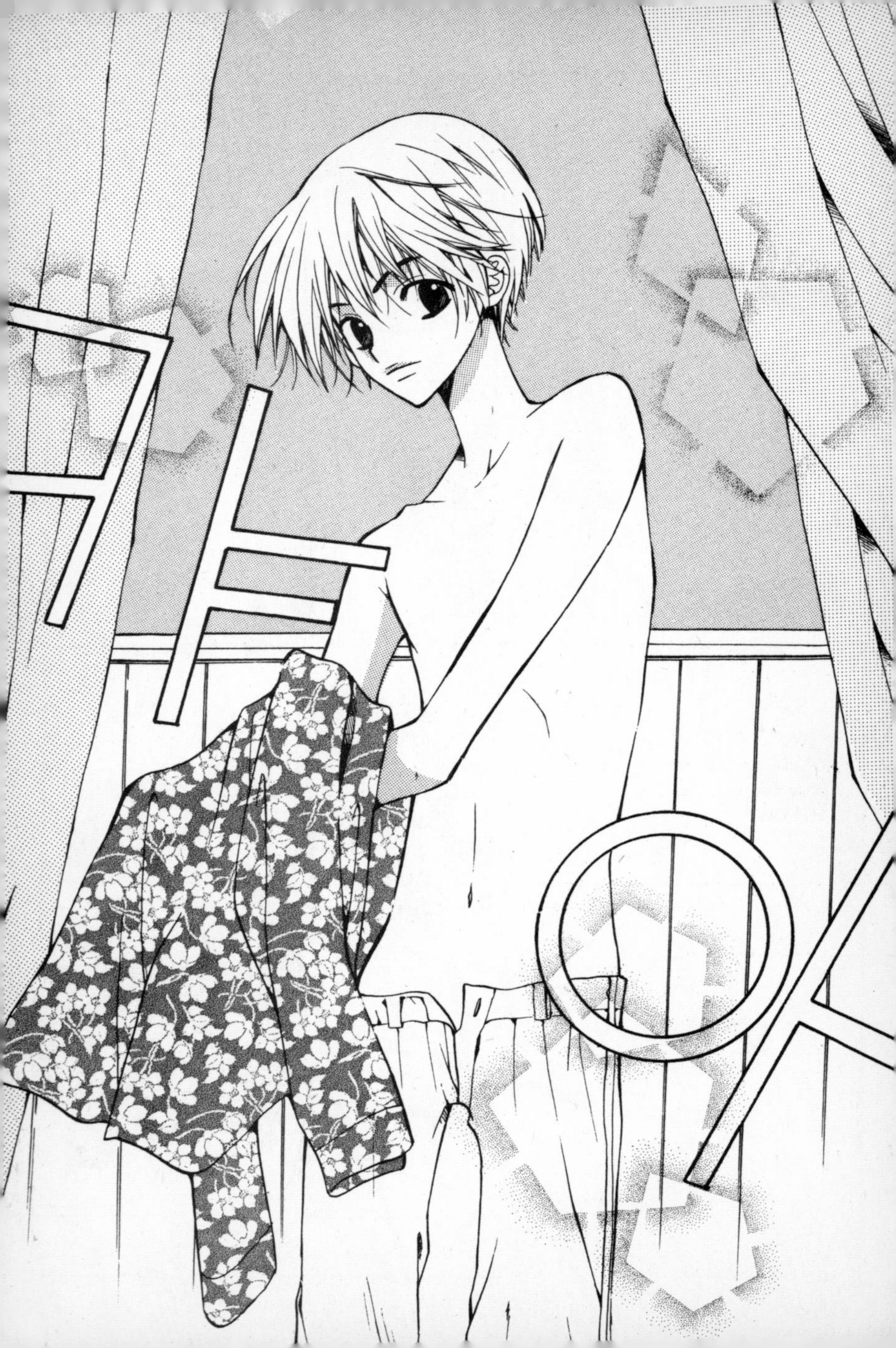

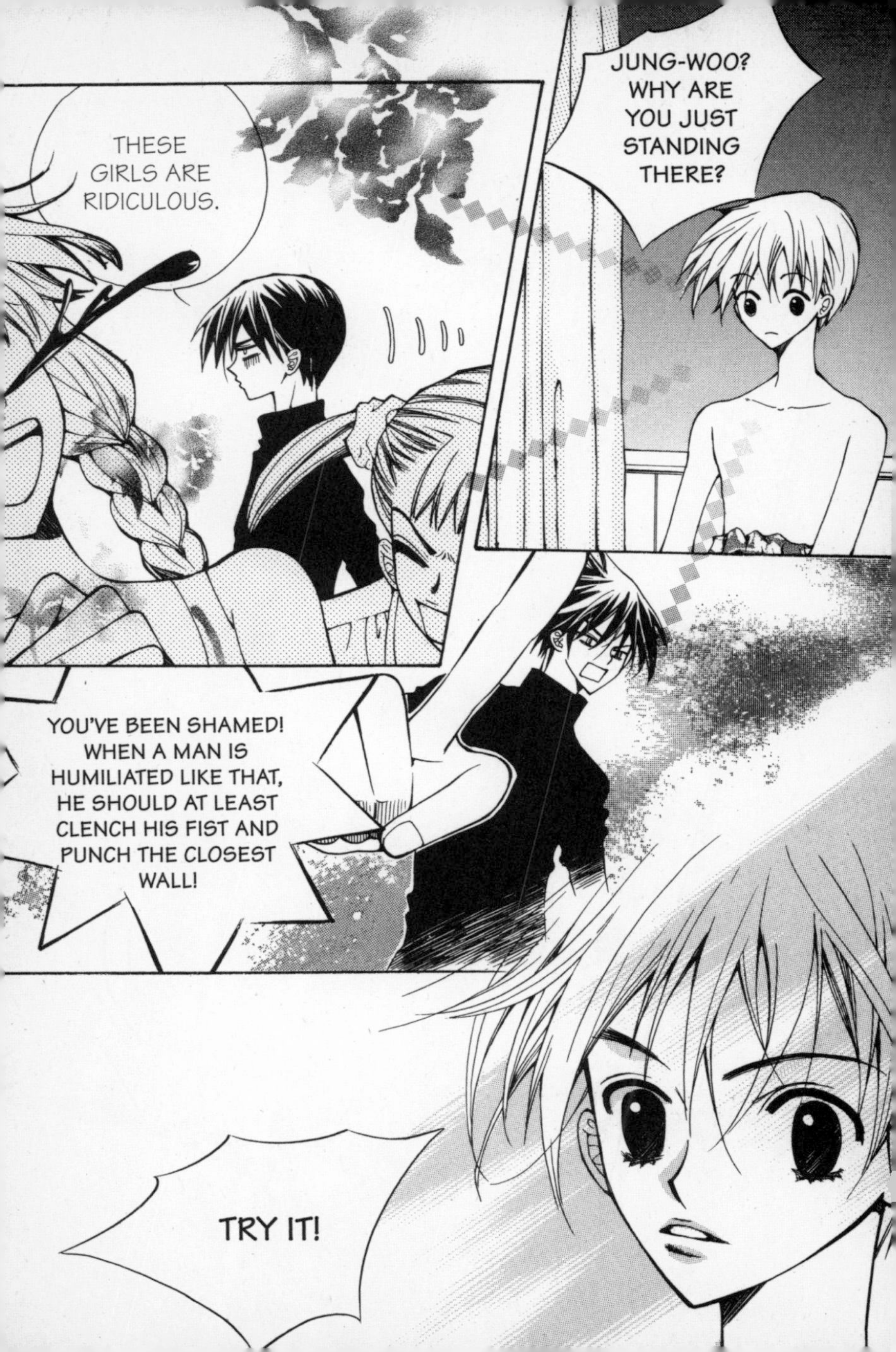
THESE GIRLS ARE RIDICULOUS.
JUNG-WOO? WHY ARE YOU JUST STANDING THERE?
YOU'VE BEEN SHAMED! WHEN A MAN IS HUMILIATED LIKE THAT, HE SHOULD AT LEAST CLENCH HIS FIST AND PUNCH THE CLOSEST WALL!
TRY IT!

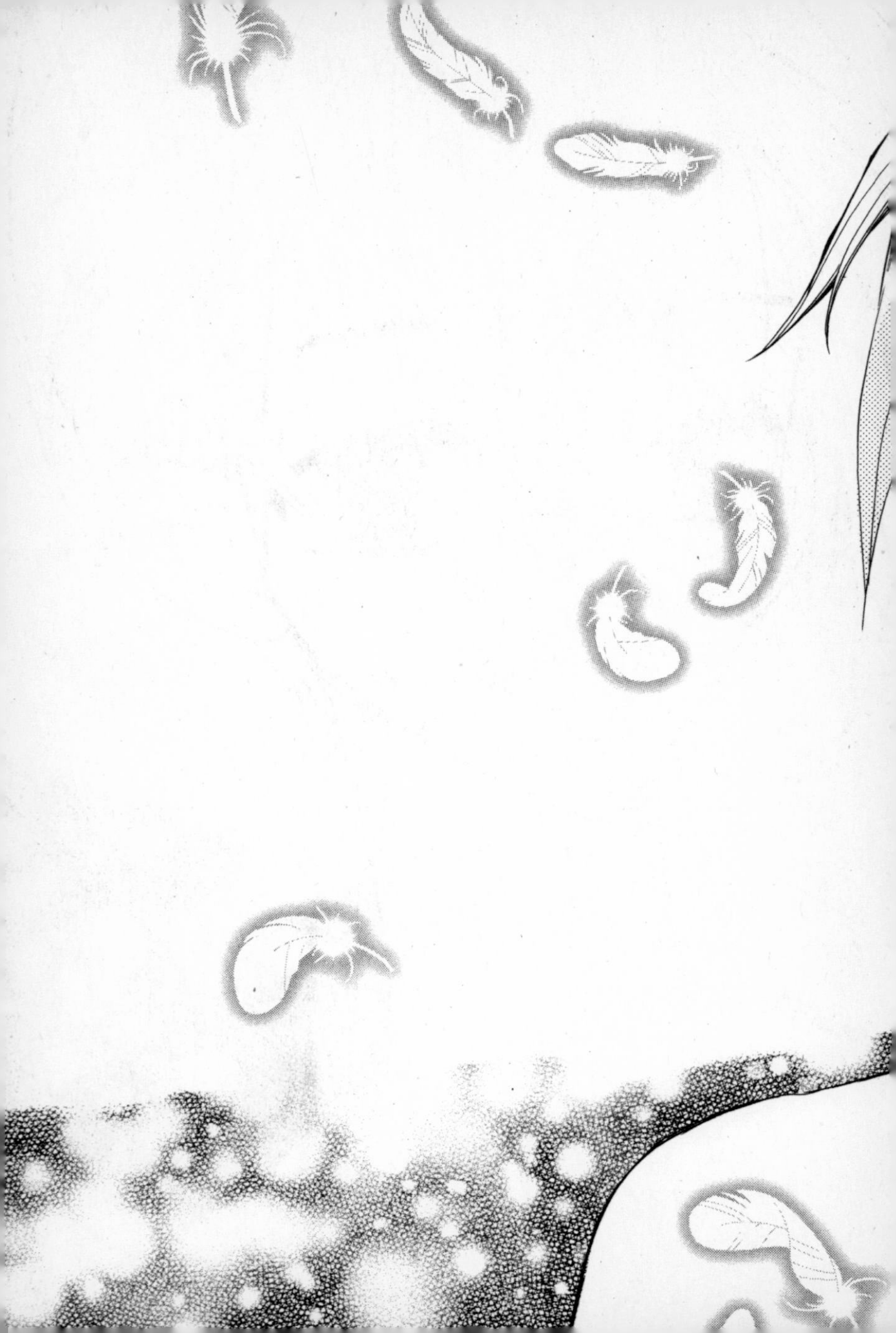

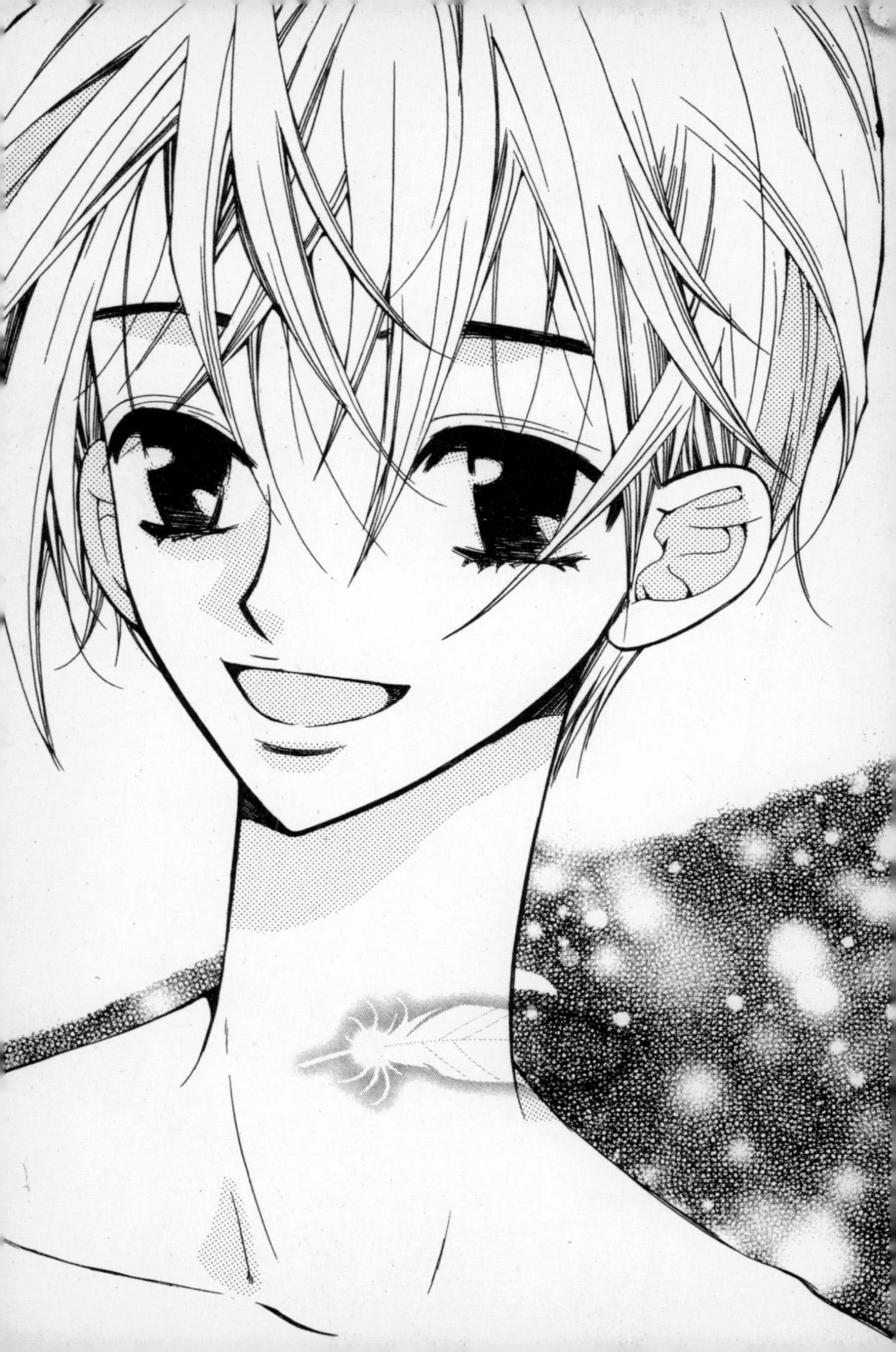

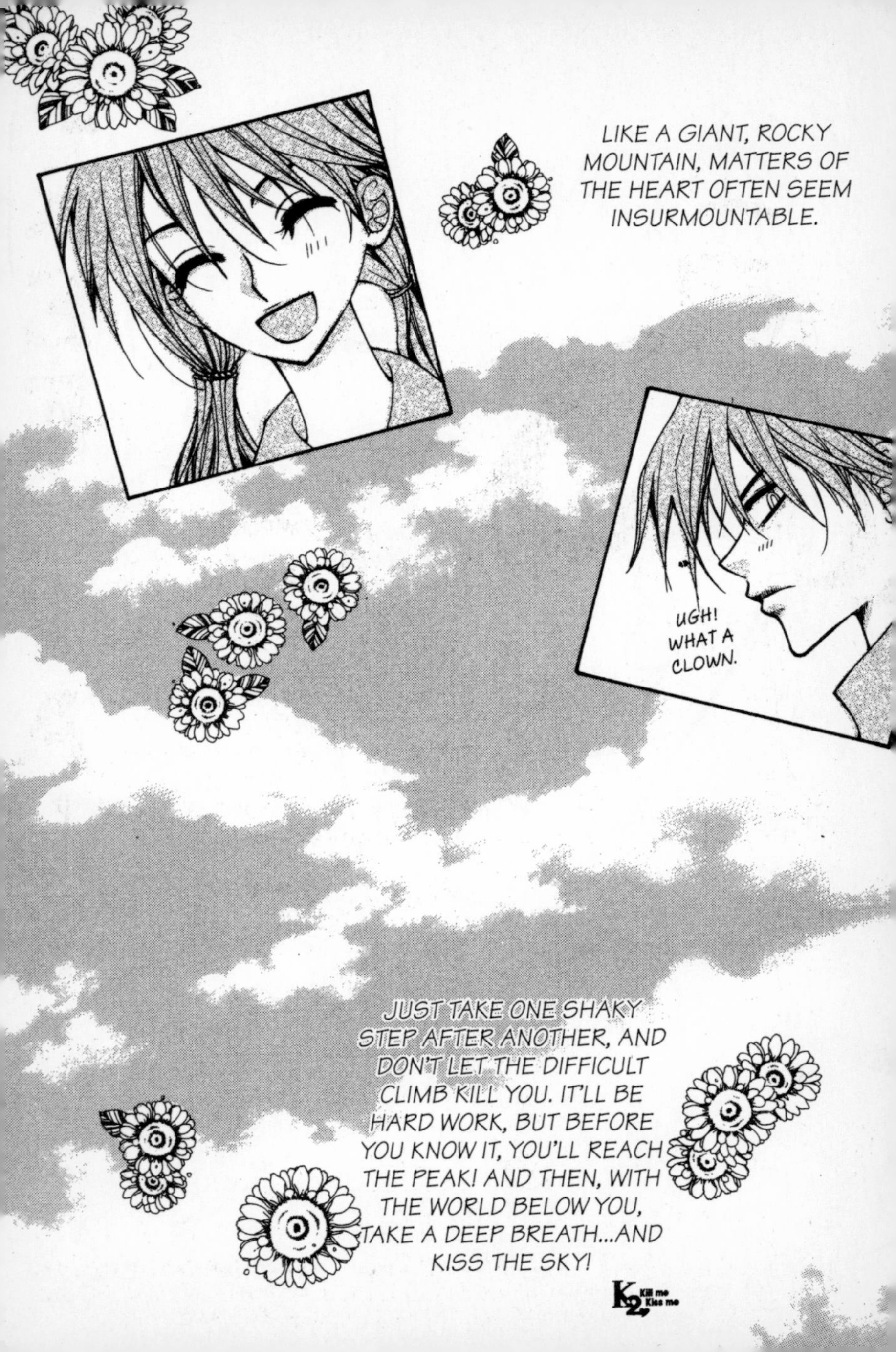
LIKE A GIANT, ROCKY MOUNTAIN, MATTERS OF THE HEART OFTEN SEEM INSURMOUNTABLE.
UGH! WHAT A CLOWN.
JUST TAKE ONE SHAKY STEP AFTER ANOTHER, AND DON'T LET THE DIFFICULT CLIMB KILL YOU. IT'LL BE HARD WORK, BUT BEFORE YOU KNOW IT, YOU'LL REACH THE PEAK! AND THEN, WITH THE WORLD BELOW YOU, TAKE A DEEP BREATH...AND KISS THE SKY!

FREE TALK

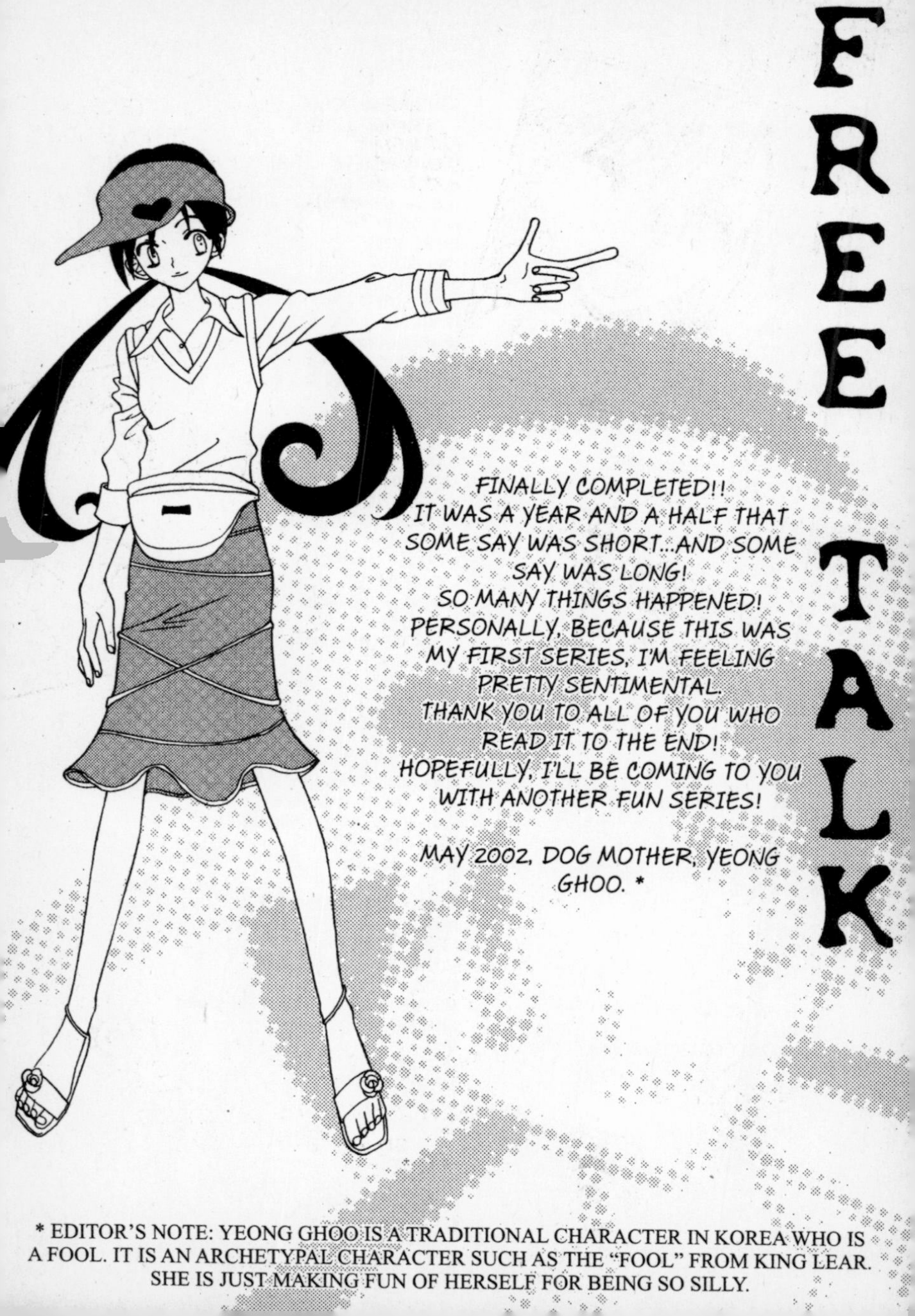

FINALLY COMPLETED!!
IT WAS A YEAR AND A HALF THAT SOME SAY WAS SHORT...AND SOME SAY WAS LONG!
SO MANY THINGS HAPPENED!
PERSONALLY, BECAUSE THIS WAS MY FIRST SERIES, I'M FEELING PRETTY SENTIMENTAL.
THANK YOU TO ALL OF YOU WHO READ IT TO THE END!
HOPEFULLY, I'LL BE COMING TO YOU WITH ANOTHER FUN SERIES!

MAY 2002, DOG MOTHER, YEONG GHOO. *

* EDITOR'S NOTE: YEONG GHOO IS A TRADITIONAL CHARACTER IN KOREA WHO IS A FOOL. IT IS AN ARCHETYPAL CHARACTER SUCH AS THE "FOOL" FROM KING LEAR. SHE IS JUST MAKING FUN OF HERSELF FOR BEING SO SILLY.

ALSO AVAILABLE FROM 🌀TOKYOPOP®

MANGA

.HACK//LEGEND OF THE TWILIGHT
@LARGE
ABENOBASHI: MAGICAL SHOPPING ARCADE
A.I. LOVE YOU
AI YORI AOSHI
ALICHINO
ANGELIC LAYER
ARM OF KANNON
BABY BIRTH
BATTLE ROYALE
BATTLE VIXENS
BOYS BE...
BRAIN POWERED
BRIGADOON
B'TX
CANDIDATE FOR GODDESS, THE
CARDCAPTOR SAKURA
CARDCAPTOR SAKURA - MASTER OF THE CLOW
CHOBITS
CHRONICLES OF THE CURSED SWORD
CLAMP SCHOOL DETECTIVES
CLOVER
COMIC PARTY
CONFIDENTIAL CONFESSIONS
CORRECTOR YUI
COWBOY BEBOP
COWBOY BEBOP: SHOOTING STAR
CRAZY LOVE STORY
CRESCENT MOON
CROSS
CULDCEPT
CYBORG 009
D•N•ANGEL
DEARS
DEMON DIARY
DEMON ORORON, THE
DEUS VITAE
DIABOLO
DIGIMON
DIGIMON TAMERS
DIGIMON ZERO TWO
DOLL
DRAGON HUNTER
DRAGON KNIGHTS
DRAGON VOICE
DREAM SAGA
DUKLYON: CLAMP SCHOOL DEFENDERS
EERIE QUEERIE!
ERICA SAKURAZAWA: COLLECTED WORKS
ET CETERA
ETERNITY
EVIL'S RETURN
FAERIES' LANDING
FAKE
FLCL
FLOWER OF THE DEEP SLEEP
FORBIDDEN DANCE
FRUITS BASKET
G GUNDAM
GATEKEEPERS
GETBACKERS

GIRL GOT GAME
GRAVITATION
GTO
GUNDAM SEED ASTRAY
GUNDAM SEED ASTRAY R
GUNDAM WING
GUNDAM WING: BATTLEFIELD OF PACIFISTS
GUNDAM WING: ENDLESS WALTZ
GUNDAM WING: THE LAST OUTPOST (G-UNIT)
HANDS OFF!
HAPPY MANIA
HARLEM BEAT
HYPER POLICE
HYPER RUNE
I.N.V.U.
IMMORTAL RAIN
INITIAL D
INSTANT TEEN: JUST ADD NUTS
ISLAND
JING: KING OF BANDITS
JING: KING OF BANDITS - TWILIGHT TALES
JULINE
KARE KANO
KILL ME, KISS ME
KINDAICHI CASE FILES, THE
KING OF HELL
KODOCHA: SANA'S STAGE
LAGOON ENGINE
LAMENT OF THE LAMB
LEGAL DRUG
LEGEND OF CHUN HYANG, THE
LES BIJOUX
LILING-PO
LOVE HINA
LOVE OR MONEY
LUPIN III
LUPIN III: WORLD'S MOST WANTED
MAGIC KNIGHT RAYEARTH I
MAGIC KNIGHT RAYEARTH II
MAHOROMATIC: AUTOMATIC MAIDEN
MAN OF MANY FACES
MARMALADE BOY
MARS
MARS: HORSE WITH NO NAME
MINK
MIRACLE GIRLS
MIYUKI-CHAN IN WONDERLAND
MODEL
MOURYOU KIDEN: LEGEND OF THE NYMPH
NECK AND NECK
ONE
ONE I LOVE, THE
PARADISE KISS
PARASYTE
PASSION FRUIT
PEACH FUZZ
PEACH GIRL
PEACH GIRL: CHANGE OF HEART
PET SHOP OF HORRORS
PHD: PHANTASY DEGREE
PITA-TEN
PLANET BLOOD
PLANET LADDER

10.19.04T

ALSO AVAILABLE FROM TOKYOPOP®

PLANETES
PRESIDENT DAD
PRIEST
PRINCESS AI
PSYCHIC ACADEMY
QUEEN'S KNIGHT, THE
RAGNAROK
RAVE MASTER
REALITY CHECK
REBIRTH
REBOUND
REMOTE
RISING STARS OF MANGA™, THE
SABER MARIONETTE J
SAILOR MOON
SAINT TAIL
SAIYUKI
SAMURAI DEEPER KYO
SAMURAI GIRL™ REAL BOUT HIGH SCHOOL
SCRYED
SEIKAI TRILOGY, THE
SGT. FROG
SHAOLIN SISTERS
SHIRAHIME-SYO: SNOW GODDESS TALES
SHUTTERBOX
SKULL MAN, THE
SNOW DROP
SORCERER HUNTERS
SOUL TO SEOUL
STONE
SUIKODEN III
SUKI
TAROT CAFÉ, THE
THREADS OF TIME
TOKYO BABYLON
TOKYO MEW MEW
TOKYO TRIBES
TRAMPS LIKE US
UNDER THE GLASS MOON
VAMPIRE GAME
VISION OF ESCAFLOWNE, THE
WARCRAFT
WARRIORS OF TAO
WILD ACT
WISH
WORLD OF HARTZ
X-DAY
ZODIAC P.I.

NOVELS

CLAMP SCHOOL PARANORMAL INVESTIGATORS
SAILOR MOON
SLAYERS

ART BOOKS

ART OF CARDCAPTOR SAKURA
ART OF MAGIC KNIGHT RAYEARTH, THE
PEACH: MIWA UEDA ILLUSTRATIONS
CLAMP NORTH SIDE
CLAMP SOUTH SIDE

ANIME GUIDES

COWBOY BEBOP
GUNDAM TECHNICAL MANUALS
SAILOR MOON SCOUT GUIDES

TOKYOPOP KIDS

STRAY SHEEP

CINE-MANGA®

ALADDIN
CARDCAPTORS
DUEL MASTERS
FAIRLY ODDPARENTS, THE
FAMILY GUY
FINDING NEMO
G.I. JOE SPY TROOPS
GREATEST STARS OF THE NBA
JACKIE CHAN ADVENTURES
JIMMY NEUTRON: BOY GENIUS, THE ADVENTURES OF
KIM POSSIBLE
LILO & STITCH: THE SERIES
LIZZIE MCGUIRE
LIZZIE MCGUIRE MOVIE, THE
MALCOLM IN THE MIDDLE
POWER RANGERS: DINO THUNDER
POWER RANGERS: NINJA STORM
PRINCESS DIARIES 2, THE
RAVE MASTER
SHREK 2
SIMPLE LIFE, THE
SPONGEBOB SQUAREPANTS
SPY KIDS 2
SPY KIDS 3-D: GAME OVER
TEENAGE MUTANT NINJA TURTLES
THAT'S SO RAVEN
TOTALLY SPIES
TRANSFORMERS: ARMADA
TRANSFORMERS: ENERGON

You want it? We got it!
A full range of TOKYOPOP
products are available now at:
www.TOKYOPOP.com/shop

10.19.04T

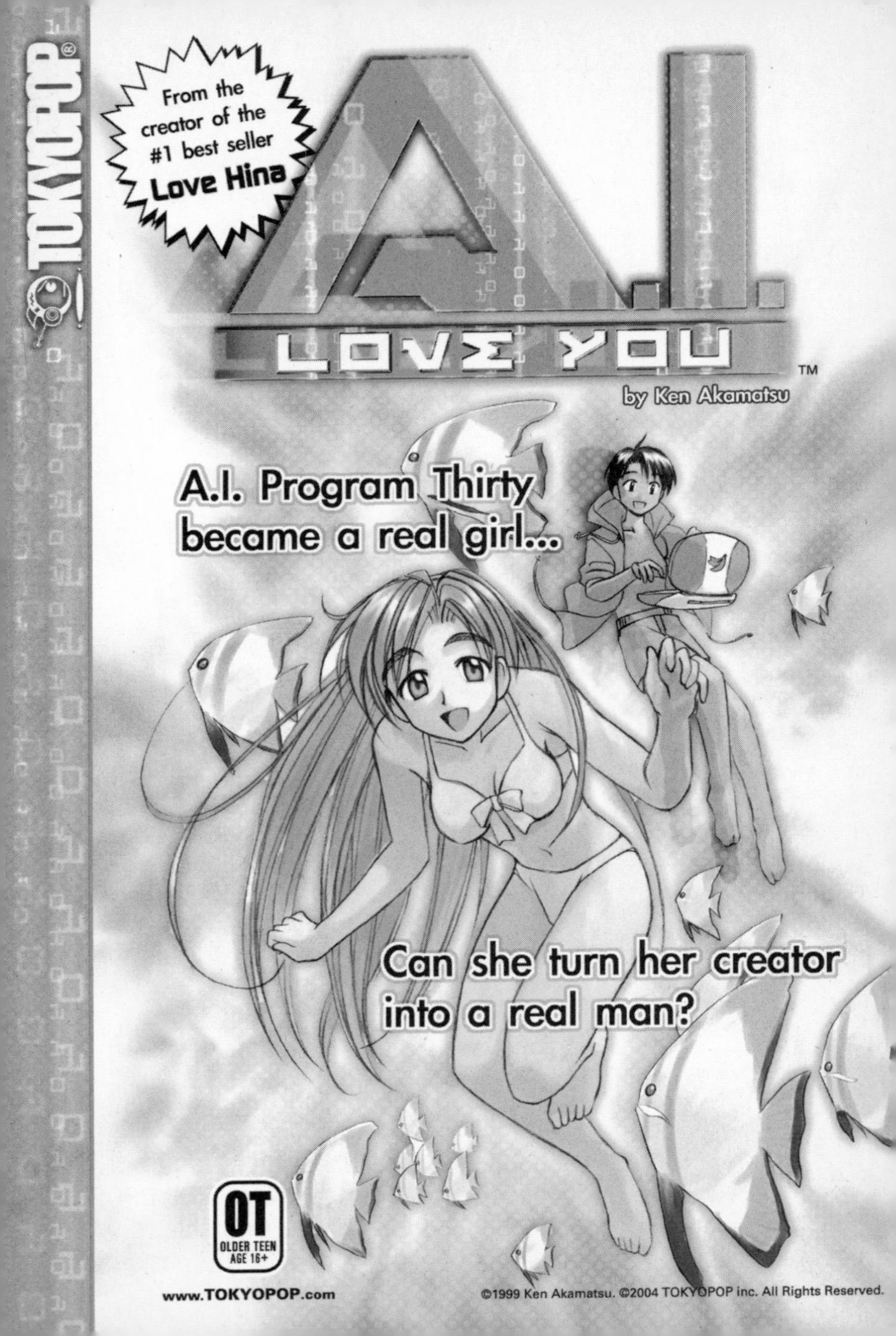
TOKYOPOP®
From the creator of the #1 best seller Love Hina
A.I. LOVE YOU™
by Ken Akamatsu
A.I. Program Thirty became a real girl...
Can she turn her creator into a real man?
OT OLDER TEEN AGE 16+
www.TOKYOPOP.com
©1999 Ken Akamatsu. ©2004 TOKYOPOP inc. All Rights Reserved.

Snow Drop ™

Like a fragile flower,
love often blooms in unlikely places.

So you wanna be
a Rock 'n' Roll star...

Gravitation

by Maki Murakami

100% AUTHENTIC MANGA

Rock 'n' Roll & manga collide with superstar
dreams in this hit property from Japan!
**Available Now at Your Favorite
Book and Comic Stores!**

OT
OLDER TEEN
AGE 16+